UNDERGROUND PETERSBURG

UNDERGROUND PETERSBURG

RADICAL POPULISM, URBAN SPACE, AND THE

TACTICS OF SUBVERSION IN REFORM-ERA RUSSIA

CHRISTOPHER ELY

NIU PRESS / DeKalb

Northern Illinois University Press, DeKalb 60115
© 2016 by Northern Illinois University Press
All rights reserved
Printed in the United States of America
25 24 23 22 21 20 19 18 17 16   1 2 3 4 5

978-0-87580-744-7 (paper)
978-1-60909-203-0 (e-book)

Book and cover design by Yuni Dorr

Library of Congress Cataloging-in-Publication Data
Names: Ely, Christopher David, 1963–
Title: Underground Petersburg : radical populism, urban space and the tactics of
   subversion in reform-era Russia / Christopher Ely.
Description: DeKalb : Northern Illinois University Press, [2016] | Includes
   bibliographical references.
Identifiers: LCCN 2016008347| ISBN 9780875807447 (pbk. : alk. paper) | ISBN
   9781609092030 (ebook)
Subjects: LCSH: Saint Petersburg (Russia)—Politics and government—19th century.
   | Saint Petersburg (Russia)—Social conditions—19th century. | Subculture—Russia
   (Federation)—Saint Petersburg—History—19th century. | City and town life—
   Russia (Federation)—Saint Petersburg—History—19th century. | Radicalism—
   Russia (Federation)—Saint Petersburg—History—19th century. | Populism—Russia
   (Federation)—Saint Petersburg—History—19th century. | Public spaces—Political
   aspects—Russia (Federation)—Saint Petersburg—History—19th century. |
   Subversive activities—Russia (Federation)—Saint Petersburg—History—19th
   century. | Russia—History—Alexander II, 1855–1881.
Classification: LCC DK568 .E48 2016 | DDC 947/.21081—dc23
LC record available at http://lccn.loc.gov/2016008347

FOR EMMA ELY AND FOR JANE ELY

Contents

Preface and Acknowledgments

T HIS STUDY OF RUSSIAN REFORM-ERA radical populism began as an inquiry into the Russian public sphere. Years ago I started out with an interest in the press, public opinion, and public spaces and events, intentionally avoiding the revolutionary radicalism that seemed already well-covered ground. Soon, however, I wound up diving back down into the hidden and subversive realms of the populist underground. This unpredicted shift of topic was both ironic and symptomatic. I came to understand that as a result of the constricted boundaries around what could be voiced without threat of punishment, reform-era public expression and underground activism were intertwined phenomena; they interacted with, and sometimes even complemented, one another. The autocratic state did not create the revolutionary underground, but it certainly created conditions in which it was likely to flourish.

The reforms of Alexander II aimed to conjure into existence a restricted Russian public that would contribute its voice yet remain politically docile. Instead, these reforms helped to create a frustrated public sphere alongside a substantial measure of discontent and subversion. Alexander's limited *glasnost'* produced politically engaged individuals who were allowed to read, think, and discuss public affairs but still had little chance to influence policy given the lack of suffrage and serious restrictions on speech and assembly. For most Russians, patience, quietism, and respect for authority remained the accepted posture. Not surprisingly, however, some lacked the patience and refused to accept the gradual path to change. Revolutionaries go underground in order to influence the public, harboring the hope of one day altering the body politic to the point that their forbidden ideals will become legitimate within a transformed political structure. Wanting to accelerate the process of change, the frustrated few put into operation a succession of strategies, one of the most effective being underground conspiracy.

As I began to explore radical populism from the point of view of its participants, I learned that it could exist and exert leverage only by finding ways to maintain a precarious autonomy in the face of heavy police pressure. Russian radicals could not have had the impact they did were it not for their ability to create and maintain elaborate, concealed organizations. In attempting to grasp the origins and contours of the populist underground they created, I discovered that many of the questions

I wanted answers for had not been raised in previous studies. Why and how did an underground come into being in the first place? How did it evolve over time? How did those who occupied the underground manage to maintain its autonomy? In what ways did members of the populist underground make use of the pre-existing spaces of the cities in which they operated? And how and why did the populist underground carry out the violent acts for which it is best known—assassinations of state officials including the tsar—in the face of a powerful state with a police force dedicated to their eradication?

Because most earlier studies have focused primary attention on the ideological origins of radical populism, and tended to see the values, doctrines, and intellectual debates of the populists as the central issue worth discussing, I found few guideposts in secondary sources to help my search for the material constraints, the tactical decision-making, and the practical strategies that built the underground into a political weapon to be used against the autocracy. All of these concerns, however, loomed large in memoir literature and police inquiries, which form the main source base for this book. The focus here on organization and activism provides an alternate vantage point from which to view the trajectory of radical populism. I hope this perspective will illuminate important features of the populist movement that have so far remained in the shadows.

Many years of gratitude have been building up since I began this project. A grant from the Kennan Institute of the Woodrow Wilson International Center in 2001 helped launch the initial phase, financial assistance from Florida Atlantic University, the Lifelong Learning Society, and a Bernadotte Schmidt grant from the American Historical Association funded summer research trips, and an IREX Short-term travel grant enabled me to complete work at archives in Moscow and St. Petersburg. The University of Illinois Russian and Eurasian Research Center was especially useful in helping me locate published memoirs and obscure sources, and two sabbaticals from Florida Atlantic University afforded much-needed time for writing. Individuals who have helped along the way include Clark and Ann McPhail and Ralph Fisher in Illinois as well as Masha Bell and Dima Nartov in Moscow. I also found extremely helpful a conference on terrorism and modernity organized by Carola Dietze and Claudia Veerhoven at which I learned a great deal from scholars such as Martin Miller, David Rapoport, Lynn Patyk, David Blackbourn, Benjamin Schenk, Richard Back Jensen and James Gelvin. For help reading all or parts of the manuscript, a huge debt of thanks goes to Dan White, Madeleine Lenke, Lucinda Ely, David Fisher, Robert Weinberg, Melissa Stockdale, and Rebecca Friedman. For encouraging words of support at critical moments, I would like to thank Mark Bassin, Joseph Bradley, Daniel Field, Richard Stites, Doug Weiner, Jonathan Wiesen, and Natasha Zaretsky. My thanks for support of a more personal kind go out to Lesley Davison, Joan Goody, Peter Davison, Tom Gleason, Patricia Herlihy, and Madeleine Ely. Without them this book would not exist.

INTRODUCTION

The activities of Russian radicals developed out of practical experience in the movement itself.

Norman Naimark

Is space indeed a medium? A milieu? An intermediary? It is doubtless all of these, but its role is less and less neutral, more and more active, both as instrument and as goal, as means and as end. Confining it to so narrow a category as that of "medium" is consequently woefully inadequate.

Henri Lefebvre

HALF A CENTURY AFTER TAKING part in violent attacks against state officials that culminated in the assassination of Tsar Alexander II, Vera Figner was still amazed at the success attained by the small band of "revolutionaries" she had joined. "While the state funneled the entirety of its extraordinary resources into fighting the evil," she recalled, "nothing—neither the bayonets of hundreds of thousands of troops, nor the hordes of guards and spies, nor all the gold in the state treasury—could preserve the ruler of 80 million, and he fell at the hands of the revolution-aries."[1] How had a few dozen radical activists managed to persevere against one of the world's most powerful states? How did they manage to attack high-ranking officials in broad daylight and escape to attack again? How did they provoke a governmental crisis, unleash a frantic police crackdown, and yet still make attempt after attempt on the life of the tsar, finally killing him on March 1, 1881? The assassination of Tsar Alexander II is one of the most familiar events in the history of imperial Russia, and the radical populist movement that accomplished it has been analyzed in enough popular and academic studies to fill a book-length bibliography.[2] Yet the populists' astonishing campaign still remains as surprising today as it was to Vera Figner in the 1920s. "In certain ways," reads a popular contemporary textbook on Russian history, "it defies imagination."[3]

All the more remarkable, at the height of the assassination campaign the organization carrying out the movement, then known as "The People's Will," was in the midst of an ideological crisis. The group that had called itself "Land and Freedom" split and disbanded in the summer of 1879, mainly over the question of whether or not to attempt regicide. Those members who reformed as The People's Will were united in their agreement to assassinate the tsar, but their political views varied widely. They did not even agree on the ultimate reason for, or outcome of, the planned assassination. Some hoped regicide would launch a revolution and inaugurate an era of peasant-based anarchic socialism; others believed it could help them build a centrally governed socialist state. And when they finally killed the tsar, the demands they made were moderate and politically liberal. They declared themselves prepared to leave the monarchy intact as long as the next tsar pledged to accept freedoms of speech and assembly and the election of a body of representatives. In short, their aims had almost no ideological consistency. As Nikolai Morozov, a member of The People's Will, wrote later, "I don't remember even one conversation in our group about socialism.... The names we went by (nihilists, terrorists, socialists, anarchists) ... almost never fit and were chosen in blind imitation of foreign parties without much sense of their meaning."[4] But if the ideological goals of the "populists" (as they sometimes referred to themselves) so lacked coherence, what lent them the fortitude to endure the ever-present threats of imprisonment, Siberian exile, and execution? What gave them the needed *esprit de corps* to operate an extremely successful campaign of terror and assassination in the face of massive reprisals and the relentless pursuit of the political police?

One reason it has been difficult to find satisfactory answers to these seemingly straightforward questions is that scholarship on Russian populism has long privileged the role of ideology above all other factors. Revolutionary populist ideals have been interpreted in a variety of ways—as selfless and liberating, as heroic but misguided, as starry-eyed and utopian—but in almost all cases the importance of ideology (of intellectual radicalization) has been the central fact upon which analyses of the movement have been based. The radical populists are often understood as the archetypal inheritors of the Russian intelligentsia as a whole, a group Isaiah Berlin referred to as "men with a degree of passion for ideas perhaps never equaled in a European society."[5] Thus the analysis of radical populism has always been closely connected to, and often nearly indistinguishable from, the history of ideas. Yet attempts to understand radical populism exclusively in terms of ideology have proven problematic time and again. Berlin, for example, in a widely read essay on Russian populism, was reduced to arguing about The People's Will that "the views of these men were astonishingly simple. They believed in terrorism and more terrorism to achieve complete, anarchist liberty."[6] Almost every part of this statement is inaccurate or misleading, from the implication that the populists shared a single collective goal, to the notion that their methods constituted a blind lashing out without limit, even to the not insignificant point that many of these "men" were actually women. Berlin's attempt to explain populist actions as a result of populist ideas reduced his usually lucid and sensible scholarship to extreme oversimplification: what motivated Russian radical populists was broader and more complex than he was willing to see.

Other historians have attempted to explain radical populism in psychological terms as a matter of pathology, or even as a kind of inverted Christian desire for self-sacrifice and martyrdom.[7] From this perspective populism did not require a clear ideological position because it was an emotional crusade based on an overriding desire to surmount the obvious inequalities and injustices in imperial Russia. In this way populism has been characterized as a kind of atheistic *ressentiment* of Christianity. The sons of priests, who constituted a disproportionate number of populism's early leaders, stood their Christian values on their heads and turned Christian personal ethics into a social and political ethics that sought to establish heaven on earth.[8] A variation of this position emphasizes the ethos of service and self-sacrifice that has deep roots in Russian history.[9] Another widespread argument suggests that populism was primarily a social phenomenon based in the relatively impoverished middle class groups known as the *raznochintsy* (people of varied ranks), who were in essence fighting a proxy class war by supporting the even less privileged peasants.[10] Finally, quite the opposite reading emphasizes the noble origins of many populists, who, racked by guilt for the world they had inherited, turned the resources of their privileged backgrounds against themselves and began to fight for the underdog.[11] Given the number of people involved in the movement, one can identify specific individuals who embody each explanation, but neither ideological nor psychological explanations adequately characterize the movement as a whole.

Whatever their original intellectual motivations, historical sources demonstrate that in the context of their time the populists were keenly attuned to practicalities, to the exigencies of the moment. Put another way, they were motivated by whatever worked to help them attain their goal of overthrowing the social order and the autocratic regime that supported it. The plans of the populist revolutionaries were constantly thwarted by imperial Russia's large and active political police force, the Third Section of his Imperial Majesty's Own Chancellery, but over and over again they demonstrated their resilience: their remarkable capacity to regroup, to learn from their mistakes, and to devise new methods and strategies. These strategic improvements eventually put them in a position sufficiently powerful to provoke what the historian Petr Zaionchkovskii aptly dubbed "the crisis of the Russian autocracy."[12] By the time The People's Will had developed into an internationally known revolutionary organization, even though their ideological goals were muddled and contentious, the voice with which they conveyed their general discontent was loud and powerful. State and society had to listen, and the substantial shifts in government policy and personnel the autocracy made in 1880 clearly demonstrate that they did. By the late 1870s both the state and the public, as well as much of the world beyond Russia's borders, had come to believe that Russia was on the brink of revolution. At the height of its power between 1878 and 1881, radical populism would be more accurately understood as a political phenomenon, a movement in search of power, than an ideological phenomenon, a movement seeking to fulfill a prescribed set of values and beliefs.

But to assert that the populists eventually came to be motivated by the seductive allure of their increasing political influence is not yet to explain how they managed to acquire that power in the first place. The process by which they gained an influence far out of proportion to their numbers and resources is the subject of this book. The level of ideological commitment was substantial and remained relatively constant, whereas tactical methods for waging revolutionary struggle underwent a long series of transformations in a dialectical process that involved the struggle against state authority and the battle for public opinion as much as, or more than, it involved populist doctrine. This study proposes that populist activism developed as it did *not only* under the influence of ideological and psychological motivations but also *in spite of* the influence of ideological and psychological motivations. Left out of attempts to account for the vehemence and violence of radical populism have been the material conditions in which the movement arose. Ideas and passions were only half the story. Practical interests and material conditions played a central role in the development of the populist movement.

In the following pages, I trace the gradual rise of what would become the populists' most effective tool: the revolutionary underground. This book seeks to offer both a general history and a thick description of the underground as it developed during the reform era under Alexander II (1855–1881). The creation of that underground involved a slow and difficult process in which other methods of revolutionary struggle were gradually ruled out, and organizational discipline, group unity, and new methods and strategies for maintaining the underground were developed and improved upon. Ultimately, the revolutionary underground established a novel way to occupy and control urban space. It set up a base of operations in the midst of the city, directly under the noses of the state officials and police forces trying to destroy it.

Thus it must be stressed that despite populism's ideological emphasis on the peasant and the countryside, the physical and social environment in which the movement played out was not rural but urban. Populism arose, evolved, and reached its peak impact in the city. Even the populists themselves used the labels "villagers" and "urbanites" to distinguish factions within their organization, and despite their well-known, if usually short-lived, experiments residing in peasant villages, nearly all of them spent the bulk of their politically active lives living and working in the large metropolitan centers of Odessa, Kiev, Moscow and, most importantly, the capital city of St. Petersburg. Cities served as the main environment in which the populist movement coalesced, and cities were essential to populism's organizational and tactical successes.

This book is not the first to point out the counterintuitive link between rural-oriented populist doctrine and the reality of the radical populists' urban-centered lives, but here the peculiar nature of the urban environment will play an especially prominent role.[13] Once we focus on the significance of the city, the evolution of radical populism begins to look less like an ideologically guided crusade for social justice, and more like a pragmatic process of trial and error leading to the acquisition of improved methods of revolutionary struggle. As we will see, populist activism involved, at different times, cultural experimentation with work and personal behavior, various attempts to express political dissent in the public sphere, the organization of secret conspiracies, teaching and propagandizing among urban workers, and treks to the countryside to interact with the peasantry. Such methods had mixed results. They helped sustain the populist movement, but they often led to jail terms and exile. And yet every success and failure offered opportunities from which to learn. Populist activists gradually discovered how to use urban space to their advantage, to form it into an instrument that made their movement highly effective as a means of destabilizing the Tsarist regime. From rudimentary underground organizations in the early 1860s,

radical populism had by the second half of the 1870s developed the necessary discipline, tactics, and techniques (and also created the tangible physical spaces) with which to build a sustainable urban underground struggle.

Terms like "revolutionary underground," "underground insurrection,"
and the like, at least in the historiography of imperial Russia, have never
been used with any scholarly precision. The word "underground," of course,
is a metaphor to describe a particular type of clandestine organization (often
with political goals). In the broadest sense, a political underground is an
organized, secret association intended to overthrow, or at least undermine,
the political system that presides over it and from which it conceals itself.
In this respect a distinction must be made between an underground and
an oppositional movement in emigration, since the members of a domestic
underground must remain hidden in order to avoid prosecution. For this
reason an underground must to some degree constitute a distinct space situated within a given polity but separated from it and answerable mainly to its
own concerns.[14] There is good reason, then, to retain the term underground
rather than "secret organization" or "conspiratorial society," since "underground" implies the necessity of a usable physical space. To sustain their
movement, the radical populists needed to construct a hidden realm within
the larger space of the city that would afford them sufficient autonomy to
operate. The populist underground, therefore, was more than a metaphor.
It was the possession of a contested space that made possible political agitation and deadly insurrectionary attacks.

Possession of that space allowed the populists to conduct the intentionally spectacular operations (assassinations, bombings, robberies, prison
breaks, etc.) that would eventually lend their movement both great notoriety
and an air of invincibility. But the most spectacular single act that can be
undertaken in an autocratic system (in which the ruler is simultaneously
the holder and the symbol of power) is regicide. Especially after the initial unsuccessful attacks on Alexander II's life (in 1866 and 1879), the tsar
had come to be increasingly well-protected, rendering assassination an
extremely difficult feat, all the more spectacular if it could be accomplished.
Between the spring of 1879 and the regicide of March 1, 1881, a succession
of attempts on the life of the tsar took up most of the time and resources
the radical underground had gained. The populists themselves understood
perfectly well that the outcome of a successful assassination was uncertain,
possibly even disastrous for their movement (as indeed it turned out to be),
but they were incapable of refraining from using the power they possessed.
It is a basic premise of this book that since the underground secured the relative safety and autonomy the populists needed to carry out their regicidal

mission, their underground organization cannot be understood as an epi-phenomenon grafted onto their ideological commitment. Instead it was their most novel and effective innovation, and it became a driving force in its own right. By the late 1870s, the underground itself had come in large measure to determine the trajectory of radical populism, from its methods and aims to the remarkable effectiveness that would eventually make popu-list terrorism the victim of its own success.

IDEOLOGICAL POPULISM

To place the formation of the underground at the center of a history of radical populism is far from standard practice. Scholarship on radical pop-ulism has, for the most part, de-emphasized tangible factors. Tactics, orga-nization, and environment have nearly always been regarded as secondary to ideas and political beliefs. One might say that the "why" of populism has overshadowed the "how." In this respect it is worth noting that, remarkable as it might seem for a movement with such concrete consequences, a sub-stantial share of the history of radical populism has been written by intel-lectual historians. To be sure, the fact that an intellectual-history approach to populist activism was possible at all attests to the important role ideology played in the movement. My intention here is not to refute the importance of ideological radicalization as a formative aspect of radical populism; rather, I want to supplement the study of ideological influences by examining the less-explored impact of environmental and strategic factors. Since all the populists shared certain underlying beliefs that helped them remain a func-tioning organization in the midst of adversity and doctrinal dispute, it will be helpful to begin with a brief sketch of those shared views.

Unlike better known radical movements (such as Bolshevism and Nazism) that have been inspired by a more or less well-articulated body of theory, Russian populism was a relatively loose affair. Its ideas developed side by side with its tactics, and it did not even acquire a name until many years after it had formed as a recognizable and definable point of view. Andrzej Walicki's description of populism as "a dynamic ideological struc-ture within which many positions were possible" is appropriately vague and useful to keep in mind. The terms for populist (*narodnik*) and populism (*narodnichestvo*) derive from the root word meaning people or folk (*narod*), and in the broadest usage Russian populism could refer to any sentiment that expressed admiration for, and a willingness to support, the poor, mainly rural and uneducated, majority of the Russian population.[15] This sense of the term populism is so inclusive as to run across the political spectrum. Even the state's arch-conservative policy of Official Nationality under Nicholas I (1825–1855) invoked an idealized *narod*. The term populist was not, however, in use until the 1870s and at that time it was associated with the radical left and revolutionary activism in the advancement of socioeconomic equality. Thus the subject of this book is properly termed "radical" or "revolutionary" populism. Still, both the broad and narrow strains of populism embraced a fundamental principle: the Russian folk, in particular the laboring peasant who had been idealized by Slavophile nationalists as well as in works of Russian art and literature, stood as the avatar and embodiment of Russian identity.

Virtually all strains of populism emerged from the educated and politically active segment of Russian society known as the intelligentsia. With the reform-era expansion of education, the intelligentsia came to include individuals from nearly all social strata, though its constitution was heavily weighted toward social elites, and while it was possible for a Russian *intelligent* to be socially conservative, devoutly Orthodox, royalist, or liberal capitalist, on the whole the intelligentsia skewed toward the left, especially in its opposition to autocratic rule. The Russian intelligentsia did not come into being at least until the late eighteenth century, and it had little impact in the public realm until the mid-nineteenth century, when semi-independent press organs began to appear. Because the intelligentsia felt that it alone served as the conscience of society, a heavy burden of responsibility for Russia's present and future direction bore down on it. It was in part the intelligentsia's sense of a sacred duty to society that inspired Russian populism.

The ideas that comprised Russian populism grew from the ground of Russia's geography and socio-political history. Across the enormous terrain of the Russian Empire stretched a vast amount of often meagerly productive farmland. To extract a surplus from this territory Russia had developed a system of lords and peasants that effectively split the country into two halves: a numerically small educated elite, expected to serve the state in some capacity in the urban population centers, and a laboring majority of rural farmers who lived at a subsistence level and generated the wealth upon which their gentry landlords lived. Until 1861 the majority of these peasant farmers were legally enserfed to their landowners. Russian society, especially by the middle of the nineteenth century, was far more complex than this snapshot suggests. Nevertheless, especially by comparison to the dynamic industrial capitalist states of Western Europe, it was inflexible, socially divided, and mired in tradition. While the Tsarist government tried to address the problem from above in a series of reforms that began with the abolition of serfdom, members of the intelligentsia began to develop their own conceptions of the problem and their own sets of solutions, from which arose the various forms of populism.

Those writers who lent populism its theoretical basis were all affiliated to one degree or another with the radical left. The most important of these were Aleksandr Herzen, Nikolai Chernyshevskii, Mikhail Bakunin, Petr Lavrov, Vasilii Bervi-Flerovskii and Nikolai Mikhailovskii. The latter five enjoyed more of the respect and admiration of the radical populist activists we will be concerned with here, but it was Herzen who had laid the foundation for populism in the late 1840s by developing the concept of "Russian socialism."[16] Herzen had argued that the political spirit of Russian peasants was innately communal as reflected in the institution of the village commune (the practice of collective decision-making and control over land distribution within a given village). On the basis of the peasantry's communal spirit, Herzen suggested, Russia would be the region of Europe to point the way forward out of the miseries of bourgeois capitalism. In Russia at this time, by contrast to Western Europe in the nineteenth century, a suspicion of private property and representative democracy cut across political lines. Many on the left (and some conservatives) believed it imperative for Russia to avoid the pitfalls of capitalism to which Europe had already succumbed. If in the West the middle classes were seen as the inheritors of the old regime, Russian populists held up the supposed egalitarianism and homogeneity of peasant life against what they saw as the egoistic and atomized world of the European bourgeoisie. In this intellectual atmosphere, Herzen's "discovery" of Russian socialism served as the foundation on which populist ideology rested, even if avowed populists were not always aware of the importance of his influence.

The idea that the peasantry contained *in vitro* the promise of a just and revitalized Russia represented a path through what populist thinkers saw as the Scylla and Charybdis of Russian conditions: the ingrained cruelty of native traditions and the potentially worse fate of Western European capitalism.[17] The intellectual idealization of peasant socialism was also typically accompanied by several other basic assumptions: that the Russian socioeconomic system benefitted the privileged few at the expense of the laboring majority, that the autocratic state did not have the will or capacity to alleviate the lot of the poor, that governmental reforms had already put Russia on the road to being reshaped in the unfortunate mold of the capitalist, industrialized, "bourgeois" West, and that the best way to combat all of these problems was, in one way or another, to overthrow, or at least moderate, autocratic rule. As populist ideals coalesced, Herzen's original theories were supplemented by other ideological influences: Chernyshevskii's passionate plea that nothing could be more important than social justice and equality, Bakunin's suggestion that Russian peasants were incipient rebels, and Lavrov's admonishment that the entire intelligentsia owed its social privilege to peasant labor. Upon these foundations, Russian populists generally accepted that the peasantry contained within itself both the desire for a revolutionary struggle to overthrow the Tsarist regime and a rough blueprint of the future utopian society they wished to institute. Populism's essential principles were already well-established by the early 1860s, and among the radical left they tended to be taken as articles of faith rather than opinions open to debate.[18]

It should be noted that although populists often evinced admiration for traditional peasant customs (and in some cases exhibited Slavophile leanings), they were not on the whole backward looking romantic nationalists hoping to revive an earlier stage in history. They opposed technological progress only if its gains could not be shared by all. In an affirmative sense, Russian radical populism can be aligned with, but not equated to, both socialism and anarchism. Some populists admired, and hoped in some unspecified way to embrace and use, the "socialist" practices of the peasantry as represented by periodic land redistribution. They saw these practices not so much as a model for governance but rather as evidence that the Russian population as a whole would be ready to accept some form of socialist revolution. Other populists emphasized the customary peasant desire to break free from outside control in order to live autarchically in their local communities. This second idealization of the peasantry rested on the anarchist aversion to centralized forms of authority as well as its celebration of small, local democracy.

In fact, this aversion to centralized authority was even closer to the center of populist values than a fear of capitalist westernization. In the 1860s and 1870s, capitalism was still a weak phenomenon in Russia, whereas the state seemed a vast and monstrous force, the ultimate source of all social ills. The large majority of populists were not writers and intellectuals but revolutionary propagandists and activists, a group that tended to focus on the immediate problem of overthrowing the social order based on the political foundation of Tsarist autocracy. For most radical populists the primary concern was getting rid of the impediments to social justice, as a result of which they saw their immediate enemy as the state and its massive bureaucratic apparatus. Populists typically harbored a furious enmity toward the autocracy and at times became quite single-minded in their quest to overthrow it. Whereas Marxism posited the motive force of history as impersonal socioeconomic relations, populists mainly believed that conscious human activity drove history forward. Given populism's theoretical open-endedness, the view that human beings made history encouraged action rather than patience and caution. If most populists harbored a deep respect for the peasants and their culture, they also doubted the peasantry's capacity to bring about revolutionary change without external impetus. It became the job of the populist to spark revolution among the peasants who needed it most.

Although from today's perspective radical populist views may appear hopelessly naïve, in the mid-nineteenth century they were espoused by the most brilliant members of the left-leaning intelligentsia. Populism's core ideals inspired a varied collection of talented and altruistic people with the passionate conviction that theirs was the only just course for correcting a Russian political and social system that had long oppressed and immiserated the vast majority of its population. The importance of these ideals and the moral values they inspired should not be underestimated, and it is not the purpose of this study to downplay their significance. However, the difficulty of adapting these ideas to a program of political change was obvious from the start. How could a movement predicated on the inherent value of a largely illiterate rural population be pushed into action by a culturally distinct and numerically insignificant minority of educated urbanites?

Perhaps as a result of the general ideological agreement on the potential benefits of peasant socialism, on a day-to-day basis issues of methods and tactics overshadowed those of doctrine and principle. Lev Tikhomirov, a key member of The People's Will, recalled a conversation with the organization's de facto leader Aleksandr Mikhailov that demonstrates just how insignificant ideological concerns could seem in the heat of battle. Although Mikhailov took great pains to safeguard the populists' underground press, which was printing a heavy stream of newspapers and leaflets (with print runs sometimes in the thousands), he was not at all concerned about the information contained therein. "Whatever is written makes no difference," he told Tikhomirov, "What matters is the mere existence of an illegal newspaper! The police search for it and cannot find it. That's what has an effect on the public. ... The ideal newspaper would be one with nothing written in it."[19] Tikhomirov had been one of the main editors and contributors to this underground newspaper, but he still supported Mikhailov's point, arguing that "the whereabouts of the press drove public discussion into a white heat. The simple fact of having a press raised us in the public's esteem."[20] What mattered here was not the content of the ideas being expressed but the power to express those ideas in flagrant disregard for authority.[21]

RADICAL POPULISM AND ITS HISTORIANS

It is not difficult to explain why historians have taken such a strong interest in populist ideology. The time and place that gave birth to the utopian certainties of Russian populism emerged within the larger context of post-enlightenment European modernity, which stretched from the French Revolution to the end of the Cold War. It was a period in European history keenly receptive to the power of ideas. The modern era, in a way that some have argued may now be passing, embraced the notion that humanity had the intellectual capacity to improve its social and material reality through the institution of new and better socio-political systems. The Russian populist faith that a revolutionary uprising could produce a bright socialist/anarchist/democratic future was not, then, an isolated enthusiasm; it was part and parcel of the wave of global revolutionary movements of the nineteenth and twentieth centuries.

In this respect, scholarship on radical populism that devoted primary attention to the ideological origins and aims of the movement was simply reflecting the fundamental concerns of the epoch in which it was written. In 1960 when Martin Malia wrote about the nineteenth-century Russian intelligentsia that "no class in Russia has had a more momentous impact on the destinies of that nation or indeed of the modern world," he had a more convincing case to make than would be accepted today.[22] Russian thinkers had contributed to shaping the world Malia described by helping to usher in the Soviet Union, which had an incalculable impact on twentieth-century global history. Given that impact, no matter what political perspective historians of populism wrote from, their primary concern was likely to be the set of ideas that seemed to link together the great chain of radical thought that had brought about Bolshevism. This scholarship tends to assume, as Claudia Verhoeven has noted, "a direct, one-to-one relation between the words (or theory) of radicals and the acts (or praxis) of revolutionaries."[23]

In fact, not only have historians generally neglected to separate the strands of populist activism from the history of ideas, but they have often represented populist violence as both the most extreme and the most characteristic manifestation of the Russian intelligentsia as a whole. The *locus classicus* of this argument is found in the brilliant pre-Revolutionary collection of essays called *Signposts*. Here, in the wake of the failures of the left in the Revolution of 1905, several essayists attempted to diagnose the maladies of the intelligentsia, over and over adducing as their key evidence the violence and extremism of the radical populists. In *Signposts* the specific political, social, and environmental possibilities and constraints that directly influenced reform-era radical populism dissolve into the rich soup of intelligentsia ideas and values as a manifestation both of Russia's uniqueness and of its unique problems.[24] It is fair to say that this idea-based tradition has remained since *Signposts* the dominant approach to radical populism.

After 1917, the stakes only rose higher. In Soviet history Marxist analysis reigned supreme, but since the Marxian perspective had been developed to account for Western European circumstances, it properly viewed radical populism as a wrong turn, an essentially "petty bourgeois" phenomenon moving against the currents of history. As a result of the ideological marginalization of populism, one might have expected Soviet Marxist scholars to ignore the populist phase of revolutionary history as a misguided and relatively trivial part of the Russian past. But revolutionary populism remained an important topic for reasons of national pride and revolutionary tradition, not to mention the fact that Lenin himself had been inspired by populist tactics and revolutionary zeal and incorporated aspects of radical populism into the Bolshevik tradition.

The contradictions between a Marxist analysis of history and the Leninist esteem for radical populism created a tricky situation for Soviet historians. Since a Marxist analysis more or less required the introduction of social class, Soviet historians emphasized the social backgrounds of the populists. They held that in the largely preindustrial circumstances of reform-era Russia, the *raznochintsy*, who had begun to attend universities in larger numbers and formed an increasingly significant contingent among the intelligentsia, created the social foundations of radical activism.[25] Ultimately, Soviet historians created a picture of the populists as heroic and sympathetic, if theoretically misguided, revolutionaries; their fight against autocracy, ill-informed as it was, could still be portrayed in Soviet/Russian patriotic terms as "one of the most glorious pages in the history of the Russian liberation movement."[26]

For their part, western scholars tended to exhibit sympathy for the political legitimacy of populist views without sharing the radical populists' revolutionary ardor. Neither Soviet nor western scholars had a great deal of contact with, or influence on, one another, but both groups shared a teleological approach to the history of the revolutionary movement. In the west, radical populism helped account for the "Russian *sonderweg*," Russia's inability to develop on a "normal" path toward healthy institutions of constitutional government and representative democracy, a shortcoming which sent the country hurtling instead toward a social revolution that put an extremist party in power. In the attempt to account for Russia's apparent historical uniqueness, the question of populism's relationship to Bolshevism became a crucial theme. If Soviet historians were preoccupied by the degree to which populism succeeded or failed to approximate a Marxist-Leninist conception of history, western historians searched for the roots of Bolshevism in the values and actions of the populists. The unabashedly teleological aspects of western historiography are reflected in the titles of two widely read studies produced in the mid-twentieth century: Avraham Yarmolinsky's *The Road to Revolution* and Franco Venturi's *Il Populismo Russo*, published in English as *The Roots of Revolution*. Both texts begin with intellectuals and ideas, both culminate in the revolutionary violence of The People's Will, and both explicitly draw out the influence of radical populism on the Bolshevik Revolution.[27]

Soviet historiography was severely limited in interpretive flexibility, but it came to abound in minute detail. Among Soviet historians, a great deal of effort went into publishing primary source collections and monographs on narrow topics. Western scholarship had greater room for maneuver, but in accord with the ideological weight of radical populism in a Cold War climate, it often broke down into pro and contra approaches that implied acceptance or rejection of populism's radical agenda. Venturi's monumental study of Russian populism, for example, treated his subjects with reverence for their part in the long, bitter and heroic struggle against an intransigent autocracy. In his work, the populists emerge as self-sacrificing freedom fighters. Adam Ulam's entertaining (if irascible and unsympathetic) condemnation of Russian populism, *In the Name of the People*, was almost refreshing by comparison. Western studies often aimed to highlight the dangers of radical ideology and its potentially destructive social consequences. For Ulam, radical populism seemed more a product of an ideologically motivated abnormal psychology than a sustained and effective revolutionary movement.[28]

In the end, these seemingly disparate and opposed, western and Soviet, accounts were united by the collective concept that the power of ideas (for good or ill) was the driving force behind radical populism. The mutual interests of opposing sides help to explain the reason for what John Klier has called "the near-obsessive interest in the revolutionary tradition that long characterized modern Russian historiography."[29] In the final decades of the Cold War, as skepticism toward western policies deepened, and social and cultural history were on the rise, some historians began to develop new approaches to the populist movement. Daniel Brower's *Training the Nihilists* examined the radicalization process, debunking the Soviet view that populism should be understood as a class-based movement by scrutinizing the social origins of student recruits. Brower instead identified as the crucible of radicalization the unifying location and experience of university education.[30] Barbara Alpern Engel's *Mothers and Daughters* examined the role of women in the populist movement, innovatively emphasizing not just female actors but the contribution of gender difference to the character of the movement as a whole.[31] And in *Young Russia* Abbott Gleason, having recognized that ideas were only one motivator of American radicalization in the 1960s, focused on other factors that had shaped populism, such as personal interaction, charisma, dress, and social mores. In Gleason's account, the movement was driven as much by cultural conflict and psychological motives as by the nature and articulation of ideas.[32]

These studies, and others published in the 1970s and 1980s, testified to the continuing significance of the nineteenth-century intelligentsia as a central subject in the historiography of imperial Russia. But in a particularly eloquent demonstration of the topic's inherent teleological basis, with the demise of the Soviet Union, the prior flood of scholarship on radical populism quickly dried to a trickle. Once the global superpower based on the ideas of Marx and Lenin had fallen apart, the topic of Bolshevism's radical origins no longer had the same relevance, and populism as a subject of consequence began to fade away. From the late 1980s, the withering away of interest in "the roots of revolution" coincided with the emergence of numerous previously unexplored topics that had begun to seem more relevant as the post-Soviet experience changed the nature of questions asked about imperial Russia. Formerly marginalized subjects such as Russian imperialism, national and ethnic identity, civil society, religion, and the family now moved to center stage. Does that mean, as some of my colleagues have suggested to me, that the study of radical populism should now be put aside as overworked and immaterial? My answer, obviously, is no. There remains a great deal to be learned about the movement, and recent scholarship has shed abundant new light on the historical context of radical populism.

One of the original explanations for Russia's path toward the Bolshevik Revolution was based on the argument that Russia lacked a middle class capable of establishing the sort of civil society that could stand up to monarchial power. Strikingly, however, as historians ceased to look for a Russian replica of western institutions and started to examine neglected aspects of Russian history, imperial Russia's missing civil society has made an appearance and helped to complicate the earlier, more black and white, reading of Russian history that pitted a hypertrophic state against a downtrodden population championed by a radicalized intelligentsia.[33] Russia did not have the equivalent of a Western European bourgeoisie, but it did have its own civil society, which played a role in historical developments. Radical populism was long treated as a symptom of Russia's "missing middle class" syndrome, but once we see the populist revolutionary movement in light of the more complex civil society taking shape in late-imperial Russia, it begins to make sense in new ways.

Also in recent years a new and quite different interest in radical populism has developed. This new emphasis is captured in the 2005 monument to Alexander II that lies across from the Cathedral of Christ the Savior in central Moscow. The inscription on the monument states that Alexander "perished March 1, 1881, as the result of a terrorist attack." This approach to the populist revolutionaries radically differs from the Soviet celebration of populists as fighters for the cause of socialist revolution. The monument implicitly locates the assassins of Alexander II in the context of global terrorism, and recent historiography has examined them in this context as well. Verhoeven, in an in-depth study of the Ishutin Circle and Dmitry Karakozov's attempt on the life of the tsar, sees Karakozov's shot as the opening salvo in the rise of terrorism as a modern phenomenon.[34] Ana Siljak's biography of Vera Zasulich emphasizes Zasulich's role in global terrorism as well.[35] And as a sign of essential change in Russian historiography, E. I. Shcherbakova's history of populist radicalism, *Renegades: The Path to Terrorism* (*Otshchepentsy. Put' k terrorizmu*), treats the movement as an upwelling of aberrant behavior that must be understood principally from a psychological point of view.[36]

In foregrounding terrorism itself, these recent studies differ from the present one. The populist movement between 1878 and 1881 constituted an important stage in the history of terrorism, particularly given the fact that the radical populists willingly referred to themselves as terrorists in attempting to define and promote their new form of violent political agitation. Ultimately this is a study of radical populism as such, not a study of radical populism as an episode in the history of terrorism. The intention here is to *ground* the populist movement in the environment from which it emerged, and the "ground zero" of radical populism was the reform-era city.

SPACES, CITIES, AND THE RISE OF RADICAL POPULISM

As a history of the rise to power of radical populism, this study inevitably rests on a set of assumptions about how power is obtained and used. One cannot understand the radical populist movement in terms of the liberal, enlightenment-based view that legitimate power originates in the establishment of democratic principles and institutions. The populists rejected that framework, in a similar way to Marx and Engels, as a means of privileging the propertied classes. Nor could Marxism itself, though sympathetic to the populists' revolutionary aims, offer an explanation for the "success" of the

populist movement, which did not proceed through a path of historical inevitability by way of industrialization and class struggle. The populists' claims
of legitimacy were clearly based on a version of what Marx and Engels called
"utopian socialism." From both the liberal and Marxist viewpoints, then, the
rise of radical populism as a revolutionary force was an aberration that did
not fall within either the approved or likely paths of historical development.

A body of theory does exist, however, in the work of Michel Foucault,
that goes a long way toward illuminating the sources of populist power.
Foucault's conception of power originated in his skepticism toward all-
encompassing world views such as liberalism and Marxism. Referring to
these "unitary discourses" of power as "totalitarian" in their assertion of
political frameworks with the capacity to account for, and validate or inval-
idate, all positions, Foucault chose to bracket out questions of broad political legitimacy and focus on the generation and use of power in localized
contexts.[37] The resulting shift in perspective enabled him to examine what
he called the "micro-techniques of power" under specific conditions and
within specific institutions and bodies of knowledge. In my view, Foucault's
work supplements, rather than overthrows, other frameworks for understanding political power, but for reasons that will become clear his approach
is much more appropriate and usable as a tool for understanding radical
populism's rise. Foucault's analysis of the dynamics of power relations puts
aside both grand narratives of historical development and questions about
ethical legitimacy, turning instead to "battlefield" questions of *how*, in practical terms, power can be acquired and effectively deployed. By similarly isolating radical populism from any all-embracing justification, or lack thereof,
we can more easily see it as rooted both in a specific time and place and in
the development of a discrete set of practices that did not require coherent ideological scaffolding. For these reasons, this study eschews moral and
political judgment in order to foreground the local possibilities and specific
constraints within which radical populism emerged.[38]

In coming to grips with the tactical and strategic operations of the populist movement, a crucial consideration must be the character of the particular environment in which those strategies were deployed, and Foucault is
helpful in this respect as well. Until recently, scholars had largely ignored the
spatial element in Foucault's work, but that has begun to change, especially
with the 2008 publication of a substantial volume of essays on Foucault's
connection to the field of geography.[39] It is now easier to recognize that
Foucault, as Chris Philo puts it, "demands sustained alertness to questions
of space, place, environment and landscape in a manner rarely encountered
from someone who is not a professional geographer."[40] Although Foucault

was most immediately concerned with the relationship between epistemology and power, and rarely made explicit the role of physical space, it is clear that what he identified as forms of "power/knowledge" were intertwined with, even dependent on, the creation of particular spaces. In his own words: "a whole history remains to be written of *spaces*—which would at the same time be the history of *powers* ... from the great strategies of geo-politics to the little tactics of the habitat."[41] Those spaces that did play a central role in Foucault's work included, among others, the hospital/clinic, the asylum, the post-renaissance city, and the prison. The most familiar example of a specific space is found in his discussion of Jeremy Bentham's "panopticon," which he reads as a sort of metaphor for modern technologies of control.

Space, even urban space, is usually conceived of as passive and inert, the backdrop upon which the stuff of history takes place, but for a number of reasons, a conception of place as a passive container is coming to seem inadequate. That specific social and physical spaces are inextricably bound up with power and historical change—one of the basic assumptions on which the present study rests—was also the central subject of Henri Lefebvre's *The Production of Space*. Lefebvre's highly abstract social philosophy speaks in a language most historians are unaccustomed to. But Lefebvre makes a powerful case for taking space seriously as an essential component of historical change. Lefebvre argues that societies plan, build, demarcate, imagine, embody, and reproduce space as a means of maintaining social stasis and affirming existing relations of power. According to Lefebvre, by "producing" a space that embodies its own form and self-conception, a society reflects, in physical form, the social relationships that underlie it, thereby asserting a kind of unstated belief structure about "the way things just are." Consequently, in its apparent immutability, as Edward Soja has put it, a given space works "to imbue all things spatial with a lingering sense of primordiality and physical composition, an aura of objectivity, inevitability, and reification."[42]

A familiar contemporary example of this relationship between space and power would be the American (and increasingly global) suburb: the network of single family homes, automobiles, highways, shopping centers, supermarkets, and so forth, which came into being during the 20th century as a result of the conjunction of a variety of technological, social, and political developments. From these developments emerged the suburb as a freely chosen living space/way of life for those who could afford it, but the suburb is also a space that reinforces and reproduces a particular vision of "ordinary" life, a vision that in turn reinforces and reproduces a particular socioeconomic and political system.[43] Within the imagined/constructed environment of the American suburb, a certain view of individualism—as well as agreed-on norms of family, community, and consumer capitalism—all appear perfectly "natural" since they constitute, at one and the same time, an image of the proper space and the *actual space* that serves to define its own normativity.

This naturalization of culture via the construction of space has its counterpart in the *disruption* of spatial norms. When a political movement appears that intentionally undermines or re-channels spatial practices, such as the familiar examples of the protest marches of Gandhi or King, the revolutionary barricading of Parisian streets, the appropriation of "People's Park" in 1960s Berkeley, the protests in Tiananmen Square in 1980s Beijing, or the "Occupy" movements of 2011, the intervention often elicits a swift and violent reaction on grounds that public order and/or property rights have been violated. Since normative space is already deeply politicized, to rethink or "occupy" it in a new way constitutes one of the most dramatic and unsettling methods of undermining otherwise apparently stable relations of power.

At this point, we seem to have ventured a long way from late-imperial Russia. The link between the above examples and the subject of this book is another specific space: the burgeoning pre-industrial reform-era Russian city. Let us return to it by way of one of the reform era's great works of literature. Fyodor Dostoevsky's *Crime and Punishment* tells the story of a young intellectual driven to murder by untenable radical views—views that resulted not only from the destabilizing power of modern thought but also from the specific experiences of life in the modern city. *Crime and Punishment* is so saturated with its urban setting that St. Petersburg seems to be one of the novel's main characters, and the impersonality and overstimulation of urban modernity (a precursor to Emile Durkheim's "urban anomie") appears to be partially responsible for Raskolnikov's madness. Dostoevsky was not subtle about this. On his way to commit murder, Raskolnikov contemplates ways to alleviate the miserable conditions of inner city St. Petersburg.[44]

While I do not agree with most aspects of Dostoevsky's interpretation of Russian radicalism, I do agree that he was searching for clues in the right place. The city was not merely the setting for his exploration of radical thought; it was in fact the actual environment within which the radical intelligentsia emerged, and indeed it is not possible to account for the phenomenon of radical populism in the absence of the urban environment that brought it into being and shaped its trajectory. The city provided a social context in which a radical movement could take shape. If "infectious" new ideas were coming to pervade modern society, particularly among its youthful cohort, those ideas were spreading in part because the urban environment served as a matrix within which new ideas could congeal and fan out. A city, especially a large and unruly metropolis, facilitates more than just the dissemination of new knowledge; it provides a space in which to forge common bonds of elective affinity from among a critical mass of like-minded others.[45] Cities also produce multiple platforms for public expression—in the press, in and through voluntary associations, in new spaces such as business and leisure venues, and even in the language of fashion communicated on the street. In this respect urbanization not only involves the formation of new streets, squares, and buildings, but it also enables the creation of new organizations, new institutions, new gathering spaces, new subcultures, and new political movements. Such developments are environmentally dependent in that they can and do take place almost exclusively in cities, all the more so in a rapidly expanding and increasingly complex city like St. Petersburg.

The period under consideration here (1855–1881) encompasses the reign of Alexander II and is commonly known as the Reform Era, the period of Alexander's "Great Reforms." The first and most important of these reforms, the 1861 abolition of serfdom, was directed toward socioeconomic conditions in the countryside, but many subsequent reforms directly concerned urban life, and the reforms intensified the already bright light shining upon the capital city as a model for the rest of the Russian Empire. The grand design behind the reforms was to redefine the role of Russian citizenship by ending passive subjection to political power and social hierarchy and unleashing the pent-up energy and initiative of society (not forgetting the implicit assumption that imperial Russian citizens would remain loyal adherents of the autocratic state).[46] Thus the reforms boosted education, decreased censorship, ushered in a flood of newspapers and journals, created a system of trials using citizen jurors, and even established elections for local municipal and provincial officials. The state intentionally instituted this transition with great caution, but the reforms provided a sufficiently dramatic set of innovations to invigorate Russian society, especially in the urban sector, and to produce the unintended side effect of increasing political dissent. As a result of the reforms, if the level of industrial modernization in Russia still lagged behind much of Europe in this era, the sense of novelty, loss, possibility and contradiction that typically accompanies rapid urbanization was keeping pace.

Russia, a latecomer to the urbanization that had long been underway in cities like London and Paris, around the middle of the nineteenth century began to catch up quickly in a rather drastic phase of accelerated urbanization that continued up to 1917. By the 1860s urbanization and intensive change were fully underway. Rapid population growth, mixed with the expansion of private enterprise and the promise of a more engaged public sphere, helped both to vitalize and destabilize large Russian cities so that the relative calm under Nicholas I began to give way by the late 1850s to the dynamism and sense of disruption characteristic of large metropolitan centers.[47] It was at this point, for example, that Petersburg residents began to exhibit increased anxiety about crime, slums, prostitution, and other "dangers" of urban life.[48] At the same time, new venues for shopping, drinking, and entertainment were opened by enterprising business owners, so that the public spaces of the city simultaneously became more conflict ridden and more vibrant. From the standpoint of urban planning, Alexandra Staub has described reform-era St. Petersburg in the following useful terms:

> The city rapidly expanded, as trade and industry led to an economic boom and a need for both new housing and other buildings such as factories, railway stations, warehouses and department stores. A briskly developing capitalism meant a temporary end to the idea of a city built according to a central master plan. Many of the recently built villas were torn down to make way for large, beaux-art-style housing blocks designed to turn a handsome profit.... The block structure created by the grid of streets became condensed and more legible.....The city now boasted a vibrant and cosmopolitan urban life, much like the Western European centers Peter the Great had sought to emulate."[49]

No doubt reform-era St. Petersburg was undergoing rapid change and development, but should we really credit the metropolitan setting as an essential component in the rise of radical populism? In addition to the reasons cited above—the city's ability to foster a critical mass of individuals, networks of sociability, easy communication of ideas, and a public platform for the expression of views—we must add that cities, especially large ones, tend to become places in which creativity and innovation flourish. The intensive interaction between diverse populations that takes place in urban environments can sometimes lead to conflict and discord, but it can also facilitate tolerance, fertilize cross-cultural understanding, and lead to creative solutions to problems. To offer a conceptually similar, but otherwise unconnected example, Matt Houlbrook has documented how the city of London in the 1920s and 1930s became the site of a flourishing gay subculture. Urban space opened room for an otherwise suppressed form of love and desire for a variety of reasons: 1) the critical mass of like-minded individuals available in a large urban setting, 2) the anonymity of the urban experience that allowed individuals to search out and engage with others, even in ways that were illegal and/or socially disapproved, 3) the density of urban space that made it possible to locate small hidden places in which to interact privately in close proximity to public space, and 4) the tolerance for non-standard views and behavior that tends to accrue in urban settings in which residents confront, and generally ignore, numerous others unlike themselves.[50] All these benefits work to the advantage of a wide variety of urban subcultures, from innovative movements in the arts, to marginal religious groups, to bohemian districts, to users of illegal substances, to out-of-the-mainstream political movements. Such groups constitute what the sociologist Claude Fischer, using the expression in an impartial sense, termed "deviant subcultures."[51]

Recent scholarship has focused on the rise of new activities and associations in urban Russia—scientific and scholarly associations, leisure activities, the spread of newspapers, the growth of theater, arts, and museums, and the rise of consumer capitalism, to name a few.[52] Studies of these subjects have often been conceived of as corrections to a Cold War overemphasis on non-normative Russian developments, such as radical political movements, the police state, and the isolation of the intelligentsia. But the argument in this study is that radical populism was grounded in the very same urban environment, side by side with the development of an enriched urban public and an increasingly active civil society. It is often pointed out that the 1917 Revolution was a thoroughly urban event. In the words of Hans Rogger, the Russian Revolution "was urban in its origins, in the social and geographical locus of its beginnings, in its leadership, and in its political vocabulary."[53] Though most of this point holds true for the populist movement as well, populism is rarely accorded such an urban provenance. The intellectual emphasis on the peasantry and the countryside is only one reason the role of the city has been obscured; another involves the fact that radical populism was not a mass movement but was largely directed by groups of intelligentsia activists.

And yet these activists and the movement they created were deeply immersed in their urban setting. As Deborah Hardy noted in her study of the formation of The People's Will, the populist movement was "an urban phenomenon, designed by urban revolutionaries for protection against the urban police."[54] Since populism favored the revolutionary transformation of society based on accessing and empowering rural values, it is not always noticed that the populist idealization of the countryside was very much a part of the wider *urban* idealization of rural life that emerged throughout Europe in the late eighteenth century. Modern urban Europeans found a variety of different ways to elevate the countryside as the pastoral lost Eden that had been abandoned by urban society in its quest for modernity. Russian populism lies on the politically leftward end of that Rousseauian "back to nature" continuum.[55] Similar to other idealizations of rural life entailing landscape painting and retreats to dachas, radical populism was an urban phenomenon. Populist devotion to and idealization of the rural *narod* ("people" or "folk") only underlines its urban character. The city was the soil from which populism sprang, and urban life shaped and directed its various shifts and developments during the 1860s and 1870s.

The most influential book among the radical intelligentsia in the 1860s and 1870s, Nikolai Chernyshevskii's *What Is To Be Done?*, makes another case in point. Every aspect of the novel—Vera Pavlovna's escape from her family, the blending of social backgrounds in her communal workshop, the rehabilitation of a prostitute, the circle of progressive young people upon which the novel's essential love triangle is based, and the feigned suicide that begins and ends the book, are all predicated on social possibilities exclusively available in an urban setting. Even the novel's exemplary revolutionary figure, Rakhmetov, undergoes what Chernyshevskii refers to as a "rebirth" only once he moves to St. Petersburg at the age of sixteen.[56] Similar awakenings were either imagined or experienced by numerous people who came to the city during this period. In the late 1850s, the radical critic Nikolai Dobroliubov wrote about life in St. Petersburg that "The voice of one's blood ties has become scarcely audible. It is being drowned out by other, higher and more general interests."[57]

Because they were free in the urban context to focus on "higher and more general interests," young Russians began to reinvent themselves in the city and ultimately went on to reshape society. In her memoirs, Vera Zasulich recalled how from the provinces St. Petersburg appeared "the laboratory of ideas, the center of life, of movement, of activity."[58] When Aleksandr Mikhailov first arrived in St. Petersburg in the 1870s, he was disillusioned by student life, but he found compensation in the city itself: "the life and people of Petersburg easily replaced for me the institutions of higher education. . . . Relations with people of various understandings and convictions, from the very highest society to the minor officials. Personal thoughts about and criticism of everything taking place before my eyes allowed me to orient myself to the new situation."[59] The city gave rise to and nurtured the populist movement as it grew. If one were to sum up the argument of this book in a single sentence, it would state that urbanization and its effects were at least as much a factor as ideology in the making of radical populism and in encouraging its turn to terrorism.

THE UNDERGROUND AS SUBVERSIVE HETEROTOPIA

A key to understanding many developments that took place in reform-era Russia is the oft-noted fact that the reforming autocracy worked at cross-purposes from its own aims. By attempting at one and the same time to institute reforms and to minimize their impact, the government of Alexander II elicited uncertainty and confusion, and eventually helped unleash dissension and revolt. As this book sets out to show, the advent of an effective revolutionary underground at the end of the 1870s was the end result of a complicated process that began by endowing the populace with the right, even the duty, of active participation in civil affairs while at the same time denying them the right to disagree with the political system and its decisions. This contradiction set in motion a long succession of efforts on the part of the opposition to express its views and organize a viable movement. These efforts included, not necessarily in chronological order, the publication of veiled criticism of Russia's political and socioeconomic systems; the writing and distribution of anti-autocratic proclamations; the creation of schools for teaching basic skills and spreading oppositional sentiment; the formation of communes and artels that united groups of people around a common goal; the writing, printing, and dissemination of illegal literature among workers and peasants; variously successful attempts to hold street demonstrations, marches, and strikes; and finally the creation of underground organizations that spread "propaganda by deed" through the commission of violent attacks that were then explained and justified in open statements to the public. As again and again revolutionary populists discovered they were unable to exert an influence on society through open activism, they came more and more to rely on the organization of an underground base from which they could engage in various forms of agitation with relative impunity.

In order to account for the effectiveness of the underground, we again turn to Foucault, whose concept of the "heterotopia" serves as a useful starting point.[60] Foucault proposed this term relatively early in his career, and although the lecture in which he first presented it was not published until late in his life, in certain ways it is a cornerstone of his work. Not surprisingly, many scholars have subsequently taken it up as a useful concept.[61] The term heterotopia, meaning quite simply "other place," attempts to describe an important spatio-social operation in modern societies.[62] By way of contrast to "utopia," an imaginary "no place," Foucault coined the term to refer to physically existing places found in one form or another in all societies. Heterotopia are carved out of the pre-existing environment but serve various distinct social functions, from reinforcing social norms and power relations to initiating social and cultural change. The importance of such heterotopic spaces involves the leverage they can exert from their removed position.[63]

While the prison, the asylum, the church, and the museum can all be considered heterotopic spaces that operate in their different ways to maintain the social order, other heterotopia have functioned to undermine existing conditions.[64] Familiar examples of such "subversive heterotopia" might include a city's bohemian district, a space recognizable by the fact that it encourages experimentation with art and alternative behaviors and values. Spaces that become identified with anti-establishment political speech, like the Palais Royal in Paris on the eve of the French Revolution, or in a different way the cabarets of Weimar Berlin, can be included among politically and socially subversive heterotopia, as would spaces that tolerate or harbor illegal activity. Radical populism created its own array of subversive heterotopia that we will encounter on these pages, from student circles and politicized bookstores to the "nihilist" commune and the terrorist's "conspiratorial apartment." The revolutionary underground was just such a subversive heterotopia, a space apart from, but at the same time precisely within, the heart of the Russian capital city. It was consciously constructed to serve a variety of subversive purposes. It was a refuge from ever-expanding police scrutiny, a locus of social and political connection for radicals and their supporters, an insurrectionary base of operations, and a remarkably effective platform for gaining visibility and notoriety for the populist movement.[65] In the construction of this subversive heterotopia, urban space did not simply serve as a context for, or a container of, events. It was a necessary precondition. The reform-era city and the underground it fostered make a good example of how, to paraphrase the geographer David Harvey, human activities create distinctive spaces, and those spaces in turn work to determine human activities.[66]

Although historians have not yet focused sufficient attention on underground spaces as a direct topic of inquiry, the concept is not at all unfamiliar in Russian history. As early as 1883, Sergei Kravchinskii (Stepniak), one of the key figures in the radical populist movement, published a widely read memoir titled *Underground Russia* that described the members and operations of the populist underground.[67] From an entirely different perspective, Dostoevsky's 1864 novella *Notes from Underground*, described St. Petersburg as a city in which those of low social status lived in a state of invisibility brought about by the alienating conditions of modern urban life. Under such conditions, certain people like Dostoevsky's unnamed "underground man," lacked social power and felt insignificant in the extreme. The root of the term Dostoevsky uses for underground (*podpol'e*) means "under the floor" as much as "under the ground," and Dostoevsky's underground man seems to represent the social invisibility of someone "under the floor" of an apartment.

But Dostoevsky's "underground" did not reflect the populists' conception of their own underground in the 1860s and 1870s. The populist underground was created by individuals from relatively elite backgrounds, people who did not at all understand themselves as insignificant, but rather conceived of themselves as the most politically conscious, humane, and critically-thinking individuals in Russia. These figures may at times have felt "humili-ated and offended" by officialdom and social elites, but even living "illegally" under false identities, they still considered themselves the best and brightest representatives of Russia's future. These young men and women went down into the obscurity of the underground intentionally. They believed doing so offered them the best chance to spread their own vision of light and social progress to Russian society. In this respect, it is curious that although the populists themselves were well aware of the importance of the underground as a cornerstone of their power, few (arguably no) historians have focused directly on the crucial role of the underground as an empowering device.

Soviet historians tended to divide and conquer the complicated history of radical populism by breaking it into separate subsections of the larger move-ment, but to separate the strands of populism risks missing continuities and internal contradictions that were equally important. What often seem to be separate episodes—attempts to make use of the urban public sphere, the carving out of heterotopic spaces for countercultural movements, the exodus to the countryside to commune with the peasantry, and the insur-rectionary activism of violent propaganda by deed—ultimately were not separate and distinct events so much as a complex web of activities that spun out from one another in dialectical processes of antagonism, amalgamation, and mutual reinforcement. The populist movement as a whole cannot accu-rately be described otherwise, and therefore I take the entirety of reform-era radical populism as my subject here. At the same time, limits are necessary, and although versions of the radical underground continued to play a role in Russian history at least up to the demise of the autocracy in 1917, this study concludes with the 1881 assassination of Alexander II, by which point the underground had outlived its first phase of power and influence.[68]

The following chapter (chapter 1) describes the opening act of radical populism, in which for a time, until the state cracked down on political activity, it seemed populist goals might be achieved through active interven-tion in the urban public sphere. A parallel movement arose in the late 1850s that called on young people to create new selves and a new cultural reality. This movement, the subject of chapter 2, was most commonly referred to as "nihilism," and it continued to have an impact in various ways throughout the reform era. Around the same time, as we explore in chapter 3, once the state effectively shut down the public expression of radical views in 1862, the attempt to carry out a revolutionary struggle went underground, with mixed results, through the remainder of the 1860s. Chapter 4 describes the process whereby new hope sprang up in the early 1870s with the movement known as "going to the people." Not long after that movement reached sizable proportions, large-scale arrests and consequent disillusionment over its effectiveness ensued. Re-centered on the urban environment in the mid-1870s, radical populism began to profit from the dynamism of Russian cities and once again returned to the urban public sphere as its center of political activism. This process is the subject of chapter 5. In roughly the same period, as detailed in chapter 6, the populists recognized the necessity of creating a sustainable urban underground, and putting into practice a variety of conspiratorial techniques, developed a resourceful and effective underground space. Chapter 7 details the tactics used in carrying out some of the operations that gave the populists the aura of power and invincibility they had attained by the late 1870s. Chapter 8 describes the underground at the apex of that power, showing how the seductions and misunderstanding it generated ultimately led to a severe undermining of the populist movement after the assassination of the tsar.

Perhaps because of the long decades of effort to make sense of populism as an ideological phenomenon, it came as a surprise to me to read the memoirs (and the few remaining letters) of the populists who had been involved. Youthful, naïve, and motivated by emotions far more than ideas, the reform-era populists depicted themselves as passionate crusaders for an indefinite cause, in contrast to the doctrine-debating Marxists who followed them. For this reason, the book makes liberal use of statements made by participants themselves, allowing them, to a degree, to tell their own story. I cite them often with the intention of bringing their own experience of the movement back into the foreground. The thesis that emerges can be summarized as follows: over the course of the reform era the radical populist movement, ever in search of power and influence in its quest to bring about a popular revolution, in part stumbled into and in part consciously created the radical underground, a new way of occupying urban space that temporarily offered populism its most effective means of political struggle. The formation of this new, organized and disciplined, subversive heterotopia allowed the anti-autocratic movement to congregate and carry out a wide variety of operations in relative safety, to print and distribute revolutionary publications, to gather funds and recruit new members, and finally to terrorize the state and temporarily undermine the government through acts of political violence. Underground terrorism was not the first, second, or even third choice Russian populists made as their preferred form of revolutionary struggle, but the underground the populists eventually created afforded them the autonomy to wage war against the autocracy. Without this underground base of operations, Russian radical populism would not have, and could not have, become what it did.

CHAPTER ONE

ST. PETERSBURG

From Space of Representation to Embattled Public Sphere

[In the nineteenth century] cities became great stages on which were played out the dramas of popular and radical politics.

C. A. Bayly

THE REFORM-ERA POPULISM THAT WOULD eventually create a politically active underground did not, like the Decembrist movement a quarter century earlier, begin in secret, conspiratorial societies. In the rosy dawn of the first years of the reign of Alexander II, at least some of those who pushed for change were able to do so openly. A significant constituency within the state, including to a degree the tsar himself, favored the expansion of societal participation in public affairs, and many among the intelligentsia sought to use the freedom of expression that seemed to be promised by the new regime to promote their views. It would not be long, however, before the habits of autocracy and the aspirations of the intelligentsia would come into conflict with one another. Within the space of about half a decade, from the late 1850s to the early 1860s, the limits of independent and oppositional expression would be reached. As early as 1861, clandestine, anti-autocratic publications began to be printed and disseminated, and secret societies began to form, while at the same time the state quickly wearied of the left-wing opposition. From this point forward, the radical intelligentsia would begin to venture deeper underground in order to accomplish its goals.

To understand the origins of the reform-era underground it is necessary to begin with populism's early ventures into the imperial Russian public sphere. The task is not simple in that conceptions of "the public" in the early period of Alexander II's reign were complex and problematic, resting as they did on a political system deeply suspicious of social interference in governance and a society unaccustomed to involvement in public affairs. One helpful starting point is a little-noted section of Jurgen Habermas's influential *The Structural Transformation of the Public Sphere* that sets out to describe the precursor to the modern concept of a "public" and "public opinion." Habermas refers to the pre-modern, or "lordly" and monarchial, counterpart to a modern public sphere as a "publicity of representation" or alternately a "representative publicness." In these rather awkward terms, Habermas seeks to capture an epoch in which public affairs were the exclusive purview of a ruler free from any need to gauge the mood of society in order to steer his favored course, a ruler who takes entirely upon himself those decisions and acts relevant to society as a whole. As the sole authority, the ruler "displayed himself, presented himself as an embodiment of some sort of 'higher' power."[1] Over time in early modern Europe, especially as greater economic power devolved to groups and individuals outside the ruling elite, new social formations began to appear, such as stock markets, civic associations, newspapers, and the concept of "public opinion," institutions and ideas that stressed society's relevance within the larger political whole.

The historical processes through which these new forms developed were far from simple and unfolded in a variety of ways, at different times, in different places, depending on social and political conditions. In Russia, for reasons involving deep-rooted socioeconomic structures and political norms, collective ways of conceptualizing the body politic either did not emerge or else emerged in ways that looked quite different from the picture of modern Europe Habermas and others have described. Longer and more effectively than in other parts of Europe, the Russian state maintained its "publicity of representation," its assumed ascendancy over the public sphere.

But the fact that a public sphere based on prototypical (and often idealized) models of Western Europe did not emerge in Russia does not mean, as some have claimed, that Russia entirely lacked a viable civil society.[2] The struggle to expand society's influence grew increasingly urgent over the nineteenth century, and the autocratic state itself at times nurtured society's participation in public affairs. At the same time, however, the state continued jealously to guard its prerogative as the primary voice and final arbiter of power, remaining unwilling to allow public opinion to infringe upon its predominance. The net effect of these contrasting impulses would be to create a particular kind of public sphere in Russia, limited mainly to a small contingent (for which was coined the term "intelligentsia") that was anxious to voice its views and frustrated by the limitations placed upon them. The public sphere that *did* develop in Russia by the mid-nineteenth century, then, consisted of a small subsection of educated urbanites and was constrained by severe limitations on speech and assembly. It developed as it could within legal channels, though at times this required significant compromise with the authorities. It also took political innuendo (so-called Aesopian language) to new heights and relied for information not only on legal publications but also on émigré and domestic illegal publications.

At the same time, and even in some ways as a result of limits on expression, Russian public discourse gave rise to a remarkable degree of creativity and innovation. Politics lodged deeply in the realm of creative literature (as well as other art forms) and unleashed a tradition of politically engaged "critical realism" that helped produce the world famous artistic renaissance of nineteenth-century Russia. This renaissance at least in part resulted from the fact that art, in its complexity and potential for ambiguity, was one of the few arenas capable of sheltering social and political criticism. Genuine political organization of any kind was severely limited, and these restrictions tended to enhance a personal and cultural politics, which helped, for example, to put women's rights and education at the center of the intelligentsia agenda. Finally, as a result of the state's extreme intolerance for political opposition, there arose a significant component of clandestine, or underground, activism. This chapter traces the trajectory of the imperial Russian public from the autocracy's original "publicity of representation" to the unique character of the reform-era public sphere within which radical populism first took shape.

ST. PETERSBURG AS SPACE OF AUTOCRATIC REPRESENTATION

For all its vaunted westernization, in the imperial Russian polity established by Peter the Great in the early eighteenth century, no formal or informal structures yet suggested that society as a collective whole should contribute its voice to governmental decision making. Over the eighteenth century, however, gradual social and political changes began to bring about a shift from an autocratic "publicity of representation" to what might be called the preconditions for the rise of a public sphere. The education and training of the nobility, beginning under Peter, was a first step, as Peter sought to create both able servitors and a Russian polite society, mainly by importing the trappings of Western European practices of his era.[3] The emancipation of the nobility from government service under Peter III in 1762 also in a limited way helped to establish a small population of private individuals, thus enabling the formation of a semi-autonomous "educated society." Later in the eighteenth century, during the reign of Catherine the Great, some of the rudiments of civil society, in a small semi-independent press and a smattering of voluntary associations, began to take shape. Similar developments continued, with gradual and intermittent acceleration, into the first decades of the nineteenth century.[4] Historians have understandably focused attention on the importance of these processes, but even these gradual changes would not be properly understood unless we keep in mind that the state continued to develop and improve its own "publicity of representation," trying to insure that the public realm would remain the domain of those in power: the state, the court, and the Orthodox Church.

Even so, when Peter I began to present the state as the guarantor of the common weal, it portended that the representation of state power would eventually have to be re-established in new forms, and in the wake of Peter's reign, Russian emperors learned to excel at self-presentation as a method of affirming their right to rule. Richard Wortman has explored in great detail the techniques Russian rulers used to assert their "publicity of representation" in the processes he refers to as staging "scenarios of power." As Wortman shows, each successive ruler used the press, the public ceremony, the parade ground, the palace, and the streets of the city as venues for the affirmation of his or her legitimate authority. While Peter's own techniques of autocratic self-presentation had included parades, proclamations, and works of art celebrating his reign, his greatest and most lasting testament to the power of the autocracy was the city of St. Petersburg itself. St. Petersburg would become one of the main stages upon which future scenarios of power would play out, while at the same time the capital city itself became an expression and embodiment of autocratic power. From Peter forward, the capital served as a monument to the rightful rule of Russia's emperors, and each successive ruler used it, and enhanced it, as a continuing expression of autocratic authority.

Peter founded his new capital city with the intention of making it an up-to-date baroque expression of Russia's glorious future. Historically, the "baroque city" used urban planning techniques to create a visual expression of state power in long boulevards, vast open squares, and monumental buildings, all of which were strategically positioned to celebrate the ruler in the age of absolutism as the embodiment of power and the *raison d'etre* of all social blessings.[5] In the monumental and spectacular space of the baroque city "the king becomes the very incarnation of the nature of the state.... The stage on which he shines is the one where the kingdom recognizes itself and honors itself."[6] The roots of the baroque city go back to as early as Pope Six-tus V (1585–1590) and his reconstruction of Rome, but as a late example of baroque (and later classical) city planning, St. Petersburg had the advantage of starting from scratch.[7] It stands today as one of the world's best examples of the monumental style of urban architecture. From its inception the city was created as a projection of imperial grandeur, stability, and modernity. Iurii Egorov has described St. Petersburg as a city of "dominants," structures that included "large government buildings, wide squares and parade grounds, broad streets, cathedrals and monuments commemorating great Russian deeds."[8] Stateliness, enormity and rectilinear planning put St. Petersburg on display as a testament in stone to Peter's original ideal of an orderly and powerful Russia embodied in the principle of benevolent autocracy.[9] In the city's central locations, with every footstep and every glance, inhabitants and visitors beheld a bold and unmistakable assertion of the power and omni-presence of the Romanov Dynasty.

Marcel Henaf and Tracy Strong attribute the rise of this new monumental and spectacular architecture to what they call, following J. G. A. Pocock, "the Machiavellian moment." They use this expression as shorthand for the early modern transformation of European rulership from an unquestioned and inevitable authority, whether on the basis of religious faith or dynastic principle, to something *potentially* contested for which legitimacy had to be made good by practice (as Machiavelli advises in *The Prince*) in the face of a newly interested society. In other words, at some point in Early Mod-ern Europe it came to be understood that in order to endow rulership with the "unquestioned authority" to which it was accustomed, new techniques to prop up and naturalize political authority had to be invented. As Henaf and Strong contend, this consolidation of power was partly accomplished through the tactics of architectural stagecraft: "the political technique of appearance, the organization of the stage of power, was for Machiavelli closely tied to a new rationality of representation." The ruler's power needed to be obvious to all, and the architectural craft of the baroque city helped to make it so.[10]

The effect of St. Petersburg's majestic enormity was compounded by the breadth of the Neva River around which it was built. The river opens vistas so wide that ordinary perception seems to get lost in the sweeping views. It dwarfs the individual and suggests something of the immense global reach of the all-powerful Russian Empire. The grandiose void of St. Petersburg's form was noticed again and again, by supporters of the autocracy like Pavel Svin'in, who tried to capture the city's grandeur by portraying it as almost empty of human interaction, and by detractors, like the Marquis de Custine, who referred to the city's massive scale as reminiscent of "the empty steppe."[11] To this day St. Petersburg presents such a formidable projection of power that visitors commonly react to its monumentality with sensations of both inspired awe and intimidating de-personalization. Imperial St. Petersburg's inhabitants regularly promenaded on the grand avenues which were, according to Lewis Mumford, "the most important symbol and the main fact about the baroque city."[12] In this way the streets themselves contributed to the city's sense of place as "power on display." Grand Petersburg boulevards, in particular Nevskii Prospekt, provided the sort of wide promenade that allowed for the display of social difference in which "the daily parade of the powerful becomes one of [the baroque city's] principal dramas."[13] Though one must be careful not to conflate descriptions and impressions of the city with the actual lived urban environment, it is hard to overlook the numerous descriptions in the early nineteenth century that portrayed Petersburg's stiff formality as a kind of soulless mask. Vasily Zhukovsky called the inhabitants of St. Petersburg "mummies, surrounded by majestic pyramids."[14] Gogol's short story "Nevskii Prospekt" is particularly striking in its description of disembodied bonnets and mustaches greeting one another as they glide down the city's main promenade.[15]

Architecture was not alone in representing and even promoting power in St. Petersburg. Strange as it may seem by today's standards, the bodily appearance of the tsar and members of the royal family themselves also filled that role. Russian tsars regularly opened their palaces to invited guests and strolled leisurely in public gardens at appointed hours. It was not unusual to see the tsar speeding along the streets in his carriage, or even working at his desk in the window of the Winter Palace.[16] Nicholas I used his own physical presence as a part of his "publicity of representation," a technique Wortman dubbed "the illusion of omnipresence."[17] For Russia's rulers, St. Petersburg served as the *mise-en-scene* for the enactment of their personal power. As A. P. Shevyrev has suggested, the person of the tsar constituted a kind of stage prop for the theatrical enactment of St. Petersburg's power and magnificence:

> One must note that given the considerable probability of some chance meeting [with the tsar]—at ceremonies, in the streets, in his carriage or out for a walk—each of these situations was arranged in such a way that the passerby felt himself to be both a witness to and participant in a theatrical presentation. The monarch himself was nearly an equal participant in such presentations. Even the private walks instituted by Alexander I, or

the impromptu appearance of Nicholas I at greeting places [*prisutstvennye mesta*], seemed to be well-staged scenes, in which both monarchs not only played their roles as actors, but also enjoyed the effect they produced.[18]

The extent to which the autocracy dominated public space in St. Petersburg even appears in the nature of Russia's first political rebellion: the failed Decembrist Revolt of 1825. With the desire to declare Russia a constitutional monarchy during a crisis of succession, a group of rebellious army officers (later known as "Decembrists") attempted to stage a *coup d'etat* in a public square. But rather than invade the palace, or at least stage their revolt at the center of political power in the Palace Square, they chose instead to protest on the smaller and less central Senate Square in front of the administrative Senate building. While this decision was based on their intention to prevent the Senate from administering the loyalty oath to the new tsar, in the language of the city's layout the location of their protest indicated that their rebellion was not against the monarchy itself so much as it was in opposition to the manner in which the ruler wielded power. Decembrist submission to ultimate authority was evident even before the rebels made a move. Corroborating their lack of conviction was the fact that their "dictator," Sergei Trubetskoi, was too frightened or uncertain even to make an appearance on the Senate Square. "The decision to appeal to the Senate," as M. V. Nechkina put it, "shows with great clarity the limits of the noble revolution—the fear of breaking the old state machinery, the attempt to base itself precisely on [the existing state] in the quest for a 'legal' form of revolution."[19] By coming forward to make demands of the tsar in front of the urban population, the Decembrists were, to be sure, boldly trampling on the autocracy's cherished conception of public space as the state's exclusive domain, and yet they only managed to flout autocratic authority in a way that acknowledged that their claims on the public sphere would remain limited.[20]

It is worth noting about the Decembrists that, whatever their actions during the revolt, they certainly *aspired* to dismantle the autocratic version of St. Petersburg in order to reconstruct it in a spirit of civic unity. This aspiration is well conveyed in Decembrist Aleksandr Ulybyshev's vision of a future St. Petersburg in his short text "A Dream," which envisioned a city drastically altered by the rise of civil society. In his dream members of the ruling family are no longer on public display in monuments or building names. In their place are the "busts of men who have distinguished themselves for their talents and services."[21] The future St. Petersburg has been transformed into a civic paradise by the rise of a new political system in which an autocratic "publicity of representation" has been replaced by a city whose buildings serve the good of the citizenry:

> It seemed to me that I was in the streets of St. Petersburg, but everything had been changed so much that I had difficulty recognizing them. At every step new public buildings attracted my glance, while the old ones seemed to be used for purposes most oddly different from those for which they had originally been designed. On the façade of the Mikhailovsky Castle I read in big, golden letters "Palace of the State Assembly." All kinds of public schools, academies, and libraries had taken the place of the innumerable [military] barracks which used to crowd the city.[22]

The Decembrists dreamed of a public "by the people and for the people" in a society that no longer had a place for absolute monarchial authority. The final vision in Ulybyshev's "Dream" is a "Temple of Justice" directly across from the Winter Palace, where every citizen "at any hour can demand the protection of the law."[23] Ulybyshev's democratic utopia never materialized, but similar liberalizing objectives would continue to animate Russia's intelligentsia and influence future reforms.

URBANIZATION AND REFORM

It is a notable irony that although St. Petersburg served as a great symbol and embodiment of the autocratic principle, it was here too where that principle would be most effectively challenged. Nicholas I dispatched the Decembrist revolt and took the throne in 1825 with the express intention of reconsolidating autocratic power and authority. In the wake of the French Revolution and the advance of liberalism in this period, much of Western Europe was coming to perceive concepts such as civil society and public opinion as normal and essential parts of a well-governed body politic. But Russia's social order of estates and ranks did not easily lend itself to the usable fiction of public opinion, in which "the public" is conceived as a collective whole capable of expressing a consensus view. Nicholas was content to maintain intact the divided and, the Decembrist Revolt notwithstanding, still relatively docile society he had inherited. At the same time, many educated Russians by this point had come to understand their country as a part of "civilized" Europe. From this vantage point, it would prove increasingly difficult to ignore the idea that the public (defined as the educated sector of society) had the right and duty to assert its opinions, thereby helping to build a just and beneficent whole.

Even the autocracy showed signs of accepting a minimal degree of public participation in political affairs. In the monarchial "scenarios of power" Wortman describes, a clear evolution in state/society relations emerges over the eighteenth and nineteenth centuries. Whereas Peter's scenarios mainly sought to ingratiate the great and powerful, at the coronation of Catherine II (in 1762) rejoicing crowds were mentioned for the first time as part of the celebration. In the following century, Nicholas I's 1826 coronation was portrayed as "a national tradition manifesting the monarch's historical ties with his people," and by the time of Alexander II's 1855 coronation, the monarch was presenting his reign as "a romance between monarch and people."[24] The growing importance of society evident in this trajectory was not exclusively the result of political influence from Western Europe. As George Munro has pointed out, "in eighteenth-century St. Petersburg there was a constant tension between the statist conception of the nature and role of urban life and the living, vital city."[25] The processes of urbanization that animated this "living, vital city" also had political effects. Unanticipated technological developments in communications and transportation, for example, helped unite separate parts of society and enliven public interaction. The daily press, the telegraph and the railroad were, as many have pointed out for a variety of modernizing societies, basic building blocks of a public with a sense of cohesion and mutual interests. These developments appeared in full-fledged form in Russia only in the middle of the nineteenth century. As St. Petersburg grew, both in absolute numbers and in the complexity of its social and economic make-up, the city became harder to control from above.

Of course, there is no shortage of scholarship devoted to the city of St. Petersburg, but at the same time it is rather difficult to find sources that treat the city according to the usual models for urban history. Something about St. Petersburg has encouraged scholars to write about it in what might be called non-normative ways. It has been studied as a court and administrative center, an incubator of art and culture, a cradle of revolution, and even as a "text," an "image," and a "myth."[26] Less often do we read something equally significant about St. Petersburg: its processes of rapid urbanization resembled those of many other large European cities in the nineteenth century.[27] Though it seems almost irreverent to say so, in many ways St. Petersburg was typical and its trajectory unextraordinary. Every city has a character and history of its own of course, but historically the rise of cities has played a role in homogenizing distinct cultures, both by introducing common practices and by facilitating cross-cultural connections.

In this regard it is insufficiently recognized that, in spite of all the peculiarities that distinguished the Russian Empire from other parts of Europe in the nineteenth century, one way in which east and west, Europe and Russia, were drawing closer to one another involved common processes of intensive urbanization.

It is important to keep in mind that during the imperial period Russia remained an overwhelmingly rural country, with only a quarter of the population living in cities as late as 1917. But in spite of Russia's overall rural character, the country's urban centers served as the primary nexus of change. Large Russian cities grew at such a pace in the late-imperial period that by 1900 Russia had become one of two countries in the world to have two cities (Moscow and St. Petersburg) among the top ten largest.[28] This intensive urbanization was not without substantial effects. In the first half of the nineteenth century, the population of St. Petersburg did not experience as drastic an increase as it would during the second half of the century. It grew gradually from about 150,000 in 1750 to half a million in 1850, but in the 1860s there began a period of dramatic expansion, in which Petersburg doubled to one million by 1890 (and doubled again to two million by 1917).[29] For the sake of comparison, reform-era St. Petersburg was smaller than London and Paris but roughly equivalent in size to Vienna and Berlin. In the late 1870s it had reached the size Paris had been in the 1830s. Though it had only just begun to industrialize, St. Petersburg cannot be counted as a small or insignificant European city in the 1860s. As the reform era dawned, the city was already undergoing its transformation from a well-ordered court capital to the vibrant and chaotic industrial metropolis it would become during the latter part of the century.[30]

Part of the transformation resulted from the 1861 abolition of serfdom, which enabled movement from rural to urban Russia. Already in the early 1860s "thousands upon thousands of peasants were descending upon [St. Petersburg]."[31] This urban in-migration "more than doubled" between 1850 and 1870 and sparked a surge in population growth.[32] During the reform era, 85% of textile production was carried out in Petersburg and the surrounding area, and mostly because of rapid railroad construction, heavy machinery was developing a large presence as well.[33] According to Reginald Zelnik, by the 1870s "St. Petersburg was without a doubt Russia's single most important and dynamic center of heavy industry."[34] As the population climbed and the social complexion of the city diversified, the number of homes expanded dramatically, the average height of apartment buildings went up several stories, and rental apartments became the norm.[35] Not surprisingly, according to the architectural historian E. I. Kirichenko, "the largest rate in construction of the apartment building took place in the second half of the 19th century."[36]

A large percentage of the urban population, especially after the emancipation, was made up of *otkhodniki*, or peasant migrants to the city from the countryside, large numbers of whom only stayed in St. Petersburg for part of the year and did not have a settled, stable life there.[37] As Petersburg struggled to cope with the pressures of its burgeoning and unsettled population, disease, drunkenness, and crime became endemic problems. Diseases such as cholera, typhus, and tuberculosis conspired to make Russia's capital among the most deadly of all major European cities by the late 1860s. Both the unsanitary conditions in parts of the city and the extremes of overcrowding contributed to the misery. The population would have been shrinking as a result of high fatality rates had it not been constantly replenished by the steady stream of migrants from the countryside.[38] In fact, large numbers of new arrivals to St. Petersburg went uncounted because so many of them were wanderers without documentation. After arrests for drunkenness in the year 1869, the second largest category arrested were residents without proper documentation.[39] As rapidly as the population was growing, the rise in arrest rates outpaced population growth, between 1861 and 1869 going from 69,000 to over 190,000.[40] By around 1860, Petersburg's reputation and self-conception as an orderly and decorous administrative center had begun to be replaced by an ever-increasing sense of discord and chaos. James Bater has pointed out that "the overriding impression of St. Petersburg during the eighteenth and early nineteenth centuries was one of orderliness," whereas by the reform era the presiding sense of decorum had begun to slip away. Conditions began to warrant Aleksandr Nikitenko's 1864 lament that the capital was developing a new atmosphere of violence, drunkenness, and disorder.[41]

The understandable shock of the new at this point can be attributed to a number of tangible factors. By the middle of the nineteenth century, the well-ordered spatial structure of the old court capital was growing "complex and unbalanced."[42] The number of eating establishments in St. Petersburg had risen to over 900 by the mid-1860s, and they were packed thickly in certain neighborhoods.[43] New alcohol-fueled public spaces, including cabarets (*kafeshantany*) and popular "dance class" establishments, facilitated the emergence of a "tavern public" (*kabatskaia publika*) that, as the journalist Vladimir Mikhnevich fretted, was growing difficult to distinguish from "the clubs and establishments of the privileged public."[44] Seeking to address the rising disorder, in 1866 the St. Petersburg police founded a new department "for the preservation of social order and calm in the capital," which organized alcohol-free events and activities in order to encourage sober forms of amusement.[45] By midcentury the most blighted area around the Haymarket Square had grown cluttered with taverns, brothels, and flop houses, including the notoriously crime and disease-ridden *Viazemskii Dom*. Mikhnevich referred to this region as the "central reservoir of wandering and impoverished Petersburg."[46] The Haymarket would be made famous within Russia as a region of misery, crime, and moral decrepitude in Vsevolod Krestovskii's novel *The Slums of St. Petersburg* (1864), and it would later become world famous in Dostoevky's *Crime and Punishment* (1866).

While the city certainly held many miseries for its inhabitants, it also promised a new social dynamism. As centers of gravity for people from a wide array of backgrounds, large cities offer many attractions that simply are not available elsewhere. Wherever they might be located, modern cities share dense populations, the relative proximity of separate social classes, and a tendency (if not always fulfilled) to immerse their inhabitants within networks of social interaction. Cities are not just population hubs; they are also crucibles of interaction that can activate previously unconsidered ambitions, ignite new ideas, generate new connections, and intensify older ones. For all the reputed "anomie," moral corruption and physical dangers of the large metropolis, people flocked to cities because they offered a vastly wider selection of choices for earning a living and making useful connections.

In a provincial setting, local and familial ties provide a deep and seemingly permanent social network. Since the urban environment, by contrast, is relatively impersonal and anonymous, it requires the acquisition of new skills in order to tolerate urban conditions. According to Georg Simmel and other sociologists of urban life, the depersonalization that accompanies urban conditions creates deep stresses and the possibility of psychological trauma, but at the same, by releasing the individual from those social commitments necessary in a smaller, more interdependent community, it provides "a kind and an amount of personal freedom which has no analogy whatsoever under other conditions"[47] Urban estrangement "permits people in the city to spin the wildest fantasies—and to act upon these fantasies whether they result in feats of genius or deeds of crime and depravity."[48]

From the provinces the city beckoned, as it did to the writer Nikolai Uspenskii, who wrote in his provincial seminary school memoirs: "Petersburg! Petersburg! How you inspire my soul with life and holy hopes! ... The thought of you lights up my heart."[49] For a Petersburg resident, the capital was an "alluring magnet ... that brought toward itself all the gifted people attracted by dreams of importance, fame and glory"[50] To which we must add that the "gifted" were vastly outnumbered by those arriving in pursuit of simple gainful employment. St. Petersburg proved attractive as a hub of power and culture, or as a realm of opportunity for elusive employment, though it could not and did not always deliver on its promise. The city was becoming "a kaleidoscope of every possible form of need and satisfaction, wealth and poverty."[51]

Inseparable from the urban experience in the 1860s was the impact of the Great Reforms. Russia's disastrous loss in the Crimean War in 1855 had revealed that her longstanding socioeconomic system (based in large part on enserfed labor) could no longer compete with the dynamism of the industrialized nations of Western Europe. Alexander II came to the throne in that same year, at a moment that seemed to demand some kind of deep structural change. It appeared that Russia could no longer sustain the path of social constriction and strict autocratic control that bottled up the energies of Russian society, and Alexander began to institute reforms intended to open "a space for public involvement in public affairs."[52] In spite of the state's reluctance to relinquish control, most of the post-emancipation reforms seem to have been calculated to put in place institutions and practices that would form a foundation for the growth of civil society. Among other changes, the press was allowed to expand and censorship laws were mitigated to facilitate the (limited) expression of public opinion, legal reforms that included trial by jury and local arbitration fostered a degree of societal participation in public affairs, and limited elective bodies allowed for a small amount of participation and representation in local governance. These policies partially undermined the implicit social contract of the old regime whereby society accepted an entirely subordinate role. Thus they helped to unleash both a new optimism and a new sense of uncertainty and instability. In Alfred Rieber's words, "the Great Reforms accelerated the evolution of a complex society."[53]

At least at first the Great Reforms seemed to constitute a substantial relinquishment of the autocracy's "publicity of representation." Government officials hotly debated the advisability of the reforms, but certainly some of them felt the state had to find ways to tap into society's potential if only in order to create the kind of economically expansive state that had a chance to keep pace with the juggernaut economies of Western Europe. To stimulate public participation, shake the intransigence of a stultified bureaucracy, and expose abuses to the light of day, a certain degree of *"glasnost'*," or open discourse, would be required.[54] But that very *glasnost'* was understood by other officials as a threat to social stability and state power. In order to induce a measure of popular participation in public affairs and yet avoid the emergence of threatening extra-governmental political activity, the autocracy experimented with something it sometimes referred to by the remarkably revealing phrase "artificial *glasnost*." As W. Bruce Lincoln has pointed out, since "the nature of glasnost' conflicted with autocracy too sharply," rather than define clear limits for the press and the public, the state allowed society to push the limits too far and then stepped in to impose discipline.[55] For example, before the 1862 censorship law went into effect, censorship had been preventative (all documents were reviewed and subjected to censorship prior to publication). The new censorship regime was punitive (writers and publishers were punished if their words were later understood to have violated pre-established standards).[56] This process of allowing society to test its limits until it had to be reined in characterized the state's overall approach to public expression during Alexander's reign.

Though the reforms marked a momentous shift in Russian political life, scholars have often placed a stronger emphasis on their limitations than their accomplishments. The reforms proved, as one historian put it, "conceptually limited, poorly executed, incomplete, unsustained and insecure."[57] Even the relatively progressive interior minister Petr Valuev believed that "only government power ... will be able to guide society to its further development on a true and lawful path."[58] And yet despite the institutional limitations of the reforms, the *spirit* of the reforms became a significant factor in Russian history. The unmistakable call for societal participation in the public realm excited and inspired contemporaries. Although many members of Russian educated society were careful to act only in accordance with what appeared to be the autocracy's wishes, others tried to push the role of society beyond what the state was willing to tolerate. In the ferment of the initial reforms, the city of St. Petersburg had the advantage of being the central meeting ground for those desiring a larger role in public affairs. The capital city's public voice had the potential to reach a national, even international, audience, which made it a tempting platform for the expression of new ideas. In *My Past and Thoughts*, Herzen captured the atmosphere of enthusiasm brewing during the early reign of Alexander II: "From 1855 to 1857 Russia was awoken in front of us. The stone was pushed from the grave and removed to the Peter and Paul Fortress. The new time could be seen in everyone, in the state, in literature, in society, in the people. Much was awkward, insincere, unclear, but everyone felt we'd been set in motion."[59]

PUBLIC SPACE AND PUBLIC SPIRIT

With the reforms the state had "set in motion" an untested civic sphere made even less predictable by rapid urbanization. As a result, the early reform era unleashed the political tempests that would storm throughout the rest of Alexander's reign. Large cities posed a distinct problem for the autocracy's exertion of power and maintenance of control. One important way autocratic power was maintained in Russia involved long-established methods of divide and conquer. The separate populations of the Russian Empire were isolated from one another across vast stretches of terrain, and through strenuous social ordering by means of the *soslovie* system, the Table of Ranks, and other social distinctions involving gender, region, religion, language, and occupation. By such divisions the Russian population remained, for the most part, laterally disconnected from other parts of society while vertically connected to the ruling powers at the top. Yet urbanization works against such methods of governance. The larger a city grows, the harder it is to maintain traditional distinctions. Urban density enables people to blend together, to influence one another, to receive information and ideas from the outside sources that arrive with a city's inflows and outflows of people, goods, culture, and information. Cities serve as hubs of many things: commerce, transport, media, higher education, government, law courts, and the arts, and although these functions generally maintain their autonomy from one another, the compact nature of urban space throws together otherwise separated spheres and individuals into new and unpredictable interactions.

In this urban context, the experimental *glasnost'* tolerated for a short time in the late 1850s and early 1860s generated a sense of excitement and desire for change that would continue to reverberate through the following decades. The early reform era energized the urban experience and made new possibilities seem endless. According to Aleksandr Koshelov, in the late 1850s Petersburgers "began to stir and move; each sought room for movement (*prostor*), wanted to know his rights and receive in them affirmation and security."[60] In his memoir about this era, Nikolai Shelgunov waxed eloquent on the expanded possibilities under Alexander II:

> The idea of freedom gripped everybody, penetrated everywhere, and carried out something absolutely unprecedented and unfamiliar. Officers retired in order to start up a small shop, a linen store, or a bookstore, get involved in publishing or establish a journal. . . . Every capable and energetic person at that time started down a new road, founded some new occupation more suitable to his talents. . . . In a word, society strained its every power in order to found for itself a new, independent position and shift the center of gravity of social initiative toward itself.[61]

Elizaveta Vodovozova similarly saw the early reform era as a moment of social awakening: "The remarkable invigoration of life at the beginning of the sixties was an entirely new phenomenon. . . . I've never since met with such bold happiness, never heard such resounding laughter. And it was quite natural: after the abolition of serfdom, the transformations continued instilling great hope for the future. ... It seemed obvious to everyone that among us had begun an entirely new and unknown civil and social life."[62] As Vodovozova suggests here, because the state itself demonstrated a degree of enthusiasm for society's involvement in public affairs, to many it seemed as though state and society were united together in a cooperative effort to create a more just, more active, and more independent society.

In a rapidly expanding sphere of variously inclined, legal and illegal, daily and monthly publications, *belles lettres* and political journalism also fed into the dynamism of the times. Between 1855 and 1860, subscription rates for the journal the *Contemporary* more than doubled, while heated debate surrounding the new journals, or novels like Turgenev's *Fathers and Children*, marked the early reform era, as did the influence of Herzen's journal the *Bell*, which was published in England but smuggled into Russia in sufficient numbers that it too gained a wide readership.[63] G. Z. Eliseev, an editor at the *Contemporary*, understood Russian public opinion of this era as something expressed almost exclusively on the pages of newspapers and journals. He used the odd term "literary bohemia" to describe the diverse groups of Russians interested in public affairs who, by publishing small pieces and writing letters to the burgeoning collection of newspapers and journals, sought to expose the "lies, hypocrisy, self-interest, arbitrariness, insolence, exploitation, effrontery" of government officials who would not otherwise have been held accountable.[64] According to Eliseev, these nearly anonymous writers used the press as a way to "awaken Russia in all its cities—and awaken it in the most beneficial way."[65]

Although it often seems in histories of this period, as it did to Eliseev, that print media was the sole arena for the exchange of opinion, to focus exclusively on reading and writing is to underestimate the role of the city itself. Russia's reform-era public sphere took shape not merely on the printed page but also in concrete locations within the city. As Vodovozova saw it, the density of urban space was crucial to the experience of young people in this period: "acquaintances lived a tightly interconnected life, frequently seeing one another and being well-informed of each other's material circumstances. These frequent meetings powerfully promoted interconnection, the exchange of ideas, and the acquisition of knowledge; they facilitated the development of social ideals."[66] One intriguing reform-era example of the urban capacity to bring together people who would otherwise have remained apart because of their social and intellectual backgrounds arose in Moscow in the late 1850s where a circle formed that humorously referred to itself as a *vertep*, which roughly translates to "den of thieves."[67] What was particularly novel and interesting about this "den" was its social constitution. It included curious Slavophiles from the nobility alongside students from the lower middle classes attracted to western socialism, and it was led by Pavel Rybnikov, from a family of Old-Believer merchants. Older intellectuals and young students spoke together, sometimes deep into the night, about political ideas and public affairs.[68] These discussions offered the older generation a chance to interact with young students, and they gave the students an opportunity to participate in the intellectual circles that had previously been restricted mainly to the realm of social elites.

Perhaps because of its novelty in reform-era Russia, interaction in public space quickly came under suspicion in the eyes of the police. Throughout the decade of the 1860s the Third Section undertook a systematic set of observations on a wide variety of public places that had no inherent political content. These places included parks, pleasure gardens, festivals, entertainment halls, theaters, restaurants, taverns, coffee and tea shops, hotels, balls, dancing venues, and even bath houses. Third Section agents kept careful records and observations on whatever "scandals" took place in these locations, maintaining a lookout for any incident that could be construed as politically subversive. But if the Third Section's mandate to observe such gatherings was based on the assumption that the very existence of public space was inherently incendiary, police agents found little to confirm that suspicion. For the most part, the "scandalous" behavior they discovered consisted of alcohol-induced personal conflicts that occasionally carried a tinge of class resentment or political grandstanding.[69] "Our agents," read one report, "keep a sharp lookout on any place where there is any public confluence of people, and they listen in on the general conversation." Yet what these sharp-eyed agents most often discovered was not too surprising: "complaints about a lack of money."[70] The blending of separate social groups seemed a danger in and of itself, which was well expressed in one agent's description of a coffeehouse that opened in 1864: "the most varied class of people gathers here: students, ragged officials, rich merchants, cabmen, and prostitutes—this whole rabble of regular visitors at the coffee house dances and sings to the music of an organ grinder."[71] Some of the more incendiary political findings included a retired police officer wearing a (French Revolutionary) red cockade on his cap and a caricaturist from the satirical journal the *Spark* mocking a military officer at a *Passazh* restaurant.[72] Eventually the Third Section abandoned the project.

But the fact that public assembly was not inherently political does not mean that spaces for anti-autocratic discussion did not come into being.

Since anti-governmental writing, speech, and public protest were illegal in imperial Russia, the most typical venue for such discussion was the private home. So common are descriptions of the stuffy, sweaty, standing-room-only apartment in which political meetings took place that it almost seems a set piece of reform-era memoir literature. Fully public spaces that facilitated political speech in the early reform era were necessarily few, and under constant threat, but some did arise. Some of the most important venues for public interaction were bookstore/reading rooms that doubled as meeting places for those interested in political topics. Bookstores facilitated close encounters between those of like mind and served as places to locate illegal, semi-legal, or simply obscure foreign publications. The best known and most politically inclined of such venues was Nikolai Serno-Solov'evich's bookstore and reading room at 24 Nevskii Prospekt, which opened in 1861. Serno-Solov'evich established his bookstore because, as he put it, "In the time we are living through it is more than ever necessary ... to have a space where different opinions can be openly and peacefully discussed."[73] His store was visited by a wide variety of people, including students, low-ranking officials, and soldiers. After the closing of the university it became a hub for student discussion and debate.[74] The purpose it served was well expressed in the government order to shut it down: "[Such bookstores] do not offer a place to read so much as they create a place for baseless conversations and a place to pass writings among visitors with the aim of spreading disorder and unrest among the people."[75] The police well understood the role of bookstores among the politically active urban inhabitants, so they limited their number and singled them out for surveillance.[76]

The Serno-Solov'evich bookstore was closed in 1862, but it was later re-opened by Aleksandr Cherkesov, who maintained its reputation for politically oriented literature. Cherkesov understood the radicals' need for the sort of heterotopic space in which discussion and debate might foster new ideas, and he used his bookstore as a venue for after-hours political meetings. He even maintained a small, covert printing press to produce illegal publications.[77] Under both Serno-Solov'evich and Cherkesov, the bookstore gained a reputation as "practically the headquarters of revolutionary sentiment among the students."[78] In another demonstration of its heterotopian function, the Serno-Solov'evich bookstore served as a venue for gender politics. It was here that a young woman, Anna Engelgardt, first took the formerly exclusively male role of clerk. "Petersburg was stunned," wrote Shelgunov, "when a pretty young woman in blue glasses appeared behind the counter. ... At that time working in a shop was an ideological act; it was virtually a form of propaganda for the new ways, a democratic refusal of class [*soslovnyi*] prejudice."[79] The city's public library played a similar role. Ivan Pryzhov described the St. Petersburg public library as a site of accelerated cultural change. He especially appreciated that young women were so accepted at the public reading room that nobody paid special attention to their presence, an attitude he believed would still have been unthinkable in contemporary Moscow. The library reading room convinced Pryzhov that "the Petersburg woman has demonstrated her readiness for public life [*obshchechelovecheskaia zhizn'*]."[80] Around the same time, the Third Section noted the same phenomenon with considerably less pleasure: "One of the main places for meetings of the short-haired and improper female nihilist is the women's reading room in the Imperial Public Library."[81]

Another politically charged public meeting place, the Chess Club opened by Count Kushelev-Bezborodka in January 1862, was less a hot spot for chess playing than it was a venue for discussion of current affairs. Many of its members were prominent Petersburg intellectuals and journalists. From its inception, the club provided an arena in which to discuss "the most vital questions of domestic politics, society, life and literature."[82] A Third Section infiltrator claimed the primary topics discussed there were "measures which would provide freedom of the press and ... the necessity of introducing a constitution to Russia."[83] The head of the Third Section in 1862, Vasily Dolgorukov, claimed the Chess Club was a front for radicals to organize a "party of opposition."[84] Engaged in what officials insinuatingly called "conversations about current affairs that lack any sort of foundation," the Chess Club was closed down within six months of its opening.[85]

Other urban spaces that created room for political speech were even more short-lived. Literary readings, musical performances, and public lectures—often arranged for charity—grew to become a common part of the lively urban scene in the early 1860s, and it was not unusual for such events to acquire an oppositional character. According to N. Nikoladze, "in a variety of schools and public halls were arranged more and more public readings and lectures, always with transparent hints about university disturbances and political events."[86] Debates and lectures sometimes provided an excuse for the expression of discontent that found its outlet in the "deafening roar" of the audience's applause when it encountered veiled but unmistakable criticism of the government. Such events could at times appear so volatile that both thrilled participants and hostile observers compared them (with obvious exaggeration) to political demonstrations.[87] Aleksandr Skabichevskii, then a university student, observed the debate on the origins of Russia that took place in 1860 between Nikolai Kostomarov and Mikhail Pogodin, but he did not attend as a student hoping to learn about Russia's early history.

For him the debate served as a pretext to voice his political sympathies: "although it was of no concern to me where our first dynasty came from ... nevertheless I furiously applauded the speeches of Kostomarov and booed after every reply of Pogodin."[88] The most incendiary lecture, given by the St. Petersburg University history professor P. V. Pavlov in March of 1862, was so openly oppositional in tone and was greeted with such applause that one observer referred to the speech and its receptions as a "riotous demonstration." The lecture led to Pavlov's exile from the city and soon thereafter the curtailment of all similar events.[89]

While the working class remained relatively small, and strikes did not play a major role until the late 1870s, the presence of St. Petersburg workers in the early 1860s created an opportunity that helped connect the different urban populations by bringing about an important opportunity for initiative from below known as the Sunday school movement. The name derives from the fact that workers only had Sundays available for extra-vocational activities like education. On Sundays educated people in different Russian cities opened formal and informal centers to teach workers basic literacy and other subjects. The movement began in Kiev in 1858, but it quickly spread, and by 1860 St. Petersburg was already the home to hundreds of worker-students being taught in at least twenty-three schools.[90] For some teachers, who included not only university students but also military officers and state officials, the schools were part of an altruistic effort to raise the level of literacy and other basic forms of knowledge among workers; for others they served as a site at which political views could be disseminated or exchanged.[91]

Since the Sunday schools were a direct result of the urban capacity to bring together otherwise separate communities, they offer an important example of the way urban space helped promote social change. The schools were, in the words of Zelnik, "by far the most important and widespread effort on the part of educated society to alter the fate of the urban worker."[92] The quick rise and spread of the Sunday school movement would be inconceivable outside of an urban setting because the schools coalesced on the basis of the physical proximity between the educated classes and the industrial workforce in urban areas. As one voluntary educator noted, Sunday schools compelled the intelligentsia "to continually enter into close relations with the needy classes of Petersburg."[93] They also opened up new spaces of interaction between urbanites of different backgrounds. The "moral significance of the Sunday schools," as Konstantin Ushinskii put it, "consists in the contact between educated people and working-class people."[94] Not unrelatedly, since many teachers were female, they helped expand the role of women in public life. At least in some cases, friendships between workers and educators continued after the state prohibited the schools, as in the case of Nadezhda Stasova, who carried on friendly relations with her working class students after her school was forcibly shut down.[95]

A far more established educational institution, St. Petersburg University (along with other Petersburg venues of higher education) also made an important contribution to the dynamism of the reform-era St. Petersburg public sphere. Under Nicholas I, Russia had been cautious about expanding education, since a well-educated populace was considered a potential threat to social stability, but in answer to the needs of state and bureaucracy Nicholas sanctioned some expansion of secondary and higher education, and the universities began to educate a larger number of students from a wider variety of social backgrounds during his reign. The Western European revolutions of 1848 induced Nicholas to place new restrictions on university enrollment and expansion, but many of those restrictions were lifted not long after Alexander II came to the throne. University enrollments nearly doubled in the first four years of Alexander's reign, and they brought in students from a wider array of social backgrounds.[96] In part as a result of the expanded student body, and in part as a response to the reforms, a new student subculture arose in the late 1850s that would have a continuing impact on the urban fabric into the next century. Though implemented and controlled from above, Russian institutions of higher education constituted the kind of heterotopic space that facilitated change and experimentation from below. By its nature the university—which throws together a variety of strangers from the same cohort for a short but intensive period of intellectual labor—forms a space apart in which personal growth and cultural dynamism are to some degree inevitable.

Students, moreover, played a potentially volatile role in Russia. The number of students in the country was infinitesimal by comparison to the population of the Empire as a whole, some few thousand by contrast to 80 million. But this small group, especially in the capital, was expected to take up leadership positions, mostly as functionaries for the state. Their potentially bright futures notwithstanding, the influx of students from outside the nobility meant that some students, who were being groomed for responsible positions, lived in crushing poverty. A member of the Third Section attributed the stubbornness of the problem of entrenched radicalism to the nexus between university and city life in St. Petersburg. As he saw it, expanded university enrollment combined with student poverty was the underlying cause of political dissatisfaction: "For thousands of *versts*, from all ends of our wide fatherland, flow into Petersburg young people in search of higher education. Many of them scarcely have the means of existence to make the journey and they flatter themselves in the faith that it will not be difficult to feed themselves by giving lessons."[97] Although there is little evidence that poverty led to political radicalism, and many students were politically moderate, non-committal, or inclined to a life in state service, from the late 1850s, state service was increasingly demonized within the student milieu as contributing to social injustice and rigid traditionalism. Aspiring to join an increasingly stigmatized institution came with the risk of becoming "part of the problem." The educational system, for example, was denigrated by Nikolai Ishutin as "a little path that led to bourgeois life."[98] According to Osip Aptekman, Russian students perceived themselves as having two opposing choices: to find service in a position with the state or to form circles of political activity with other young people.[99] The former was safer and more promising; the latter was dangerous but glamorous and self-sacrificing.

To become a student at one of St. Petersburg's institutions of higher education was also to become an inhabitant of the city, a part of its life and culture, and for many young people both the move to the city and life in the university felt liberating and exhilarating (in spite of widespread poverty). As one memoir recalled, students got involved in every aspect of urban life "since so many of us constantly ran in the most varied strata of Petersburg society."[100] The university was where for the first time young men could throw off their regional and familial ties and begin to forge new connections of their own. Students took comfort in forming independent associations that allowed them to assist one another. These groups were often associations of students from a given home region (*zemliachestva*), but student circles could also take the form of non-regional mutual aid funds, collective libraries, collective dining rooms (*kukhmistery*), or just study groups. In the new and exciting reform-era atmosphere, university students pioneered a method of interaction and dispute resolution for which they used a term from the peasant commune: the *skhodka*. Because such meetings were established to develop a consensus view, they tended to produce a sort of "consciousness raising" and unity-building effect.[101] An anonymous correspondent for Herzen's *Bell* considered the *skhodki* to be schools of "accountability and responsibility," but he also believed they potentially led to "anarchy and chaos inside the universities" because they enabled students to form their interests and methods without guidance from university administrators or state officials.[102]

Student disturbances started out local and limited, over minor issues like whether smoking was allowed or beards could be grown, but over

time student politics evolved to the point of taking up nationally significant concerns. So important was the role played by the universities that
contemporaries often understood Russian radicalism as, in essence, a stu-
dent-based phenomenon; many detractors on the right used the derogatory
words "student" and "nihilist" interchangeably. Popular lecturers at the university, which typically meant left-leaning professors and included Pavlov,
Kostomarov, Konstantin Kavelin, Mikhail Stasiulevich, and Boris Utin, used
their lectures as platforms to discuss contemporary issues, and the hundreds
of students who attended these lectures did not leave them in the classroom.
As Pryzhov put it in 1861, in a statement characteristic of the enthusiasm of
the time: the students carried lecture hall ideas "out into the world, onto the
streets, into family life" and served as "the advance archers of a future army
of Russian enlightened society."[103] Pryzhov was right that students' activism
spilled over into their actions outside the university walls. Even court historian, Sergei Tatishchev, acknowledged the breadth of 1860s politicization:
"The ferment embraced the so-called leading circles, and in particular university students . . . but it took on even larger proportions . . . [and] included
people of both sexes, various social classes, young writers, officers, doctors,
younger students, teachers and even university professors."[104]

THE EXPERIMENT ENDS

In the early years of reform the public was far more united in spirit and
enterprise than it would be during the rest of Alexander II's reign. The special good will toward the state in these years, even among generally critical
members of the intelligentsia, sprang largely from Alexander's determi-
nation to carry out the abolition of serfdom, by any count a difficult and
momentous undertaking. During the honeymoon phase of this enterprise,
the autocracy was widely hailed for its reforming efforts. But the sense of
political unity that hovered over the late 1850s and early 1860s proved to
be brief. The general spirit of cooperation broke down in the early 1860s,
and the rupture culminated in widespread disillusionment. Shelgunov's
point that "Alexander II himself kindled revolutionary feeling by awakening
exaggerated expectations" helps explain the rapid shift.[105] Both the initial
optimism and the failed hopes were unrealistic given the extreme complex-
ities of abolishing Russia's longstanding socioeconomic foundation, and an
autocratic political system in which power is vested at the top is always in
danger of promoting higher expectations than it has the capacity to deliver
on because it appears to (but does not) have unlimited room for maneuver.

Unhelpfully, the state continued to jealously guard the public sphere as its own domain, deeming off limits nearly all political speech critical of state policy. Unable to protest without the threat of censure or arrest, from the early 1860s radicals began to take it as axiomatic that the autocracy had offered too little too late and had to be abolished itself before any social progress would be possible. Over the course of the next two decades the left would become increasingly revolutionary, and the state would become increasingly embattled and intransigent. The educated society that stood between them sympathized with certain radical aims while at the same time it thirsted for order and stability. It was on the basis of this stalemate that radical populists began the long search for a workable form of political agitation that would eventually culminate in the creation of a violent revolutionary underground.

By the early 1860s the student movement had moved far beyond internal issues and begun to take an interest in problems like Polish independence and the push for a constituent assembly in Russia. So destabilizing had student disturbances at St. Petersburg University grown that in the fall of 1861 the administration chose to shut the university down. In response, students decided, against all convention, to march across the city to the home of the university administrator Grigorii Filipson. This unexpected event was perceived by contemporaries as the very first street demonstration in St. Petersburg.[106] Although the matter at hand directly involved only students, as a result of its novelty it attracted large crowds and was greeted as a subversive act.[107] A government associate of Valuev's said in response to the student march that Russia had now "crossed the Rubicon," a reaction that suggests the autocracy's abiding intolerance of the usurpation of its "publicity of representation."[108] The tsar himself saw the event as "the first attempt of the revolutionary party to test its strength."[109]

Though in some ways official Russia's fear of a student demonstration was an overreaction, in other ways there was reasonable cause for concern. Events that took place in the imperial capital were automatically national events, so a Petersburg march inevitably took on greater significance than it would have elsewhere. Even the students themselves understood their demonstration as much more than a student issue. A pamphlet they published prior to the march held that "we are legion because behind us are common sense, public opinion, literature, the professors, the countless circles, critically thinking people, Western Europe."[110] For the students themselves their newly acquired role as politically active members of society in the capital city had an intoxicating effect. As one of them put it, "You were expecting something new, special, bravura. Everyone felt an irresistible longing to show his worth in some desperately courageous, heroic action."[111] Organized student demonstrations and conflicts with the police would continue into the fall, and large numbers of students would be arrested.[112] Little more than a week after the Petersburg student march, Moscow University students organized a 600-strong march to the grave of the liberal scholar Timofei Granovskii as a pretext for what became known as the first street demonstration in the city of Moscow.[113] The ferment of revolt in this period gave rise, in the words of another student, to the exuberant premonition that "something of enormous significance was going to happen, perhaps even in the very near future."[114]

The unauthorized usurpation of what the state still considered its exclusive space of representation seemed a violation that called for decisive action. As disturbances mounted, the state finally decided to jail a large number of student activists, and it shut down the university for the next eighteen months. In response students and professors set up a "Free University" that met in various halls within the city, including the municipal duma. This "university," which was in essence a wide-ranging series of public lectures given by university professors sympathetic to the students' inability to continue their studies, quickly became popular and managed to operate with the cooperation of about two dozen professors. But it did not last long. When Pavlov's lecture (described above) was greeted by enthusiastic applause, the state regarded the event as tantamount to a political demonstration.[115] To protest Pavlov's exile, the students ceased attending the lectures, and the "Free University" experiment came to a close. It had lasted less than three months.

Another example of the state's wary attitude toward popular involvement in public affairs involved the Sunday school movement. Sunday schools were a relatively innocuous form of urban activism, but the state considered them a threat because they promoted a "dangerous" blending of social classes. The schools threatened the social order because they educated people considered to be "unprepared" for knowledge.[116] At first, the Ministry of Education insisted on limiting Sunday teaching to basic skills, like literacy, math, and religious instruction, and assigned clergy members to watch over the teachers. Eventually in June 1862, citing the infiltration of "criminal ideas against the state," the Ministry shut down the entire movement.[117] As a fleeting experiment in public participation, the Sunday schools provide a microcosmic illustration of the development of the imperial Russian public sphere. Initiative from below was tolerated initially, even encouraged in some ways, and yet any possibility of a threat was perceived as perilously subversive and therefore was quickly curtailed.[118] The state's fear of the Sunday school movement was exacerbated by the fact that some teachers hailed from non-elite social backgrounds and were themselves considered unreliable. As Zelnik pointed out, "the closing of the Sunday schools represented a victory for those elements within the government who feared the participation not only of the masses but of any independent social group, above all the so-called middle strata (roughly defined as educated non-nobles, or educated nobles who did not serve in an official capacity) in the solution of Russia's social problems."[119] As had been the fate of the student protestors, arrests were made, teachers were sent into exile, and opportunities for involvement in public life narrowed that much further.

While the state anxiously quelled public initiatives, it continued to use St. Petersburg as the stage for its own "publicity of representation." State-sponsored spectacles that took place in the early 1860s included a ceremony in which hundreds of peasants offered bread and salt to the tsar in celebration of the emancipation, the celebration of Russia's millennial anniversary in 1862, and the fiftieth anniversary celebration of the 1814 Russian occupation of Paris in 1864.[120] At such celebrations the autocracy used public space to model its view of how subjects should understand their place within the Russian body politic. Public and private buildings were hung with state flags, garlands, and lanterns; garlanded busts of the tsar were placed in shop windows, military orchestras played in shops and public places, and at night Nevskii Prospekt was lit up with "luxurious illuminations."[121] The intentional staging of such "scenarios of power" revealed the authority and rightful place of the autocratic government as presented before the people, who themselves were represented as the quiescent and obedient part of the Russian polity. At times certain spontaneous public gatherings also arose and were tolerated by the state because they conformed to its conception of the proper political use of public space. These included the crowds that thronged to Palace Square to condone Russia's defeat of the Polish Uprising in 1863 and those in 1866 celebrating the failure of Dmitry Karakozov's attempted assassination of the tsar.

State efforts to dominate public space and minimize non-state initiatives remained effective during the reform era, and state spectacles and celebrations always seem to have drawn large crowds. And yet the appearance of spontaneous, tolerated demonstrations suggests the possibility of a gradual shift from state dominance of the public sphere to an increasing amount of public activity initiated from below. The state's use of public space for its own prerogatives may have helped in part to undermine its traditional dominance of the public sphere: by awakening an interest in large public gatherings and creating models for how such gatherings could be carried out, the state inadvertently encouraged unofficial public activism. Indeed, radicals went so far as to co-opt official displays of power in ways that worked to their own benefit. Government sponsored "civil executions" of political criminals, for example, came to be attended by groups of spectators on the left, who intentionally hushed voices of condemnation from the crowd. By 1864 a full co-optation of the civil execution ceremony took place when Nikolai Chernyshevskii underwent the process.[122] By removing their hats in unison, shouting their support, and throwing flowers toward the accused, the spectators transformed Chernyshevskii's erstwhile humiliation into a farewell celebration in advance of his Siberian exile.[123]

From this point forward, again and again the left would find ways to turn the state's "bully pulpit" to its own purposes. In the absence of any right to hold public protests, they would turn trials, public sentencing, and public funerals into moments of anti-autocratic demonstration.[124] Public condemnation of political criminals regularly brought forth spirited support for the accused and condemned. In the case of those convicted in the Nechaev Affair, once they were taken from the scaffold and placed in a carriage: "a whole crowd of young people went to shake their hands, and ran alongside the carriage."[125] A similar cheering crowd was to be found at the sentencing of the populist radical Aleksandr Dolgushin in 1875.[126] The police eventually came to acknowledge the problem. An anonymous Third Section report on the use of public punishment and civil executions pointed out that while on the surface public punishment might appear a good way to keep people in line, in practice such events could have the opposite effect:

> The criminal often publicly protests from the scaffold against the government's sentence, undermining faith in justice. With respect to political criminals in particular ... conducting public punishments leads to a result that runs entirely against the views of the government. ... The criminal, shouting down the [military] drum beat, with defiant body movements addresses himself to the people, appealing to their indignation, insulting the government, etc. Faces in the crowd being, so to speak, electrified by these appeals, join together with the disgraceful conduct of the criminal and become the victims of such enthusiasm."[127]

In the search for a way to engage in public protest while under threat of prosecution for anti-autocratic speech and assembly, a new method was born in 1861, inaugurating a period Shelgunov would later dub "the era of proclamations." In the summer of that year a series of unauthorized leaflets, expressing various levels of anti-autocratic sentiment, flooded the streets of St. Petersburg. Proclamations printed abroad and smuggled into Russia were supplemented by documents published in secret on small printing presses, and the city provided an excellent matrix for their rapid distribution. Between the summer of 1861 and the spring of 1862, around a dozen distinct proclamations appeared on the streets, each of them intended for a different constituency within the population.[128] Proclamations were addressed to, among others, the student youth, army officers, society at large, and the peasantry. The most famous and incendiary of these, titled "Young Russia," called in lurid terms for violent attacks against state power and class enemies: "To the axes and beat the imperial party, without pity, as they do not pity us now, beat them in the squares if the lowly swine dare walk onto them, beat them in their homes, beat them in the narrow lanes of the cities, beat them in the wide streets of the capitals, beat them in the villages and towns."[129] Though "Young Russia" was not greeted particularly warmly by the youth for which it claimed to speak, it was the clearest cry of hopelessness that a legal and public solution to political change would be possible. In its appeal for a bloody revolutionary overthrow of the prevailing system it was a harbinger of the violent underground that would soon begin to take shape.[130]

Other less violent proclamations premised their calls to action on the injustice of prohibiting freedom of expression in Russia. Shelgunov's "To the Young Generation" condemned the government for its fear of exposing the public's views to greater scrutiny. This proclamation held that for the state, "public opinion does not exist just as Russian society does not exist, just as for the landowner the opinions of his peasants do not exist."[131] Shelgunov's friend Mikhail Mikhailov was arrested for distributing the document, and in his celebrated trial he testified that he himself had written it "for lack of public opinion" in Russia. "If you're interested in how the thinking public views the government," Mikhailov testified, "just take out the instrument and the music will play."[132] Although in principle populists like Shelgunov and Mikhailov fought in the name of the rural and laboring poor, time and again the populists would turn to those interests that affected the urban sector most directly: rights of speech, assembly, and electoral power. As they would so often point out, the lack of such rights made their struggle to improve the lot of the peasantry far more difficult than it would otherwise be. Particularly during those moments in the early 1860s and late 1870s that Lenin would later label (with considerable exaggeration) "revolutionary situations," the demand for political liberties came to the fore.

The final paragraph of Shelgunov's proclamation suggested why the distribution of proclamations quickly became a favored method of political combat. "If each of you convinces only ten people," it read, "our business in a single year will have gone far."[133] Perhaps one reason for the hope that proclamations could have a revolutionary effect involved the fact that they were disseminated boldly and openly on the city streets. They were placed on theater chairs, posted to walls in public places, sent out by mail and even, mirroring and reversing the city's infamy as a hub for pickpockets, "quietly stuffed into pockets."[134] The rapid spread of proclamations terrified the government, which established a commission to combat "the publication and dissemination of ill-intentioned writings."[135]

But in spite of their widespread dissemination, the proclamations did not produce the desired galvanizing effect. Not long after the appearance of "Young Russia," a series of fires of unknown origin broke out in the central section of St. Petersburg. Some argued the fires were the deadly and destructive acts of desperate radical arsonists. Others suggested police agents had set them intentionally in order to pin the blame on the radicalization of society. The origin of the fires has never been resolved, but for the state they supplied the final justification for a backlash against tolerated public spaces and activities. In the summer of 1862 public lectures, the Sunday schools, the Chess Club, bookstores, public reading rooms, and several journals were shut down almost simultaneously, both to curtail what the state considered "an alarmed state of mind" and to prevent discussions among "inhabitants of the capital who don't have any basis on which to discuss contemporary events."[136] The closings were followed by arrests of key figures on the left, including Chernyshevskii and Serno-Solov'evich. At the same time that it was shutting down "dangerous" public interaction, a state commission also reminded people of their public duty "to bring to the attention of the government anything that concerns or harms general well-being."[137] From this point forward, strict limits on political activity, set by the state and enforced by the Third Section, would play a major role in shaping the direction and form of revolutionary activity. In an 1865 rescript to the Moscow Assembly of Nobles, Alexander II wrote, "No one before Me is destined to take it upon himself to intercede for the general welfare and needs of the state."[138] The public sphere was to remain the provenance of the ruler and his designated representatives.

By this point in imperial Russia almost every kind of political activism had become, as Lev Deich would later put it, "connected to risk."[139] Not until the early twentieth century and the Revolution of 1905 would activism within the public sphere become sufficiently viable to produce a decisive effect. The impossibility of left-wing activism in the public realm created a situation in which lines were drawn and sides were chosen. Sergei Bulgakov saw "the merciless and unremitting pressure applied by the police" as one of two factors that shaped the radical intelligentsia. In his view, such extremes of police pressure "intensified that 'underground' mentality which was part of [populist radicalism's] innate character."[140] Unable to effect change within the public sphere, the radical populists would begin to put other methods of political struggle to the test. One response sought to bring about social and political change through the transformation of private life. Another response was the creation of the first underground movements that sought by various means to instigate a popular uprising. These two distinct strategies form the subjects of the next two chapters.

CHAPTER TWO

NIHILISM

Self-Fashioning and Subculture in the City

> The Metropolis was now much more than the very large city. ... It was the place where new social and economic and cultural relations ... were beginning to be formed.
>
> Raymond Williams

W HEN IN THE EARLY 1860S the state began to shut down left-wing participation in the public sphere, it was hoping that without a voice the oppositional movement of the late 50s and early 60s would collapse and live on as nothing more than a passing phase, a forgotten anomaly. Instead Russian radicalism managed to survive by transforming itself into a different sort of movement. Several clandestine organizations arose in the 1860s that attempted, under the cloak of secrecy, to carry out various forms of anti-governmental activism. At the same time there was a turn toward the politics of culture and private life in a looser movement that attempted to change society by reformulating everyday values and practices. The psychological and cultural politics of this latter group, which we refer to here as "nihilism," had already gotten underway during the early years of the reform era and reached its peak in the early to mid-1860s. This chapter examines nihilism while the next focuses on the ideologically related but tactically different secret organizations of the early underground movements.

What was a nihilist? Unfortunately the question does not have a simple answer since few terms in late-imperial Russia were more over-determined than "nihilism." Fortunately, Russian use of the word at least has a definitive origin. By the late 1850s it was clear that a new subculture was coming into being among university students and young postgraduates that involved various combinations of oppositional politics, rejection of conventionality, and high regard for materialist and utilitarian ideology. At first those involved did not go by any particular name (other than the word "student," used broadly to indicate a kind of generational sensibility). In 1862, however, attempting to capture the new "type" in his novel *Fathers and Children*, Ivan Turgenev chose the relatively obscure term "nihilist." No matter that this word was a fictional device and not particularly applicable, a collective term for the young intelligentsia of the early reform era was clearly needed, and Turgenev's label stuck with a vengeance. It quickly came into fashion as a term of opprobrium used by those who disapproved of the incipient youth culture, and from there it was not long before some of those described as nihilists chose, with varying degrees of acceptance, to embrace the word as an inaccurate but tolerable designation for the countercultural values they favored.

Except in the crassest formulations, the word "nihilism" in Russian never implied the kind of wholesale repudiation it still suggests in other languages. Some "nihilists" rejected much that had come before (for instance sentimental and lyrical art, idealist philosophy, conventional morality, traditional religion, and class prejudice), but they understood themselves in turn as introducing and embracing alternate values (for instance, empiricism, utilitarian ethics, service to those in need, and usually one or another version of socialism). In spite of its extremely common use in late-imperial Russia, one is tempted to reject the word "nihilism" as so misleading and imprecise as to be virtually meaningless. I retain it here for a particular purpose: to refer to an aspect of populist radicalism that reached its peak in the early 1860s and continued to inform the populist movement throughout the reform era. Nihilism may be said to describe that phase of the populist movement during which it seemed possible to change the world by changing oneself and reconstructing one's community.

For the young radical intelligentsia of this era the personal was political and the political was personal. The core values of Russian nihilism involved opposition to and transformation of conventional culture in a personal and communal form of political struggle that played out mainly on the urban stage of public and private life in St. Petersburg and other large cities. Nihilism as such was often scorned by later populists, who saw its focus on personal transformation as both self-serving and futile, but it also quite clearly continued to inform the mores and attitudes of the radical community throughout the 1860s and 1870s. For this reason an understanding of nihilism is crucial for understanding the formation of the populist underground. Most importantly, the culture of nihilism would provide a common set of values and norms that facilitated the group unity that would later be so necessary to sustaining underground organization and discipline.

The customary way for historians to make sense of nihilism still remains, even if in rather vague terms, an appeal to social origins, in particular an emphasis on the influence of that non-noble but educated middle strata known in the nineteenth century as the *raznochintsy*. The midcentury rise of an intelligentsia of mixed social origins certainly put its stamp on the cohort of the 1860s, but to identify nihilism in specific, or the 1860s intelligentsia in general, with a particular social class is extremely problematic, a fact readily apparent even to casual students of the subject. As Daniel Brower long ago pointed out about the Russian students who comprised nihilism's first flowering, the theory that nihilism emerged as the direct result of an influx of *raznochintsy* into the universities has "no basis in fact."[1] Soviet scholars tended to portray the *raznochinets* as a relatively dispossessed member of the middling social strata fighting against social injustices they could more easily understand because they were closer to the lower classes. In this reading, a member of the *raznochintsy* becomes a representative of the ill-treated masses and a fighter for their rights. Such impulses were certainly involved in the development of nihilism, but the rapid rise of the radical intelligentsia cannot be understood on the basis of any simple class antagonism. Many on the left came from among the nobility, and among the members of the *raznochintsy* a disproportionate number were sons of clergymen.[2]

Rather than treat the *raznochintsy* as a distinct social formation with special class interests, a better way to approach its relationship to the radical intelligentsia is to emphasize the word's prefix, meaning "varied." The unprecedented forms of association, new values and ideas that took shape in the "sixties" had their origins in what we might call the new "meeting grounds" supplied by the university and the reform-era city. People of "varied" classes had a greater opportunity to connect with and influence one another than had been possible before the reform era. Members of the radical intelligentsia from many different strata of Russian society were working, in the urban context described in the previous chapter, to establish new connections, new ideas and new identities that rejected social background as relatively meaningless. Urban environments enable people more easily to substitute *elective* values and practices for legally mandated and supposedly fixed social origins. The initial venues in which the new forms of association could take place were very often places of higher education where "old class distinctions disappeared readily and new forms of association developed."[3]

The new connections made at the universities simultaneously developed elsewhere in the socially mixed spaces of the reform-era city, and the dominant subculture/identity that took shape in these environments is that which ultimately would be labeled nihilism. Nihilism, in this respect, was not a class rebellion, nor was it any kind of organized movement. Sociologically the nihilists are best described as a mixed *soslovie*, voluntary subculture, the single demographic consistency of which was youth. Nihilism was not centered on class; it was rather, as Richard Stites put it, united by a common ethos: "a cluster of attitudes and social values and a set of behavioral affects—manners, dress, friendship patterns."[4] Defined in this way, nihilism is the outlier in this study. It was not a revolutionary movement, though it certainly had its political aspect, and rather than concealing itself underground, it instead sought public recognition in order to serve as a beacon pointing the way forward to the rest of society. The two intertwined processes that brought this nihilist ethos into being were a personal/psychological project of self-fashioning and the creation of an urban subculture. Both processes were dependent on the culture and space of the city.

SELF-FASHIONING

Given the restricted position in which the left intelligentsia found itself as a result of severe post-1862 limits on speech and assembly, it is hardly surprising that a politics of image and identity (as opposed to a politics of public persuasion or street activism) gained momentum. Although some radicals in this period chose to form underground associations, for those who were not prepared for conspiratorial activity it was still possible to express criticism in concealed and symbolic ways that were difficult to outlaw or keep out of print. Some individuals possessed the rare opportunity to express themselves in published journals, and they resorted to disguised (Aesopian) language as their method of political expression. The majority of dissenters, however, lacked a mouthpiece in the press and chose instead to demonstratively transform their mode of existence as a message of defiance and critique. This was the nihilist approach. Nihilists shared certain values that lent them a degree of ideological unity, but ultimately nihilism was more performative than programmatic: the left-leaning youth of the 1860s turned to clothing, attitude, and unconventional behavior as a way to identify one another and as a means of creating a recognizable protest against conventional politics and morality. One large advantage of their cultural politics was that sartorial, stylistic, and behavioral expression were relatively safe from prosecution, but the nihilist capacity to generate an effective social protest went much further than that.

For contemporaries and historians alike, it has been easy to dismiss nihilism as a superficial transgression that lacked underlying knowledge of, or commitment to, a greater cause, but in its time and place nihilism presented a countercultural critique that attracted the young intelligentsia and made the rest of society take notice. "Feeling themselves less the carriers of a particular political program than the creators of a new culture," Sergei Kalinchuk has written, "the young revolutionaries perceived the world through the prism of this culture and correspondingly strove to organize their everyday life [*byt*]."[5] It was their approach to everyday life that Chernyshevskii, an original exemplar of nihilism, wanted to describe when he dubbed the nihilists "new people." Chernyshevskii believed that human beings could refashion themselves, their communities, and ultimately the entire modern world by making rational choices about their everyday lives, as long as these choices were unprejudiced by conventional thinking. Thus nihilism was not merely a way of rejecting and communicating disdain for the inherited world, but it was also an attempt to create a new personal identity. It was at one and the same time a recreation of the self and a staging of the self. For these reasons the nihilist project can be understood as an exercise in "self-fashioning."

The term "self-fashioning" was originally used by Stephen Greenblatt in his 1980 study *Renaissance Self-Fashioning* to describe a process he saw taking place in the vastly different historical context of Renaissance England.[6] Greenblatt was interested in how English writers during the early reformation began to exhibit a deep, angst-ridden interest in the self, in personal identity as well as in the difficulty of maintaining a stable identity within their particular social and political context. Greenblatt's expression has often been misused to describe a simple act of image cultivation, but in fact he had in mind a much more complex and ambiguous process that might be thought of as the creation of an "expressive identity," or a personal sense of *self* that was also, and equally, a way to establish a *role* among others. To unite personal identity and projected image within a coherent sense of self is certainly not possible under all circumstances, but this description suits the radical intelligentsia of the 1860s remarkably well. For nihilists, identity and image did not need to be uncoupled since they were two parts of the same strategy used in the struggle to reshape the world in what they hoped would be a more rational and democratic form.

In spite of the different historical contexts, Greenblatt's conception of self-fashioning provides a useful approach to Russian nihilism because discussions of personal identity are prone to get trapped in the dichotomy of externally projected image versus genuinely experienced selfhood. This bifurcation of the personally immanent from the socially projected implies that identity is one of two things: either an image, and thus false or delusional, or authentic, and thus true, undivided selfhood. By this logic, when Russian radicals experienced the adoption of a nihilist identity as "ridding oneself of vulgar, obsolete prejudices" and "awakening to a new life," we would have to believe they were either undergoing a deep character transformation, and unaware of projecting an image, or else playing false roles for political gain.[7] When the populist Aleksandr Nikol'skii intentionally slept on the floor without blankets, or when Aleksandr Lutsernov refused to wear shoes even in the winter, they were certainly behaving in order to create an admirable nihilist persona.[8] But were they carving out a sense of self or were they parading an attitude? Greenblatt's version of self-fashioning refuses this dichotomy, accepting that a consciously developed persona and a change of self can take place as part of the same process.

It is also worth keeping in mind here the notably broad scope of Greenblatt's discussion of self-fashioning. Although focused specifically on early modern England, Greenblatt understood the need for active self-fashioning that began in the early modern period as something endemic to modernity itself. Indeed, the epilogue of Greenblatt's book includes a discussion of his own personal endeavors at self-fashioning in the 1970s. Greenblatt conceived of the struggle for a usable identity as a necessary, even reflexive, aspect of the modern consciousness. In the early phases of modern, urban identity, the working out of a functional sense of self was becoming an essential requirement for the navigation of an increasingly complex and atomized world. By comparison to the world of the medieval court or village, in which because of social rigidities the self could not afford to be flexible and open to interpretation, in a modern context selfhood was becoming something like a device through which to gain a measure of power within one's social environment. From this broad perspective, self-fashioning can be understood as a project shared by English Elizabethans and Russian nihilists alike.

Of course St. Petersburg's nihilists had little in common with the Englishmen Greenblatt studied. The defiant, politicized, scientistic, and group-oriented nihilist of reform-era Russia could hardly have been more unlike Greenblatt's well-connected, fiercely individualistic, politically cautious and often religiously devout Tudor gentlemen. But despite the obvious differences between the two groups, certain intriguing commonalities emerge. To begin with, both found themselves on the cusp of a new age, trying to make their way in unfamiliar circumstances that allowed (even encouraged) them to cobble together from the raw material of their lives what might be called "usable public personae," or contextually acceptable personal identities. For Greenblatt's subjects, intensive interest in personal identity was a response to the astonishing open-endedness and promise inherent in a period of rapid modernization and social change. Something similar can be said for those trying to find their place in the dynamic new world unleashed by Alexander's Great Reforms. Both eras can be called, following Greenblatt's characterization of Renaissance England, times of "radical and momentous social crisis" in which a "disintegration of the stable world order" was taking place.[9] Like Greenblatt's writers, who felt both the promise and the anxiety of change and modernization in post-Reformation England, the nihilists experienced a mixture of expectation and dread amidst the unprecedented possibilities and new dangers that accompanied Alexander's modernizing reign.

In this respect, the fact that Greenblatt's book originated in his encounter with Michel Foucault is of central importance.[10] Foucault considered the self, or individual agency, less stable and inflexible than it is often conceived to be. For Foucault the self is folded into, and built up out of, institutional discourses and generalized forms of knowledge. Foucault wrote in his essay *What Is Enlightenment?* that "Modern man ... is not the man who goes off to discover himself, his secrets and his hidden truth; he is the man who tries to invent himself. ... Modernity does not 'liberate man in his own being'; it compels him to face the task of producing himself."[11] The modern self, in these terms, cannot be understood as "natural," or as a product of free will. Rather individual subjectivity is constructed through a complex negotiation with power (political, social, institutional, etc.) because the self must find a suitable place within a pre-existing set of social and political parameters. Greenblatt by no means rejected Foucault's insight that institutionalized discourses played a role in creating the individual subject, but he sought out the ways in which, at the birth of the modern era, individuals might negotiate selfhood, developing personae or identities that could render individuality more productive in its given context. Nihilism can be similarly rethought in terms of self-fashioning because it involved the construction of socially and politically effective identities within the difficult and intimidating, but also potentially liberating, context of reform-era Russia.

It must also be said that any self-fashioning process is inconceivable in the absence of the social and spatial environment in which it takes place. If the circumstances of sixteenth century London and nineteenth century St. Petersburg radically differed from one another, both cities did have at least one important similarity: new, fragile, and dangerous public spheres in which people could be, and often were, imprisoned or otherwise punished for subversion. Writers in the city of London in the sixteenth century found themselves "displaced from a stable, inherited social world" and had to build themselves anew in an urban and increasingly cosmopolitan setting.[12] In London, as later in St. Petersburg, the density; mutually reinforcing sociability; and cultural, intellectual, and political exchange characteristic of thriving cities encouraged the creation of new possibilities and new selves. St. Petersburg and other large Russian cities likewise served as the primary matrix of sociability in which nihilism coalesced.

THE NIHILIST PERSONALITY

Projects of personal and cultural reconstruction in the interest of political change already had a long history in Russia before the advent of the reform era. Whether we are speaking of the cultivation of the "Decembrist type," a Hegelian "reconciliation with reality," or any number of projects of personal transformation in the private sphere, the cultivation of personal identity within a relatively well-defined circle or social sphere made sense in a Russian polity that, as noted in the previous chapter, intentionally held public participation in political affairs to a bare minimum.[13] Once the short experiment with public expression of the late 1850s/early 1860s was curtailed, it must have been an almost reflexive reaction to return to a politics of group-centered personal transformation. In this respect, what might be called the basic operating principle of nihilist self-transformation was Chernyshevskii's concept of "rational egoism," a sort of personal corollary to the collective utilitarian ethic of organizing for the greater good. The radical optimism of Chernyshevskii's conception of rational egoism is concisely adumbrated in the words of the character Lopukhov in *What Is to Be Done?*: "If someone can give pleasure to another person without causing himself any discomfort, then in my opinion calculation demands that he do so, because he himself would receive some pleasure from it as well."[14] Not only in his fiction, but in his philosophy and political economy, Chernyshevskii envisioned a world in which reasonable people would master their problems with dispassionate calculation. The ego in "rational egoism," contrary to common usage, refers mainly to the gratifications of selflessness rather than the usual idea that gratification results from the satisfaction of personal needs and desires. As Dmitry Pisarev echoed in his review of Chernyshevskii's novel, "The personal good of the new people corresponds with the general good, and their egoism instills the widest love for humanity."[15]

The unique nihilist combination of altruism and egotism raises understandable confusions. Sergei Bulgakov, for example, wrote about the inherent contradictions of nihilist intelligentsia thought that "concepts of *personal* morality, *personal* self-perfection, development of the *personality*, are extremely unpopular with the intelligentsia [although] the intelligentsia's outlook is itself a case of extreme self-affirmation of the personality, its self-deification."[16] The explanation for this apparent paradox lies in the intentions behind the complicated nihilist self-fashioning process. Marked individuality and open-ended personal freedom seem to conflict with rational egoism and utilitarianism, which are premised on the notion that once the faulty conditioning structures of a severely distorted society are removed, the healthy individuals that result will all need and want more or less the same things. It was this relatively generic persona conceived in the utilitarian imagination which the nihilist sought to embody. Though it seems self-contradictory, nihilist work for the betterment of society was understood as identical to working to satisfy one's own personal desires, for upon close consideration, ran the theory, the clearest means of achieving personal satisfaction lay in doing the greatest good for the greatest number of people.[17] Once the individual had rid himself of his immature conventional desire for direct personal satisfaction, the identification of personal utility with social gain would become the obvious default position. The goal then became to carve out a highly moral personality adaptable to utilitarian ethics. Under the tutelage of Chernyshevskii and other prominent figures, rational egoism provided a recipe for living that, when put into action and displayed before others, would convince society of the ultimate benefit and good sense of strict rationality and dispassionate materialism. For these reasons, as one contemporary pointed out, the nihilists tended to ignore political issues and instead focused on "the arrangement of personal and family life."[18] Or to put it differently, the nihilists found their political issues *within* personal and family life. The focus on personal identity and cultural norms allowed the nihilist to denounce those who did not hold similar views and instead unite as a group of people around what amounted to a moral program of individual and group cultivation.

As the original prophet of nihilism, Chernyshevskii himself underwent a sort of ur-self-fashioning process, in which he developed a workable personal identity outside the confines that his family and education had provided for him. Chernyshevskii's biographers have elucidated the process of personal cultivation through which he put himself in detailed examinations of the diary he kept in the 1840s and 1850s. In particular, Irina Paperno's book-length study functions in a broad sense as an analysis of

Chernyshevskii's self-fashioning project. Chernyshevskii sought to create a usable self-conception and self-presentation as an outsider in the intimidating context of St. Petersburg under Nicholas I: "For Chernyshevsky, a prototypical personality was to be formed not only in works of literature but also in private life. The task involved subjecting one's personal life to the demands of a public role ... but it also entailed a deliberate psychological self-organization, in which one's private personality, one's psychic life itself, was shaped to conform to a historical mold."[19]

On the basis of the feelings of marginalization and disenfranchisement Chernyshevskii experienced when he arrived in St. Petersburg in 1846 as the son of a provincial priest from Saratov, he gradually invented a personal style and set of values that afforded him a measure of confidence within Petersburg society. The persona he originated would eventually become one of the cornerstones of the nihilist identity. As Nikolai Berdiaev put it, Chernyshevskii fashioned out of this persona a kind of "moral capital of which less worthy people who come after [would] avail themselves."[20] Through an elaborate and time-consuming process that involved the emulation of an older peer and an inventive approach to marriage, Chernyshevskii transformed his social awkwardness amidst the glittering backdrop of Petersburg rank and nobility into the moral authority of a politically active journalist and social critic with, eventually, a loud and persuasive voice. The combination of persona, political stance, and utilitarian personal ethics he created for himself would have an important influence on young people of lower social status, who often came to Petersburg in a similarly awkward and intimidated state, and it also produced an equally magnetic effect on young people from among the elite who were searching for a way to distinguish themselves. Though it would be an extreme exaggeration to say that Chernyshevskii's model *created* nihilism—which was a much more complex phenomenon than could be embodied in a single person—there can be little doubt that the tone of Chernyshevskii's writing in the *Contemporary*, and even the effect of his character and image in personal encounters, did a great deal to shape the identity and culture of nihilism.

The nihilist personality was meant to act as a statement projected to the outside world, while at the same time it rested on a self-conception of moral and intellectual superiority. Another crucial moment in the coalescence of the nihilist identity is found in Pisarev's review of *Fathers and Children* in which the young reviewer accepted the character of the nihilist Bazarov as a flawed but largely accurate reflection of his contemporaries, claiming that "all the aspirations and ideas of our entire young generation can be recognized in the characters of this novel."[21] The "Bazarov type" for Pisarev had shed the desire to maintain connections with the hierarchical power structure of his society and therefore no longer required the affectations and mannerisms that had long oiled the machinery of polite society. Pisarev interpreted Bazarov's blunt manner as a reflection of his generation's personal independence: "[the nihilist] feels a natural, insurmountable disgust toward excess eloquence and verbosity, toward sweet thoughts, toward sentimentality, and generally toward all pretense not based on the real and tangible. Such aversion to everything removed from life and everything that has turned into empty phrases lies at the heart of the Bazarov type."[22]

Pisarev, following in the footsteps of Chernyshevskii, was a thoroughgoing "rational egoist," and it was well understood that his approval for the rejection of elite mores was also a call for personal transformation. His rejection of "society," a relatively small and privileged elite that was after all inextricably intertwined with autocratic power, constituted a rejection of the socio-political system as a whole. It was therefore an act of serious, if only implicit, rebellion. The nihilists formulated a new ideal of selfhood by contrasting a materialist and positivist ethic, based loosely on an appeal to the natural sciences, against the idealist, humanist ethic of the prior generation. Pisarev's contrast between positivist materialism and philosophical idealism was meant to inform personal choices and generate a new way of being and a new set of interpersonal codes. According to Pisarev's way of thinking, the formation of a new self made it possible for the nihilists to "choose sides" with the as-yet-unrealized world of the bright future they dreamed of. Particularly infuriating to the older generation, even to those like Herzen who had devoted their lives to the fight against autocratic Russia, was the sense of innate superiority the nihilist rejection of social niceties seemed to entail. Pisarev, for example, described Bazarov's relations with the older generation (and by extension the relationship of his entire generation with the preceding one) as that of an adult in a roomful of children, in which the adult is the member of the younger generation and the children his benighted elders.[23]

Petr Kropotkin would later describe the allure of the nihilist attitude in a similar way: "The life of civilized people is full of little conventional lies. Persons who hate each other, meeting in the street, make their faces radiant with a happy smile; the nihilist remained unmoved, and smiled only for those whom he was really glad to meet. All those forms of outward politeness which are mere hypocrisy were equally repugnant to him, and he assumed a certain external roughness as a protest against the smooth amiability of his fathers."[24] The idea that condemning the hypocrisies of conventionality reflects a superior moral stance and intellectual viewpoint has played an endemic role in the culture and politics of modern societies, especially among young people, dating back at least to the epoch of the French Revolution. It remains a common way of fashioning a personal identity to the present day. One young woman who despised the world she believed she had inherited, "that thing of everyone trying to be nice and well-mannered, and behind the scenes, people weren't really" opted to reject it: "I ripped my clothes, scalped myself, pierced my ears." She was not far in attitude from Pisarev or Kropotkin, though she was part of the punk generation of 1970s London.[25] Although nihilism (like punk rock) was very much a performative assertion of identity and rebellion, it was also an attempt to gain an inner sense of liberation.

Chernyshevskii was a generation older than the nihilists of the sixties, but in descriptions of the persona he created for himself what would come to be considered nihilist characteristics are unmistakable. Abbott Gleason's description captures its essence: "his whole bearing was an affront to the existing order, and he conveyed the impression that he would not make the slightest social concession. To smile and murmur a few ceremonial words to put an interlocutor at his ease would be, somehow, to betray his whole position. Sincerity was everything."[26] The intentional and provocative reversal of cultural norms through the expression of awkwardness, curt manners, and negligent dress was, according to Paperno, "deliberately cultivated, both by those who were naturally ungracious and by those trained in the social graces."[27] Members of the older generation, like Konstantin Kavelin, saw Chernyshevskii as "a tactless, smug person," but in fashioning this "tactless, smug" persona Chernyshevskii had created an identity the young generation thoroughly admired.[28] It would become a leitmotif of reform-era underground groups to devise plans to free the beloved Chernyshevskii from his distant Siberian imprisonment after he was exiled in 1864. Even in the late 1860s, years after Chernyshevskii's exile, the memory of his character was still revered as "the sort of genuine person especially needed in Russia as an example."[29] As Isaiah Berlin put it, "his personality and outlook set their seal on two generations of revolutionaries."[30] As the populist movement developed and transformed, it would continue to draw strength from the shared nihilist persona Chernyshevskii and his contemporaries had done so much to construct.

A NEW MODEL: WHAT IS TO BE DONE?

Though nihilism rested on a foundation of personal transformation, it was also a collective endeavor. The most important means by which

Chernyshevskii helped shift the personal/psychological project of early nihilism into a full-blown countercultural project was through the publication of his novel *What Is To Be Done?* What came to be called nihilism was already a recognizable phenomenon when Turgenev gave it a name in 1862, but with the 1863 publication of *What Is To Be Done?* nihilism crystallized into something much closer to the subcultural phenomenon it would be understood as afterward. Chernyshevskii's novel had an almost immediate impact on the development of nihilist counterculture. In part its influence owed to the esteem in which its author was already held. Chernyshevskii wrote *What Is To Be Done?* from prison, where his trumped-up arrest had already gained him a martyr's status. The novel was intentionally presented and clearly received as something far more important than a work of fiction. It was read, as one memoirist put it, "in a kneeling position."[31] As Georgii Plekhanov later maintained, an intelligent person reading the novel would come away "cleaner, better, braver, and bolder under its philanthropic influence."[32]

What Is To Be Done? became a mainstay of the development of the Russian revolutionary movement for decades to come, even though because of strict censorship Chernyshevskii could do no more than make veiled appeals for revolutionary activism. Instead he used his novel as a revelation of the spirit of rational egoism, utilitarian ethics, and communitarian values. *What Is To Be Done?* answered the question it asked. Though Chernyshevskii rejected the word nihilist, he wrote his novel as a kind of blueprint for a nihilist counterculture. It was, as one of Chernyshevskii's contemporaries put it, "a program for action."[33] By painting a portrait of a group of "new people" (Chernyshevskii's preferred term for nihilists), it pointed the way toward an exit from stultifying tradition that would, it was strongly implied, enable the next generation to usher in a new and better world. "Good, strong, honest, capable people," Chernyshevskii wrote in the book's preface, "you have only just begun to appear among us; already there's a fair number of you, and it's growing all the time."[34] The novel's main characters (Vera Pavlovna, Dmitry Lopukhov, and Aleksandr Kirsanov) clearly come across as figures to be emulated, and the novel as a whole offered itself as a guide to a better life in an overt way that was similar to didactic fiction like Rousseau's *Emile*. *What Is To Be Done?* was an instructional guide for molding a new type of person and a new culture.

So much does the novel focus on individual initiative that it might well be considered a socialist version of Samuel Smiles's *Self-Help*, which had been published in England four years earlier. Unlike Smiles's non-fictional advice manual, *What Is To Be Done?* was based on a fictional plot, but it was a kind of fiction that was, as Chernyshevskii himself was at pains to point out, little more than an excuse for a lesson in hard work, proper attitudes and reasonable behavior. This reading was corroborated by Pisarev's 1865 review, which characteristically refused to discuss the novel as an aesthetic object but spent some fifty pages demonstrating that its characters must serve as beacons for the personal development and cultural standards of his contemporaries. In particular Pisarev emphasized the work ethic and moral values that placed them head and shoulders above the "Philistines," "adult children," and "civilized primitives" of the previous generation.[35] One of Chernyshevskii's main characters, Lopukhov, behaves in the novel with such seemingly impossible altruism and self-sacrifice that generations of readers have questioned his plausibility. Pisarev, on the other hand, harbored no such skepticism:

> People like Lopukhov are rare at present, but such people are in no way above ordinary human beings. Anyone not born an idiot can develop in himself the same capacity for thought, can strengthen himself through useful labor, can rise to a proper and clear understanding of his relations with others, and when this happens, the actions of a Lopukhov will appear entirely simple and natural, and he will inquire with sincere bewilderment: but could it be possible to behave any other way?[36]

If acceptance of Turgenev's Bazarov as a prototype had been hesitant and contentious, the young intelligentsia took to Chernyshevskii's characters without hesitation. Educated young people "wandering aimlessly around Petersburg," as Eliseev put it, "began to do exactly what they were supposed to do according to the ... novel."[37] *What Is To Be Done?* eased adoption of the behavioral changes it proposed by offering numerous examples of how to arrange one's everyday life, from the grand ambition of establishing cooperative business and living ventures (a challenge that would be taken up by many followers) to suggestions for changes in clothing, diet, and interpersonal relationships. Because Chernyshevskii's characters rejected conventional norms in their easy elevation of "rational" behavior over "irrational" tradition, they seem wooden and unrealistic in the manner of unconvincing science fiction, but all the same they had magnetic appeal to decades of Russian radicals. The tremendous popularity of the novel, along with its promotion of "nihilist" ways, helped turn nihilism into an almost cultish phenomenon. As Aleksandr Skabichevskii put it, after the publication of *What Is To Be Done?* nihilism began to take on a "sectarian character of isolation from the rest of Russia" in which "as in any sect, the people belonging to it considered only themselves the faithful, the chosen, the salt of the earth. The whole remainder of humanity was considered a crowd of unhappy nothings and despised Philistines."[38]

In this respect, the reception of *What Is To Be Done?* can be considered the turning point at which nihilism was transformed from an act of self-fashioning into an act of counterculture formation, from a celebration of a nihilist type of individuality into a new cultural norm in which individuality was less important than group coherence. While Pisarev continued in his articles to portray nihilism as an attitude of individual strength and certitude that enabled the individual to reject the outdated conventions of previous generations, the nihilism found in *What Is To Be Done?* is different. With the exception of the character Rakhmetov, Chernyshevskii's novel relegated individual personality to a lower level. Its model "new people," through their logical embrace of rational egoism, seemed to develop personal strength and confidence in an entirely unspectacular fashion, almost as a matter of course. One might say that Chernyshevskii was less interested in promoting individual personality than he was in establishing a shared personality type. In describing Lopukhov and Kirsanov, both almost impossibly confident and talented characters, Chernyshevskii held that "all of their most outstanding traits belong not to the two individuals but to a type."[39] In the novel's countercultural fantasy, it was the accumulation of similar types that would usher in revolutionary change and finally enable people to say, as Chernyshevskii suggests they soon will, "Well, now life is good."[40]

Among all of the countercultural reconfigurations of Russian society proposed by *What Is To Be Done?* the most essential was undoubtedly its suggested reconstruction of gender norms. The novel's plot rests on conflicts involving love and marriage, and its essential pathos emerges from the characters' ability to surmount these problems by rejecting traditions that subordinate women to men. Chernyshevskii did not pioneer these questions in Russia. His novel was only one of many contributions to the intelligentsia's ongoing discussion of feminism, the so-called "woman question," but he emphasized gender relations as a way to generate both a critique of and alternatives to the social norms of his day. Chernyshevskii's novel closely followed Mikhail Mikhailov's articles on "the woman question," an earlier set of texts on gender roles that had had an important impact on the nihilist movement. Mikhailov argued for an end to cultural differences and separate spheres for men and women, supporting higher education for women and marriages based on "equal status."[41] For its part, *What Is To Be Done?* can be considered a sort of *bildungsroman* about its female protagonist Vera Pavlovna. Unlike the ordinary people around her, Vera Pavlovna takes it as axiomatic that substantial differences between men and women do not exist.

As she puts it: "I realize a woman's voice is contralto and a man's baritone. What follows from that?" Vera Pavlovna's quest for autonomy in a patriarchal society is both a central feature of the book's feminist message and a platform on which Chernyshevskii can imply the need for rational (meaning utilitarian and socialist) solutions to economic and social arrangements. What emerges from Vera Pavlovna's reshaping of her life are sexual independence within marriage, mutual respect between men and women, cooperative labor workshops, and a series of dreams that point to the inevitability of undefined but sweeping socialist revolution.

It would become particularly characteristic of the reform-era intelligentsia that men worked side by side with women to promote women's rights. Women and men on the left emphasized the importance of women's education, and a group of distinguished professors in St. Petersburg eventually opened a series of courses in 1868 intended to prepare women for higher education.[42] The "Alarchin Courses" gave a small number of Russian women sufficient educational background to pave the way for university study abroad, and at the end of the 1870s women's higher education was finally made available in public universities.[43] Already by the late 1870s, proportions of Russian women in secondary and higher education exceeded numbers in the rest of Europe, only to be outdone by the proportion of female students in the United States.[44] For the nihilists and populists, the struggle for women's autonomy did not turn into the "battle of the sexes" that sometimes arose in other European countries. Among the populist intelligentsia, respect for women's rights was generally assumed. In his study of Russian feminism, Richard Stites contrasted Russian and European feminism, arguing that "If Russian men were more numerous, more active, and more sweeping in their advocacy of women's rights, this is because the Russian intelligentsia, by its nature and from its inception, exhibited a social and intellectual style dominated by the compulsion to live a life that was fully consistent with its ideas."[45] The radical populist undergrounds of the 1870s would have been remarkably different (and most likely less effective) organizations had they not brought together men and women on an equal footing.

What made the gender question among the Russian intelligentsia a central issue? It would be difficult to argue that Russian men were innately opposed to women's social subordination, or that Russian women were more assertive in their demands for independence than their European counterparts. Perhaps the primary reason the "woman question" loomed so large in reform-era Russia involves the compromised nature of public discourse. In the political context of a state that refused to tolerate freedoms of assembly, political parties, and many forms of political speech, a more easily masked, and less easily prosecuted, politics of culture and identity arose to play a relatively larger part in Russia. The politics of personal life that developed in Russia stressed gender inequality as a repudiation of patriarchal standards, and this emphasis led to the somewhat surprising phenomenon of an advanced feminism in an otherwise stultified political arena. Suffrage was, of course, a non-issue in the absence of democratic institutions, but by the 1870s, as Stites held, "in quality and range of women's higher education, Russia had no peer in Europe."[46]

Indeed the entrance of women into the public sphere was an essential feature of the time, welcomed on the left and decried on the right. In the late 1850s, as Vodovozova remarked, "among women there began a furious search for employment: they sought lessons, worked at the telegraph office, as typesetters, in binderies, became saleswomen in bookstores and other shops, became translators, readers, midwives, feldshers, copyists and stenographers."[47] To find employment, women who had the economic and social advantages to be able to do so went to the cities "where they dreamed not only of obtaining a position, but of finding conditions of life fairer and more reasonable, corresponding better to their contemporary needs than those they met in their antediluvian families."[48] Unfortunately, employment opportunities for women were difficult to locate and generally offered poor compensation. As a result, the promotion of women's education became a movement in its own right. It was an important success for reform-era activists that in spite of the state's refusal to allow women educational opportunities, some of the first women in Europe to gain prominence in fields like medicine and mathematics were Russian.

The emphasis on gender equality in Russia ultimately sprang from the same source as that of nihilism itself: the compelling idea of carrying out revolution at the level of everyday life. It is here where urban space came into play as a formative aspect of nihilism. Just as the non-noble classes in Western Europe used the inherent potential of the city to create a new, and eventually dominant, class of people that came to be called (after the city itself) the bourgeoisie, the nihilist effort to transform the world was firmly rooted in the urban environment. As noted in the introduction to this book, the formation of "new people" demands an urban environment. It is true (and quite characteristic of typical urbanite aspirations) that Chernyshevskii's vision for a bright post-revolutionary future is presented as a post-urban world that has transcended urban space all together. But it is not surprising that the post-urban world of Chernyshevskii's imagination only exists in the realm of Vera Pavlovna's dreams. All the behavior Chernyshevskii models as a way toward that future—from founding artels, to saving prostitutes, to forming circles for intellectual development—depends on the proximities and new possibilities only to be found in an urban context. In *What Is To Be Done?* the prostitute Kriukova meets the young Lopukhov by chance while walking the streets of St. Petersburg, at which point he is in a position to teach her that a better way of life is available. The streets are a place where society may fall apart but also where it can reconstitute itself as something better.

NIHILISM AND THE THEATER OF URBAN LIFE

As Chernyshevskii's ideal of rational egoism proposes it should, individual identity among the nihilists came to be closely entwined with collective identity. Like contemporaneous artistic bohemians in other parts of Europe who were beginning to experiment with new personal images and behaviors, the nihilists found that personal transformation could offer a sense of meaning and community. In contrast, however, to the bohemian model of acting out against the grain of conventional morality in order to "shock the bourgeoisie" by cultivating an identity as far as possible out of the mainstream, nihilism often took a separate path by raising conventional morality to uncharacteristically high standards and expecting those same standards to be met by other nihilists as well. The nihilist desire to flout outmoded convention and reject social norms typically worked by displaying restrained, even ascetic, personal behavior. The moral and ascetic aspect of nihilism is one reason it has sometimes been described as an atheistic inversion of Christianity.

E. I. Shcherbakova has described a self-improvement list written by a young nihilist that includes the following eleven wishes for personal improvement: temperance, silence, order, decisiveness, moderation, hard work, sincerity, fairness, self-possession, tidiness, and calm.[49] In spite of what detractors wrote about the supposedly dissolute behavior of the radical intelligentsia, such personal goals were commonplace among them. Vladimir Debagorii-Mokrievich would claim about a later populist circle in Kiev that it rested on a kind of righteous self-abnegation: "we had to . . . reject the life of privilege and begin to live the way the people [*narod*] live. We had to remove ourselves from everything demoralizing."[50] Such austerity appealed to women as much as men, as noted by E. D. Dubenskaia: "Not ascetic by nature and habit, nevertheless [radical women] led an ascetic life and dressed poorly. Many among the brilliant assemblage of women of that time, who had been raised in luxury, threw out their frilly linens and dressed in rough underthings and simple dresses, and didn't wear any other kind of clothing throughout their lives. They also ate meager provisions and not only did not have comfortable apartments but sometimes lacked even their own rooms."⁵¹ Someone who "lived in the nihilist fashion," according to Lev Tikhomirov, "did not allow himself any luxuries, not in the form of decent food, nor of warm and comfortable clothing."⁵² At times this self-abnegating asceticism resembled bohemian admiration for "romantic" poverty; at other times it smacked of smug sanctimony. Either way, by departing from norms of conventional behavior, nihilists and bohemians were equally successful in shocking their more conventional contemporaries.

In the context of late-imperial Russia, the nihilist identity, with its seductive combination of rebellion and integrity as well as its communal reassurance of unity and mutual support, influenced generations and helped generate a type of political power where none had existed before. That identity, expressed through socially marked forms of dress, language, and behavior, was readily recognizable to outsiders and insiders alike. Contemporaries (including both observers and participants) who defined nihilism in terms of appearance and attitude were so commonplace that nihilism can almost be understood *as* appearance and attitude. When the older generation of intellectuals, even among left-leaning political allies, took the nihilists' bait and expressed horror at the young generation, it only rendered the nihilist identity a more powerful tool for enabling young radicals to identify like-minded peers and unite around common values. To project "external roughness" against "smooth amiability," proclaimed one's place in a larger community, and sustained confidence among young individuals who often lacked status, wealth, and power.

In cultivating a nihilist image, the social context and spatial environment played a central part. An image is of course meaningless in the absence of an arena in which it can be effectively displayed. To be successful as a political statement, nihilism had to be "performed," and therefore it required a stage on which its performance could take place. Many such stages were used, and their scale varied from the family drawing room and the provincial secondary school to the streets of Moscow and St. Petersburg. Perhaps the most familiar and characteristic display of nihilism involved clothing. In this respect, nihilists followed long-established trends in urban history. As Richard Sennett has argued, prior to the modern era the clothes a person wore on the street in front of strangers served primarily as a badge of class origin or vocational affiliation, hiding the self behind (or perhaps revealing the self within) a known group identity. But later in the more open-ended and impersonal conditions of the burgeoning nineteenth century metropolis, clothing began to serve as a revelation of individuality, an expression of deeply felt *personal* identity.[53] In Russia fashion continued somewhat longer to adhere to traditional expressions of group identity since dress remained more tightly wedded to rank (uniforms) and the traditions of one's *soslovie*. Not until the reform era did sartorial possibility begin to open up in a similar fashion to the process Sennett found unfolding at a somewhat earlier period in Western Europe.

While some reform-era Petersburgers clung to their uniforms, it was in this period that, among certain people, personal expression through dress burst forth in a new array of personal, social, and political possibilities. "Fashion," as Christine Ruane has written with respect to the reform era, "allowed individuals to create imagined communities ... whose sartorial nonconformity frequently led to political confrontation."[54] The wealthy official Nikolai Selifontov, for example, dressed in fantasy imitation of a peasant, wearing a red shirt and velveteen trousers tucked into greasy boots.[55] Most notorious of all was the writer Pavel Iakushkin, whose outrageous clothing and drunken way of life served, as Gleason has described, as "a public criticism of 'official Russia,' a slap in the face of right-thinking people, and a bad example to the young."[56] Iakushkin's ragged and dirty persona was meant to signify a kind of alternative authenticity; his extremism in dress served as both a political demonstration of a common identity with the Russian peasant and a symbol of his countercultural rejection of the status quo. Like Western European dandies and bohemians, who presented their lives and personae as works of art in the city streets, Selifontov and Iakushkin used the urban public sphere as a stage to proclaim the possibility of alternative ways of living and thinking. Members of the so-called "Smorgon Academy," a Petersburg circle that formed in the late 1860s, took downwardly mobile dressing even further, naming themselves after an old gypsy bear-training camp in the forest because "our grooming and manners had something in common with wild bears."[57] The unsympathetic journalist Mikhnevich mocked populist writers like Zlatovratskii and Zasodimskii, saying they found "civic valor" in baste sandals and cheap peasant boots, while they saw "sin and falsehood" in fashionable tricot slacks and calfskin German shoes.[58]

Nihilist style, since it involved group unity as much as personal individuality, tended toward the adoption of a fairly narrow set of choices, and in a way it became a uniform in its own right. Clothes were worn, as Skabichevskii put it, "demonstratively, in order to openly express belonging to the chosen crowd."[59] Nihilist dress was composed of a few basic components that distinguished one's allegiance to the group. A short list of typical features for men would include long hair, high boots, a rough plaid overcoat, blue-tinted glasses, and perhaps a canvas shirt with a sash and a rough-hewn walking stick. Because of the greater variety and luxury of women's fashions, nihilist women stood out even more. They cut their hair conspicuously short, and they typically wore a flat, black woolen dress, blue glasses, and sometimes a plaid shawl. Short hair for women was such a clear demonstration of group identity that nihilist women were sometimes referred to simply as *strizhenitsy* (shorn women). Women's short haircuts and unkempt fingernails, in keeping with nihilism's ascetic image, desexualized them, while men left their hair uncut and uncombed, giving it at times a romantic appearance, or as Lev Deich expressed it, an appearance of "picturesque disorder."[60] The point of these standardized fashions, as with relatively standardized nihilist behavior and lifestyle choices, was to outwardly portray an inner anti-conventionality before the rest of educated society, while at the same time demonstrating allegiance to the nihilist community.

The desire to build community helps explain why lack of adherence to the code could lead to marginalization, even ouster from the group. Aleksandr Sleptsov, for example, a writer for the *Contemporary* and the founder of a well-known "nihilist" commune in the early 1860s, was every inch the populist radical in ideological terms, but he also happened to be rather fastidious in questions of dress and furnishing, which thereby rendered him suspect among his peers. Nihilism intentionally presented itself as the antithesis of urbane society, and just as proper social behavior had to be learned in polite society, sometimes at the cost of painful social embarrassment, so too did the image, style, and sociability of nihilism need to be painstakingly acquired. As Vodovozova explained, "[the] rules were not set forth in writing, but since one could be subjected to censure and ridicule for not obeying them, anyone who did not wish to be labeled a hard-boiled conservative had them firmly committed to memory."[61] Nihilist cultural forms underwent a turbulent evolution in the dynamic life of the capital city, and to master the fluctuations required jockeying for authority by means of the most successful deployment of ideas, language, dress, and manners. If one deviated from the cultural pattern, one's nihilist "credentials" could be tarnished. Such attitudes persisted long after nihilism proper had been discredited as a viable political stance among the populists. As late as the mid-1870s, Deich maintained cold relations with his future comrade-in-arms Plekhanov because "his outward appearance . . . didn't at all suit that of a nihilist."[62]

NIHILIST COUNTERCULTURE

Nihilism, then, offered a pattern by which to develop an individual sense of self, which at the same time revolved around a common set of tacit codes for speech, bearing, and dress that served as a marker of group belonging.

For this reason, terms like subculture and counterculture suit the nihilist movement well. As Peter Pozefsky has argued, group unity helped sustain the movement over time. By marking their lives in the form of dress, speech, and social conduct, the nihilists "succeeded in distancing themselves from the social mainstream and, in doing so, created a distinctive subculture with sufficient dynamism to survive the historical environment in which it initially appeared."[63] Nihilism as a cultural form had coalesced in an urban context, and it continued to rely on the theater of urban life in order to stage presentations of its distinct values. "Bohemia does not exist and is not possible, except in Paris," wrote Henri Murger, and although a variety of bohemian subcultures would later crop up in other cities, it is not surprising that the urban dynamism of nineteenth-century Paris rendered the French capital an ideal space in which a hitherto unheard of counterculture could emerge.[64] One might well say the same thing about nihilism and the city of St. Petersburg. Nihilism could only have come into being in an environment with both the critical mass of educated young people and a ready audience for the spectacle of the alternative culture they created.[65] Not only was it easier in the city to get copies of books, thick journals and illegal foreign publications that supplied some of the ideological foundations of nihilism, but urban space provided a crucible for the cultivation of dress, manners, posture, expression, and turns of phrase that came to be considered characteristic of nihilism.

It is a common assumption about large cities, particularly of the gigantic and impersonal industrial metropolis that arose in the nineteenth century, that they impart to their inhabitants a sense of isolation or "anomie."[66] Following Emile Durkheim's work on urban environments, sociologists have shown how large cities can isolate their inhabitants, stranding them within the "lonely crowd."[67] It is perhaps less often noted that cities also foster sociability, new connections, new ideas, and new projects. One might say that for every isolated and overwhelmed Raskolnikov one can also find an engaged and adventurous Razumikhin. A large metropolis offers ample opportunities for overcoming isolation and anonymity, while the intimidating overabundance of the metropolis generates a need for community and mutually supportive personal relationships. Georg Simmel, who bemoaned what he considered the depersonalization engendered by urban environments, also wrote that the creation of new groups "compensates for the isolation of the personality."[68] The potentially alienating metropolitan *Gesellschaft* (society) is also capable of fostering a plethora of new *Gemeinschaften* (communities). It is these latter communities that are referred to, at least in a modern urban context as "subcultures." Such subcultures have ranged from diasporic communities, to religious and cultural movements, to criminal gangs, to the sort of countercultural and politically motivated phenomenon found in nihilism. In the simple terms used by an urban sociologist: "cities provide persons—whatever their idiosyncratic tastes, needs, values, or life styles—the opportunity to find others who share the same tastes, needs, values, or life styles."[69] Urban space can be lonely and anonymous and at the same time conducive to an environment in which creative individuality and community building flourish.

If an urban environment tends to breed subcultures, politically motivated countercultures are even more closely connected to urban conditions. To quote the sociologist Claude Fischer: "Discontented citizens are found everywhere, but cities permit the militant ones to meet, to organize, to mobilize. Thus cities produce insurrectionary movements."[70] Nihilism in the 1860s was a far cry from the quasi-insurrectionary movement that would come into being in St. Petersburg in the late 1870s, but because of its clear intention to present a model of difference from the conventional culture that dominated the capital city, it is most accurately labeled a "counterculture." If the term "subculture" suggests only separation from the mainstream, the term "counterculture" better captures the assertion of superiority and social criticism involved in nihilism. As we have seen, particularly in the person of Chernyshevskii, self-fashioning offered a means of generating social power where it was not otherwise available; it was a way of turning weakness into strength. The formation of a group identity among disaffected students and marginalized young intellectuals reinforced this social power by creating conditions in which mutual recognition, unity, and social notoriety facilitated political solidarity.

Because of its camouflaged but unmistakable political aspirations, Russian nihilism is sometimes erroneously conceived of as an early, if awkward, eruption of the radical political traditions that eventually led to the Bolshevik Revolution. Nihilism certainly contributed to the revolutionary climate that would continue to gather strength into the twentieth century, but it should not be confused with the activist political undergrounds that developed side by side with nihilism, but remained distinct from it. Though nihilism, like underground movements, united its adherents around a set of ideas and practices, it did not limit its activities to a vetted cohort of like-minded associates and conceal them from ordinary society. Quite the contrary, nihilism served to link together unconnected individuals with potentially similar views and to profess to the outside world an ideological affiliation that drew a line between ordinary citizens and those who belonged to the nihilist "tribe." Thus nihilism was not an exclusively political phenomenon. It makes just as much sense to align nihilism with the history of youth subcultures that have gone to battle not against governments but on the field of cultural codes and personal values. Umberto Eco's description of countercultural style as "semiotic guerilla warfare" would be a good description of nihilist tactics.[71] For that reason it has always been difficult to connect nihilism's collective adherents to any well-articulated ideological doctrine or political movement.

Even though its cultural emphasis rendered nihilism less an obvious threat to the state than were explicitly politicized movements, the "danger" nihilism's particular brand of subversion seemed to pose was still understood on the right as a political threat. In the panic that followed Dmitry Karakozov's attempt to assassinate the tsar in 1866, simply wearing nihilist clothing came to be considered by the police an "insolence deserving not only of condemnation but of prosecution."[72] In some indistinct way, nihilism seemed to be at fault for subversive acts. Social links between standard nihilist cultural warriors and violent political radicals can be identified, and were in fact identified by the police throughout the 1860s and 1870s, but perhaps a better reason for the perceived threat has to do with nihilism's success in the arena of cultural politics. As Dick Hebdige has pointed out, it is never particularly difficult for a counterculture to distinguish itself from "mainstream culture" since the mainstream has "a tendency to masquerade as nature, to substitute 'normalized' for historical forms."[73] In a way, conventional culture's claim to embody the normal way, or the *only* way, had everything to do with the success of nihilism.

By presenting reform as the order of the day, the autocracy implicitly requested Russian society to question its standards and decide whether they remained valid and relevant in a changing Russia. Of course those in power would never have been able to imagine the seemingly unquestionable assumptions nihilism would call into question and attempt to undermine, but to a degree the young *shestidesiatniki* (sixties people) of the nihilist era were merely playing the role they were given when the state attempted to draw on the participation of society. Countercultures, by "repositioning and recontextualizing" the standard order of things, emphasize the ways in which what has been made to look natural is actually constructed.[74] Since nihilism engaged in this act of rethinking traditions and conventions to a substantial degree, it is not surprising that the alternative order the nihilists promoted would go on to serve as a cultural foundation for the revolutionary tradition for decades to come.

The most attention-grabbing countercultural practices of the nihilists involved two customs described in detail in *What Is To Be Done?* These were fictitious marriages and alternative living and working arrangements in communes and artels (worker collectives). The "fictive marriage" became a not-uncommon practice among nihilists and populists in the 1860s and 1870s, perhaps because it offered something important to both parties involved. For women the goal was independence. In order to break the chain of submission, first to the will of parents and second to a husband, fictive marriages were contracted to give a woman autonomy from her family. Such marriages did at times culminate in mutual affection, but their primary *raison d'etre* involved, as Vera Kornilova (who engaged in such a marriage to Nikolai Griboedov) put it: escape from "the bourgeois life at home."[75] But how did the fictive husband benefit from such an arrangement? Except for cases in which he was hoping the façade marriage would eventually lead to a genuine attachment, a development also modeled in Chernyshevskii's novel, the attraction was altruism. Contracting a fictive marriage allowed the male partner to demonstrate within his countercultural community that he deeply valued women's autonomy. He could also sometimes boast that by offering his "bride" independence he had added another fighter to the cause.

If fictitious marriages scandalized the public, the nihilist commune provided even more shock value. It is sometimes suggested that imitation of *What Is To Be Done?* was the sole reason for the popularity of cooperative living and working arrangements, but while Chernyshevskii's novel played the central role in the propagation of communal experiments in this era, Chernyshevskii had originally modeled his commune on attempts that had already been made in reality.[76] The most important of these attempts may have been the original model for Vera Pavlovna's women's sewing artel. The "Women's Publishing Artel," founded by Maria Trubnikova and Nadezhda Stasova around six months prior to the appearance of Chernyshevskii's novel, was a cooperative business venture that translated and published foreign texts for Russian readers. It became a viable operation that lasted to the end of the 1860s. It was funded by an arrangement of collected shares of both capital and labor, and it offered women employment and an otherwise elusive personal freedom.[77]

Artels, communes, and circles for discussion and debate had a significant impact in shaping the lives of reform-era radicals. As Petr Tkachev recalled in 1874: "Since the benches of gymnasium I have known no society other than the society of youths absorbed in student meetings, conspiring secretly, establishing Sunday schools and reading centers, directing artels and communes."[78] Such societies offered great social rewards to those who participated in them, but they also required large amounts of time and effort.

When Aleksandr Mikhailov got involved in his first commune, for example, he found that it "swallowed all his attention."[79] As a result of the practical difficulties of communal and cooperative ventures, as Vera Zasulich recalled, although communes "sprang up like mushrooms," they often fell apart in such acrimony that the disputes they engendered had to be resolved in court.[80] Even so, communes and artels remained an important part of populist practice into the 1880s.

The nihilist commune makes an excellent example of the city's capacity to facilitate the proliferation of new spaces and new spatial practices. We tend to think of space as extensive. For instance, when we use the adjective "spacious" it denotes abundance of space, room for movement. Equally important, especially in an urban context, is spatial intensivity, or the proliferation of space inward. Imagine, for example, a medium-sized room of thirty by thirty feet. Such a room may appear to be relatively small and a standard-sized container for the contents within it. One might, however, subdivide that room with partitions into several smaller rooms, all of which would be diminished in size but still serviceable as separate rooms. And if the room has high ceilings, it would further be possible to subdivide it vertically into another layer of an equal number of rooms. If, moreover, one were to add to this quantitative subdivision of space a qualitative set of distinctions—each room is painted a different color, holds different furnishing, is used for different activities, etc.—we have now, in a sense, created a great deal of space where it did not seem to exist before. Urban environments put to work a similar combination of quantitative and qualitative subdivision that enables the expansion of not just blandly uniform separate spaces but a potential abundance of heterotopic forms and functions that are sometimes imposed from above but also generated from below.

The desire to enact the model forms in *What Is To Be Done?*, accompanied by the dynamic conviviality and concern for social and cultural innovation that had come to characterize the reform-era Russian city, enabled nihilist counterculture to perform a spatially intensive reconstruction from within. Communal living in these spaces could include sharing of rooms, food, property, and even clothing, both in order to minimize expenses and as a way to practice the principles of an imagined future by "putting socialist principles into practice in personal life, and repudiating the values of the 'old world.'"[81] Communes served as "centers for drawing young people together, increasing the influence of the more developed and mature on those just arriving," and they were especially important for women "who thirsted for knowledge and strove for independence."[82] And given the dense population and complex interstices of a large urban environment, there was little that official Russia could do to restrain the adoption of communal living.

The most famous of the communes to appear in the wake of *What Is To Be Done?* was the Sleptsov commune on Znamenskaia Street [present-day Ulitsa Vosstaniia]. By later standards it was a tepid experiment in collective living, based very loosely on the plans of Charles Fourier. It managed only a rough approximation of shared resources, employed servants to do much of the household labor, and held a salon on Tuesdays for curious visitors.[83] The commune's open-door policy, which had been intended as a way to publicize its forward-thinking living arrangements, led to malicious rumors and fictionalizations that portrayed it as both licentious and impractical.[84] A Third Section report described the commune as made up of "young people of immoral and harmful character" who "repudiate all the laws of public order, do not recognize parental relations or marriage, which they replace by the equal rights of both sexes to intimate relations among themselves."[85] The information here was based on nothing more than gossip, but the report does at least demonstrate that the commune was sending its intended message of rejection of convention. Sleptsov's commune lasted only from the fall of 1863 to the spring of 1864. The reason for its demise seems to have involved a clash of personalities, money problems, and a general lack of interest in household chores.[86]

Absent the accusation of immorality and the unfounded allegations of promiscuity, most members of the Znamenskaia Commune did, to an extent, repudiate the old order, seek equality between the sexes, and favor a degree of communal property. Artels and communes were consciously planned heterotopic spaces in which new experiments in life and work could take place and through which such experiments could be presented and performed for the benefit of the rest of society. Such spaces tended, like many other countercultural associations, to establish an us/them mentality. "I considered only the members of the commune to be decent and honorable," recalled one participant, "while all the rest were idiots or scum."[87] Another St. Petersburg commune at the corner of Arkhiereiskaia and Kamenoostrovskaia Streets was founded by a group of women studying to be midwives in the mid-1860s. Like so many nihilists, they wished to demonstrate their humility and lack of pretense, which they did by eating horsemeat, but at the same time they were ill-prepared to do housework, so they hired a cook.[88]

Whatever their shortcomings, these nihilist experiments in urban heterotopia established one important foundation of the undergrounds that would arise later. Certain underground organizations would take shape on the basis of experiments in cooperative living, and the most successful of them would make requisite the sort of subcultural corporate spirit that such experiments sought to perfect. Beyond that, the practices of fictive marriage and of creating usable spaces known only to the community of young radicals were essential foundations for the networks of conspiratorial apartments that would later serve as the safe refuge of the radical populist underground during its terrorist phase.

CHAPTER THREE

UNDERGROUND PIONEERS

In Petersburg they put together a commission of ministers to uncover the reasons why the young were creating secret societies. . . . The reason is simple: if they do not allow the creation of open associations, then of course they will be created in secret.

Sergei Goloushev

AROUND THE SAME TIME THAT nihilism was reaching the peak of its notoriety in the early 1860s, another method of protest was slowly taking shape. A series of small but influential radical groups began to adopt clandestine methods of organization in the service of those populist aims that had not managed to get a good hearing in the limited public sphere of the early reform era. In these small organizations, the populist underground was gradually forming, but the learning process was slow and difficult. Elena Vilenskaia, one of a few historians who has chosen to focus directly on the underground itself, concluded that in the early 1860s secret anti-autocratic organizations had become "a persistent and steady element in Russian social life."[1] From this point forward, as Vilenskaia maintained, one secret organization or another somewhere in the Russian Empire would be making plans to overthrow the government. But in spite of the growing importance of such organizations, underground movements emerged slowly, haphazardly, and mostly in isolation from one another. Leaders of these organizations took some notorious missteps, and it would be years before any underground movement would become an effective tool of political subversion or attain any degree of sustainability.

In view of the last chapter, it should be noted that nihilist counterculture and underground radical activism were not mutually exclusive. Nihilism was an open movement that put its cultural politics on display, but at the same time there was no reason that demonstrative nihilists could not also be covert revolutionaries. Even the distinction between legal and illegal, open and secret political activities could be blurry. From the early 1860s a large gray area existed in which both quasi-political activities and clearly illegal activism took place. Indeed, throughout the reform era it was a common story for future revolutionaries to begin with the intention of working in an open and legal manner but to wind up hindered by official prohibitions and radicalized by the frustration that there was no option left other than to act in secret. Nikolai Serno-Solov'evich, for example, a leader of one of the earliest undergrounds, had begun his career as a government official. It was he who, in 1858, openly approached Alexander II in the palace gardens and handed him a manuscript suggesting how to correct current policy errors. Within three years Serno-Solov'evich had retired from government service and begun to devote his full energies to conspiratorial efforts to bring down the government for which he had worked.[2] A later example, Iakov Stefanovich, had worked peacefully in pursuit of rather modest goals supporting Ukrainian education and identity, but when the state frowned on his efforts and blocked them he came to feel that since it was not possible to carry out peaceful activism his only option was to fight for a new government that would tolerate his private efforts to benefit society.[3] Such dashed hopes for tolerated dissent were not uncommon forms of disillusionment on the journey underground. One radical wrote about the official handling of those with moderate views that "highly placed idiots think their clumsy measures will prevent anything: if only they knew that with each new oppression the circle of honest people closes more and more tightly."[4]

If cities create excellent conditions for the rise of subcultures, they also create excellent conditions for the formation of underground movements, and for many of the same reasons. The density that facilitates elective association with like-minded others also creates conditions of anonymity, of living in a crowded environment that encourages lack of interference in the affairs of others. The associations more easily formed in cities, like student groups, discussion circles, Sunday schools, nihilist collectives, and bookstores (almost all of them in the larger Russian cities), made possible the kinds of social interaction that allowed secret organizations to coalesce.

The early undergrounds found various models to emulate, including pre-existing Russian associations and published accounts of foreign underground movements. The Decembrist Revolt still loomed large as a reminder that a few decades earlier a serious challenge to autocratic authority had emerged from a network of secret societies. Possibly even more important was knowledge of the French Revolution and the Revolutions of 1848 (and later the Paris Commune), which offered numerous models of overt and covert revolutionary activity. Finally, the writings of European revolutionaries like Mazzini and Buanorotti described techniques for escaping detection, like leaderless cells and invisible ink.[5] In more general terms, practical experience with conspiratorial organization arose quite easily in the atmosphere of a suspicious state supported by a well-developed political police force. Under such conditions, underground connections and activities emerge as a matter of precaution, become reflexive, and all the more readily take hold among the political opposition.

And yet effective underground discipline, organization, and tactics were not learned easily. As opposed to the underground organizations that emerged in the late 1870s, the secret associations of the 1860s struggled to make effective use of urban space and to develop the microtechniques of underground concealment that could have afforded them the capacity to work toward their revolutionary aims. The four most important undergrounds to arise in the decade after 1862 were the following: 1) the first Land and Freedom, 2) the circles surrounding Nikolai Ishutin, 3) the circles surrounding Sergei Nechaev, and 4) the organization named after Nikolai Chaikovskii. The first three of these all collapsed not long after they had begun, and they must be considered little more than aspiring underground movements. The Chaikovskii Circle, on the other hand, did create a relatively sustainable underground. The rudiments of that underground, including some of its personnel, the habits it instilled, and some of the tactics it pioneered, would serve as a basis for the formation of every major radical organization in the 1870s all the way to the 1881 assassination of Alexander II.

THE FIRST LAND AND FREEDOM

The first well-known underground organization in the reform era called itself "Land and Freedom." A great deal of effort has gone into the examination of this shadowy conspiratorial association. In affirmation of Lenin's characterization of the late 1850s/early 1860s as Russia's "first revolutionary

situation," Soviet scholars often exaggerated the era's revolutionary potential, in part by inflating the significance of Land and Freedom.[6] Following
their lead, Franco Venturi argued that this organization "played an important role in history," and he devoted a full chapter to it. In one respect the first
"Land and Freedom" (the name would later be adopted by a more consequential organization) deserves the attention it has received since it was the
first serious attempt in this era to organize a revolutionary underground, but
on the whole its significance has been considerably overestimated.[7] To this
day it is unclear who belonged to it, and in terms of revolutionary activity
it accomplished little more than to produce a few scattered publications.
Moreover, because of its secretive nature, it could not, as later organizations
would, provide a recognizable model to follow, reject, or rework. From the
viewpoint of underground organization, Land and Freedom deserves our
attention mainly as an example of the problems and obstacles encountered
in the attempt to form a revolutionary underground in reform-era Russia.

It is likely that Land and Freedom was led by several well-known figures
among the radical intelligentsia, most of whom had connections to the two
most influential left-leaning publications of the time: Herzen's *Kolokol* (the
Bell) and Nekrasov's *Contemporary*. The name Land and Freedom derived
from an expression of Herzen's that summarized what he considered the
peasants' two main needs: farmland and freedom from external control.
The name itself points to a characteristic of every subsequent underground
movement during the reform era. All were established, in one way or
another, in the interest of stimulating an uprising among the rural peasantry. They aimed mainly to alleviate the suffering and oppression of the
predominantly rural lower classes. And yet their membership consisted
almost exclusively of educated urbanites. As would become increasingly
clear throughout the reform era, the disconnect between the urban activists
and the peasantry they sought to represent would plague would-be populist
revolutionaries by depriving them of a clear and obvious course of action.
At the same time, on the other hand, the gulf between rural laborers and the
urban intelligentsia would help to sustain and regenerate radical populism
because the distance between the urban and rural spheres kept alive the
sense of altruistic struggle that bathed political subversion in the light of
heroic necessity.

For an underground movement to form, it required a group willing to
brave the dangers of acting in defiance of the autocracy and its vigilant
watchdogs in the Third Section. By 1862 a sufficient number of such people
who were disillusioned by the limitations on public activism had located one
another and formed Land and Freedom. This organization, founded in the

summer of 1861, seems to have been the brainchild of the brothers Nikolai and Aleksandr Serno-Solov'evich, in consultation with Herzen and Nikolai Ogarev. Though it is not absolutely certain, the meager available evidence suggests that its core leadership included Chernyshevskii, Sleptsov, Nikolai Serno-Solov'evich, Nikolai Obruchev, and Dmitry Putiata.[8] The wave of arrests that occurred in the spring of 1862, and led to the imprisonment of two of these five figures, insured that other members would have to carry the movement forward without them. Those listed above were also members of an open organization for the distribution of books for use among the working classes, an organization that was possibly used as a shield to conceal the activities of Land and Freedom itself. As an open organization it was able to make use of public meeting places like the Chess Club and Serno-Solov'evich's bookstore.[9] Vilenskaia cites a set of regulations composed by Putiata that reveals the secretive nature of even these legal operations: "do not keep unnecessary records of meetings, lists of members, etc. Each active member writes for himself only that which is necessary to him alone for a specific business, always preferring where possible, quick verbal actions over formally written ones."[10]

A programmatic statement of Land and Freedom's aims declared their ultimate goal "to overthrow the imperial despotism that is blocking the free development of the life of the people." More dramatically, the same document also held that "only the price of blood can purchase the rights of the people."[11] These were unmistakably revolutionary aims, but how was one small and disconnected organization to accomplish them? Judging by remaining documents connected to Land and Freedom, its members seem to have envisioned their core group as a node around which to unite the various strands of discontent within Russian society, at which point a revolution would, in some yet-to-be-determined way, ignite on its own. Before he was arrested, Serno-Solov'evich argued that "elements inimical to the inept government are growing by the day, but they do not threaten it while they remain without ties, unity or trust in one another. To unite them and arouse them to united action is the business before us."[12] Similarly, one of the Land and Freedom proclamations declared: "we now openly call on all Russian citizens to serve the great cause of popular freedom."[13] The goal of uniting the various strands of discontent in Russian society was certainly the task before them, but unfortunately the organization with its center in St. Petersburg was made up almost exclusively "of people in literary circles and those connected to them."[14] These educated, elite conspirators could only make good on their appeal to popular freedom by directing readers toward a nebulous organization through the use of an anonymous publication.

The members of Land and Freedom understood that their options were severely limited. The contemporaneous but distinct Zaichnevskii Circle that put out the proclamation "Young Russia" was much more open about its activities, as a result of which its members were quickly arrested, imprisoned and dispersed.[15] One must keep in mind that at this point (apart from the very different Decembrist movement nearly forty years earlier) there was no track record of success or failure for underground movements, and no basis upon which to infer what might or might not result from a political conspiracy or the distribution of incendiary publications. Land and Freedom attempted to project an image of power, while in reality it was still just casting about for new members.[16] Both the Zaichnevskii Circle and Land and Freedom discovered that their ends stood in contradiction to their means. They desired a mass movement, a popular uprising, but their small numbers and underground defensive posture cut them off from the peasantry and the urban lower classes. A great deal of the energy and creativity that went into underground activism over the next two decades would be based on the quest to overcome this essential contradiction.

The fact that the members of Land and Freedom did not clearly perceive these contradictions must be attributed to the loose, even somewhat fictional, nature of their enterprise. In an effort to keep the police from discovering their leadership and "cutting off the head," they used a tactic that has since come to be called "leaderless resistance." Land and Freedom was based on groups (or cells) of five individuals. Each member was to have a limited connection to only the other members he knew personally, the intention being that if caught he could only incriminate a small number. Sleptsov described this structure as follows:

> The organization of fives consisted in the fact that each member organized around himself his own group of five, etc. In this way, if in the five were members a, b, c, d, e, then each of them would be a member of an independent five and consequently around each of them would be no more than eight who knew him personally: four of the five to which he was united and four of those he united to his own group of five. If one among the group should be exposed, eight people of two different groups of five would know about it. If babbling took place, then only eight people would suffer.[17]

This method of forming cells of individuals mutually unaware of other members in the organization had two advantages: it was much safer, and it gave the appearance of vast untapped reserves of power. At the same time it suffered from the distinct disadvantage of isolating its members to the degree that, as one of them later explained, "at times doubt arose as to whether this Land and Freedom really existed."[18] For such an organization to operate effectively, it requires steadfast prior commitment, since it provides little means of sustaining enthusiasm for the cause, and it also needs the solid guiding hand of a committed leadership. Land and Freedom had neither. It lacked what nihilist communes had and what future underground organizations would struggle to create: a heterotopian space in which to operate. Without a gathering place they could not unite their members, easily recruit new ones, or effectively plan and carry out revolutionary acts. The defect of a lack of autonomous space was not easily rectified in a state that employed a large and powerful political police force, and revolutionary organizations would grow increasingly aware of the need to maintain a space apart in order to function.

Not surprisingly, Land and Freedom was unable to last much beyond 1863. Their underground press published a small leaflet at the beginning of that year and two abbreviated "journals" in subsequent months, but by the end of 1863, in Herzen's words, Land and Freedom was already "a myth."[19] "Even in St. Petersburg itself, the heart of the movement," Venturi conceded, "an undisputed central authority was never able to assert itself."[20] The leaderless structure of Land and Freedom made it difficult to organize, but perhaps the main lesson learned from this failed attempt was that sentimental and ideological unity alone would not accomplish revolutionary aims. In addition to carving out their own clandestine spaces, successive underground organizations would take pains to develop greater degrees of both hierarchy and rigor. It should be noted that as a conspiratorial operation, Land and Freedom did set in motion some tactical methods that would be used by later undergrounds, like recruitment from the universities and the establishment of an underground press, but in the end the main thing it contributed to the development of underground traditions was the general impression that a populist underground with revolutionary aspirations was a real possibility in Russia. In this respect, its nebulous nature may have been an advantage in that it promoted the idealized vision of Land and Freedom as an organization with great revolutionary potential, a vision that lived on as an inspiration to future conspirators.

THE ISHUTIN CIRCLE

Because of its involvement in Karakozov's attempt on the life of Alexander II in 1866, the organization led by Nikolai Ishutin has loomed larger in the history of the revolutionary movement than it might have otherwise. As a result of the investigations and trial that followed the assassination attempt, we have more information on this group of radicals than on others of comparable size, and the information is useful for shedding light on the development of underground movements in the mid-1860s. Ishutin's circle first emerged in 1863 among students at Moscow University who were part of a *zemliachestvo* from the provincial region of Penza. It began as a student association, but a core group, inspired especially by the writings of Chernyshevskii, quickly dropped their studies and began to devote full-time effort to political activism.[21] Early on, members of the circle were aware of the existence of Land and Freedom and considered joining it, but they chose to move in their own direction.[22] Ishutin's "Organization," as it was sometimes called, was disorganized, overextended, sometimes even ridiculous in the far-fetched aspirations behind its various schemes, but its frantic search for viable methods of revolutionary struggle provides a snapshot of developing aims and tactics that reveals an effort to grow beyond the limitations that had crippled Land and Freedom.

The Ishutin circle faced the same problem as Land and Freedom and all other populist undergrounds. Its revolutionary aims were the basic ones of the populist movement: "to end private property in land and put in its place communal usage."[23] With this peasant-centered goal, their primary mission would be to make a sufficient number of peasants aware of the injustice of their situation in an effort to arouse their revolutionary ardor and instigate a mass uprising. The Ishutintsy benefited from the fact that they had not begun, as many of the leaders of Land and Freedom had, as public figures, and their relative obscurity enabled them to remain unknown to the police while engaging in a wide variety of separate operations. Though their aim was, as Ishutin stated, "to draw close to the people," they recognized that goal could not be achieved in the near term without intermediate steps taken first.[24] The only viable starting point seemed to be a clandestine urban movement, through which they hoped eventually to "unite into a single whole the entire young intelligentsia of Russia to force it in a single revolutionary direction."[25] If they could not yet reach the peasantry directly, at least they might be able to create an urban organization with the capacity to bring together a much wider group of sympathizers.

Some members of Ishutin's circle were happy to work gradually through patient educational efforts; others favored practicing nihilist asceticism as a demonstration of revolutionary inner fortitude. Some even clung to the hope of "transformation by means of street demonstrations."[26] One of the Ishutintsy testified that, "we members did not have a single goal, did not agree on any means, [and] were not in any way committed either to each other or to the society."[27] The activities of The Organization spun off in a dizzying array of directions so that eventually any connection between their different operations became more a hope than a reality. They established a book-binding cooperative from which they drew new recruits; they attempted to organize a cooperative of coach drivers; they planned trips into the countryside to spread propaganda among the peasantry; they considered founding an agricultural commune on the Amur River in East Asia; they planned to set up a network of provincial libraries staffed by radical librarians; they created a cooperative of seamstresses modeled on that found in *What Is To Be Done?*; they organized mutual aid societies for the benefit of students; they invested in a cotton processing factory in Mozhaisk outside Moscow and tried to put its workers on a cooperative footing; they sought to do something similar with an iron smelting plant in the province of Kaluga, from which they hoped to turn a profit in order to help fund their other ventures; they had plans to establish both umbrella- and shoe-making workshops; they created a school for children intended to train future revolutionaries; they set up a dining hall for university students; they plotted to free both Chernyshevskii and Serno-Solov'evich from prison; and they did successfully help carry out the freeing of the Polish prisoner Iaroslav Dombrowskii as he was being transported to Siberia.[28]

Few of these projects got very far off the ground, and those that did make progress seem to have been carried out with frantic motion and lack of discipline. Taken together, the various projects of the Ishutin Circle suggest that, with a core membership of no more than a dozen people, the organization was both overextended and directionless. Yet if the Ishutintsy never managed to unite around a single plan or goal, there was still some method to the madness. Since the spring of 1862 populists no longer had the advantage of an urban public sphere in which to speak and act, and the Ishutintsy sought to address the absence of a public space in which revolutionary activity was possible. The majority of the projects listed above represent attempts to establish subversive heterotopia as leverage points for building up a consolidated revolutionary movement. Ishutin himself seems to have been partial to the idea that bookstores, libraries, and reading rooms could be set up across Russia in provincial cities within which "the librarians would personally spread revolutionary ideas."[29] The actual establishment of artels, factories, and schools constituted efforts toward the production of revolutionary space. They were used to engage new recruits, to generate funding for other operations, and to consolidate larger revolutionary networks.

The spaces created by the Ishutin group ranged across a broad spectrum from nihilist collectives to highly conspiratorial undergrounds. Their artels, for example, were not just economic cooperatives but also venues in which political views could develop and be passed on to new members. In these spaces experiments in collective labor were used in nihilist fashion in order, as one of them put it, "to create a social force and turn society's attention our way."[30] At the same time, the Ishutintsy intended such spaces as distinct locations in which to draw potentially interested parties closer to their views. As one member put it, they served as "fishing ponds," in which to catch new revolutionaries and as centers "in which to unite the progressive youth."[31] For example, the women's seamstress collective was planned both as a vehicle for the "emancipation" of its women workers and as a "support base" in which to enlist new revolutionary recruits. The most far-reaching venture was the school for boys opened at the end of 1864 that, at least according to some members, was planned as a training ground for "revolutionary cadres."[32] Whatever else was taught at this school, lessons included such math problems as whether 1 or 72,000,000 was a larger number, the answer providing evidence of the tsar's personal insignificance relative to the size of the Empire's population.[33] A natural history teacher used the state insignia of the double-headed eagle to make his point: "The eagle is, to the highest degree, a bird of prey. It kills birds and animals and devours them, which is why the government that crushes its own innocent subjects has this bird as its symbol."[34]

The Ishutintsy hoped that by establishing different kinds of spaces and associations they would be able to create a loose affiliation of linked activities around an inner core of conspiratorial revolutionaries. The outer circles consisted of worker groups in the process of indoctrination and of student circles cutting their teeth on relatively safe activism in university politics, while the inner circle was made up of full-time revolutionaries attempting to guide and connect the various movements while simultaneously developing plans that aspired sooner or later to overthrow the government. The core group itself lived together in a communal apartment named for its landlord Ipatev, for which reason Ishutin's inner circle was sometimes known as the Ipatevtsy. This inner circle included a few revolutionaries who had, as the common expression went, "burned their boats behind them." Having been arrested or exiled, they now lived illegally, without identification and under false names. The number of such "illegals" would continue to grow as arrests were made, and these people would eventually comprise the heart and soul of the revolutionary underground. Starting from the core group, then, the Ishutin underground developed ways in which open or "semi-legal" activities could be linked to the underground leadership in a way that the more cautious structure of Land and Freedom had prevented. The Ishutintsy could use their more open activities to propagandize and recruit new members while letting these operations serve as a shield that deflected suspicion from their more subversive aims.

The main problems that confronted Ishutin's circle were lack of secure space and lack of funds. Ishutin was attuned to the key importance of securing safe spaces in which all of these operations could be carried out. His long-term plan was "to organize a center in Moscow, to arrange a library, schools, associations" upon which "the members would spread out into the provinces and organize schools and associations there."[35] Bookstores, well known as meeting points for "nihilists," served as useful gathering and recruitment points, but since the police were also aware of the radical use of certain bookstores, they could be vulnerable to spying and infiltration. It was extremely difficult to find any kind of space capable of bringing together the various parts of the larger operation. Even more difficult, funding the array of activities they had taken on in the absence of any legal status or public presence was a constant burden. Ishutin's Petersburg associate, Ivan Khudiakov, referred to the lack of money as the Ishutintsy's "most important obstacle."[36] One core member from the nobility, P. D. Ermolov, devoted a good deal of his family money to the cause, and the Ishutintsy engaged in charitable entertainments like musical performances and literary readings, ostensibly in order to raise funds for cover organizations like their schools.[37] Since these funding sources were insufficient, they tried to open profit-making ventures like cooperative factories, though these never got off the ground. The "expropriation" of funds from post offices and treasuries (apparently never carried out) was also entertained as a possible source of funding, as was a plan to poison the merchant father of one of the members in order to donate the son's inheritance to the cause.[38]

Given such endemic problems, it is not surprising that, according to the testimony of the member D. Iurasov, by 1865 the Ishutintsy were splitting into two camps: "the extremists wanted to produce a revolution by means of agitation and verbal propaganda, the moderates wished to act through schools, associations and the distribution of books."[39] Among the revolutionary extremists, like Ishutin himself, a favored slogan, "conservatism in words and progress in action" hints at the core group's fondness for conspiratorial methods.[40] Although their precise intentions remain uncertain, in the final few months before their arrest, the inner circle seems to have been developing the kernel of a militant underground that called on its members to sacrifice their lives and those of others to the cause. Ishutin, who, to use Venturi's phrase, "introduced a particularly Machiavellian note" into the revolutionary movement, seems to have been the guiding force behind these militant tendencies.[41] Based on the testimony of other members of his circle, Ishutin clearly sought to maintain strict control in his own hands. He demanded extreme devotion and was not averse to using mystification and intimidation tactics in order to maintain his leadership role. He even kept secret tabs on peripheral members in order to insure their reliability.[42] He tried to cultivate the aura of a powerful figure through what seems to have been a kind of stagecraft authority, as well as proposing to undertake dramatically violent plans both to intimidate and inspire his fellow members.[43] Some members of the core group called him "General." In spite of his intimidation tactics and efforts to keep leadership in his own hands, he was unable fully to maintain power over the organization. The members of his group seem to have considered fighting off his leadership by force at one point, and his inability to restrain the Karakozov assassination attempt, which quickly destroyed the entire organization, provides an obvious example of his underlying lack of control.

The Ishutin Circle never became the underground of violent conspirators its leader seems to have favored, but plans for this transformation were apparently underway by the time the operation was discovered. A key moment in the shift toward violent tactics took place when Ishutin met with Khudiakov in St. Petersburg shortly after Khudiakov had returned from a trip to Europe in late 1865. The two young men both aspired to hasten political change, yet both of them were suspicious enough to speak in vague terms that could easily be exaggerated in the mind of the other. Ishutin returned from his meeting with Khudiakov excited about a "European Revolutionary Committee" that was supposedly prepared to back up a revolutionary struggle in Russia. What this committee was, or whether it existed at all, is open to debate, but Ishutin certainly used the idea that he had its backing to push for revolutionary activities that might have more immediate results. The secret and extremist inner core was to be known as "Hell." Claudia Verhoeven has pointed out that "it is probably not possible to ever get a definitive answer to the question of 'Hell's' existence," and to read the extensive trial testimony makes Hell seem like everything else the Ishutintsy did: an impatient casting about for a viable revolutionary method. Some testimonials treated Hell as little more than a joke, while other members seem to have taken "the joke" rather seriously. Even if Hell were, as some have suggested, pure fiction made up under the influence of alcohol, the fiction itself throws light on the early planning stages of underground insurrectionary tactics.[44] At a minimum, the concept of Hell suggests that a desire to establish a violent, revolutionary wing constituted one part of the Ishutintsy's underground activities.[45]

For our purposes what is most interesting about Hell is what the idea reflected about the potential development of underground methods. Hell was said to call for members to live under assumed names, to abandon ties to family and friends, and to live exclusively for the goal of revolution. Its emphasis on extreme secrecy and cutting ties with the past went hand in hand with the new interest in violence as a revolutionary strategy. Ishutin claimed that the "European Committee" had the means to supply his circle with equipment for making an "Orsini bomb," a pre-dynamite, hand-held explosive device that had been used in an assassination attempt in Paris against Napoleon III in the 1850s.[46] In the absence of a secure underground, the commitment to engage in violent acts carried with it a likely death sentence for the perpetrator, so anyone who would actually carry out a violent act needed in some way to break from society. Those engaged in potentially violent activities were supposed to make themselves "drunk and dissolute in order to deflect any kind of suspicion that they held any political convictions."[47] Envisioning violent attacks on government officials, including regicide, the revolutionaries were supposed to carry a ball of mercury in their teeth so that, should they be caught, they could bite down and create an explosion that would render their faces unrecognizable. In the pocket of the mutilated radical, testified one member of the group, would be found a proclamation explaining the reasons for his crime, the demands of the revolutionaries, and threats of further violence if those demands were not met.[48] The pocket proclamation would announce that "there exists a huge revolutionary society, that its strength is immeasurable ... [and] that if the inheritor of the murdered tsar does not agree to grant the wishes demanded by the revolutionary society, then there will follow a second shot, then a third, a tenth, etc."[49] Such strategies suggest that one faction among the Ishutin Circle had, at least in part, relinquished the idea of direct appeal to the peasantry and begun to fantasize about methods devised to terrorize the government and send a message to the Russian population at large.

All of this may well have been nothing more than the product of animated discussion, but some aspects of the Hell concept ran parallel in interesting ways to the tactics that would be adopted later by more developed undergrounds. Aliases, false passports, the use of hand-held bombs, schemes to murder government officials, regicide, and proclamations to explain the acts of violence all anticipated actions that came fully into play among the terrorist undergrounds of the late 1870s. Whether any of these ideas would have been adopted is impossible to know because on April 4, 1866, largely against the will of the Ishutin Circle, Ishutin's mentally unstable cousin Dmitry Karakozov was arrested in St. Petersburg after having shot at the tsar in an attempt to assassinate him. Karakozov clearly acted independently from the rest of the group. He was isolated, ill, and suicidal, and Ishutin and others tried to stop him, though perhaps a bit half-heartedly. Ishutin seems to have had grave doubts about the impact of an attack on the tsar, but he also seems to have been intrigued by the possibility of a revolutionary effect.[50]

Revolutionary violence was far from new, of course, but its suggested use in these cases did not seem to be based on any logical purpose other than the desire to generate attention, in which case it appears that the Ishutin Circle had begun to flirt with what would later come to be called "terrorism." Ishutin even told one member that he was considering the use of explosives "to blow up a fortress or a railroad," again in an evident bid for recognition and publicity.[51] Karakozov himself believed a successful assassination would send a message to the laboring classes of Russia that the extremes of poverty and inequality in Russia were the fault of the tsar and his government. He intentionally left behind a letter explaining to the workers of St. Petersburg the reasons for his act. In view of this letter, even though Karakozov did not act with the approval of the Ishutintsy, his assassination attempt may be seen as the first example in Russia of an effort to communicate a political message by way of a violent attack. It was the first example of "propaganda by deed" and was in fact discussed in these terms (*avant le mot*) by Ishutin and Khudiakov, both of whom referred to Karakozov's attempt as "de facto propaganda" (*fakticheskaia propaganda*).[52] Khudiakov denied that it would be effective (but only in oblique terms) by suggesting that "the people are insufficiently prepared" for it. Ishutin and Khudiakov at least recognized the hope that other terrorists have had ever since, that a violent act would have the power to shift the winds of opinion.[53]

Because the Ishutin Circle grew famous as a result of Karakozov's attempt to assassinate Alexander II, it is mainly remembered as an organization of revolutionary violence, even though most of its projects before the end of 1865 were peaceful efforts to find that elusive path from educated urbanite to laboring peasant. Their anxious and unsuccessful search for a means to establish this connection presents them as a sort of microcosm of the development of the revolutionary movement during the reign of Alexander II. They searched for a revolutionary methodology but found themselves constantly stymied by the combination of an indifferent society and a watchful political police. And while they sought to carve out a succession of subversive heterotopic spaces, they had to confront the difficulty of these efforts in the face of potential and real police surveillance. Perhaps as a result of these impediments, with Ishutin's leadership began the tendency to deceive and coerce not only non-revolutionaries but even fellow members of the underground. Finally, Ishutin, as we will see more clearly with Nechaev and The People's Will, revealed how easy it was in an underground organization to be seduced by the notion that one could "by means of some kind of grand and terrifying fact ... embolden and awaken the sleeping people."[54] It was still just the beginning of such a dream.

THE NECHAEV CIRCLE

Karakozov's shot missed the tsar, but it had a profound effect on Russian society and an even greater impact on radical populism since it reinforced the government backlash against the revolutionary movement. Its position strengthened by the failed assassination attempt, the autocracy was emboldened on July 22, 1866, to sanction the closing of "any public meeting, club, or cooperative association (*artel'*) they deemed a threat to state order or public security and morality."[55] Membership in a secret society would now be considered a criminal act. Shortly after the assassination attempt, Alexander dismissed Third-Section leader Dolgorukov and appointed in his stead the young and enthusiastically harsh Petr Shuvalov. The expression "white terror" came into use at this point as shorthand for the government reaction, and very little underground activity took place between 1866 and 1868.

Questioning of the Ishutin Circle had revealed the enormous ambition of populists seeking to bring about revolutionary change in spite of the formidable obstacles that stood in their way. The events of 1869–1871 that came to be called the Nechaev Affair reveal a similar picture of vast ambition and meager success. Sergei Nechaev was a singular character in the revolutionary tradition. The underground he formed, unlike that of Ishutin, was mostly of his own making. It was overblown and disorganized and the least effective of any well-known underground movement in reform-era Russia, but it has received an enormous amount of attention, mainly with regard to the romantic, reckless, violent, and unfulfilled dreams espoused by its leader.

Nechaev's importance in radical populism has been vastly exaggerated.[56] Probably the most significant impact Nechaev and his organization had on the development of the radical populist underground was as a counterexample, a model of what to avoid. One problem with the ideology-based approach to the populist movement is its tendency to engage in definition by extremes, in which the most radical views are read as the most charac-teristic. Nechaev's "Catechism of a Revolutionary" may be the most familiar text produced by any radical populist apart from *What Is To Be Done?*. But the oft-encountered presentation of Nechaev and his famous text as typical products of radical populism is extremely misleading. Nechaev's fanciful pronouncements convey a picture of desperado radicalism that make for fascinating reading, but his portrait of revolutionary extremism existed almost exclusively within his own fervid imagination and those, perhaps, of a few of his close collaborators. Although none of Nechaev's plans ever came close to fruition, what he did put into practice was a remarkable episode of deception and mystification by a masterful, and possibly psychopathic, con artist with a cause.

Nechaev's various writings, some of them composed in collaboration with Mikhail Bakunin and Petr Tkachev, are a good starting point for understand-ing his place in the populist movement. The above-mentioned "Catechism" (a text meant to be learned by heart) calls on radicals to subject themselves to complete underground submersion. For Nechaev, the revolutionary must isolate himself not only from society, but from any and all sociability: "[he] has no personal interests, no business affairs, no emotions, no attachments, no property, lacks even a name" and must shun "all romanticism, sentimen-tality, attractions and delights." He is driven exclusively by "cold calculation" in order to devote the entirety of his attention to accomplishing the over-throw of the government.[57] Given this paean to dispassionate action, it is ironic that Nechaev was among the most romantic individuals radical pop-ulism ever produced, both in his blind faith that destroying the old regime would in some unspecified way unleash a utopian future, and in his vision of the unparalleled "satanic" power of the committed revolutionary himself. With respect to a sustainable plan beyond revolution, Nechaev had almost nothing to offer. He believed in pure anarchism: "the savior of the people can only be that kind of revolution which annihilates at the roots any gov-ernment and exterminates the entire state tradition, order and social class in Russia."[58] As for the ideal revolutionary, he is a "doomed man ... who knows that in the very depths of his being, not only in words but also in deeds, he has broken all the bonds which tie him to the civil order and the civilized world with all its laws, moralities, and customs, and with all its generally accepted conventions."[59] Harkening back to old romantic traditions (inspired in part by Bakunin) Nechaev preferred to envision a future dominated by "the world of the wild robbers, who are the only true revolutionaries in Rus-sia."[60] Of course there has always been a healthy dose of romantic idealism in any revolutionary movement, but it was Nechaev more than anyone else who conjured up the specter of the all-powerful individual working toward total transformation, a figure modeled on the likes of Prometheus, Satan, Faust, or Napoleon—as the elemental force of populist rebellion.

Nechaev came from a modest background that gave him a minimal education, and he was largely self-taught.[61] When he encountered radical politics and began to search for a means to foment revolutionary change, at first he experimented with a variety of different tactics, from street demonstrations to propaganda among the peasantry. But he soon perceived these options as painstaking, dangerous, and unlikely to yield quick results.[62] It was not long before he turned toward the tactic of violent conspiracy, apparently inspired by reading Buanarotti's history of Babeuf's Conspiracy of Equals.[63] After his failure to begin a movement in St. Petersburg—and a subsequent trip to Europe during which he collaborated with Bakunin—Nechaev went to Moscow to create a new organization of about forty people, recruiting them mostly from among the students at the Petrovskii Agricultural Academy in what was then the outskirts of the city. By this point, Nechaev had abandoned any pretensions toward a grass roots revolutionary movement and was interested in a centralized, disciplined conspiracy controlled by himself from above.

Students at the Petrovskii Academy had more freedom than in most institutes and universities of the time, and Nechaev promised them the opportunity to get involved in the political activism in which they longed to engage.[64] That Nechaev so easily misled these students into participation in his otherwise non-existent organization provides an important insight into the populist movement as a whole. If Russian populists shared a general concern for righting the social injustices of Russian society, the more acute motivation for joining a revolutionary underground often had to do with the simple personal ambition to get involved in the struggle for a cause. As Tikhomirov wrote about the members of his own university student radical organization from around the same time that "the youth were not interested in reading, nor science, not even in the truth ... but in *action*."[65] Nechaev seemed to offer them a chance to participate in an endeavor in which they might contribute to the greater good and make a difference in their world. In contrast to most of them, Nechaev's working-class origins made him seem a "man of the people" uncorrupted by an elite upbringing; they admired his "authenticity" in a way that calls to mind students at The University of California at Berkeley in the late 1960s, who showered devotion on the more "authentically oppressed" Black Panthers in Oakland.

The authority Nechaev derived from his social position and his promises of political action enabled him to stake his claim among the students as a revolutionary leader, while at the same time he worked to make himself appear only a small cog in a much larger revolutionary machine, which was centered in Western Europe and extended throughout Russia. The members of his organization did not know him by name and referred to him as "Pavlov," while in the guise of Pavlov he spoke of "Nechaev" in the third person as a fallen leader.[66] Nechaev himself had written that, "with the aim of merciless destruction the revolutionary can and often must live in society, pretending to be something entirely different from what he is."[67] Accordingly, he fabricated parts of his biography, making himself look like a martyr and even faking his own arrest as a way of generating sympathy for his cause. The fictional Nechaev, or the persona of Nechaev's imagination, had been involved in prison breaks and had crossed Russia on foot, getting to know the sufferings of the people. Now as Pavlov he served as the liaison for a huge European revolutionary organization that maintained cells all over Russia.[68]

Nechaev managed to create the semblance of an organization through his remarkable faculty for mystification and manipulation. "Nechaev," later recalled one of his followers, "possessed the amazing ability to persuade people to become members in the association; he could present the thing on such a grand scale, make it seem like such an important affair that on the strength of these arguments alone he attracted people to himself."[69] Nechaev/Pavlov also managed to scare his student recruits into cooperation by claiming that the "Central Committee" for which he worked had its own police spies who kept a close watch on all the members.[70] To compound the sense of secrecy and deadly seriousness, members were often referred to by number rather than name.[71] Once it was exposed, of course, Nechaev's organization quickly unraveled. According to Pryzhov, soon after the organization's demise it became clear to all involved that "Nechaev had absolutely no distinct plan at all."[72]

Although Nechaev himself focused mainly on igniting a revolutionary uprising, the organization he had formed also engaged in more peaceful activities. In both the Ishutin and Nechaev Circles two distinct paths toward revolution competed with one another. One involved gradual propaganda and "consciousness raising" among the various disenfranchised sectors of the population, while the other favored militant action intended to catalyze an uprising. Both circles maintained members engaged in the former, while both Ishutin and Nechaev entertained different ways of accomplishing the latter. Nechaev placed representatives in the countryside, and others among the Nechaevtsy sought to learn a trade in order to draw closer to the workers and peasants.[73] In anticipation of the large student movement of 1874, before Nechaev's circle collapsed, many of its more peripheral members planned trips to rural Russia to help out with education and improvements, while also conducting anti-government propaganda.[74] At the trial of members of Nechaev's organization, the Ministry of Justice used Herzen's later-popularized phrase "going to the people" to describe such activities.[75] Nechaev himself, according to his associate Kuznetsov, wanted his organization to draw close to the peasantry, and Nechaev's espousal of populist ideas seems to have been a prime factor in attracting members to his circle.[76]

In spite of this element of interest in the rural sphere, as with virtually all other important underground organizations that arose in Russia, Nechaev's was firmly entrenched in an urban setting. He himself had first gone to St. Petersburg in order to escape what he found to be the stultifying provincial city of Ivanovo, which had nothing to offer him but "mud."[77] He arrived in St. Petersburg in 1866 without great political interests, but left in 1869 a thoroughgoing revolutionary. The center of the organization Nechaev subsequently established in Moscow was the Cherkesov bookstore managed by Petr Uspenskii.[78] Nechaev used the bookstore, as well as the Mamontov hotel, for recruitment and meetings.[79] Like the Ishutintsy, Nechaev was attuned to the importance of space. Not only did he work to build subversive heterotopia, like the bookshop or the circles located among the living quarters of the students at the Petrovskii Academy, but he also sought to enlist pre-existing urban spaces and personal connections in his revolutionary activities. In his general rules of operation we find advice for creating hideouts, for making contact with people at all levels of society from prostitutes and criminals to the wives of government officials, and for learning the structures of police and governmental administrations.[80]

Although Nechaev's efforts did not result in the production of a large number of concrete heterotopic spaces like those established by the Ishutin Circle, his writings demonstrate a clear need to infiltrate various distinct places and institutions. One of his programmatic statements on revolutionary activity read that: "The revolutionary must penetrate everywhere, into all the lower and middle estates, into the merchant's shop, into the church, into the noble's home, into the world of the bureaucrat, the military, into literature, into the Third Section and even into the Winter Palace."[81] With these aims in mind, members of Nechaev's circle took on different tasks of outreach to various communities, like propagandizing among the peasants, or women students, or gathering donations from merchants.[82] Some historians have found it surprising that the older and perpetually drunken Ivan Pryzhov, who came of age in the 1840s, became a member of Nechaev's inner circle. Pryzhov's own reasons for joining Nechaev's circle remain obscure, but his ties to the urban underworld made him valuable to Nechaev, who gave him the task of making connections with potentially revolutionary elements within Moscow. He was supposed to focus on non-industrial workers from the working classes: "porters, drivers, bakers and letter-carriers," and was given the responsibility of spreading propaganda among the patrons of taverns as well as "swindlers, the lowest kinds of prostitutes and such people who had cause to hide from the police."[83] Nechaev appears to have found the criminal sector of urban society a more fitting place to gather revolutionary recruits than from among paid laborers. He even convinced two students in his circle to abandon their plans to work in the village and follow Pryzhov's lead into Moscow's criminal underworld in the region of the Khitrovka Market. As it turned out, his recruits quickly abandoned their plans to "get to know the people" when a sympathetic prostitute told them they were about to be robbed.[84] Though Nechaev's organization never materialized in such a way that his plans for making use of the urban environment could be put into practice, it is worth noting that later organizations used similar tactics of infiltrating various substrata of the urban population to great effect.

In spite of the fact that Nechaev's actions caused a good deal of grief, including the notorious murder of one core member (an act that effectively brought to an end Nechaev's schemes), it is impossible at times not to notice an element of grim humor about the whole affair. Nechaev's sometimes clumsy attempts to draw in followers, combined with their own staggering naïveté as a result of their deep desire to be "of service," makes the Nechaev Affair in retrospect seem more a dark comedy of errors than a functional operation. When the curtain was finally pulled back on Nechaev's operation, among the former members of his organization "arose the awareness that no Committee, no proximity of a popular uprising, no widespread organization—none of this existed. It was only they alone, deceived students, accidental conspirators."[85] It had all more or less been the work of one man. Not unrelatedly, as Vera Zasulich later noted, Nechaev "had not the least sympathy" for the members of his circle, and seemed "a man from another world, as though from another country or a different century."[86] As Martin Miller has pointed out, Nechaev's plans and manifestoes anticipated later developments in the populist underground in important ways. For the time being, however, they were to remain in the realm of imagination since neither Ishutin nor Nechaev managed to create the kind of underground organization capable of carrying out a coherent set of plans. In both cases, the powers they managed to achieve quickly slipped out from under their control. It would require both a much more disciplined organization and a reliably autonomous space in which to operate if the latent potential of underground operations were to be actualized to any degree.

THE CHAIKOVTSY

The brief existences and insurmountable complications experienced by Land and Freedom and the circles of Ishutin and Nechaev point mainly to the limits of the early undergrounds of the 1860s. All were searching for an organizational form that could be sustained and a set of tactics that could disseminate their views and lead to radical change, but in these aims none were successful. Still, these were not the only populist organizations in existence in Russia. By the late 1860s there began to appear a number of small groups, usually circles of self-education, that developed in various locations, not only in the large cities but in small provincial cities as well. One such circle that began to coalesce in St. Petersburg at the end of the 1860s chose to operate on a different set of principles than those of the Ishutin and Nechaev organizations, and it managed to attain much of the success the others had not, as well as to last significantly longer. A salient difference between this group and the earlier organizations was that its origins were to be found as much in nihilist counterculture as in political conspiracy, and it would appear that the group unity of nihilist subculture provided much of its long-term strength. This circle originated in the Vul'fov Commune, named for its location on Vul'fov Street in St. Petersburg. It was at first led by Mark Natanson and Vasilii Aleksandrov. The Vul'fov Commune was a shared living space as well as a place where students and other young people gathered to talk politics. It gained such a reputation as a center for politically minded students that it was nicknamed "the Jacobin Club."[87]

With the picture of Nechaev's movement fresh before their eyes in the form of the 1871 public trial of the Nechaevtsy, Natanson and Aleksandrov intentionally turned away from Nechaev's secret, conspiratorial tactics in hopes of founding a more open, inclusive, and morally grounded association. It must be noted that most populists reacted negatively to the Nechaev Affair. Pavel Aksel'rod, for example, compared Russian radicalism unfavorably to comparable European movements because Russia had produced the "dark, crude, barbarian force" of Nechaev.[88] And yet in spite of their general disapproval of Nechaev's "Jesuitical system [and] blind submission to some unseen center," the trial of Nechaev's co-conspirators was a catalyzing moment on the populist left.[89] The trial publicized the fact that, in spite of Nechaev's shortcomings, revolutionary organizations were not only possible but genuinely existed after the post-Karakozov crackdown. Learning the details of Nechaev's underground, other populists were simultaneously inspired to found politically active circles and persuaded to reject and redirect Nechaev's methods. For the Vul'fov group, whatever Nechaev did was perceived as "something absolutely negative that we must not repeat in our own activities"[90] Natanson in particular came out strongly against Nechaev, arguing at various *skhodki* that revolution is impossible until you exhaustively understand the political situation, and thus the most rational plan was not to launch a conspiratorial organization, as Nechaev had, but to begin with extensive "circles of self-education."[91]

Natanson's circle not only rejected strict organizational hierarchy, but also in contrast to Nechaev, remained adamantly nonviolent.[92] Its members believed, as Kropotkin put it, that "a morally developed individuality must be the foundation of every organization, whatever political character it may take afterward, and whatever program of action it may adopt in the course of future events."[93] At around the same time in southern Russia, entirely unconnected to Natanson's circle, the Nechaev Affair inspired in Aksel'rod a similar desire to found a network of interconnected study circles.[94] It was as though Nechaev had produced a needed demonstration that a revolutionary movement could not succeed if founded on a weak moral and intellectual basis.

The shift from Nechaev to this new model underground seemed, as one historian described it, "as though from the stifling underworld you suddenly dropped into a sweet-smelling meadow filled with sunlight."[95] The central source of this "sunlight" came to be known as the Chaikovskii Circle after Nikolai Chaikovskii, one of its most prominent early members. Chaikovskii was less a leader than a recruiter for the organization, and the fact that the circle was not remembered for a particularly central leader, in contrast to Ishutin and Nechaev, suggests something of its character. Memoirs of the Chaikovskii Circle, of which there are many, all agree that its members were seeking to forge a new kind of group dynamic rather than just accomplish external goals. This focus may be one reason why the "Chaikovtsy" managed to create a sustainable organization where others had failed. If the structure of Land and Freedom maintained intentional distance between its members as a means of security, and Ishutin and Nechaev tried to lead through coercion and deception, the Chaikovskii Circle functioned on an egalitarian basis in which consensus decision-making and mutual admiration were considered *de rigeur*. In this way they managed to develop "an atmosphere of intimate camaraderie and high idealism."[96] A foundational moment of the new organization occurred in a rented dacha outside St. Petersburg in the summer of 1871. Here the essential membership came together on the basis of a merger between the members of the Natanson/Aleksandrov Commune and a group of women studying at the Alarchin courses that included Sofia Perovskaia and the Kornilova sisters. When the dacha proved too exposed to police scrutiny, the new group set up a communal apartment in the city on Kabinetskaia Street that would serve as their main base of operations.

One member of the circle, Sergei Kravchinskii, later wrote that the Chaikovtsy had more the character of a brotherhood than a political society. Its members had to learn the self-abnegating discipline of submitting freely to the "general will," or the opinion of the majority, because "truth must be on its side."[97] Whereas Nechaev had carefully written up his future aims, a set of regulations and even a catechism, the Chaikovtsy intentionally eschewed established rules and regulations, preferring to operate on an informal basis of mutual consensus. The political ideals of the Chaikovtsy coincided with Rousseau's ideal polity outlined in *The Social Contract* in that both held interpersonal bonds and individual self-worth to be mutually reinforcing. For Kravchinskii, the Chaikovtsy resembled a family with no secrets from one another, even in private life, a transparency possible only because members of the circle were all people with "hearts of gold and steel."[98] "It is difficult for me," wrote Aksel'rod, "to express the atmosphere that reigned in this circle. Between the members was felt a brotherly closeness, that heartfelt simplicity of relationships that sometimes can be found in a good and friendly family."[99] While many memoirs used the term "brotherly" to describe the circle, it stands out as highly distinctive that the Chaikovtsy membership included a substantial number of women. The influence of women within the group is corroborated by the early removal of its original co-leader, Aleksandrov, for his unwanted attitude and behavior toward women.[100] It is also worth noting that this "family," befitting its urban origin, included members from disparate backgrounds. Although it began with male students, it came to include both genders, diverse ages, military personnel, and even practicing professionals like Kropotkin.

Joining the Chaikovtsy offered Kropotkin a chance to experience what he considered the full and meaningful existence he had not found elsewhere in Russia. Among the Chaikovtsy he experienced "that exuberance of life when one feels at every moment the full throbbing of all the fibers of the inner self."[101] A similar exuberance was reported by most of the early members. Nikolai Morozov felt that the group was united "not only by the general task but by love for one another."[102] Terms like "fraternity," "family," "sect," and even monastic "order" have been used to describe the organization. As another member, Leonid Shishko, recalled, "in the circle we realized full equality and absolute respect for every member."[103] Nikolai Charushin called it "a tight-knit family with high demands on the spiritual and moral character of each member."[104] One observer familiar with the group described its "moral cohesion, close spiritual unity, nurtured by a boundless faith in one another, and ... mutual delight in one another."[105] Kropotkin, even though he was often at odds with the group for ideological reasons, later recalled that "never did I meet elsewhere such a collection of morally superior men and women as the score of persons whose acquaintance I made at the first meeting of the Circle of Chaikovsky. I still feel proud of having been received into that family."[106] Such a degree of adulation was later heaped on the Chaikovskii Circle in populist memoirs that at times it seems excessive (as though perhaps later populists needed to believe a utopian moment had taken place in their movement), and yet the consensual and mutually admiring character of the group became a basic model on which populist underground organizations would be based for the next decade and beyond.

Among nihilists, as in other countercultural communities from religious sects to Bohemia, common personal and cultural attributes functioned to separate "us" from "them," and the Chaikovskii Circle also developed a somewhat cultish quality. Morozov, for example, delighted in the romantically unglamorous living arrangements he discovered among the Moscow wing of the group, later expressing warm nostalgia for using his worker's kaftan as a blanket, sleeping on whatever surface was available, and resting his head on anything he could find for a pillow.[107] Like the nihilists, the Chaikovtsy found Spartan living arrangements morally upright (as a sign of their kinship with the unprivileged) and at the same time a rebuke to the "luxuries" of daily life among the educated classes. They were proud of scrimping by eating horsemeat, for example. In fact, one group reportedly dined on the flesh of puppies from a stray dog, thereby demonstrating their capacity both to economize and to "struggle against prejudice."[108]

The Chaikovtsy also took seriously the nihilist injunction to actively reorganize traditional gender arrangements. Like the heroes of *What Is To Be Done?* and the nihilists it inspired, Sergei Sinegub proudly undertook a fictitious marriage in order to liberate a female acquaintance from an unhappy marital proposal arranged by her parents.[109] In general, women and men held equal importance among the Chaikovtsy, and both showed a willingness to perform the same duties. Some of the Chaikovtsy women even dressed like men in order to ease chores and exercise as well as move around more freely in public.[110] Inspired by nihilist values, women's position among the Chaikovtsy as fully equal and committed revolutionaries was later emulated and became standard practice among populist revolutionaries, a practice that would have a significant impact on the character of future undergrounds.

The Chaikovtsy were held together in equal measures by a general sense of disapproval for Russian social and political conditions and by bonds created in their own interactions as part of their countercultural experiment. According to Kropotkin, "our youth … were not theorists about socialism, but had become socialists by living no better than the workers live, by making no distinction between 'mine and thine' in their circles, by refusing to enjoy for their own satisfaction the riches they had inherited from their fathers."[111] The cohesiveness of their association, as Pavel Miliukov would later point out, had a great deal to do with the practice of communal living, which "brought them spiritually closer to one another and contributed to the elevation of the moral standards that governed their interrelations."[112] They worked to create a social structure that would stand outside of everyday Russian life, a structure that was unimpeachably upright and maintained the populist reverence for the laboring majority. Consequently, as in certain religious associations, the Chaikovtsy developed methods for mutual policing of the other members. It was required for members to maintain, as Charushin put it, "absolutely clean hands, free from any sings of dirt" and to "confess" one's faith in populist convictions.[113] Keen to reinforce common values and purge undesirables, they engaged in "criticism of each by all—that is, objective analysis of the characteristics and particularities of a given personality at the general meetings."[114] This emphasis on transparency and forced conformity has, of course, many analogues in later communist movements.

Among the Chaikovtsy, the process could become almost puritanical in its emphasis on moral rectitude. "The circle was more concerned with morality than any other circle at any other time," wrote Tikhomirov, who was involved with both the Moscow and St. Petersburg branches.[115] They were suspicious of those who occasionally drank to excess or took an inordinate interest in the opposite sex. They even considered those who wore "gloves or starched shirts" to be suspect.[116] Standing members of the Chaikovskii Circle would not allow into their group people who, no matter how capable as revolutionaries, "by their personal qualities did not satisfy their moral requirements."[117] Kropotkin recalled that "before a new member was received, his character was discussed with the frankness and seriousness which were characteristic of the nihilist."[118] One potential member of the Chaikovtsy was kept out because she allowed herself unnecessary clothing purchases, demonstrating her insufficient dedication to the cause. Given their moral rigor, it is not altogether surprising that Chaikovskii himself had a religious conversion and abandoned the group named after him in 1874 to travel to the United States and establish a new religious community.[119]

Like the Ishutin Circle, the Chaikovtsy were quite energetic and managed to start a successful enterprise that helped to expand their revolutionary base. In the summer of 1871 they came up with the idea of the "book project" (*knizhnoe delo*). The project bought and printed inexpensive books, distributing them among workers and peasants, and sold revolutionary literature to educated readers, all at reduced prices made up for by donations brought in from their connections in "liberal society." These activities allowed the Chaikovtsy to display an impressive work ethic, and they stimulated the development by the early 1870s of a broad organizational network connected to large and small cities throughout much of European Russia. They even purchased a printing house of their own in Switzerland. According to Vasilii Bervi-Flerovskii, "they conducted affairs better than any Petersburg or Moscow book sellers or publishers and could serve as an example of efficiency and effectiveness for all of them. They had agents in all the cities, even in the middle of nowhere [*v medvedzh'ikh uglakh*] . . . and all their agents behaved with the same selflessness as in the central organization."[120] This statement exaggerates their reach, but the book project enabled them to become the first group of radical populists to possess something resembling a national organization based in the capital. On the pretext of distributing literature, they began to make treks into the countryside as early as the summer of 1873, anticipating the full-fledged movement "to the people" of the following year.

While the book project was largely legal, as a result of police harassment it wound up helping to push the Chaikovtsy further underground. The Third Section was not unaware of the success of the circle's venture and knew that some of the books they distributed included radical propaganda. They made arrests, confiscated books, and generally tried to shut down the operation. As Chaikovskii himself pointed out, it was the interference of the state that "pushed our cultural workers onto the path of political struggle and terrorism."[121] The Chaikovtsy never engaged in anything like the political violence that would come to dominate radical populism by the end of the 1870s, but they did pioneer some of the underground tactics that allowed "terrorism" to take place. As early as the period of the commune on Vul'fov Street, police harassment induced the young populists to develop strategies for guarding meetings, warning off outsiders, and escaping detection.[122] Sofia Perovskaia, for example, the scion of a wealthy and well-connected noble family, acquired a false passport and disguised herself "in a cotton dress and men's boots" as the wife of an artisan in order to rent the dacha that became their early gathering place.[123] As a hideout, this dacha proved a miserable failure because the "bohemian" lifestyle of the Chaikovtsy drew so much attention that the police took notice. Subsequently, they set up their "headquarters apartment" in a working-class Petersburg neighborhood. In an anticipation of the conspiratorial apartments of later organizations, it was kept secret from both the public and the police. It must be said, however, that the Chaikovskii Circle's strategies of concealment were primitive compared to those of later underground groups. Their apartment was squalid, uncomfortable, and filled with various people coming and going. In stark contrast to later sophisticated methods of concealment and discretion, the Chaikovtsy's practices were less than subtle, as Tikhomirov noted in his recollection of searching for the apartment for the first time and hearing one of the Chaikovtsy whistle to him from the window to come inside.[124] Despite such rudimentary conspiratorial techniques, the Chaikovtsy began to develop a network of safe spaces in the city in which to pursue their goals. Intensive police scrutiny also induced them to develop secrecy methods such as the use of invisible ink or cipher in their letters.[125] Unbeknownst to the Chaikovtsy, their defensive efforts to build up a web of protected spaces and their use of coded communication were establishing the groundwork for the extensive and consolidated heterotopian space that would become the base of operations for the revolutionary underground later in the decade.

Eventually the combination of increasingly ambitious activism and increasingly persistent police surveillance led to the eradication of the original Chaikovskii Circle. By early 1872, the Chaikovtsy had begun to build an underground version of the Sunday school movement, teaching literacy and other basic skills to urban workers, this time clearly intending to instill a radical point of view. They established multiple centers for teaching and propagandizing among workers, while at the same time other parallel populist organizations got involved in similar types of outreach and propaganda. By the end of 1872 populists were giving regular lessons and meetings with small numbers of workers in all the major industrial regions of St. Petersburg. Rather than go directly to the factories, the Chaikovtsy tended to make connections at worker taverns and tea houses, and in some cases rented apartments in which to live and teach in working class areas like Narvskaia and Petrogradskaia Storona. According to Kropotkin, workers were so attracted to these meetings that the populists had to "restrain the zeal of our new friends" who otherwise "would have brought to our lodging hundreds at a time."[126] This number is no doubt an exaggeration, especially considering that, as Kropotkin pointed out elsewhere, workers were keen to maintain their independence and only rarely interested in the revolutionary goals of the radical populists.[127] Still, a growing degree of mutual interest and interaction between workers and radicals arose at this point. It would continue to expand over the course of the 1870s.

For its part the state saw fraternization between the educated and uneducated members of society as a serious threat, and the populists had to remain "very secretive and strictly conspiratorial" to carry out their propaganda efforts among workers.[128] Toward the end of 1873 a series of arrests decimated the Chaikovtsy and made it difficult for them to fully recover in their original form.[129] The increasing need for security from the police began now to necessitate the creation of concealed apartments that would shelter the revolutionary underground later in the decade. In the interim, however, just as members of the Chaikovtsy were being imprisoned for their activities with workers in the city in the winter of 1873/1874, a wave of interest in direct contact with rural Russia was coming to dominate the populist movement. In fact, members of the Chaikovtsy who were still at large helped pioneer the mass movement "to the people" that would reach its peak in the summer of 1874.

CHAPTER FOUR

TO THE PEOPLE AND BACK

Poets enticed the *intelligent* with the spaciousness of the steppe and the silence
of sleepy forests; moralists with the absence of vanity and sin. Economists
moved him with the need to introduce technical innovations into rural life;
teachers, knowledge; jurists, jurisprudence. Meanwhile, the cultured individual continued to flee the countryside, and with such haste that the decade
1870–1880 will probably be called 'the exodus from the countryside.'

Sergei Krivenko[1]

A CONTRADICTION APPEARS WHEN WE contrast two traditional
accounts of reform-era radical populism. On the one hand, the sharp
leftward turn that took place in the late 1850s has been attributed
to the rise of the struggling, non-noble classes—the *raznochintsy*—who
are said to have exerted a powerful influence on the direction of Russian
society during this era. On the other hand, the turn to populism proper
(with its focus on interacting with the rural peasantry) that took place in
the early 1870s has been associated with class guilt, particularly the guilt
carried by wealthy and/or noble students who saw themselves as gaining an
education and a comfortable living by relying for material support on the
wealth generated by the agricultural labor of the Russian peasant. Was radical populism, in essence, a movement based on *raznochintsy* solidarity with
the lower classes, or was it in essence a movement based on the privileged
classes seeking to redress the injustices in Russian society by overthrowing
class distinction?

The question is misleadingly reductive, and neither explanation accurately captures the complicated situation, but it needs to be asked since both explanations have been offered at various times, often without acknowledging the complex origins of the populist movement. The better answer would be to say that both of these phenomena existed side by side within an urban environment that allowed individuals from different backgrounds to influence one another. The *raznochintsy* and people from more privileged backgrounds made connections in the universities and cities and created the left-wing intelligentsia as a complex amalgam of interests that helped give radical populism its unique character.

The urban intelligentsia of this epoch created and held in common a shared culture: educated, cosmopolitan, well read, politically conscious, averse to tradition, skeptical of the autocratic government, and largely alien to a life of rural manual labor. By the summer of 1874, the youngest members of that intelligentsia had begun, under the influence of various published theories, to seek entry into the world of the Russian peasantry. Almost unexpectedly, for reasons that have never been fully explained, during the winter of 1873–1874, around four thousand students and other (mostly young) people began to prepare for excursions into the countryside in order to acquaint themselves with the peasants, who had long been considered the authentic exemplars of Russian identity and the greatest hope for Russia's future.[2] In hindsight, the journey *en masse* into rural Russia has come to seem almost a fad, a fleeting craze, but it was also a serious and politically dangerous movement that would have decisive consequences for the fate of radical populism as a whole.

The populist watchword "to the people" was originally Herzen's, and the concept of making a pilgrimage to the people in the countryside dated back to an 1861 article in his journal the *Bell*. Since that time, in small numbers Russian populists had been "going to the people" for many years. Even earlier, in 1859, one member of the *vertepniki*, M.Ia. Spiridenko, had moved to a village in Kherson Province and dressed and worked as a peasant in order to learn about peasant lives and political views.[3] In 1861 Chernyshevskii seconded Herzen, admonishing educated people to find ways to get close to the peasantry. He proposed a bit naïvely that one must "speak to the peasant plainly and he will understand you; be concerned for his interests and you will win his sympathy."[4] Petr Zaichnevskii was arrested in the village in the summer of 1861 for propagandizing among peasants, and in 1862, Nikolai Peterson, a later member of the Ishutin Circle, went to the village to work as a teacher at a school for peasants that had been established by the writer Tolstoy. By 1864 he was consciously working to incite revolutionary sentiment among the locals.[5]

As Kropotkin later recalled, the exchange of texts and mutual exhortation underlay the movement to the people: "In every quarter of St. Petersburg, small groups were formed for self-improvement and self-education. . . . The aim of all that reading and discussion was to solve the great question which arose before them. In what way could they be useful to the masses?"[6] The mass upsurge of enthusiasm for venturing into the countryside that arose in the early 1870s was most immediately based on views espoused by Petr Lavrov and Mikhail Bakunin, both of whom gave their names to different wings of the populist movement of this epoch.[7] Some had been inspired by Bakunin's 1868 call for radicals to incite the peasants to rebellion.[8] Others were inspired by Lavrov's 1870 *Historical Letters* which held that the leisure and education enjoyed by Russia's wealthy minority was possible only because of the wealth generated by Russia's laboring majority.[9] Both Bakunin and Lavrov, in their different ways, exhorted readers to repair the age-old breech between educated society and the rural working class. The conjunction of their distinct but complementary views inspired and justified the exodus to the countryside. Over the course of 1873 it began to seem obvious to many that the way to bridge the gap between educated urbanite and laboring peasant was simple: collapse the space between the two cultures by physically moving to the countryside, and thereby directly connect the two worlds together. A member of the Chaikovskii Circle by the name of Sokolovskii, for example, held that if the intelligentsia remained in the cities the people would continue to see in them only their oppressors, so in order to demonstrate their solidarity they would have to shed their privileged exterior, move to the countryside, and enter into the lives of the working people.[10]

"Going to the people" marked a sharp departure from the psychological and cultural interests of nihilism, though it continued the Chaikovskii Circle's rejection of the conspiratorial methods that had been upheld by the Ishutintsy and Nechaevtsy. The movement to the people sprang up in a flurry of half-hidden meetings and inspirational speeches. By contrast to the early undergrounds, "going to the people" lacked secrecy, formal organization, and centralized direction, and its open-ended nature enabled larger numbers of people to get involved, while also ensuring that the event would unfold without any coherent, overriding aim. Although serious preparation did take place, "going to the people" was based less on careful planning than on a variety of romantic visions of confronting the unexpected, the other, and drawing close to it. Thus although the numbers involved in the movement did not amount, for example, even to the number in a single crowd on the streets during the Revolutions of 1905 and 1917, "going to the people" is

accurately described as a mass movement. It united into a single phenomenon, by way of values, principles, and actions, many hundreds of educated
young people who had never met one another but were motivated by a similar form of inspiration.

Even though the populists were leaving the city in large numbers on their
way to Russia's vast agricultural hinterlands, no stage in the populist movement was so fully and blatantly urban as this one. "Going to the people" was
organized in cities, inspired and assisted by urban "circles of development,"
and it proved extremely difficult to sustain, in large measure because the elements of urban life that had made the movement possible in the first place
were absent in the countryside. Focus on the rural world helped unite the
varied populations of the urban sphere. "The very word 'populist,'" Stepan
Shiraev noted, "became known to me only in Petersburg."[11] Even the opponents of "going to the people" exhibited notably urban concerns in their
attempts to curtail the movement. Hundreds of propagandists arrested in
the peasant villages were brought back to the capital, held in Petersburg jail
cells, and put on trial in Petersburg courts, thereby fanning the flames of
unrest in the capital. In fact, the urban prosecution of those who ventured
into the countryside would become an essential contributing factor in the
development of the urban underground in the later 1870s. "Going to the
people" was less an anomalous detour away from the city than it was a formative stage in the urban rebellion that had been developing throughout
the reform era.

PREPARATIONS

By the spring of 1874, the desire to visit the village had built up to a fever
pitch, and preparations for rural visits were underway in many of Russia's
cities and university towns. It is a complicated problem to explain why so
many leapt all at once into such a potentially dangerous direct action as these
treks to the countryside. One factor that came into play was simple curiosity.
Having long read about the admired yet enigmatic peasant in a theoretical way, many young Russians were eager to meet the exotic other in their
midst, that exemplar of Russian culture and identity they had long admired
and pitied, idealized and disdained. For the Chaikovskii Circle, while the
"book project" had been a success, such long-term efforts that did not yield
immediate fruit had begun to seem timid and ineffective. As Charushin put
it, they had grown restless "to test their strength and readiness for service to
the people in new, simple and unaccustomed living conditions."[12] A Third

Section report from February, 1871 described a group of "students" living among the peasants in the countryside, working with them, as well as reading to them and (purportedly) discussing political issues.[13] It was also in that year when the Chaikovtsy began searching for ways to spend time among the peasants. The curiosity had been building for years by the time it burst into genuine activity in 1874.

Another motivating factor for the young populists was experience with the peasantry who lived closer to home. In the foreword to the second edition of his "Russian Workers in the Revolutionary Movement," Plekhanov succinctly and accurately described the populist line toward rural peasants and urban workers in the early 1870s:

> The populists of the 1870s looked at the peasantry as Russia's primary revolutionary strength, and on the peasant commune as the source of our country's progress toward socialism. The development of ... large-scale capitalist industries seemed to them a lamentable phenomenon, unsettling the firm ground of the old "foundation" of the economic life of our people and thereby forestalling the arrival of social revolution. Thus, activity among the working class never occupied an important place in the populist program: the workers were of interest only to the extent that they were capable of *supporting* a peasant uprising, which according to the populists could only arise far from the industrial centers.[14]

The disdain for urban workers expressed here was typical at the time, but it is worth pointing out that in the early 1870s the vast majority of urban workers were still peasants, both officially by passport and also in the more tangible sense that most maintained close ties with the villages from which they came.[15] Although populists tended to idealize peasant life and institutions, many were afraid to interact with peasants, feeling that their extremely different backgrounds had opened up a socially awkward distance between the educated and uneducated members of society. Part of the difficulty interacting with peasants, as Aleksandr Kviatkovskii later confessed, was that the peasant village remained "terra incognita" for the majority of populists.[16] For this reason, the first attempts "to penetrate into the popular masses," as Shishko put it, "took place ... in Petersburg itself" because of the readily available opportunity found in interaction with peasant-origin urban workers.[17]

By 1872 the Chaikovtsy had begun secret, face-to-face interaction with factory workers.[18] In spite of his initial misgivings, Plekhanov later described this process in positive terms: "the populists were energetic people who didn't like to sit on their hands. Many of them, finding themselves in the city, drew close to the workers in order to not lose valuable time."[19] As they drew closer to the workers, they came to realize that such interaction would assist them in learning how to interact with the peasants. Plekhanov, for example, who worked as closely with urban workers as any of the populists, entirely changed his attitude about making personal connections with the peasantry: "a rapprochement with the people, which had earlier frightened me with its difficulty, now seemed simple and easy."[20]

Populist interaction with workers largely consisted of teaching basic literacy, as well as broaching topics like history and math. Under the right conditions, such lessons could open up discussions of a social, political, or religious nature. Although some populists considered workers "spoiled by urban life" (i.e., no longer as "authentic" as the peasants in the countryside), they did have significant success instilling new ideas in the worker population.[21] In fact, some workers began gradually to take on some of the habits of their urban surroundings, and a handful even began to feel inspired by their populist teachers to become politically active themselves. As Plekhanov recalled, "little by little urban life made [the worker] yield to its influence; unconsciously he took on the habits and views of the urbanite."[22] It is also interesting to note that, as Deich pointed out, "in a material sense, many of them lived better than we members of the intelligentsia."[23]

The successful change in worker mentalities and living conditions is hardly surprising since workers represented a subset of peasants who had already demonstrated the initiative to begin new lives by migrating to the cities. Now they resided in an environment that exposed them to new people, ideas, and values on a daily basis, and while increasing urban sophistication may have distanced workers from their peasant roots, it also began to make some of them political allies with the radical populists. The cultural discrepancy between workers and peasants seemed to the populists to be evident in microcosm in the difference between industrial factory (*zavodnyi*) and factory workshop (*fabrichnyi*) workers. The populists considered the industrial workers to be more sophisticated, more settled in the city, and the workshop workers to be both less sophisticated and more temporary. In terms of culture and education, Plekhanov ranked the industrial factory workers between the average worker and the intelligentsia and the workshop workers between the average worker and the peasants.[24] Under the assumption of this distinction, some populists sought to work with the industrial workers, assuming they were more prepared to accept revolutionary doctrine, while others preferred to work with the workshop workers, who remained more attached to their peasant roots and were more likely to return home to the village for summer work.

Although efforts to "enlighten" urban workers were successful on a small scale, the idealization of the rural sphere among the populists rendered such urban activities little more than practice for the main event: meeting peasants on their home territory in rural Russia. One early venture into the countryside proved woefully prophetic for the rest of the movement. One of the first groups to make a concerted effort to propagandize among the peasantry was known as the "Dolgushintsy," after their leader Aleksandr Dolgushin. This group began its operations a year before the mass movement of 1874. They carried out their outreach efforts almost openly, and thus were captured and brought to trial relatively quickly. The Dolgushintsy began their activities, as would many others who traveled to the countryside, with discussions held in St. Petersburg, where they began to develop their plans in the fall of 1872.[25] Half a year later, in the spring of 1873, they moved together to a dacha the wealthy Dolgushin had built on land he purchased outside Moscow, in an attempt to gain a foothold among the local peasants of Zvenigorodskii District. The plan was to set up, as Dolgushin put it, "a comfortable shelter from which to undertake dangerous activities."[26]

From 1873, based partly in Moscow and partly in the rural outskirts, the Dolgushintsy began to write, print, and eventually distribute proclamations to the local peasants.[27] In addition, they published addresses to educated urbanites, those they referred to as "cultured people." Proclamations aimed at the intelligentsia contained appeals to "go to the people" and made the argument that no other solution to the problem of fomenting revolution remained possible. According to the Dolgushintsy, earlier forms of activism—including joining an artel, working with the *zemstvo*, engaging in charity work, and becoming a teacher—were already hopelessly compromised by their involvement in the Tsarist establishment.[28] In place of these activities, they urged that by taking up residence in the village "nowhere will you be so useful as a propagandist for a new and better life than among the people."[29] As the Dolgushintsy would be among the earliest to discover, however, the countryside was a much more dangerous environment than the city in which to distribute subversive material. It was immediately obvious to locals who the strangers distributing revolutionary pamphlets were, and word traveled quickly to village officials. Dolgushin's dacha had not been a safe shelter after all, and their efforts collapsed amidst arrests. Still, in spite of their failure the Dolgushin Circle had helped to pioneer and propagate a new form of political activism in Russia.

In another preliminary adventure, two of the most ambitious members of the Chaikovtsy, Sergei Kravchinskii and Dmitry Rogachev, made a widely discussed trip to the peasants in the summer of 1873. The two of them dressed as traveling workers and had a series of adventures that seemed to them to suggest that the peasantry harbored a degree of interest in radical views, even perhaps that a latent revolutionary spirit was to be found beneath their complacent exterior. Upon returning to their cohort in St. Petersburg, Kravchinskii and Rogachev reported that their work among the peasants had been a great success and that all one had to do was "learn some skill and dress more simply, and then it would be possible to boldly move around the countryside to spread propaganda."[30] Word of such ventures, even when they led to arrest, aroused high optimism among students and populists to the point that the winter of 1874 "was distinguished by a completely unusual liveliness of the young generation everywhere in Russia ... an animation especially great in Petersburg."[31]

Not only as a result of connections with the workers, but in other ways too the movement to the countryside could not have existed without certain advantages offered by the city (particularly the capital) as a space of preparation. Ekaterina Breshko-Breshkovskaia intentionally traveled north to St. Petersburg from Kiev in order to get ready to depart for the countryside back in Southern Russia because "the work [of preparation] was more concentrated and intense in Petersburg than elsewhere, and young people from all parts of Russia sought advice and guidance there."[32] Meetings took place almost daily, all of them inspired by an enthusiastic vision of healing Russia's social apartheid through spreading propaganda and inspiring popular revolt. As Mikhail Frolenko recalled, these Petersburg meetings were "far from small, secret gatherings; on the contrary they were large, overflowing halls, packed to the rafters with noise, arguments, and people interrupting one another."[33] At meetings organized to assist preparation, according to Charushin, "everyone was talking about the [peasantry], about its sufferings, its increasing poverty and its systematic oppression, about the fact that the situation could not go on any longer, that it was finally time to open the eyes of the people to the cause of this evil and thereby force it to exit its incapacitated position."[34]

Some of the earliest urbanites to go out to the countryside were actually workers themselves, encouraged by populists who knew that workers would find the task of assimilation less daunting.[35] According to Shishko, "the first push toward the journey to the people was given in Petersburg by the workers, who were not finding in their factory environment sufficient grounds for a mass worker's movement."[36] As Frolenko put it, "Their language, their manner of expressing their thoughts ... made them seem more understandable to the peasants."[37] So obvious appeared to be the cultural schism between the educated and laboring classes that many populists tried to learn to pass as peasants themselves, accepting that the only way to enter the peasant world would be "to renounce their cultural habits and appearance and present themselves before the people as simple types, all the better as someone with skill in a useful and needed trade."[38] Believing, with remarkable arrogance, that they could pick up skilled trades in the space of a few weeks or months, young intelligentsia urbanites who had never before worked with their hands struggled to master the trades of dyer, blacksmith, cabinetmaker, shoemaker, locksmith and carpenter, and began to dress themselves in peasant/worker sheepskin coats (*polushuby*). The brevity and awkwardness of these attempts would account for some of the quick detections and arrests that ensued once the populists entered the villages. All the preparation—mental, physical, and social—had taken place in the familiar environment of the city during the winter and spring of 1874. That summer they would enter into the other sphere of Russian life.

THE CALL OF THE VILLAGE

For most of the Russian radicals who ventured into the countryside, their efforts and enthusiasm were based less in any particular doctrine than in their faith in the peasants and a passion to improve their situation. Deich, who would later identify himself as a supporter of Bakunin's revolutionary activism, went to the people in 1874 without any compelling ideological reason: "I not only didn't clarify where my sympathies lay, with the Lavrovists or Bakuninists, but the questions didn't even come up for me at that time."[39] For Deich, as for most other young populists, going to the people was simply the right thing to do. What might actually happen in the village began as an exciting mystery.

Reasons for making the pilgrimage varied widely. At a minimum, they included the following: teaching useful skills, such as reading and writing; learning about peasant culture and institutions; learning from the folk wisdom of the peasants by imbibing certain intangibles like the physical endurance of hard work, depth of faith, and a close relationship to the land; familiarizing themselves with the needs and requirements of peasant communities; sharing in the plight of the peasantry's economic hardship; merging with peasant culture as part of a genuine Russian experience, as opposed to life in the westernized and inauthentic urban world; and, certainly not least, leading the peasants toward an awareness of the injustice under which they lived in order to convince them that fighting back against the government and the local landlords was a legitimate and potentially successful course of action. Many populists prioritized the goal of igniting revolutionary fervor among the peasants, but it would seem that at least as large a number wanted to experience what they believed were the peasants' innate characteristics of, as Vera Zasulich later put it, "altruism, justice and a mass of other peaceful virtues."[40] Other visitors were less likely to trust this idealized view of the Russian peasant. As Dmitry Klements pointed out, some of them made the journey almost as a specialized form of tourism: "they went to the village to have a look at the people about whom so much was said in Petersburg ... with the aim of seeing personally how the people lived and thought."[41]

Without a doubt, "going to the people" was the most hopeful phase of reform-era populism. Echoing optimistic statements from the era of proclamations, the argument ran that if a propagandist in the countryside could only make ten converts to the revolutionary cause, "then that *ten* in turn [would beget] *one hundred* followers and so on."[42] Ippolit Myshkin later began his famous speech at the trial of the 193 by denying any connection between "going to the people" and the urban underground: "I cannot call myself a member of a secret association because my comrades and I ... do not represent any kind of separate entity connected by an external unity common to the whole organization. We form one part of the multitudinous social-revolutionary party that now exists in Russia."[43] He added that "given all the differences of opinion on different questions, the adherents of social revolution come together on one thing: that the revolution can be accomplished in no other way than by the people itself."[44] Although by late 1877, when Myshkin made this speech, some of his former comrades had turned back to secret association as a method of struggle, Myshkin had been in prison since 1875 and his speech captured the optimism of the earlier period in which so many felt that living in the village among the peasantry would finally transcend the separation of the urban intelligentsia from the rural masses and unite the whole of Russia into a single mass movement.

Part of this optimism involved the widespread notion that the peasantry had been hoodwinked into blindness to the unfair conditions in which they lived. It was thus the duty of the intelligentsia to awaken their rural compatriots to revolutionary consciousness. In recollections of his student and radical youth, Vladimir Korolenko remembered how his contemporaries were attached to populism not by theory but by a general sense of injustice: "That is why the ideas of revolutionary populism took such a quick and complete hold on the minds of people of our generation. Social injustice was a fact that hit one in the eyes."[45] Solomon Chudnovskii shared a similar view. He believed that he and his cohort went to the countryside "remembering our debt to the people, remembering that we obtained our knowledge by means of the shackled [*katorzhno*], laboring, and perpetually hungry people."[46] By the early 1870s many populists had come to believe they were in a position to right that injustice by reconnecting the divided halves of Russia: to unite educated elites with poor laborers, city with country, Europeanized Russia with genuine rural Russia. Debagorii-Mokrievich recalled how it felt to champion the cause of the rural majority: "We all had great faith in the future then. . . . We felt in ourselves the presence of an unusual strength and the consciousness of this strength rested on our faith in the people. . . . Such faith made it possible to hope for success and ignore the rest of society. And that's what we did. We ignored society, recognizing only ourselves, the revolutionaries, and at the other end the peasants, rejecting as unnecessary anything external to us and the peasantry."[47]

To the romantic ideal of such freedom fighting we must add a deeper psychological element. The populists mainly lived in big cities, with their social divisions and injustices front and center as an accustomed part of everyday life. Going to the village and communing with the "uncorrupted" part of Russian society seemed a way to regain cultural purity. As Richard Wortman put it, "The village appeared as a realm apart from the depraved egoism of the city."[48] One populist stated that "going to the people" grew popular because people believed the "sea of rural culture" would wash away "sorrow, bitterness and disappointments."[49] Not unrelatedly, life in the countryside offered many people a satisfying opportunity to actively help less-fortunate others, an opportunity that had been difficult to find since the closing of the Sunday schools in 1862. "Every minute," wrote Vera Figner about her experience in the village, "we felt we were needed and not extraneous. Consciousness of one's usefulness was a magnetic force attracting our youth to the village; only there was it possible to have a clean soul and a peaceful conscience."[50]

As larger and larger numbers of politically active young Russians heard the call, an unspoken but powerfully spiritual sentiment overtook the movement. "All were gripped in an impatient thirst to renounce the old world and dissolve into the popular element in the name of its freedom," wrote Charushin, "It was in its way a pure religious ecstasy, in which neither judgment nor sober thought had a place."[51] The characterization of "going to the people" as a religious pilgrimage based on spiritual passion seems far-fetched when looked at from the perspective of the revolutionary struggle to overcome raw socioeconomic disparity, but those involved in the movement repeated it so often that it cannot be ignored. Kravchinskii called the movement "a kind of procession of the cross" and held that populists went to the village less to fulfill practical, political aims than "to satisfy a deep need for personal moral cleansing."[52] Aptekman, who called the experience of the countryside a source of "shattering spiritual uplift" for members of his generation, converted from Judaism to Orthodoxy in order to more fully participate in the peasant world view.[53] Kropotkin went to church with the peasants and kept the same fasts. The whole sense of spontaneous, confident, joyful, and spiritual enthusiasm was captured in a memorable passage from Kravchinskii. For him the movement to the people resembled:

> A powerful cry that arose from nowhere certain and spread through the land, beckoning all those with true compassion to the great deed of saving the motherland and humanity. And all those compassionate people responding to this cry, filled with sorrow and indignation for their prior life, abandoning their homes, their wealth, their honors, their families, gave themselves over to the movement with the sort of joyous enthusiasm and ardent faith that knew no bounds.... It would be hard to call this movement political. It was more like a crusade, with all the contagiousness and utter devotion of a religious movement. People strove not only toward distinct practical aims but also toward the satisfaction of a deep need for personal moral purification.[54]

Perhaps most tellingly, "going to the people" played a role in forming a new religious movement called "Godmanhood." This new religion was created and espoused by a populist in Orel Province by the name of Aleksandr Malikov, who had been tangentially connected to the Ishutin Circle. Malikov managed to persuade a number of people, including Nikolai Chaikovskii himself, that "going to the people" could form the basis of something far more than a mere propaganda effort. He believed it could serve as the source of a global spiritual transformation in which individuals would find a connection to the divinity within themselves and thereby usher in a new utopian age. Chaikovskii became a devoted disciple, began to wear long robes tied at the waist with a cord, and moved to Kansas in the United States to help found a new religious commune based on Malikov's teachings.[55]

Such flights of spiritual enthusiasm capture an important aspect of "going to the people," but as with any movement that includes large numbers of participants, motivations were extremely diverse. Sinegub saw his journey as a ticket out of the humdrum business of everyday life and said he went because he wanted to keep from "getting stuck in the swamp of everyday official or bourgeois existence."[56] German Lopatin acknowledged that going to the people was an unknown experiment, carried out hopefully but without certainty about the result: "a solid acquaintance with the people would allow us to form a clear understanding and to choose in the future the path to follow that would be sure to bring the greatest use to those who feed and support society."[57] Nikolai Morozov claimed scholarly motives as part of the reason he went: "I didn't so much want to preach new social and political ideas as to study the popular masses, to personally enter their working life and finally clarify for myself whether the peasantry could really offer some form of assistance to the intelligentsia in its difficult struggle for freedom and enlightenment."[58]

It must also be said that not all motivations involved self-sacrifice. Aksel'rod noted that in addition to the idealization of peasants as "instinctive socialists and potential revolutionaries," those who went to the people were also motivated by "an adventurist inclination."[59] The temporary adaptation of another mode of existence among a population relatively remote might be compared to the more recent interest in volunteer programs like the Peace Corps or various similar forms of outreach, but only if we add in a strong element of political inspiration grounded in the populist "scorn for urban civilization" and "idealization of peasant life."[60] Although romantic and escapist impulses were only part of the movement, it is not surprising to find such feelings among participants who were seventy percent aged twenty-five and younger.[61] Like Tolstoy's character Levin in *Anna Karenina*, who dreams of fully immersing himself in the peasant milieu, many populists wanted more than merely to help and sympathize with the peasants: they wanted integration and identification with them. They wanted, as Aptekman put it, "to live with [the people's] joys and sufferings, to share with them their bright hopes and bitter sorrows."[62] Such characteristics as hard work, authenticity, and "innate socialism" might well be learned through simple proximity to the peasants, and many memoirs reveal an unmistakable competition for the most complete immersion in village life.

Many of the more idealistic visions of the Russian peasant are difficult to disconnect from the Slavophile romanticism in which they had their ideological origin. A generation earlier, the Slavophiles had developed a version of romantic nationalism based on unique Russian traits shared by educated gentry and urbanites and (as they saw it) the uncorrupted and innately Russian peasantry. Populists similarly made comparisons between the cold and hyper-civilized, industrial capitalist west and the warm, authentic, and unspoiled world of the Russian peasant. On his return from Europe, Debagorii-Mokrievich recalled how the peasants in the train had helped him return to his Russian roots: "every muzhik and baba who got into my wagon felt like family to me. I looked at them as though I'd never seen them before. . . . Once I'd shaken off my cosmopolitanism, the world took on a new coloring. I felt that life had more beauty and meaning."[63] This sense of passionate identification also inspired Debagorii-Mokrievich to bring a horse thief into his populist circle because of the man's innate "revolutionary nature." As it turned out, once the thief was arrested (for his association with the populists) he denounced his intelligentsia comrades.[64] Later, Debagorii-Mokrievich realized he had misjudged the peasantry as a result of excessive admiration: "I had idealized the peasant environment, even though I had been rather well acquainted with it. It goes without saying that this idealization was all the greater among those who had grown up in the city and never saw any peasants apart from those outside the windows of their rooms."[65] Another populist, S. A. Viktorova-Val'ter, referred to such idealization as "the basic sin/mistake [*grekh*] of our generation."[66] Charushin would eventually claim that even as the movement to the people was unfolding he considered it a romantic dream, but he brushed off his anxiety "because of the firmness of our faith and the vitality of our idea."[67]

It is also clear from populist memoirs that the countryside itself charmed urban outsiders. While they went to the peasantry as their primary purpose, they entered the rural sphere as though stepping into a new and more beautiful world. One group of radical students who took up residence in a village on the outskirts of Moscow went into the fields to harvest rye, some of them dressed, peasant style, in baste sandals and long canvas shirts tied with a rope. At least temporarily such labor felt like a vacation. As one of them wrote: "in a completely new situation after the stuffy, bourgeois academic environment, I found myself in an especially joyful mood, looking at the yellow sheaves of still uncut rye and at the long row of working peasants and youths, most of them students from Petersburg."[68] In this respect, "going to the people" can be understood not only as the expression of a uniquely Russian political movement but also as one example of a widespread urban romance with the countryside and nature that began to arise throughout the western world during the second half of the eighteenth century. At one end, we find the wilderness cults prevalent in places like the United States, Australia, and Canada; at the other is the fascination with the agricultural realm so prominent in England, France, Germany, and Scandinavia. To be sure, the charged political atmosphere, in which the peasantry stood as the key to unlock a popular revolution, was unique to the Russian Empire, but that should not blind us to the fact that (just as throughout Europe in the nineteenth century) rural life came to represent innate, positive characteristics that seemed to be vanishing with the advent of modernity. Populist excursions into the countryside carried a similar romance with "nature."[69]

Ordinary Russians not motivated by political concerns in this period also began venturing into the countryside as a form of leisure travel.[70] Points of comparison between leisure travelers and populist activists include the fact that both hailed mainly from cities, both were only temporary sojourners, in both cases the rural sphere was prized for its authenticity, and in both cases in the actual event of visiting the countryside the reality of rural life was often found with chagrin to be less than ideal. The otherness, the peacefulness, and the beauty of rural Russia were remembered in populist memoirs years later. Aptekman's description of his friends' excitement at their summer plans has the ring of adventure travel. When asked their destination each would reply triumphantly: "Na Volgu! Na Ural! Na Don! Na Zaporozhe!"[71] Aksel'rod found it thrilling to live "without any scholarly preparation, without the university that meant to tie us in to urban culture."[72] Once in the countryside, the populists had some harrowing and maturing adventures. Morozov got lost in a blizzard, nearly froze to death, and drank vodka to the point of vomiting inside a peasant hut. His memoir glamorizes all the hardships as experiences that forced him to grow up and later gave him stature and respectability among his peers.

Another aspect of Morozov's adventures in the countryside did not involve the peasantry at all. Even when he was ostensibly studying the peasants and spreading propaganda among them, he continued to collect "lichens, mosses, woodland mushrooms, and various stones and fossils."[73] Elsewhere he wrote: "I wanted to run skipping, embrace a tree, kiss the tender, modest wildflowers."[74] Morozov was a particularly starry-eyed romantic among his populist peers, but his enthusiasm about his experiences in the countryside was not uncommon. G. F. Cherniavskaia-Bokhanovskaia retained "the most poetic recollections" of a walking trip through the countryside that was part of her time in the village, and Deich remembered his enjoyment, on his first trip into the countryside, of "the picturesque banks of the Dnieper" and "the trills pouring forth from the nightingale."[75] It is hard to differentiate Deich's reaction from that of someone on vacation: "under the influence [of the rural environment]," he recalled, "I soon forgot the bitter and unpleasant feelings I had prior to my departure."[76]

To locate "going to the people" in cultural attitudes that link radical populists with the European bourgeoisie runs in stark contrast to most scholarship on the movement. Following Lenin, Soviet scholars inserted the populists into the pantheon of pre-Marxist heroic radicals. Any similarity to their bourgeois foils could only be regarded as superficial or coincidental. Indeed, the populists themselves conceived of their movement as a direct ideological contrast to bourgeois values, even as an intentional forestalling

of the rise of western bourgeois ideals in Russia. Perhaps one way to understand the similarities between the populists and western leisure travelers
would be to conceive of the two modes as a Janus-headed reaction to a larger
historical development: rapid urbanization and the concomitant separation
of the urban and rural spheres. The urban sphere was the crucible within
which Russian populism formed and developed, so it is not surprising to
find the Russian populists reacting to rural conditions with an urban mentality. Among both bourgeois leisure travelers and revolutionary populists,
perception of the countryside was affected by a distance that made agricultural labor and its hardscrabble rewards easier to idealize.

AWASH IN THE PEASANT SEA

Having been raised in provincial cities or on noble estates, many populists already had some experience of rural Russia. But experience of estates
and provinces was by no means equivalent to familiarity with the world of
the Russian peasant. Lopatin, who referred to the peasantry as "a mysterious
sphinx," said about the populists that "the majority, having left the provinces
for the university while almost still in childhood, possessed the most insignificant acquaintance with the actual conditions and life of the people."[77]
Plekhanov later admitted that when he went to the people, his knowledge
of them was "murky and indistinct." "Loving the 'narod,'" he wrote, "I knew
it very little, or better to say, I entirely did not know it, although I grew up
in the countryside."[78] The distance between peasants and populists based
in Russian socioeconomic conditions could not be overcome by enthusiasm alone, and that distance challenged the populists over and over again
during their time in the countryside. While distributing revolutionary literature, Morozov discovered that one of his more interested peasant recruits
had torn out a page of his propaganda materials to roll a cigarette. "Sorry,
cousin," the peasant apologized, "I badly wanted a smoke, and that paper is
so clean, so good."[79]

The peasants could not, and did not, live up to the external ideal the
populists imposed on them. Many of them preferred the idea of private,
as opposed to communally owned, property; most of them saw the tsar as
a beneficent figure; and some of them considered the populists dangerous
outsiders, not unlike the "foreign" landowners and local officials they often
despised. One female propagandist was taken for the local landowner's
illegitimate daughter.[80] However, in considering the theme of unbridgeable
cultural distance between peasants and populists so often found in populist

memoirs, one must also keep in mind Daniel Field's skepticism about the veracity of the populists' accounts of the peasants' negative attitudes toward them. Field held that much of the memoir literature on "going to the people" was written later under conditions in which it was in the interest of the populists to play down their level of success in connecting with the peasantry. Working with documents from closer to the time of their arrests in the mid-1870s, Field discovered a greater degree of willingness on the part of the peasants to heed the political aims of the populists and concluded that "a level of trust, a certain *sblizhenie* [drawing together] was achieved."[81] In certain cases this conclusion is warranted, and yet it must be added that connections were rarely lasting and certainly never managed to rouse an effective rebellion.

Whatever the precise level of connection, it is certain that most populists returned to the city within a few months, some of their own accord and some under arrest. It may well be that although the two parties failed to achieve a long-term connection, the source of the disconnect lay less with the peasants and more with the populists themselves. Slow, painstaking and dull work was not something young enthusiasts were keen to carry out, especially in the absence of the animated urban environment to which they were accustomed. We find a remarkably uniform consensus in populist memoirs that life in the village was dreary, alien, and difficult. Figner summarized the populist difficulties in her oft-cited line: "I confess I felt alone, weak and powerless in this peasant sea."[82]

The sea makes a woefully apt metaphor for the way a member of educated urban society, even one who had grown up in the countryside like Figner, could react to the seemingly infinite human misery she found in the peasant milieu. Rural poverty, ignorance, and disease seemed to stretch on endlessly, and whether the point was to help the peasants, cure their diseases, or ignite a revolution among them, any individual act felt like trying to empty the ocean with a spoon. The populists were fully prepared to reject the familiar and detested world of Russian elites, but embracing the hard realities of peasant life did not turn out to be as easy as they had imagined. Though Figner elsewhere described the peasants she encountered as "simple souls with a captivating charm," she also confessed that, "I had the desire to come to the aid of the people, but this desire came not from direct acquaintance with its impoverished condition, but from . . . a negative assessment of the life around me, an existence which seemed to me empty, colorless, and egotistical."[83]

As a result of the distance between peasant and populist, one anonymous document (found by the police in the possession of an arrested student), called "What State is Most Effective for Drawing Close to the People?," warned against acting scholarly, expressing literary or technical knowledge, or exhibiting awareness of medicine or law.[84] Were the populists to approach the peasants straightforwardly as themselves, in other words, they would be rejected. Tikhomirov later pointed out the contradictory nature of their position: "[left-leaning journalists] wrote that for no reason was it necessary to lie to the peasants. But what were we doing today? We lied at every step and lied in the name of truth."[85] The peasants' negative view of outsiders in their midst was one factor that prompted the populists to disguise themselves in the countryside. Men sometimes dressed in the rough peasant coat called an *armiak*, and women sometimes donned the sleeveless peasant dress known as a *sarafan*. Some populists even wore traditional homemade bark sandals. And yet peasant attire could seem strange on those raised in an entirely different environment, so the less distinctive clothing of urban workers traveling through the village was more often preferred.

The well-intentioned urban visitor was such a novelty in the village that when Dmitry Klements spent time in the countryside outside Novgorod, doing a few favors for the local peasantry under the assumed name "Vladimir," rumors began to spread that Grand Prince Vladimir Aleksandrovich was wandering the countryside seeking to "help the sick and the poor."[86] Dressing like workers or peasants and covering over one's education and polish probably helped some of the populists gain access to the peasants, but it was only a first step and does not seem to have awakened a great deal of trust. Frolenko recalled that Vera Zasulich and Marusia Kolenkina looked awkward and were difficult to recognize when they wore peasant clothing, but when they dressed "in urban clothes they were entirely transformed" and looked, "beautiful." "Clearly," he remarked of Zasulich, "here was a purely urban inhabitant."[87] Some populists like Klements were painfully aware of the irony that they had to play a role in order to associate with the part of Russian culture they admired and hoped to unite with.

Populist visitors also felt acutely the lack of their usual amenities. It is worth keeping in mind that many populists had, only a few years earlier, left their residences at country estates or provincial cities in order to become part of the only realm in Russia that seemed to have significance for the educated: one of the big cities (or at least a university town). Before she ever went to the city Vera Figner had already grown "dissatisfied with our quiet, village life, the pointlessness of it."[88] Learning about her friends who had left, she grew more and more ready to escape: "one wanted to be in harmony with one's surroundings, to be healthy, happy, beautiful and strong ... but all around was the village. Mud and poverty, sickness and ignorance."[89] In addition to the morally dispiriting aspects of the village, physical challenges could also create problems. For Cherniavskaia-Bokhanovskaia, unaccustomed to a peasant woman's workload, the village was "complete physical torture" that left her hands covered in blisters, even though emotionally she claimed to have felt a deep sense of peace and ease.[90] Similarly, though Deich had at first appreciated the scenic charm of the countryside, within days of actually beginning to work with peasant laborers, he was growing discouraged: "to unbelievable physical exhaustion was added total loneliness."[91] While Deich managed to stick out the physical rigors of the village, his companion with a weaker constitution soon gave up and returned home.

Not only educated populists but even workers themselves who returned to the village sometimes felt as though they had entered an alien environment. "The reason was always the same," Plekhanov surmised about the workers he knew, "village morals and order became unbearable to a person whose character had begun to develop even a little. And the more gifted the worker, the more he thought and studied in the city, the sooner and the more decisively he broke ties with the village."[92] Aptekman described a worker named Nikolai who had come to the city and quickly gained a solid education. When he returned to the village as a propagandist in a setting similar to the environment in which he had been raised, he had difficulty tolerating it. His sensitive character "chased him out of the village." "In a word," wrote Aptekman, "[he] was a man of the city."[93] Indeed as a rule most of the workers associated with the populists were reluctant to return to the countryside.[94] Andrei Zheliabov, who hailed originally from a peasant milieu but left to get an education, set out to work sixteen-hour days side by side with the peasant family that had invited him in. His exertions left him with little time for propaganda but much greater insight into the "zoological" existence in which the peasantry had to labor. Under such arduous circumstances, the notorious conservatism of the peasantry began to make much more sense to him.[95]

Given the nature of the Russian rural environment, it is not surprising that outsiders would find conditions difficult. Figner's medical work brought her into close contact with the miseries of village life, and her description can stand as an example of the common reaction:

> It was impossible not to look at the sick indifferently; illness aged everyone: the adults had rheumatism, headaches lasting 10–15 years; almost everyone suffered from skin diseases; few villages had a bathhouse; in the vast majority of cases they washed on a Russian stove. Incurable inflammations of the stomach and intestines, wheezing in the chest audible from several steps, syphilis that didn't spare any age, scabs and ulcers without end, and all of

this amidst such indescribable filth in their homes and clothing, with such meager and unhealthy food that you were left in a daze wondering whether this was the life of human beings or animals.

As a result of long work amidst these conditions, Figner was prompted to ask: "is it not ironic to speak to a people entirely oppressed by physical ills, about resistance, about struggle?"[96]

Beyond their confrontation with disease and deprivation, most of the populists experienced boredom and alienation in the village. Mikhailov felt cut off and powerless in the deeply traditional and religious Old Believer village he visited in 1877:

> You can't imagine . . . how torn away from the whole world you feel, living in the hinterlands pretending to be from the people. You can't get newspapers or journals, you can't receive letters from your friends, and you can't read books other than simple, popular ones. . . . After the first days of novelty, little by little emerges the sense of your complete helplessness and loneliness, all the more when they are arresting your comrades in the city month after month, and the new members don't even know who you are. You feel that as each day passes you are more and more disconnected from those who think like you, as though you alone remain in the world among others removed from you in spirit.[97]

"It was possible," as Figner put it, "to fall into despair from the revolutionary isolation in which we lived."[98] When friends met Maria Kovalevskaia in the village after a long stay without the company of her peers, "she spoke without stopping, as though trying to make up for . . . the long days of loneliness."[99] One of Aptekman's friends came to believe he was losing his sanity in the village. He "so wanted to speak a little in our language" that he had a conversation with the stove.[100] The populist sense of seclusion in the village would grow even more agonizing for those who went out to the peasants during the later 1870s, once activism in the cities had increased and the populists in the countryside began to feel they were missing out. "When news began to reach me about street demonstrations in the cities and about the beginning of the struggle for freedom that I had long awaited," Morozov recalled, "I could no longer be patient."[102] It was not long before he rushed back to St. Petersburg.

The sense of alienation only increased as populists discovered that they were unable to have much effect on improving peasant conditions or inspiring revolutionary ardor. According to Mikhailov, at meetings in 1876 many of his fellow populists confessed that their "influence on the people was superficial."[103] Aleksandr Ivanchin-Pisarev complained that "less than one in a thousand ... took an interest in my ideas."[104] As Debagorii-Mokrievich put it, "to be honest, for revolutionaries there wasn't much ground for work among the peasants.... Our peasants were far from being in a revolutionary mood.... We saw around us practically universal illiteracy (and what kind of widespread propaganda is possible among an illiterate population?)."[105] Even when a peasant received a propaganda lesson with good humor, he "listened to the revolutionaries just the way he listened to the church father preaching to him about the kingdom of heaven [before leaving] the church [to go] about his business just as before"[106] The thorough failure of village propaganda struck those who had earlier been so enthusiastic about its prospects as a painful and demoralizing defeat. Figner described the sense of helplessness they felt as a "moral shock": "hopes were ruined for many; the program that had seemed so possible, did not lead to the expected results: faith wavered in the correct arrangement of affairs and in their own personal strength; the stronger the enthusiasm of someone who had gone to the people, the more bitter his disappointment."[107]

Perhaps the exaggerated original idealization of the peasantry was almost guaranteed to culminate in a painful collapse. Aleksandr Solov'ev found the peasants "depraved by drunkenness, held in bondage by local *kulaks* [wealthy peasants] and innkeepers, and steeped in ignorance that had no end to its depths."[101] Since he had originally seen them as "the bearers of justice, preservers by their very way of life of the ideal, embedded in their souls, of the correct construction of the communal society," Solov'ev was driven to depression by the necessity to reassess the peasantry.[108] He attributed his later willingness to attempt assassination of the tsar to the insuperable disappointment he experienced in the countryside.[109] By 1876 most populists had come to recognize, in the words of M. M. Chernavskii that "between the revolutionary youth and the popular masses as yet there was no common language."[110] Ultimately, activism that followed the prescriptions of populist theory was beginning to appear either impossible under Russian conditions or at least a form of struggle that would require a lifetime, perhaps even several generations, of effort. The majority of those who went to the countryside realized the village was ill-suited to agitational activity, and many of those who had not been arrested soon returned to the cities in a dispirited state.

PROPAGANDISTS AND REBELS

Dismay and demoralization were common reactions to the difficulties encountered among the rural peasantry, but some populists remained in the countryside, a few into the late 1870s and beyond, mostly giving up revolutionary propaganda and focusing instead on helping with practical needs like medicine and education.[111] For most the populist program of revolutionary agitation, deflated by the facts on the ground in the Russian village, seemed to require a fundamental rethinking. Many populists simply quit and returned to their everyday lives. Many had been arrested and awaited trial in prison. Others remained in the village off and on all the way to 1878 and had difficulty leaving even when their comrades called them back to the city.[112] Still another group took a new and controversial approach, an approach that ultimately failed but would have a significant influence on the populist movement in the years ahead. The new strategy belonged to a faction in Southern Russia/Ukraine which came to be called the "rebels" (*buntary*). The rebels recognized the failure of trying to foment revolution by spreading propaganda among the peasantry. More importantly, they understood that propaganda methods that condemned the state and Russian society as a whole had little influence with most peasants, who were almost exclusively interested in local conditions and problems and understood political power in almost mystical terms.

When Debagorii-Mokrievich (a leader of the rebels) went to the countryside he found that the peasantry still trusted the tsar to give them the land they believed was theirs. "Everywhere I went," he recalled, "I heard about the Russian Tsar, who was the true political ideal of the Slavic people, ... just but strict, strong but kind; friend of the simple folk and enemy of the landowner."[113] Faith in this mythical tsar's good intentions precluded the possibility of rebellion and instilled an attitude of "extreme passivity."[114] Another rebel leader, Iakov Stefanovich, was highly critical of this characteristic peasant mentality. In his formulation of the problem one can see how disillusionment with idealized notions of the peasants spilled over into a willingness to mislead them: "We saw that the Russian *muzhik* is full of all kinds of prejudices. He believes in God and it is only to religion that he turns for an explanation of everything around him; he is ready to consider the tsar his benefactor and pin all his hopes on him; finally, he is a despot in his family and beats his wife."[115]

Serfdom had ended, and at least in theory the peasants were now a part of the larger citizenry of Russia. But with respect to culture, geography, and the terms of emancipation that kept them tied down by debt, the peasantry remained separate and isolated from the rest of society. Not surprisingly under these conditions, they did not abandon their traditional values and beliefs. The peasants, as the rebels understood, still cherished the age-old myth of the tsar as their defender and patron, whose willingness to assist them was thwarted only by the local landowners and government officials. The rebels, aware of these beliefs and resigned to the notion that they could not explicitly convince the peasants to rebel against the state, instead chose intentionally to deceive a particularly susceptible group of peasants into believing that the tsar was commanding them to revolt. In ideological terms, the rebels found support in Bakunin's enthusiasm for "creative destruction," claiming that the incitement of peasant rebellion was their fundamental task and had to be pursued by whatever means available .[116]

In other words, the rebels were not prepared to abandon the countryside but had come to believe that the original motives and methods of "going to the people" had to be fundamentally reworked. By 1876 Debagorii-Mokrievich and Stefanovich had organized a new group that quit trying to contribute to a broad and general diffusion of revolutionary ideology in order to focus instead on effecting an uprising in a single local region. Their aim was "to adapt to the character of the peasant worldview . . . to be a radical insofar as a peasant could be radical."[117] Reasoning that all the major peasant uprisings in Russian history had been instigated by a pretender to the throne, they began to conclude that "it would only be possible to call forth an uprising in the name of the Tsar."[118] Reliance on this cynical tactic resulted less from the rebels' growing disdain for the peasantry than it did from their conviction that urban and rural Russia were irrevocably split. Russia had developed two such entirely distinct cultures that the views and methods of one could not be practically and usefully applied to the views and methods of the other. Rather than attempt to produce an actual pretender to the throne, they printed documents that appeared to be orders issued by the tsar (including a forgery of his signature). In 1876 Stefanovich assumed a false identity as a peasant in possession of this "royal" decree, which commanded the peasants to band together in secret societies in order to overthrow the local nobles. The new method was remarkably successful and drew hundreds of peasants to the cause of a tsar-inspired rebellion against the landlords. Eventually Stefanovich told the peasants that no further help would be forthcoming from the tsar, and that now they themselves had to organize and carry out their rebellion.

Though this grand deception (named the Chigrin Affair for the region in which it took place) had managed to inspire a degree of rebellion, before it could ever get off the ground it was discovered and put down by the police. Debagorii-Mokrievich later claimed that although the rebels felt guilty about using trickery, they went forward with their plan because they believed Russian history had given them no other options. In a sense, their trickery was simply a more elaborate version of the deception and pretense—altering their clothing, language, and identities—the earlier populists had relied on for propaganda purposes. Ironically, however, this more extreme deception allowed most of them to abandon the earlier practice of pretending to belong to the peasantry. Other than Stefanovich, the rebels did not feel the need to affiliate closely with the Chigrin peasants. For one thing, they stayed away from the peasants because they didn't want to be denounced by them as earlier populists had been. According to Debagorii-Mokrievich, only four out of fifteen members of their circle sought acquaintance with the local peasants in whom they tried to incite rebellion. He even believed that "it would have been incomparably more logical for the majority not to live in the villages at all but to stay in the cities until they were needed as armed brigades."[119] And although some did remain in the countryside, they lived their lives there among fellow educated urbanites "all of whom lived in the same student-bohemian fashion."[120] When they could spend time together "they talked, drank, sang, joked, and made fun of the neighbors and the local peasants in general."[121]

The Chigrin Affair of 1876 constitutes a pivot point between the spontaneous, open-ended "to the people" movement of 1874 (and after) and the organized, clandestine use of violence that would emerge in the later 1870s. The main difference between the rebels and the later urban terrorists is that the former continued to view the countryside as the center of revolutionary activity. Like the later urban groups, the rebels developed a taste for weaponry. In 1876, according to Debagorii-Mokrievich, "we all had revolvers and daggers that we carried with us at all times. We bought multiple rounds of ammunition and systematically practiced shooting. As a result we became excellent marksmen."[122] The arming of populist radicals that took place in the rural sphere in1876 would erupt two years later in Kiev and Odessa into violent retaliatory attacks against officials and armed resistance to police raids.

In a further parallel that anticipated the urban underground's attempts to master the space of the city, the rebels in the countryside began intensive tactical planning and scrutiny of the terrain of their chosen battleground: "We found it useful, even necessary, to study the locality where the uprising would take place. ... We rode around to acquaint ourselves with the environs, ordered detailed maps published by the general staff of the Kiev, Podolskii and Khersonskoi provinces, and often unrolled them on the table and studied the relevance of the country roads, forests and creeks."[123] If in these ways the Chigrin rebels anticipated the tactics of the later urban revolutionaries, by contrast to the underground that was taking shape in St. Petersburg the rebels in the countryside found it nearly impossible to generate sufficient funds.[124] Because of the need for greater funding for armed rebellion, the logic of the populist movement was leading back to the cities where resources were much easier to amass.

THE RETURN TO THE CITY

In September of 1879, half a decade after "going to the people" was at its height, a St. Petersburg radical looked back on the episode as though gazing upon his idealistic and naïve youth: "Do we not recall the peasant-goer of our propagandists in '74? All he had to do was go to the peasant. As long as he wasn't interfered with in getting to him, everything there would be beautiful; all that had to be done was talk to the peasant, who would judge reasonably and do everything he asked. The result turned out the same everywhere: the peasant cruelly betrayed the rosy hopes of the propagandist just as the Tsar-Father betrayed the peasant himself."[125] In the optimistic days spent preparing to go to the people in 1873 and 1874, it seemed to almost all the inspired and enthusiastic populists that their actions would break down the walls between the separate halves of Russia and serve as the beginning of a longed-for rejuvenation of Russian society.

Ultimately, lack of success encouraged them, as Tatishchev expressed it, "to change the ways and means of their activity."[126] In the case of the rebels, that meant adopting new methods of struggle in the countryside, but for most populists it would come to mean "a whole new direction, powerfully moving the center of activity . . . from the villages to the cities."[127] It is probably true, as some participants later pointed out, that had the authorities not essentially agreed with the populists that inciting rebellion among the peasantry was a real possibility, the state would not have pursued the populists in the village with such vigor, would not have arrested so many, and would not have put so many on trial after long prison stays. Under these circumstances, perhaps radical populism would have withered away from inertia as a result of the deep dissatisfaction and lack of propagandistic momentum experienced in the village. Instead, mass arrests created martyrs, long prison stays aroused bitterness and a desire for revenge against officialdom, and the courts became a pulpit from which to preach the righteous creed of populist values. Those populists lucky enough to have escaped arrest found themselves back in the cities, trying to regroup and groping their way toward some new solution to overcoming what most still unwaveringly considered the unconscionable injustices within Russian society. While many remained faithful to the program of rural propaganda and continued periodically to return to the village, an increasing number of populists had begun to recognize the basic impossibility of fomenting revolutionary change in the enormous and alien world of rural Russia.

But in this case failure would have its advantages. Debagorii-Mokrievich argued that even if the movement to the people in the mid-1870s failed to achieve the goal of a peasant uprising, on the other hand "it helped us achieve something we did not work toward—sympathy from the thinking strata of Russian society"[128] Because so many were arrested and put on trial, the Russian public was able to learn about how the populists had sacrificed their freedom for something they believed in. In this way too "going to the people" is properly understood as an urban drama played out against the rural backdrop of the peasant village. As Philip Pomper has noted, as a result of the unfulfilled hopes of peasant propaganda, the populist movement now at least possessed "a much better idea of what was possible in both the countryside and the cities."[129] In particular, a new appreciation for the possibilities available in the urban sphere was taking shape. After two months away from the city, Charushin recalled, "Despite its many negative sides, I sincerely fell in love with St. Petersburg. In one way or another, here was the center of the intellectual life of the country, all ideological tendencies issued from here and then spread throughout the land, and before everything else it was here that the bold plans for revolutionary struggle had so powerfully gripped us."[130] Though they had pinned their revolutionary aspirations so firmly on the peasantry, St. Petersburg remained the intellectual and social home base of Russian populism. As a large city, it was also the kind of progressive, unstable, dynamic environment in which a great deal could change in a short period of time. Change did come quickly, but as we will see in the next chapter, it came from an entirely unexpected quarter.

CHAPTER FIVE

CITY SYNERGY

But here I am again in Petersburg, again back in civilization; I've again reappeared on the surface of the waves, after four months of being submerged in the depths of the people.

Lev Tikhomirov

Petersburg, as if by force of law, formed a central point where all the dissatisfied could find sustenance and satisfaction.

Minister of Justice K. I. Palen

AFTER THE HIGH HOPES AND exaltation of "going to the people," the radical propagandists of the mid seventies who had not been arrested returned to the cities deflated, dejected, and unclear about the way forward. Numerous memoirs refer to the years 1875 and 1876 as a low point for the populist movement. And yet there was a certain serendipity to the timing of their return. Just as the populists were reluctantly coming to accept that the dream of igniting the peasantry into flames of revolution had been a vain ideal, the possibility of a new way forward began to suggest itself. Since the early 1860s the state had managed to minimize activity in the urban public sphere, but in the middle of the 1870s public involvement in political affairs began to spring to life once again. The new public spirit had nothing to do with populism, and it did not even originate in Russian affairs. The change was set in motion by foreign events in the far-off Balkan Peninsula which helped to initiate a new phase in Russian domestic politics.

In 1876 the movement to support the Balkan Slavs in their quest for independence from the Ottoman Empire suddenly began to grip the ordinarily quiescent and apolitical Russian public, and the summer of that year witnessed the rise of a new form of spirited activism on the city streets. Radical populists got directly involved in the movement by collecting donations and enlisting as volunteers, but more importantly the public response to Balkan events renewed their interest in urban activism and helped to redirect populism toward activity in the urban sector and away from the peasants in the countryside. Though urban activism created an obvious dissonance with the rural-focused principles of populism, the numerous advantages of the urban sphere would prove too compelling to ignore for years to come.

BALKAN INTERREGNUM

In 1875, the gathering storm of rebellion among various populations of Balkan Slavs against the ruling Ottoman Empire began to interest small sectors of Russian public opinion. A Russian movement of support for the national independence of Serbs, Montenegrins, Herzegovinians, and Bulgarians began to take shape within conservative Pan-Slav Circles.[1] Especially in the wake of harsh Turkish reprisals in Bulgaria (the famous "Bulgarian atrocities"), the movement then grew to include all sectors of Russian public opinion and unleashed a firestorm of activity by the summer of 1876. Unless we count the quite different famine relief efforts of 1891, the active show of public support for "freeing the brother-Slavs from the Turkish yoke" was the only substantial and sustained mass movement in the Russian public sphere that took place prior to the twentieth century. It was not surpassed in numbers of street demonstrators until the Revolution of 1905.

Nevertheless it has received scant attention from historians and remains poorly known. The reason for the unfamiliarity of these events can be attributed to the fact that the Balkan-Slav movement was both short-lived and anomalous. Perhaps even more significant, it does not fit into any established trajectory of the development of Russian history. As a campaign that pushed for foreign war, it was not part of the revolutionary "liberation struggle," and as a mass movement with supporters who ranged from radical to conservative, it did not conform to a state-centered vision of Russian national unity. Moreover, the fact that the urban public was gripped by events in the Balkans, and participated with remarkable energy and enthusiasm, belies the common assertion that Russia lacked any tenable civil society in this period. The campaign to support the Balkan Slavs eventually achieved its main goal of pushing Russia into the Russo-Turkish War of 1877–1878, and in the process it managed to reawaken a spirit of popular participation in public affairs that had mostly lain dormant since the early 1860s. This reawakening would have consequences both for urban society and the autocratic state.

Probably owing to the general sense of unity with other Orthodox Slavs, and certainly as a result of an effective initial campaign by Pan-Slav organizations, Russian society took a strong interest in the Balkan conflicts.[2] The Russian general Mikhail Cherniaev spearheaded a volunteer army of Russians to join the Serbian campaign against Turkey, and by the hundreds (eventually thousands) Russian volunteers shipped out to join the fight. Scores of medical teams accompanied them. Millions of rubles were raised in collection campaigns in the capitals and throughout the provinces. Readers clamored for news from the Balkans to such a degree that newspaper circulations skyrocketed, nearly doubling within six months.[3] The editors of left-wing journals such as the *Cause* (*Delo*) and *Notes of the Fatherland* (*Otechestvennye zapiski*) began to advise readers to donate to a cause led by conservative nationalist Pan-Slavs.[4] In this climate, the usually sober-minded liberal journalist Aleksandr Pypin conceived of the movement as an awakening of civil society:

> From all corners of Russia, from all classes of society, an echo of ardent sympathy for the Slavic affair has resounded and reinforced the first awakening and first tentative steps. The movement has reached such a scale that even foreign observers find that since 1812 there has been nothing like this universal burst of enthusiasm, ... proof that no matter how many times it has been reproached for its immobility and lack of concern for its own interests, Russian society is closely attuned to its fundamental national interests and capable of offering much personal sacrifice and devotion because the question of the freedom of the Southern Slavs is a question of fundamental national importance for ourselves.[5]

Another liberal observer pushed the point of domestic significance further in a private letter, speculating that the movement's influence on Balkan affairs was negligible compared with its potential to bring about a *"res novae"* (implying revolutionary change) within Russia itself.[6]

As a rule, the autocracy frowned on the public expression of political sentiment, but the wave of political demonstrations in support of the Balkan Slavs that broke out in the summer of 1876 proved difficult to hold back, especially since supporters of Russian involvement were widespread, included strong advocates of autocracy, and extended right into the royal family itself. Because few scholars have taken an interest in Russia's response to the Balkan Crisis, what actually took place in 1876 has remained subject to serious misinterpretation. Approaching the public reaction primarily in terms of the political influence of a relatively small interest group (Russian Pan-Slavists), historians have failed to notice one of its key features: the movement was led by Pan-Slav Committees, but it radically transcended Pan-Slav interests. The Balkan Slav movement did not spring from what one scholar has puzzlingly labeled "Panslav public opinion"; on the contrary, its surprising strength was based on its capacity to unite a variety of different interests in the single aim of the liberation of ethnic Slavs from the Ottoman Empire.[7]

Radical populists, for example, were involved from early on as supporters of any and all popular uprisings against an oppressive ruling class. An underground committee to help the Southern Slavs was set up by populists in Odessa as early as the fall of 1875. Active participants in the movement included two notable members of the Chaikovskii Circle, Klements and Kravchinskii, as well as several others who went to the Balkans to fight or serve as medics and nurses.[8] Two of them died there. The populist volunteers found themselves together with some very strange bedfellows: Pan-Slav nationalists hoping to extend Russian authority in Eastern Europe and liberals backing the Southern Slavs' struggles for national independence. Revolutionary activists, populist intellectuals, left-wing journals, liberal to centrist newspapers, nationalist agitators, and many high-ranking government officials (including the tsarina, the tsarevich, and other members of the royal family) all sought to aid the Balkan Slavs, and most of these groups favored Russian military intervention.[9]

By early August, Alexander II, unwilling to go to war for sound reasons of statecraft and diplomacy, complained of pressure from "the present mood of public opinion" and "inflammatory articles in the Russian press."[10] An article in the August, 1876 edition of the left-wing the *Cause* tried to capture the exultant mood on the streets in that summer:

> Never in Russia have newspapers been read so avidly as now! Never has the information therein been disseminated among the non-reading and illiterate so quickly and grasped by them so hungrily as now. . . . Never in any epoch of its history was Russia so deeply and unanimously agitated as now; the Serbian affair has become a national Russian affair and it is impossible not to be frightened of the consequences of this passion. . . . The

Russian people for the first time is experiencing a solemn moment of noble enthusiasm, for the first time is imbued with the consciousness of popular political ideas.[11]

Far from conflicting with the state, public demonstrations daily exhibited support for the tsar, national unity, and military strength, and the demonstrators were eager to present their goals in terms the autocracy could easily embrace as a celebration of Russian moral authority and international power. At the same time, the conviction that political change was on the horizon, repeated over and over again by commentators across the political spectrum, attests to the widespread sentiment that the role of public influence in Russian society was rapidly gaining strength and would not limit itself to popular patriotism.

By June of 1876 the cities of Moscow and Petersburg had begun to take on a new look and feel. Portraits of Cherniaev, who had thwarted the will of the tsar in gathering and leading the volunteer army to Serbia, were published by the thousands and began to appear in shops and offices throughout Moscow and Petersburg. Newspapers described banners flying from so many windows they lined the streets in "striking effect," while street-corner collectors, dressed in military and Red Cross uniforms, occupied strategic locations for the gathering of donations.[12] In August a feuilletonist for the newspaper the *Voice* (*Golos*) humorously proclaimed the rise in Russia of the "public man," a figure keenly sensitive to the news of the moment and always ready to "cater to the whims of the social temperament, which we've come to call public opinion." The summer of 1876 ideally suited this new public man, who "floated in the wide stream of the agitated popular mood like butter in oil."[13]

As newspaper circulations increased, consumption patterns also changed. Newspaper reading became a more public, communal activity. "Newspapers are hungrily snapped up," wrote one observer, "beer gardens, eateries, taverns and streets have turned into reading rooms."[14] The mood on the street was celebratory rather than confrontational, but at the same time it rested on a spirit of popular independence. "Petersburg was in an uproar," remembered Klements, "Some, like the late attorney Ol'khin, ran around the city with a newspaper in his hand reading telegrams from the theatre of battle in the streets and squares"[15] Although the left-wing publicist Nikolai Mikhailovskii was generally put off by the profit motive that drove the popular daily the *New Time* (*Novoe Vremia*), he nevertheless admitted with gratitude that "this newspaper and its publisher have suddenly become the leaders of magnanimous social sympathy."[16] The daily news was helping to constitute an imagined space of national discourse; it contributed to the sense that Russia had joined together in a united and socially diverse public conversation.[17] Because of the impact of the press, worried government officials lashed out at it for disseminating harmful ideas, but they remained at a loss for a way to censure open expressions of patriotism.[18]

The most prominent events of the pro-Slav movement were large public dispatches of volunteer troops at railway stations. These send-offs typically began as pre-arranged processions accompanying the volunteers on their walk to the stations, while singing and shouting out pro-Slav, anti-Turk slogans. Widely varied estimates have been given for the size of these gatherings, ranging from hundreds to above ten thousand. Whatever their size, they took place with regularity, and the crowds increased as the summer wore on, to the extent that during demonstrations it became difficult to approach the departing trains or even enter the railroad stations.[19] By late August such masses flocked into the stations that sometimes volunteers themselves failed to reach their trains. Shouts of encouragement to the tsar and the Serbo-Croatian "*zhivio*" to Prince Milan of Serbia resounded so loudly they were said to have drowned out the sound of the departing locomotives.[20]

In spite of the outpouring of patriotism, large, uncoordinated public events were, as ever, anathema to the autocratic regime. As early as July a police agent reported that the public was allowing itself "to sharply criticize the government for its passivity," and warned that such freedom was "growing to great proportions" and could get out of hand.[21] By the start of September, Third Section officials claimed, with a degree of exaggeration, that the railway send-offs had grown to such an extent as to have become "the boldest possible demonstrations."[22] Officials like Moscow Chief of Police I. L. Slezkin worried that all the new influences in public life were engendering what he called "an abnormal frame of mind."[23] More specifically, the police were concerned that large send-offs could "serve as the basis for grumblings against the government" or that "ill-intentioned elements" could take advantage of the demonstrations in order to stir up dissatisfaction.[24] In a letter to the future Alexander III, Konstantin Pobedonostsev tried to persuade the heir to the throne that the movement to aid the Balkan Slavs had become a grave threat: "[the government] must take control of the popular movement, take it in hand, direct it, or it will spread further and further, wildly, distortedly, beyond the government, into lack of faith and even enmity toward it. Then things will be very, very bad."[25]

Government fears were not entirely unfounded. As early as July the left-wing journal the *Week* (*Nedelia*) referred to the movement not only as a struggle to help the Southern Slavs but also as a possible basis on which to expand Russian political freedoms. As pro-Slav sentiment exhibited increasing degrees of civil independence, they argued, the movement was acquiring a new meaning in domestic life: "Earlier donations could arouse only philanthropic feelings, now alongside that must be included political considerations. . . . We can be sure that our donations [to Southern Slavs] serve as the firm foundation for our own well-being."[26] Indeed, while the early volunteer send-offs limited their interest to the faraway Balkans, as the movement developed crowds began to use them as a platform for criticizing the autocracy's inaction. A departing medical officer made a speech in late August that challenged the government to send its own troops to the Balkans, and the crowd greeted his words with "enormous approval."[27] Petersburg's Governor-General, Fedor Trepov, reported in August that when the police prevented a departing military officer from reading out a call for donations, "the military officers and the public began to complain loudly, and from all sides were heard threats that such police restrictions would be publicized in the newspapers."[28] Because they faced the possibility of post-facto censorship, newspapers reported on events with great caution, but they did begin to carry on a polemic with Russian officials, requesting a public reckoning for police attempts to shut down demonstrations.[29] A Muscovite merchant and pro-Slav activist named Porokhovshchikov told Minister of War Miliutin that the danger of public opinion "will be a threat to the state if it continues its inaction and indifference to the Slav affair." Though Miliutin considered such presumption from an ordinary citizen an unthinkable breach of etiquette, he conceded that "in the current mood . . . the talk of Porokhovshchikov will make an impression."[30]

Some officials even expressed concern that the movement could devolve into full-scale anti-governmental agitation, as in the following Third-Section memorandum:

> A firm conviction has formed at all levels of society that the government, having for so many years received the full cooperation of society in its reforms and undertakings, must now be led politically by this clearly defined public opinion [on the Balkan Slavs]. This view has even penetrated into the industrial and working classes, among the student youth and in general into that part of society which has lately demonstrated the greatest inclination for revolutionary propaganda. . . . [It is] founded on the idea that the government, not taking an active part in arranging the fate of the Slavs, has managed to facilitate the revolutionary movement, powerfully supported by social ideas as well as the notion of general Slavic freedom through Slav revolution.[31]

Finally in late August, Moscow's city leadership acted to minimize the demonstrations and their "political tendencies" by terminating evening train departures that took place after working hours, and instead instituting morning departures, "during which public congregations will be far smaller."[32] The Third Section in St. Petersburg followed suit by allowing send-offs only during working hours.[33] A few days later, government censors went further and forbid prior mention of times and dates for volunteer departures "since such announcements serve as a cause for street demonstrations."[34] In the end, however, the clamor for war won out. In a speech on October 29 that, in the context of public demands for state action some considered "the first political speech the Emperor made to the people," the tsar gave an ultimatum to the Ottoman Empire that soon led to a declaration of war the following spring.[35] In essence the movement had successfully achieved its goal, and its success brought it to an end.

CENTRIPETAL FORCE

Once the public outcry subsided, future developments would show that most urban Russians felt comfortable voicing their views in public only insofar as they were broadly accepted and not considered illegal. In subsequent years, long imprisonments for participants of non-tolerated demonstrations gave a solid reason for this reluctance. Did the summer of 1876, then, generate little more than the harmless pretense of an active civil society? Was it a kind of short-term role-playing at public activism? At the height of the movement in late August, a feuilletonist made an observation that suggested as much: "Strange thing! Although every day our hearts beat with sympathy for the pain and suffering . . . of our oppressed brothers, it's been a long time since we had so much fun as we did this summer."[36] Although the writer opposed the movement and sought to diminish it with this sarcastic taunt, his sarcasm captured a certain shift taking place in Russia's public culture. Civic activism is a communal enterprise and public space is, by definition, social space. By finding a means of engaging in political activity in the summer of 1876, just as in the initial stages of many revolutions, Russians brightened their urban landscape and discovered a way to inject into their lives a meaningful sense of belonging to a greater whole.

The feeling of enjoyment went hand in hand with a sense of self-worth. "At the moment," wrote a Russian observer from abroad, "Russians feel more like people because they can speak openly about their sympathies."[37] The newspapers made similar comments in different terms. The *New Time* affirmed the public's political influence within Russia: "In the year 1876 public opinion finally appeared in Russia! We must thank the Slavs that they helped us find it; before this we'd never used it."[38] The *Voice* emphasized future liberalization: "Our movement ... strengthens the national spirit and chases away the melancholy and dejection of our pessimists. It airs out and freshens our stores of popular strength."[39] The left-leaning journal *Notes of the Fatherland* declared that "No one in Russia ... thinks about anything, can speak about anything, wants to read about anything but news about what is happening beyond the Danube. In Russian books, in Russian journals, in Russian newspapers, on the streets, in cafés, at concerts, in the theatre, on the railroad, at markets, in taverns—all they search for, all they read about is information about the Bulgarians, about their lives and sufferings under the Turkish yoke."[40] The breathless tone of this passage, as well as its celebration of the public sphere, is as revealing as the phenomenon it claims to describe. Urban Russia had grown excited about its newly active public, and the "Balkan Slav moment" suggested that public opinion had a role to play in civic affairs. Of course in an autocratic regime public opinion lacked any definite purpose, but for a time the public seemed to have become a player in Russian decision making rather than a passive bystander in thrall to an active state. After 1876 that role was no longer so easily dismissed.

The liberal left was particularly excited about what it saw as the public's new influence, and even some populists were willing to be optimistic. P. A. Gaideburov, the publisher of the *Week*, made the point explicitly in a letter to the liberal academic Konstantin Kavelin: "I think the present enthusiasm for the Slavs is just what we need [*nam na ruku*]. It facilitates precisely that separation from the official frame of mind toward which we are striving."[41] The populist Mikhailovskii cautiously agreed with this point of view on the pages of *Notes of the Fatherland*: "to a degree, we now have the opportunity to express our feelings ... and however you minimize the significance of the situation, in the end this is something new in Russian life."[42] The *Week* explained its support in the following terms: "If Russia, through its blood and sacrifice to Serbia and the Slavs, can gain a consciousness of its own national strivings, if she makes only a single step forward in her domestic and foreign political maturity ... won't this be for us the greatest political lesson and the most precious gift?"[43] Mikhailovskii even tentatively suggested that Russia had attained a new degree of civic independence:

> I have placed my hopes in the Turk-Slav events and Russian society's passionate response to them ... an unexpected thing in Moscow and other cities—these hundreds, even thousands of people, crowding onto the

squares and into the railroad stations, filled with one thought and one feeling (no matter what its source), loudly proclaiming their sympathy, seemingly in accord with government policy but still independent from it. Without getting carried away by the hope that all that is truly alive in Russian society will suddenly emerge, it's been possible, with worry and expectation, to hear the sound of freedom.[44]

Not surprisingly in this hopeful atmosphere, it was in 1876 that the radical populists began to focus their energy on urban organization and activism. The writer and activist Vladimir Korolenko later recalled that he had planned to apply the sentiments and experiences gained in his support for the Balkan Slavs to "the struggle for the freedom of our own people."[45] In August 1876 the future revolutionary leader A. D. Mikhailov moved to St. Petersburg, writing in his memoirs that "instinct told me serious forces and extensive plans would only be found at the center, where all experience converged."[46] M. A. Timofeev, who came to Russia as a student in 1876, said that during this period, for liberals and radicals alike St. Petersburg "bubbled like a cauldron," and in the cities were gathering "thousands of searchers for new paths of revolutionary activism."[47] Many revolutionaries continued their efforts among peasants in the countryside, but as early as 1877 radical populism was coming once again to be understood as an urban phenomenon. Perhaps most significantly, Plekhanov recalled that "the whole summer [of 1876] we . . . went mad for demonstrations."[48] Although Plekhanov attributed this enthusiasm to a comparatively minor funeral/demonstration for a deceased populist that had taken place in March, it is impossible to imagine that the daily demonstrations for the Balkan Slavs, which dominated public attention from the late spring through the early fall, did not play the more influential role in generating his excitement. In fact, a populist demonstration was planned for November 1876 under the pretext of commemorating Russian volunteers killed in Serbia.[49]

Debagorii-Mokrievich recognized that by 1877 "more or less everyone [among the populists] was infected with skepticism. . . . The village that had earlier beckoned was now put on the back burner. Revolutionaries started to accumulate in the cities."[50] Morozov agreed with him: "Having experienced conclusive defeat in the countryside, the movement again turned to the urban people."[51] Some populists came back dejected; others told themselves they would return to the city to fight for the civil rights they needed in order to express their views openly in rural Russia. When Aptekman, a staunch proponent of rural propaganda, returned to St. Petersburg in 1876, he recalled that "student circles and meetings were strikingly lively. . . .

Propagandists from the various ends of Russia had returned to the cities, as if it had been agreed upon. The very same question tormented them all; they all searched for an exit from this transitional state."[52] The Third Section also affirmed the populist return to the city. According to an official report, it was the failure to change peasant minds in the summer of 1874 that convinced the "students" to regroup in city centers in order to work among the urban workers in the factories.[53]

In spite of the undeniable doctrinal imperative for populists to focus their main efforts on peasants in the countryside, the opportunities created by urban conditions continued to outshine the dull, troublesome, and dangerous act of living and working in the village. According to Mikhailov, "the fall of 1876 for the radicals was very animated. Many people came to Petersburg from all parts of Russia . . . many separate people, like me searching for truth and work, even further exaggerated the general animation. . . . In the countryside success was very weak, in the cities affairs went better."[54] Frolenko noted the predictable populist cognitive dissonance involved in making the transition from country to city: "At first leaving for the city, several kept alive the hope of returning again to the village and made new plans and projects, but soon all this was abandoned. Entirely new urban activities were begun. The liquidation of spies and traitors, the freeing of [imprisoned] comrades, setting up a press took time and extended further and further, decisively chaining people to the city."[55] S. P. Shevtsov referred to the year 1876 as "a turning point in the mood of the leading groups, which began a broad social movement."[56] Aptekman believed that "The youthful cohort fully shared our populist aims and viewpoint, but it was much more attracted to the city, with its intense emotions. . . . The village it loved 'from the beautiful afar.' . . . In the village it was necessary to work long and tirelessly, without much going on [*bez shuma*]. In the city at just this time began to appear the new direction, beckoning the youth to itself."[57]

With the populist return to the city, the dissonance within individual activists was mirrored by a division within radical populism as a whole. Some populists wished to find a new way forward in the cities, while others remained faithful to the original goal of a peasant revolution and wanted to use the cities primarily as a staging area for continued incitement of rural rebellion. In the context of these two separate goals a new organization arose in the fall of 1876 that, over the next half decade, came to have a huge impact on radical populism, and eventually on Russia as a whole. It borrowed its name from the first populist underground, becoming the second iteration of Land and Freedom. As before, the terms "land" and "freedom" indicated the two primary aims of the peasantry, so although the organization was centered in St. Petersburg, it continued to express its objectives in the populist language of peasant rebellion. At this point Land and Freedom still conceived of its main task as propaganda among the peasants, but it was also now far more willing to enjoy the advantages available in an urban setting. It is clear from its initial charter that Land and Freedom was establishing the basis of a new urban underground; organizational discipline, strict secrecy, and active efforts to undermine the autocracy had become priorities.[58] The members of Land and Freedom now began to draw up plans to penetrate governmental institutions, the military, the zemstvos, factories, and groups among the liberal professions, in whom, according to Figner, they hoped to "incite all kinds of protest and declarations of dissatisfaction with government measures."[59] While they did not abandon the earlier populist emphasis on the countryside, they reoriented populist methods by expanding their aims to include many new forms of activism in the urban sphere.

From this point forward, as we will see, work in the village would become increasingly detached from the main aims of radical populism, as Land and Freedom gradually emerged as an urban organization with a rural wing. Those who remained true to the original spirit of Russian populism felt that the urban members "were occupied with fireworks, the brilliance of which distracted the youth from the main affairs, from the world of the [rural] people who so needed their strength."[60] For the next several years, however, the urban core of the populist movement increasingly ignored populist doctrine and listened instead to the voice of practical experience, forging a movement based on effective methods of unsettling the government and focusing the attention of society on their revolutionary aims. Although they had all the ideological legitimacy on their side, populists who continued to stress work in the village would fade from importance and gradually grow peripheral, while the urbanites went from strength to strength, exerting a profound influence on educated society and the state, and eventually gaining the attention of the entire world.

Another force pulling the populists back to the cities was rising dissatisfaction among liberals and moderates. For several reasons, the political ferment that had begun in 1876 did not settle down for the rest of the decade. When Russia went to war against the Ottoman Empire in 1877, events at first brought further displays of patriotism, but it was not long before the patriotism gave way to dismay over high battlefield losses and disgust for some well-publicized episodes of mismanagement and scandal in the war effort.[61] Patriotic fervor would again swell temporarily in 1878 after Russia defeated Turkey and concluded the Treaty of San Stefano, which gave Russia huge gains in Eastern Europe. But within a few months that treaty was dissolved and re-negotiated by a concert of European powers at the Congress of Berlin, which to the great chagrin of Russian nationalists overturned most of Russia's territorial gains. Part of this final settlement included the Russian autocracy's acceptance of a newly independent Bulgaria under a constitutional government. To Russia's liberals this concession seemed a strong signal that the Russian autocracy might be willing to grant a more democratic form of government to its own population. When it became clear, however, that no new Russian constitution was forthcoming, it fueled the desire to push for greater freedoms from below. In light of the Bulgarian Constitution, some elected, liberal *zemstvo* organizations began to argue it was time to make themselves the basis of a nationally elected body. By March of 1879, the leader of the Chernigov *zemstvo*, I. I. Petrunkevich, was calling for fundamental political change from a liberal perspective: "At the present time the *zemstvo* must write on its banner three tenets: freedom of word and print, the guarantee of civil rights, and a call for a constituent assembly."[62]

The degree to which liberal public opinion had an effect on shifting the direction of radical activism is difficult to gauge, but populist memoirs about this period often credit the shifting landscape of liberal public opinion with energizing the revolutionary struggle. Nikolai Morozov, returning from a three-year incarceration to the streets of St. Petersburg in the spring of 1878, noted a fundamental change in the urban environment: "coming into Petersburg I suddenly felt that I was going into something new, great, already taking place in our large cities."[63] According to Tikhomirov, in 1878 "all of Russia, i.e., educated Russia, was then in a rather revolutionary frame of mind. ... Everyone was certain there was some kind of upheaval on the way, which would soon lead one way or another to a constitution."[64] Plekhanov pointed out that events in the spring of 1878 led the "Russian public" to begin to lose patience with the arbitrary methods of autocratic government.[65] A year later, in October of 1879, the populists' underground newspaper, the *People's Will* (*Narodnaia Volia*) recalled that in 1878 both foreign and domestic political conditions grew more complicated and intertwined in Russia: "the agitational movement enlarged with increasing speed; events called forth, and seemingly hastened, one another."[66] According to D. T. Butsynskii, by 1878 it was no longer rural immiseration that was rousing the indignation of students [in St. Petersburg] but political events in the capital.[67] In the late 1870s, certain liberal circles even began to discuss forming an underground movement with their own underground newspaper.[68] Because of fundamental ideological differences, populists and liberals could never easily see eye to eye, but in spite of their hesitation, as Tikhomirov put it, "the liberal public conducted itself in such a way that revolutionaries could not but think that they sympathized with them."[69]

Under these conditions, for the five years beginning in 1876 and continuing into 1881, St. Petersburg became a crucible in which a sort of synergy of goals and interests took place. Minister of Justice Palen, shamed by the outcome of a trial that became a *cause célèbre* in favor of the opposition, blamed St. Petersburg as the root of the problem, because the capital city served as a magnet to attract opposition and give them "sustenance and satisfaction."[70] Palen was trying to exculpate himself, but he was also right. Adding into the mix of a thriving urban environment an active (if limited) press, jury trials, and the promise of a role in public affairs emboldened a variety of groups and individuals to push for change. Liberals began to militate for their own causes as well as to demonstrate support for the radical populists, while populists were energized by the public mood of discontent with the government and its restrained but perceptible sympathy for radical activism. As populist tactics entered the new urban arena of the late 1870s, they in turn were shaped by evolving conditions. The two main stages in the theater of urban life on which the populists managed to assert their views and tell their story were courtrooms, particularly in a series of intently observed trials of arrested populists, and demonstrations on the city streets. Finally, connected both to the courts and public demonstrations, the Zasulich Affair in 1878 gave rise to violence as a form of political activism. The synergy of these varied urban phenomena and events brought into being the world in which populist terrorism would emerge in full force.

THE URBAN STAGE: TRIALS

In the spring of 1875, one member of the Dolgushin group who was sentenced to a prison term in Siberia chose to turn the state's punishment method of public shaming against itself. Standing before a large crowd, Nikolai Plotnikov began rhythmically and repeatedly to shout "Down with the Tsar! Down with the Boyars! Down with the aristocrats! We are all equal! Long live freedom!" A crowd of students, estimated at 500 (with probable exaggeration) by the chief of the Third Section, began to show their approval for Plotnikov, joining in with his shouting, and following his carriage back to prison. Thirteen were arrested and charged with subversion.[71] This act was one of many demonstrations in which the state's attempt to expose and shame political activists as criminals wound up backfiring. It has often been pointed out that the large trials of populist propagandists created a public platform that enabled the populists to share their aims and ideals with the rest of society. As Laura Engelstein has noted, the courts were extremely useful in this regard because they provided "a protected zone of free speech in which subversive ideas not only found utterance but reached the widest possible audience."[72] Like Plotnikov's civil execution, political trials were yet another instance in which the autocracy's "publicity of representation" was co-opted and turned into a forum for public expression.

To an extent, in fact, the transformation of political trials into left-wing demonstrations goes back as early as 1861 with the trial of Mikhail Mikhailov, about which Shelgunov wrote: "everyone felt a part of himself in Mikhailov, and his trial became everyone's personal affair. Cards of him were bought up on the spot, large crowds gathered at the Senate building to meet and accompany him, just to get a look at him. . . . There was a holiday atmosphere about it all."[73] When, a decade later, those on trial for connection to the Nechaev Affair managed to turn their trial into a battle for public sympathy, an anxious Third Section observer noted of the Nechaev defendants: "Their role has been changed; it isn't society and the state that is the accuser in the form of the court, but on the contrary they have become the accusers and accuse on the strength of the eloquence of their fantastic convictions."[74] It seemed to this police observer that the platform of the courts had afforded the revolutionaries a "moral influence on public opinion."[75]

That the state did not abandon public trials against political offenders after the trial of the Nechaev Circle seems in hindsight rather remarkable. Officials knew that such trials could be turned against their original intentions, but, insulated at the top, they regarded populist propagandists to be such heinous offenders that putting them on trial seemed capable only of publicly exposing the evils and errors of their subversive acts. Perhaps the autocracy's long-term, exclusive arrogation of the "publicity of representation" to its own ends made it seem to high-ranking officials that they still had the capacity to dominate the public sphere in whatever way they wished. Whatever the reason for the state's incautious use of public trials, the political theater such trials made possible only grew more damaging to the autocracy in the late 1870s. The first large trial of arrested populists, known as the "Trial of 50" for the number of defendants tried, was made public so that Russian society would have a chance to see for itself the debased and harmful actions taken by the radical populists spreading propaganda in the rural villages.[76] However, after powerful speeches made by the serene and self-sacrificing *intelligent* Sofia Bardina and the impassioned radical worker Petr Alekseev, who claimed to be seeking justice for the millions, the trial had very much the opposite effect from that which the state intended. It made police officials look inept and cruel in their arrests and incarcerations, while those arrested came across as brave and altruistic, acting in good faith for the betterment of the entire society.

The Trial of 50 ended in March 1877, and many later remembered it as a pivotal moment in the transition toward increased public sympathy for the populists. It was at this point, as Vera Figner later recalled, that the populists "began to gain moral authority and the halo of suffering" in the public eye.[77] Redemption gained in the courtroom in spite of the severe sentences handed out made it seem to her that "the very destruction of the socialists facilitated the growth of the movement."[78] Populist defendants were far from innocent about these public relations benefits, and they used the courts quite deliberately as a megaphone to amplify their collective voice before the public. They even sought to increase the size of that public by forging tickets to the trial and selling them on the street. Valerian Osinskii managed to sell one hundred forged tickets on the first day of the trial before he was arrested. He had plans to sell at least 1000.[79]

The state learned its lesson from the Trial of the 50, and as a result the later, larger trial that began in 1877 and ended in January of 1878, known as "The Trial of 193," placed strict limits on press reports and public attendance. Word about its dramatic events got out, however, in a sanitized version given by the newspaper *Government Messenger* (*Pravitel'stvennyi vestnik*), and in much greater detail with the opposite bias, in the underground press. Perhaps in part because of its secrecy, the Trial of 193 managed to become an even bigger popular sensation than the Trial of 50. Many of those arrested came from elite families whose sympathies were often liberal and who had difficulty understanding how nonviolent acts of propaganda could bring long spells of imprisonment and exile. Even those who did not approve of populist views tended to see the actions of the propagandists as youthful transgressions based on sympathy for the peasants and concern for the country as a whole. By keeping populists locked up in prison, for over three years in some cases, the government helped make itself look either cruel and incompetent. Thus when the populist defendants at the Trial of 193 spoke out about their noble cause in high-flown language, the public was ready to sympathize. As Sofia Kovalevskaia wrote: "the government was not clever enough to take into account that in a country like Russia, with its vast distances and the absence of a free press, political trials were a fine instrument of propaganda. . . . As a general rule, the defendants provoked lively sympathy in the most diverse circles."[80] To compound this effect, descriptions in the underground press, issues of which, according to Deich, were grabbed up "like hotcakes" because of the dearth of information in the legal press, "produced an enormous impression on the youth, the workers, and society."[81] In this way, the trial also facilitated the spread of underground publishing, which would play an increasingly prominent role in Russia's large cities over the next few years.

The defendants also intentionally used their court appearances as a means of conveying their message to the public. Not long after the Trial of 193, the defendant M. D. Muravskii wrote, "We wanted to clarify, as nearly as possible, our affairs to society, and to reveal before it the essence of the indictment . . . to let Russia see us, our strivings and acts just as they are and then let them judge for themselves."[82] Ekaterina Breshkovskaia later noted how the defendants approached the trial as an opportunity for publicity even before it had begun. Prior to the trial they exchanged "numerous conversations and letters on the subject, so that a whole series of formulas, of different degrees of caution or of radicalism, had been worked out carefully."[83] The sensational high point of the trial occurred in a speech given by the populists' best orator, Ippolit Myshkin, in which Myshkin declaimed that the entire trial was "an empty comedy, or something worse, more disgusting and shameful." Having insulted the senators presiding over the trial, as he was being physically wrestled out of the courtroom, Myshkin famously continued that the trial was "more shameful than a house of prostitution; there women trade their bodies out of necessity, while here senators because of baseness, because of servility, because of rank, and because of large salaries, speculate in other people's lives, in truth and justice, in everything that is most precious to humanity."[84] Myshkin wound up receiving one of the trial's harshest sentences and died in prison seven years later. Since details like this speech got out to the public, those prisoners who were later released became minor celebrities in Petersburg society. "They came and looked at us," wrote one of the released defendants, "like people who had returned from the other world."[85]

A Third Section report later acknowledged that the trials had aroused anger not only among the families of defendants but even in some ways provoked "the dissatisfaction and grumbling of the entire society."[86] The same report also conceded the political character of the trials, saying that the speeches at the Trial of 193 "aroused endless conversation in society" and that the press "half-openly announced its sympathy not only with the defendants but with their teachings."[87] As Pavel Miliukov would succinctly express it later: "The political trials made the revolution popular."[88] From this point forward, appeals to society would play an increasingly important role in populist tactics, and such appeals would even become a tactic of state policy as well. It was no longer possible to leave public opinion out of

the equation. Most of Russia's civil society was not yet prepared to participate in hot button political disputes, as it later would in the lead-up to the
Revolution of 1905, but it had come to constitute the third side of a triangle
in which its sympathies informed and conditioned both populist activism and the autocracy's reaction to it. The approval of society heartened
and energized the radical populists, while public opinion would become
an increasingly important concern for the state. The "artificial glasnost'"
of the reforms was starting to look like a genie that refused to return to
its bottle.

THE URBAN STAGE: STREET DEMONSTRATIONS AND STRIKES

Between 1862 and 1876, the state had effectively kept a lid on the use
of public space for nearly all political purposes save its own. Though the
Balkan Slav movement would have a more sustained and decisive impact
on the development of the public sphere, the earliest foray onto the public
stage in 1876 was actually carried out in March by a group of populists. It
was once again accomplished through the co-optation of a sanctioned event.
One method that enabled protestors to voice their views without actually
organizing a demonstration involved the transformation of funerals for
public figures into politicized events. Funerals and memorials that either
cautiously or boldly crossed the line into some form of political demonstration were numerous in the reform era. Some of these included the well-
known funerals of Taras Shevchenko (1861), Dmitry Pisarev (1868), Nikolai
Nekrasov (1877), Fyodor Dostoevsky (1881), and Ivan Turgenev (1882).
To these one must add anniversary gatherings at grave sites, like those of
Timofei Granovskii in 1861 and Nikolai Dobroliubov in 1871. But such
demonstrations were not necessarily limited to memorials for famous writers. At times during the late 1870s, funerals of little known figures were also
used as excuses to march in the streets. In the year 1878 in St. Petersburg
these included the funeral for Anton Podlevskii; the service for those who
died in an explosion at a cartridge factory; the service for G. P. Sidoratskii,
who died in the disturbances after the Zasulich Trial; and in Kiev a march
to Baikove Cemetery to place a cross on the grave of a worker who had died
of typhus.[89]

The first, and one of the largest, of such funeral-demonstrations took
place on March 30, 1876, in honor of the relatively obscure imprisoned
populist Pavel Chernyshev. Upon Chernyshev's death on the 26th of March,
it was quickly decided to turn his funeral on the 30th into "a political

demonstration that would express the protest of the Russian youth."[90] In the event, the funeral grew into an even larger demonstration than expected: "as the procession moved along new groups kept joining in" and the crowd began to number in the hundreds, if not, according to one estimate, as many as 4,000.[91] According to one source, as it wound through the Petersburg streets, the march of populist "mourners" was joined by members of educated society, including doctors, lawyers, and officials.[92] This trumped up funeral march took on a rather festive mood, considering the solemnity of the occasion, perhaps because the crowd understood that, according to one participant, it was "the first time that 'criminal propaganda' was openly carried out on the streets of Petersburg."[93] Part of the excitement had to do with hoodwinking the police, who, "unprepared for such a demonstration ... grew confused before what seemed to be an ordinary funeral and took no counter measures whatsoever."[94] The organizers found a priest to lead the procession and intentionally stopped in front of the house of detention in order to conduct a requiem. Unsuspecting police guards even helped them cross traffic on the way to the cemetery, but once they reached the burial site an orator gave an incendiary speech in Chernyshev's honor.[95]

After the Chernyshev funeral, measures were put in place to insure that the politicization of funerals would no longer be tolerated, but Chernyshev's funeral had demonstrated, in the words of Tom Trice, that "Petersburg youth had found a highly imaginative, provocative means of gaining precious access to physical and rhetorical space ... to expand Russia's public sphere in new, unfamiliar ways."[96] Deich later noted that radical populists in 1876 had begun to seek out various ways to exploit the public sphere through "student unrest, worker strikes, demonstrations, sympathy for political 'criminals,' mass protests against administrative abuses, etc., etc."[97] In all these potential avenues of collective expression, they sought to speak to the public and the government using the public stage created by the space of the city itself. By 1876 radical populists had begun to emphasize activity in the urban sphere above all other tactics. In Aleksandr Mikhailov's words, they had come to the point at which they were prepared to express their views "openly, to all the people, no matter what the consequences, to pour out their feelings and thoughts ... to pronounce in some populated public place a speech before the open eyes of society."[98]

The first fully open and unambiguously political populist demonstration took place only three months after the height of the Balkan Slav demonstrations. In December of 1876 a group of populist revolutionaries, students and workers literally unfurled their banner (a red flag with the words Land and Freedom) on one of the central squares of St. Petersburg, in what Aptekman referred to as "the first and most important experiment of the revolutionary-populists in the 'agitational business.'"[99] The demonstration took place on St. Petersburg's main thoroughfare of Nevskii Prospekt in the square in front of Kazan Cathedral. It could sustain itself no longer than a few minutes before it was quashed by a collection of police forces and unsympathetic bystanders. As contemporary participants noted, the Kazan Square demonstration was an acknowledgment of the failure of "going to the people" and a recognition that the populists were now searching for new methods of struggle.[100] The Kazan Square demonstration, so soon after the pro-Slav demonstrations, must be seen as an attempt to continue the momentum of public speech and assembly begun during the summer with the Balkan Slav events, even as it also endeavored to push that momentum in a very different direction.

As a demonstration site, Kazan Square made perfect sense. Ana Siljak has pointed out about this demonstration that everything about it "was chosen for maximum effect."[101] Not only was the cathedral centrally located, but the semi-circular construction, Greek columns, and raised parapet imparted the feel of a theater in which anyone within the semi-circle below the columnar portico was transformed into a potential audience. The idea behind the demonstration, which according to Plekhanov had in part been called for by St. Petersburg workers militating for a demonstration of their own interests, was to bring together the different elements of the urban left, including populist activists, students, and politicized workers. As a means of uniting workers and students and parading their interests before the public at large, the Kazan square demonstration sought to use the advantages of the city as both a social nexus and a performance/display space, as an arena in which to declare their political colors in the sort of immediate way that was only possible in an urban context.

Under different circumstances, the Kazan Square demonstration might have served as the springboard for a new activism of public protest, but such was the state's antipathy toward assembly and protest, which it feared as a step toward revolution, that the demonstration proved an abysmal failure. First of all, few students and populists, and even fewer workers, had the courage to participate for fear of reprisal. This fear was compounded by the inability to spread the word of such a demonstration, an act that was itself cause for arrest. When the demonstrators arrived, they were still not certain that a demonstration would take place until Plekhanov called them together and began to speak.[102] The number that did take part was no more than two to three hundred. In addition, having thoroughly imbibed the state's sense of the public sphere as its own exclusive "publicity of representation," some bystanders appear to have seen the Kazan Square demonstration as a "bold condemnation of established legality."[103] The leading demonstrators, surrounded by a crowd of a few hundred participants and a large number of curious bystanders, unfurled their flag at the same moment that Plekhanov made a brief speech. Once Plekhanov concluded, they began their planned march to the palace square a short distance away, but so outrageous seemed this unlawful usurpation of public space that police and bystanders immediately fell on the march and attacked those who seemed to be participating. This reaction ran precisely counter to the original plan, which had been set in a crowded square in order to "attract as many from among the people as possible."[104] The march quickly dissolved into a brawl and numerous demonstrators were arrested.

A Third Section report referred to what happened as "an insanely bold demonstration," and participants would later be charged with having committed a highly actionable "state crime" (*gosudarstvennoe prestuplenie*) or treason for having taken part.[105] But as one of the accused later pointed out, "The law code contained no article for the punishment of demonstrations. It seems its compositors did not consider the possibility of such a phenomenon."[106] Organized public assembly and protest had taken place, of course, as early as 1825, so it would seem more likely that the very acknowledgment of such a possibility in the law code was considered a dangerous precedent, and such "extremism" was to be dealt with in secret by the political police under the more general heading of treason. At the trial, the general charge for participating in the demonstrations was four to six years of hard labor.[107] A few participants, however, received stiffer sentences up to fifteen years for aggravated behavior, like fighting back against the police or carrying weapons.[108]

Where the Balkan-Slav demonstrations had been accepted as troubling but legitimate, a populist demonstration was quickly construed as criminal.[109] In a special anti-revolutionary meeting of state officials in the summer of 1878, "street disorders" were placed in the same category of severe criminal transgressions as murder.[110] The Third Section feared little as much as the danger of anti-governmental public assembly. It argued for the need "quickly and energetically to put down street disorders, and especially in the capitals to anticipate, block or disperse the unhappy crowd."[111] They made it clear that anyone involved in such demonstrations should, for the sake of public order, receive swift and harsh punishment: "Energetic dispersal of any kind of unreliable crowd is not as necessary as quick retaliation against its participants. Only the rapid investigation and punishment of the guilty has a calming effect on public opinion, convinces residents of the presence of the power of the authorities and saves them from the recurrence of disorder."[112] The unmistakable point here, a point that the members of Land

and Freedom and others on the left comprehended in full, was that the state would not tolerate the use of public space for overtly anti-governmental aims. The Kazan Square demonstration offered officials an opportunity to send a clear message about this lack of tolerance. By clamping down hard on public protest, just as they had in 1862, the state once again set the stage for the expansion of the underground. Thus the Kazan Square demonstration marked a critical transition point in populist tactics. It was the moment at which public demonstration was tried and, as it seemed to most populists, proven untenable. Not only did it announce the populist presence in the city, but its quick and complete failure seemed to demonstrate the need for new forms of political activism that did not risk the punishments of acting in the public sphere. It would not be long before that new activism emerged in the formation of the terrorist underground.

In addition to intelligentsia-led demonstrations, as the populists refocused their activism on urban centers, they re-established ties with workers that helped to enable the expansion of labor demonstrations and strikes. In the early 1870s the populist student Serebrennikov, while walking in the Aleksandrovsk Park in a working-class section of the city, sat down on a park bench and struck up a conversation with two workers who, it turned out, had already been in search of "students" to give them lessons. Serebrennikov offered them reading lessons, and within a few years both workers were radicalized, joined the populist movement, and eventually wound up arrested for different forms of political activism.[113] In the early 1870s, workers were only beginning to gain a political consciousness with the help of populists like those among the Chaikovtsy, but by the late 1870s, in yet another instance of urban synergy, both the young labor movement and radical populism began to influence one another. As the population of workers grew, and as more workers over the 1870s began to settle permanently in the city, there arose a greater recognition of common interests between workers and populists.[114]

For the populists, connections with workers could be both disheartening and enlightening. On the one hand, for example, N. A. Golovina-Iurgenson, who temporarily worked as a factory laborer to gain insight into factory conditions, was struck with horror by the conditions of her fellow workers in a tulle making factory. She was disturbed not only by the poor conditions and twelve-to-fourteen-hour days she shared with them, but also by the fact that they were interested in little more than new clothes and "the most unvarnished depravity as early as the age of fourteen."[115] On the other hand, Plekhanov often found workers, "comparatively quite cultivated people, with whom I could speak as easily, and consequently as sincerely, as with my student acquaintances."[116] A few workers even began to dress in nihilist fashion, and it was a revelation to Plekhanov to realize that some of the workers had begun to live in greater comfort than his intelligentsia acquaintances, including two mechanics who lived in a furnished apartment, read books, and dressed fashionably.[117] "The more I got to know the Petersburg workers," Plekhanov later claimed, "the more I was struck by their high degree of culture. Lively, eloquent and possessed of the ability to stand up for themselves and relate critically to their surroundings, they were *citizens* in the best sense of the word."[118] Cases of well-off workers were not the norm and only possible under optimal circumstances, but they do point to the gradual social blending that had begun to take place as part of the urbanization process. Curiously, as the workers adopted urban dress and manners, the populists did what they could to dress down and look unassuming. Both forms of dress were, as Plekhanov rightly pointed out, forms of protest against cultural norms and stereotypes.[119]

As time went on and the radicals and workers found more reason to cooperate, "the worker milieu generally got used to regarding the revolutionaries as natural friends and partners, and to regard their secret . . . press as a weapon of publicity [*glasnost'*] entirely at their disposal."[120] Whether because of this partnership or merely as a result of increasing political solidarity among the workers, the late 1870s in St. Petersburg witnessed a spike in labor unrest, which contributed to the politicized climate of the city. Over one hundred strikes took place in Russia in the years 1878 and 1879, the largest of them occurring in St. Petersburg.[121] The first significant strike was organized in the winter of 1878 at the *Novaia Bumagapradil'naia* Factory. A "wave of sympathy" from society helped provide material support for the strikes, which in turn helped unite populists, liberals, and striking workers around a single cause.[122] It was still a far cry from a united front, but it was a starting point for the kind of interaction across class divisions that would characterize the revolutions of the twentieth century. Toward the end of 1878, workers and populists organized a march from the *Novaia Bumagapradil'naia* to the Anichkov Palace, the home of the heir to the throne. There they intended to make an appeal to the future Alexander III (who was wrongly presumed to sympathize with the left to a greater degree than his father). Whether or not they counted on a positive response from the man who stood next in line to the throne, the event was intentionally planned as an excuse to "go out in the streets and call forth the sympathy of the public."[123]

Shortly after this march, in the winter of 1879, another event took place that facilitated a team effort between workers and radical populists. The aforementioned explosion at a cartridge factory killed eight people, while many others were severely burned and injured. Workers and radicals decided to arrange a demonstration at the funeral for the dead workers.[124] Although the police attended the funeral *en masse*, one of the workers made a speech in which he compared the sacrifice of the working class in the Russo-Turkish War to the sacrifice of his deceased fellow workers. The police tried to arrest him, others resisted, and a struggle took place in which several of the workers were beaten. The skirmish served as a pretext for arresting more workers later.[125] As this episode demonstrates, police officials understood worker demonstrations to be as pernicious as those held by the populists. The state's tight control over such events can be seen in Plekhanov's description of the atmosphere around a labor strike. When a strike occurs, he wrote, "around the [factory] streets there was already a particular look that our worker regions often take on when there is even the least smell of rebellion. Police agents dart back and forth, the beat cops run around apprehensively, at the cross streets stand piles of police, and sometimes even the Cossacks appear."[126] Political assembly and collective action of any kind was the nightmare of the Tsarist state, and state representatives defended against it more effectively than against any other political transgression.

THE URBAN STAGE: VERA ZASULICH AND HER TRIAL

In the midst of the various strikes, demonstrations, and trials of this period, another event took place that, more than any other, galvanized society and powerfully influenced the tactical direction of radical populism. In retaliation for the beating of a prisoner who had been arrested for participation in the Kazan Square demonstration, and equally as a symbolic protest against autocratic oppression, Zasulich and her co-planner, Maria Kolenkina, plotted the simultaneous double assassination of two high-ranking officials. The two women intentionally carried out their plan just after the close of the Trial of 193 so as not to prejudice its outcome, and while Kolenkina's attempt to kill the prosecutor Vladislav Zhelekhovskii was thwarted, Vera Zasulich shot and severely wounded St. Petersburg's Governor-General Fedor Trepov in front of several witnesses, whereupon she dropped her weapon and was taken into custody. Because of the overtness of Zasulich's act, the state saw the trial as an open and shut case and chose to try Zasulich in the criminal courts, which remained open to the public. Having failed to learn the lesson of earlier political trials, officials considered the trial of a cold-blooded assassin like Zasulich an excellent way to demonstrate to the public just how ruthless and contemptible were the populist revolutionaries.

Though she was tried in criminal court, Zasulich's lawyer politicized her defense by characterizing her as a defender of justice against incessant government abuses. This defense tied in effectively with the outrage produced by the earlier trials and the mood of general antagonism toward the government in 1878. Zasulich was not only acquitted but set free to a raucous ovation from the well-heeled crowd of spectators who had managed to acquire tickets to her trial. Even Minister of War Miliutin admitted about this elite segment of Russian society that "very many, if not the majority, were delighted by the acquittal."[127] A ranking member of the Third Section wrote that the trial "electrified the public."[128] The acquittal made Zasulich a sensation throughout Europe, rendering her such fame that she inspired several dime novels and a play by Oscar Wilde.[129] The populists themselves greeted the Zasulich verdict with unfettered glee, interpreting it as a watershed event that had proven the public's support for the revolutionary cause. Shortly after the trial the underground newspaper the *Starting Point* (*Nachalo*) wrote that "along with [Trepov] were nailed to the pillory the entire administration, the whole system of government, the whole internal order of Imperial Russia."[130]

Outside the courtroom, thousands of people were waiting to learn the verdict. Upon her acquittal and release, they greeted Zasulich with triumphant enthusiasm and carried her through the streets in what amounted to yet another political demonstration. The police quickly found a pretext to re-arrest her, but the crowd defended her, sequestered her away, and after a few weeks smuggled her out of the country, where she lived out much of the rest of her life. One participant in this riotous celebration, a young man named Sidoratskii, died in a scuffle with police (possibly he was a suicide), another was severely wounded, and many were beaten. Sidoratskii's death was initially perceived as the result of police brutality, and it became the pretext for yet another demonstration three days later. So demoralized or overwhelmed were the police at this point that Sidoratskii's funeral was allowed to proceed in spite of the fact that printed invitations to the event were circulated around St. Petersburg and speakers used the funeral to denounce the "despotism" of the regime.[131] The Sidoratskii funeral, at least according to several memoirs, was attended not only by young radicals but also by people of "solid social standing."[132] A meeting of top officials would refer to the events surrounding the Zasulich Trial as "street disturbances and demonstrations of a political nature."[133]

Four days after the trial, partly emboldened by the events in St. Petersburg, a group of students and radicals arranged another demonstration in Moscow. A convoy of political prisoners was being transported through Moscow on their way from Kiev to Siberian exile. The Moscow populists learned the prisoners were to be taken in closed carriages from one Moscow railway station to another, and they decided to arrange for them something like a send-off similar to those held for the Balkan volunteers in 1876. The demonstration turned into a piece of street theater as the student radicals tried to engage bystanders in doffing their caps to show support for the prisoners. As with the send-offs of Balkan volunteers, the crowds grew large and "stretched like a disorderly snake along the thin Moscow streets for half a *verst*."[134] Once the demonstration hit the center of the city, however, as if by a signal, both the police and the shopkeepers in the *Okhotnyi Riad* region attacked the marchers and severely beat anyone dressed like a student or a "nihilist." The fact that the march had been allowed to proceed into the center of the city may indicate that the attack had been a deliberate ambush.[135]

What seemed new and inspiring to so many people with respect to the Zasulich Affair was not so much Zasulich's act or acquittal as it was a temporary optimism that the various parts of society had come together in opposition to the government. As Tikhomirov put it, "the acquittal of Vera Zasulich, to the applause of the public, by itself constituted a demonstration that for purposes of agitation, exceeded all attempts on the part of the revolutionaries."[136] Not long after these events, another wave of populists still ensconced in the countryside returned to the city to take part in the newly energized urban activism. Morozov succinctly captured the impact of the Zasulich Affair: "after Vera Zasulich's shot, I instinctively felt that the center of the revolutionary activity had moved to the city."[137] Being away from St. Petersburg at this time grew increasingly unbearable for Morozov: "Almost every day news was brought to me about some kind of revolutionary event in the big city. ... My face wore an expression of passionate yearning to quickly return to the capital to take part in these affairs."[138]

Part of the populist enthusiasm about the Zasulich Affair rested on the desperate hope that "society" had now awoken to the revolutionary cause. Aptekman believed for a time that at this moment "the sympathy of society, or at least its better part, had irrevocably switched to the side of the revolutionary youth."[139] Even the popular centrist/liberal newspaper the *Voice* called the post-Zasulich period "the dawn of a new era" and claimed with obvious reference to the trial that "the rise of high hopes and expectations gripped nearly everyone."[140] "Events are moving quickly," wrote Mikhailovskii shortly after the trial, "It is impossible to hold back the movement of history. The *affairs of society must be placed in society's hands."*[141] Public sentiment was, of course, mixed, and difficult to assess, but a Third Section file attempted to take the pulse of public opinion about the Zasulich Affair by collecting intercepted letters and noting down statements of ordinary citizens. Many views were expressed, from dismay at the assassination attempt to full support for Zasulich and other populist radicals. One letter expressed the possibility that a revolution was on the horizon.[142] Another argued that Zasulich's acquittal "raises Russia higher in the eyes of Europe. . . . [When they see] that *we want truth and legality* then they will cease to consider us barbarians."[143]

In the brief epoch surrounding Zasulich's trial, in which the public seemed to sympathize with the revolutionaries and the revolutionaries seemed to have re-politicized the streets, the populists might have chosen peaceful protest in the public sphere as their primary tactic. Populism found itself at a crossroads, and the Zasulich Affair pointed them in two different directions at once. On the one hand, the general approbation for Zasulich's act suggested that the time had finally come for public protest to turn into a mass movement. On the other hand, the state had shown little leniency for public assembly when it involved anti-governmental expression. As tempting as public demonstration may have seemed at the time, it also appeared destined to meet with failure because of the autocracy's stubborn imperative to curtail it at all costs. When Morozov arrived in Moscow hoping to use the momentum of the earlier march to organize a new demonstration, the students he met with refused to participate because they were disheartened by the brutal beatings received by the marchers in *Okhotnyi Riad*.[144] In conjunction with the failure of the Kazan Square demonstration, it is not difficult to understand why public demonstrations appeared to have too high a cost. The state won its battle to keep the populists off the streets. For the time being, speech and assembly would remain limited to those forms of expression that did not threaten autocratic authority.

At the same time, Zasulich and her acquittal had demonstrated another way to register a protest and generate enormous attention. A violent attack against a public official had not only enraged and frightened the government, but it had even been sanctioned by the approval of the cream of Petersburg high society. Perhaps violence *was* the answer. The cost/benefit ratio of as little as one individual expended (by being sent to prison or the gallows) in return for enormous publicity began to seem tempting. It would not be long before political violence became a regular occurrence in Russia. As much as political demonstrations can serve as a means of seeking public approval, acts of political violence can also be carried out in the interest of garnering public support. As Kravchinskii would later point out, Zasulich's shot seemed to sanction terrorism by lending it a "halo of self-sacrifice."[145] As we have seen, violent struggle had been advocated by the populists in the countryside during the Chigrin Affair, but it was quite clear to everyone that Zasulich had engaged in something new: symbolic violence as a way to make a political point. It was a method that the populists would soon, and even proudly, claim for themselves as acts of "terrorism."

Not long after Zasulich's acquittal, the government formed a committee of top-ranking ministers that sought to shut down the growing disorder. Conforming to long-established custom, this committee remained particularly attuned to student unrest and anti-governmental agitation. One committee member anxiously opined that "the propagandists, unhindered, are printing their proclamations, freely sending them out everywhere in great quantities, and without caution attaching them to private homes and even government buildings. The daring of these madmen has reached such an extreme that they boldly create street disturbances in the daytime."[146] As was already becoming clear in the rapidly strengthening Land and Freedom organization, however, proclamations and "street disturbances" were not the main thing the government had to fear. As Plekhanov would later comment, in the wake of the Zasulich Trial "a thirst for action and struggle awakened in the most peaceful people."[147] No serious public demonstrations would take place during the remainder of Alexander's reign. The populists had already made their choice. Political violence carried out by underground terrorists would be the order of the day.

CHAPTER SIX

ORGANIZED TROGLODYTES

Building up the Underground

One must be amazed how such complicated work, carried out in the midst of the capital, could remain unseen.

Lev Tikhomirov

Invisibility is a superpower.

Banksy

EVEN THOUGH ACTIVISM IN THE city seemed to contradict the populist tenet that revolution would inevitably arise among the peasants, by the middle of 1878 the magnetic pull of the capital city was undeniable. Some populists did remain in the countryside, but they were increasingly marginalized, frustrated, and irrelevant to the movement. Vera Figner later tried to explain why, even counter to established doctrine, the city exerted such attraction:

Anyone familiar with [the revolutionary movement of the 1870s] says that Petersburg was its main hearth, the center of government and the focal point of all the country's intellectual forces. Year after year it was the place in which the oppositional elements accumulated. Precisely here were formed the most serious all-Russian revolutionary organizations ... the provinces were pulled into Petersburg and received their impetus from here. ... All of the most important political trials, with their enormous agitational significance, took place here, and it was here that revolutionary uprisings found their greatest response. In Petersburg were concentrated the main literary strengths of Russia, along with those groups that sided most with revolutionary ideals. Revolutionary organs were published only in Petersburg and from here they were spread throughout Russia. ... The population of workers in Petersburg ... was more prepared to grasp socialist and revolutionary ideas. Propaganda at the factories and workshops had been carried out longer here, more systematically and to a greater extent than in any other industrial center. ... The students of Petersburg were more numerous than in any other city and more advanced than all other students in Russia: the student unrest in Petersburg universities gave the first signal to the movement and went in advance of it.[1]

In spite of the many advantages Figner enumerates here, most populists continued to consider a mass peasant uprising the only valid form of revolution in Russia. Yet because the power to spread their message and destabilize the government was only available in the capital, it seemed almost necessary to believe that an urban fight against the government was their most effective use of limited resources. The unrealistic but comforting faith began to take hold in populist circles of the late 1870s that an urban uprising would, in some vague and as yet unknown way, spark a peasant rebellion. As Nikolai Kibal'chich hopefully expressed the common refrain: "the first urban success can give the signal to an uprising of millions of hungry peasants."[2]

At around this same time, a growing number of radicals had become "illegal," meaning that they lived with false passports under assumed names in undisclosed locations in order to avoid re-arrest. These hidden revolutionaries usually referred to themselves as "illegals," but Klements jokingly nicknamed them "troglodytes," suggesting that they lived in such secrecy and obscurity they had come to resemble primitive cave dwellers.[3] The name stuck. It was these troglodytes who in 1876 came to form the nucleus of the second organization to call itself "Land and Freedom."[4] And it was this group that began to discuss the need for what they referred to as "disorganization," meaning an urban-based campaign to sabotage and destabilize the government. By the middle of 1876 many populists were now convinced that, as Figner put it, "no uprising will be granted success if part of the revolutionary forces is not directed toward struggle with the state and preparation for a blow at the center."[5] According to Deich, "at the end of 1876 a turning point undoubtedly arose in our mood: we started to go from words to deeds: now here, now there revolutionaries started to perform deeds under the heading of "self-defense" or "disorganizing activities."[6] Between 1876 and 1878, the interest in "disorganization" took on greater and greater momentum, undergoing a transformation from one possible tactic among many into the essential and defining strategy of the populist movement.

What explains this enthusiastic adoption of "disorganization"? Why did the populists choose to cling to the uncertain hope that a blow to the state in the urban centers would ignite a peasant revolution? Nothing in the foundational principles of populism suggested the need to destabilize and overthrow the government, but among those inspired by a powerful desire to overcome injustice, practical expediency can easily overpower doctrinaire ideology. Disorganization and its extension into the violent tactics that after 1878 would come to be called "terrorism" grew to be the favored form of populist praxis mainly because the populists had created a new weapon: a tightly organized, highly disciplined, and well-concealed underground base of operations. The underground of Land and Freedom in the late 1870s, as a result of its careful planning and elaborate structure, so overshadowed the haphazard underground movements of the previous decade that the two phenomena would almost seem to require different names. By 1878 even the Third Section recognized that in the mid-1870s the populists had grown "more unified and persistent, and had dedicated themselves wholeheartedly to carrying out their plans."[7] It was the possession of an autonomous and sustainable underground space that enabled radical populism, over the course of three years, to become the scourge of the autocracy, to gain worldwide renown, and finally to assassinate the tsar. This chapter examines the complex "architecture" of the populist underground. It analyzes the underlying structures that allowed the underground to remain intact and produce a powerful effect on Russian state and society, even as the police pursued it with ever-increasing vigor.

THE CARETAKER

According to Isaiah Berlin, the radical populists of the late 1870s "virtually invent[ed] the conception of the party as a group of professional conspirators with no private lives, obeying a total discipline."[8] Berlin's point is slightly off target since the idea of total group commitment originated with the Chaikovskii Circle, while Ishutin and Nechaev had tried to impose strict discipline. Land and Freedom, however, was in part established by former Chaikovtsy, and it was certainly the first to demonstrate that a well-organized underground could be used as a powerful political tool. The desire for better organization was apparent among some populists in St. Petersburg as early as 1875, and it was particularly stressed by former members of the Chaikovtsy like Sofia Perovskaia, now living illegally, and Mark Natanson, recently returned from exile.[9] When Aksel'rod first encountered Natanson's group in 1875, he found them "absorbed in organizational problems."[10] Figner, also instrumental in the formation of Land and Freedom, recalled that, "the question of organization was one of the most serious questions and its resolution turned out to be enormously important for revolutionary affairs."[11] Natanson in particular played a leading role in turning disparate troglodytes into an organized party. His fellow populists referred to him as "Ivan Kalita" and "gatherer of the Russian lands" as a comic tribute to his work re-uniting the populist left after the debacle of "going to the people."[12] According to Figner he possessed a remarkable ability to "attract people, organize them and unite them in a common goal."[13] The difference between the old organization of the Chaikovtsy and the new Land and Freedom under Natanson was substantial, largely because of the guiding hand of Natanson and his successors. According to Zasulich, from the mid-1870s Land and Freedom "both in practice and experience . . . exceeded the Chaikovtsy like grownups compared to children."[14]

As important as Natanson had been in this transformation, he was re-arrested in June of 1877, which deprived the young organization of his leadership.[15] Three figures stepped in to replace him: his wife Olga (Shleisner) Natanson, Aleksei Oboleshev, and Aleksandr Mikhailov. The first two were arrested in the fall of 1878, and Mikhailov, who possessed the bulk of the organizational talent and driving energy among them, soon became the undesignated leader of the new organization. Although technically Land and Freedom was led by a group of key members which later took the name "Executive Committee," until his arrest at the end of 1880 Mikhailov was the only leader with complete knowledge of all its affairs.[16] Because of his hyper-cautious leadership he made certain that most other members did not have more knowledge than they needed at any given time. No figure was more important in this phase of the populist movement than Mikhailov, and it is curious that he has received less attention than some other members since without him Land and Freedom (and later The People's Will) could never have accomplished what it did. As Tikhomirov put it, "The soul of the organization was Aleksandr Mikhailov. He united everybody, ran everywhere, knew everyone, directed everything."[17] Earlier and more completely than anyone else, Mikhailov had grasped that an effective underground movement in Russia would require a close-knit, hierarchical, and highly secretive organization.

According to an autobiographical statement Mikhailov wrote while under police custody, it took until the spring of 1878 to reach a "conclusive" reorganization of Land and Freedom.[18] Mikhailov had been in the countryside during part of 1877, holding to the original tenets of populism by working among a group of rural Old Believers, but like many others he was caught up in "the mood of the prevailing moment" and returned to the city to embolden and strengthen Land and Freedom's "disorganization" wing.[19] The organizational task in front of him was enormous. Part of the problem Mikhailov faced involved the old Rousseauian principles of consensus-based decision-making, which the Chaikovskii Circle had favored. All core members, at least in principle, had an equal say. But for a constantly imperiled conspiratorial operation with revolutionary ambitions, this kind of loose organization was far too unwieldy. Leadership had to be vigilant lest too much independence jeopardize the operation, and Mikhailov fought to overcome the egalitarian and easy going tendencies of his fellow populists. In his own words: "In the character, customs and morals of the most prominent members of our association much was clearly destructive and harmful for the growth of a secret society; the insufficiency of constant watchfulness, the absent-mindedness and sometimes the simple lack of will and awareness got in the way of the transformation. . . . So Oboleshev and I began the most stubborn struggle against the broad Russian nature."[20] For doing so they had to bear the criticism of their comrades who chastised them for acting like "Jacobins, generals, dictators."[21] Fedor Iurkovskii called Mikhailov "tyrannical" and claimed that he hindered the freedom of the organization by focusing on "trivia."[22]

Most of the members of Land and Freedom went by nicknames, and Mikhailov's, *Dvornik*, was one of the most descriptive. The *dvornik* of a Russian building, which might be translated today as something like "superintendent," acted both as caretaker and watchman, keeping guard and making sure that everything remained in order. Mikhailov led his group primarily by making every effort to ensure the entire operation ran smoothly. According to testimony given by Nikolai Kletochnikov, "Mikhailov's specialty was so-called conspiratorial activity: constant motion day after day, morning to night, from one member of the party to another."[23] He made no claims for exalted status among his fellow members in the manner of an Ishutin or Nechaev, but he was clearly the leading organizer and as such indispensable in maintaining discipline among a group unused to it. He was, as one populist referred to him, "our strict professor in the subject of conspiracy."[24] Figner called him "the all-seeing eye of the organization and the guardian of discipline, so necessary in revolutionary affairs."[25] Over and over again, memoirs recall Mikhailov as someone with an almost incomprehensible genius for the orchestration of a complex operation. He raised funds quickly and easily, organized the creation and dissemination of false passports (once Oboleshov had been arrested), presided over the underground journals, kept careful tabs on the police, and laid down a set of rules that allowed the underground to continue to function even after successive waves of multiple arrests, including those of seemingly indispensable members.

As had Natanson, Mikhailov stressed centralization, which meant hierarchical leadership concentrated in St. Petersburg. Under Mikhailov, the members of Land and Freedom were split in several ways. At the top was the so-called "Executive Committee," the core group of some two-dozen leaders, which Figner referred to as "the organization within the organization."[26] Though the members of the Executive Committee had nominal control and met as a group at times to debate important questions, even this core group was split into sub-specialists, who remained in the dark about the activities and whereabouts of other members. Beyond the core members were outside members, split into groups of three and only connected to one member of the core. This outer level functioned in a similar way to the groups of five that made up the first Land and Freedom, the crucial difference being that they were guided by a central leadership in control of all operations.[27] At times that leadership consisted of Mikhailov and a few associates; at other times it was Mikhailov alone.

By 1878 Land and Freedom had formalized their association in a charter (of seven sections, consisting of fifty separate paragraphs) that spelled out their various goals and functions in clear detail.[28] As among the Chaikovtsy, any individual entering into Land and Freedom (and later The People's Will) was expected to sacrifice everything to the group. Once the new member entered, "he gave up to the cause all his personal property, sympathy, friendship, love, and his very life ... judgment and conviction, the influence of social opinion, which everyone submitted to voluntarily and willingly."[29] Perhaps most importantly, the Executive Committee doled out the party's limited resources. Mikhailov, in cooperation with his closest associates, like Olga Natanson, Oboleshev, and later Tikhomirov, held the purse strings. In order to maintain discipline and security, he intentionally withheld information from other party members, even from members of the Executive Committee. He "systematically introduced the most strict conspiracy," according to Tikhomirov, "each member ... must know in detail only that with which he is occupied.... The rest must only have the possibility to find out if it becomes necessary."[30]

Land and Freedom's original statutes from 1876 began by broadening the organization's aims beyond rural propaganda and introducing the essential importance of activism in the cities among students, workers, and liberal members of society. They also introduced the concept of "disorganization" as the injunction to sow discord in the realm of state power. The original text described disorganization as "undertaking various acts to weaken the government."[31] Gaining tangible results often depended on a willingness to deploy human lives for instrumental purposes, a talent Mikhailov possessed in full measure. Rosa Plekhanova described him as "a man of stone [*chelovek-kremen'*], a rigorist, extremely demanding of himself and others, prepared without wavering to sacrifice people ruthlessly when the situation called for it."[32] Mikhailov was a practical figure, and his organizational focus emerged from a steady preference for pragmatism over doctrine. He believed that a strong form of order and discipline had to be imposed in order to produce results. As he himself put it, "awareness of the need for an organization does not arise from abstract ideas; it is a product of living wisdom, understanding the conditions of active work and adapting to them."[33] Careful organization and strict discipline were the basic building materials from which the radical populist underground was constructed.

BUILDING A SUBVERSIVE HETEROTOPIA

As Mikhailov well understood, effective "disorganization" first requires effective organization. The scope and complexity of Land and Freedom's operations is astonishing even today. The actions of a moment often required months of preparation and the mastery of a multiplicity of minute details. Their projects demanded manpower, significant expenditure, cutting-edge technology, and the gathering of large amounts of information, all in complete secrecy while in close proximity to a large and vigilant police force desperate to prevent further outbreaks of violence. Only a tightly knit and highly disciplined organization could put all these operations into action and survive them, and such an organization was only possible under certain conditions. In the countryside, as we have seen, even dressed as peasants and secluded in the vast hinterlands of European Russia, the populists of 1874 were arrested in large numbers and quickly dispersed because they stood out too prominently against a background that had little social variety for camouflage. The work of "disorganization" was possible only in a large, diverse, and chaotic urban environment that afforded a different kind of cover. Although some attacks and other operations took place outside the major cities, all efforts toward destabilizing state power were orchestrated and funded from St. Petersburg.

One way to gain and maintain power is to control a given space and the language and activities carried out in that space. In officially sanctioned institutions like a town or a factory, writes Edward Soja, "disciplinary power proceeds primarily through the organization, enclosure, and control of individuals in space."[34] For this reason cities are in many ways more easily subject to disciplinary control from above: "cities are specialized nodal agglomerations built around the instrumental 'presence availability' of social power. They are control centers, citadels designed to protect and dominate . . . through a subtle geography of enclosure, confinement, surveillance, partitioning, social discipline and spatial differentiation."[35] The autocracy sought, through police-enforced discipline and control, to maintain its self-conception as a "well-ordered police state," particularly in the cities where the need to impose order and discipline grew from an environment of increasing complexity. In Russian cities the state maintained a system of passport regulation that identified all citizens by gender, *soslovie*, place of origin, and other attributes. Russians were also more marked by clothing and uniforms than in many other parts of Europe, while St. Petersburg apartment buildings had in-built forms of surveillance in the person of the caretaker (*dvornik*) who was expected to willingly cooperate with the police to keep tabs on the city's inhabitants.

In describing cities as "control centers" Soja was referring to the control of established institutions of power, methods the autocracy used to the best of its ability. Much the same can be said of the practices of organization, enclosure, and control devised and applied by the radical underground. The capacities of the underground derived in part from the fact that Mikhailov and company developed their own methods for controlling urban space and separating their operations from those methods of control that were supposed to be keeping *them* in check. In this respect, it might be said that what Land and Freedom accomplished under Mikhailov was the creation of a new "disciplinary technology." As Mikhailov pointed out, the urban center was a necessary command post for Land and Freedom: "Because the arena of [Land and Freedom's] activities was the capital . . . it attracted to the movement intelligentsia strength from the youth, society and the military; it led the press organ of the party; . . . it obtained material means for the organization's business; it had a bureau for classification of the necessary information, and for the supply of necessary passports. In a word, it led all the general functions of the organization."[36] Under these circumstances, as E. I. Shcherbakova has noted, as the underground developed, "the circle of revolutionaries closed all the more tightly; the boundary separating it from the rest of the world became sharper," so that in time "underground Russia lived by its own laws, sharply distinct from the laws of the Russian Empire."[37] By "closing the circle" Land and Freedom created a space that could be used to subvert prevailing forms of urban discipline and control.

If, to repeat Soja, "disciplinary power proceeds primarily through the organization, enclosure and control of individuals in space," then it follows that those forms of disciplinary control can be subverted and undermined by carving out a space free from that control. As the prefixes of words such as "subvert" and "undermine" indicate, an underground provides a position from which that subversion can be accomplished. The populist underground came to possess all the various properties of a Foucauldian heterotopia. It was, for instance, "outside of all places even though it may be possible to indicate [its] location in reality," and it had "the curious property of being in relation with all the other [social] sites."[38] Elaborating on Foucault's discussion of the heterotopia, Edward Casey has emphasized its potential as a fulcrum of power: "to make a difference in the social fabric, a heterotopia must possess a focus for the application of force. This focus can be found in the marginal location of the heterotopia itself: from this location force can be exerted more effectively than if it stemmed from the center."[39] At the same time, as Foucault has pointed out, proximity to the powers being subverted is essential: "resistance to power ... exists all the more by being in the same place as power."[40] An underground must at once be both marginal and close to the center of power because any movement that wishes to subvert that power can only be carried out in close proximity to its seat of authority. In labeling the populist underground a subversive heterotopia, the point is not to praise or condemn it but to grasp what enabled radical populism in the late 1870s to generate a substantial counterforce to the otherwise all-powerful autocratic state.

The populist underground used the heterotopia's mixture of proximity and marginality to its advantage, developing a toolkit of "microtechniques" that allowed it to remain intact and carry out its small insurrectionary struggle against the huge Russian state. These techniques included secret forms of communication, detailed knowledge of urban space, methods for infiltrating the police, networks of support among the general population, document forgery, and disguises for the creation of false identities. Most importantly, the populist underground maintained an archipelago of "conspiratorial apartments" throughout the city that allowed them to execute their operations while living undetected in central districts of Russian cities, even in the midst of intense police scrutiny. When combined into a functioning operation, these practices gave the underground the autonomy to become, as Kravchinskii called it, "the unconquerable force" that for a few years it seemed to be. By turning the system to their own ends, the populists managed to inhabit the same streets and neighborhoods as the state officials and police who were trying to capture them. Armed with a sufficiently autonomous space, they carried out one of the more spectacular and influential (though by its own standards unsuccessful) terror campaigns in modern history. The following several sections describe the most effective tools and techniques used to make that campaign possible.

False Identities

It is a great irony that one of the most important factors allowing the populists to live undetected in the city was put in place by the autocracy itself in order to keep control of the Russian population. Every Russian citizen had to have a passport, and it was a criminal offense to reside anywhere in the Empire without valid documentation.[41] The passport system, however, was so overburdened and ineffective that many thousands of people were able to live without documentation.[42] Interior Minister S. S. Lanskoi in 1857 calculated that 30,000 people that year had been arrested in Russia without a passport, and the numbers would continue to grow.[43] Nevertheless, in spite of population growth and increasing violations of the system, "between 1857 and 1894, passport rules changed little."[44] So much did urban officials rely on passports that when radicals possessed viable false documents that accorded with their external appearance, they worked as a kind of shield, enabling the holder to go about his or her business in the light of day without being troubled. A character in Kravchinskii's memoiristic novel *Career of a Nihilist* points out that in the late 1870s, while it was not at all unusual for an innocent person to be questioned by the Third Section even for simply being accused of associating with a revolutionary, illegals often felt safer than the ordinary population because "all our sins are washed away from us when we throw into the fire our old passports and reappear with a fresh one. Provided it is a good one, and we keep our eyes open, we can manage very well."[45] As the expression went, a false passport could "wash you clean."[46]

Russia's internal passport system thus made it easier for urban populists to live underground. At first, populists became "illegals" as a result of fleeing arrest or ignoring exile status. Morozov, for example, having heard he might be re-arrested after an earlier incarceration, "went illegal" to keep from being sent into exile.[47] The hundreds of arrests connected with "going to the people" also produced an upsurge in the number of illegals, since questioning and examination of documents uncovered the names of many others involved in the movement who had not yet been arrested. Those identified who had the means to do so usually left the country, but those who could not leave or wanted to stay often chose to make use of false documents. Some who had gone abroad and wanted to return to Russia could only come home by acquiring a false passport.

Eventually many populists voluntarily chose illegal status because of the independence it gave them to operate as underground revolutionaries. Deich pointed out that living illegally "not only did not create hindrances but presented many conveniences," including the fact that it was more difficult to locate and arrest somebody living under an assumed name.[48] Deich, who had escaped from prison, had no choice but to "break all ties with the past" and live illegally indefinitely. His new false status made him feel "almost complete separation from the rest of the world."[49] In this way illegal status not only afforded a kind of freedom, but it also may well have made it a little easier to contemplate and carry out reckless acts against the society from which one was now, in a sense, banished. As Deich put it, an illegal tended to develop "an inclination for danger, a complete indifference to his future, readiness at any moment to part with his freedom and even his life."[50]

Dependence on false documents necessitated keeping one's real name out of circulation, so along with false documents the populist conspirators all used nicknames and assumed names. When Mikhailov received information from the mole he had placed in the Third Section, in order to maintain absolute secrecy he only identified himself by the common name and patronymic, Petr Ivanovich.[51] Every member of the inner circle of Land and Freedom had at least one nickname, and some members of the underground only knew one another by these names. S. E. Lion pointed out that he was saved from imprisonment or execution by the fact that his radical acquaintances knew him only as "Kas'yan." The police knew about Kas'yan's activities but were never able to discover the real person behind them.[52]

Nicknames were, to be sure, essential to the maintenance of secrecy, but they also suggest something of the light-hearted camaraderie the members of Land and Freedom maintained as a way of releasing stress. Many nicknames, like *Dvornik* for Mikhailov, were both descriptive and humorous. The list of usable names went beyond the standard Russian shortening of first names or patronymics and included such colorful monikers as Cat, Top Hat, Sparrow, Alchemist, Jacobin, Grandad, Little Tiger, American, and Lawyer. Nikolai Bukh, for reasons English and German speakers of Russian will understand, was called "*Kniga*" (book). Other nicknames were simply shortened versions of first names, and in some cases nicknames described

NICKNAMES AND PSEUDONYMS USED BY MEMBERS OF THE UNDERGROUND

Osip Aptekman—Os'ka
Aleksandr Barranikov—Semen/Sen'ka
Aleksei Bogoliubov—Andreich
Ivan Bokhanovskii—Kazak (Cossack)
Nikolai Bukh—Kniga (Book)/Ivan Vasil'evich
Sergei Chubarov—Amerikanets (American)/Kapitan (Captain)
Vladimir Debogorii-Mokrievich—Mishka
Mikhail Frolenko—Mikhailo
Lev Gartman—Alkhimik (Alchemist)
Ignatii Grinevitskii—Kotik (Pussycat)
Anna Iakimova—Baska (Basque)
Fedor Iurkovskii—Sashka Inzhener (Little Sasha the Engineer)
Iosif Kablits—Dedushka (Grandfather)
Nikolai Kibal'chich—Tsilindr (Tophat)
Nikolai Kolodkevich—Kot (Tomcat)
Nikolai Kletochnikov—Agent (Agent)
Maria Krylova—Bogoroditsa (Virgin Mary)/Tetia Maria (Aunt Maria)
Aleksandr Kviatkovskii—Aleksandr I (Alexander I)
Solomon Lion—Kas'yan
Dmitry Lizogub—Dmitro
Leon Mirskii—L'vov
Aleksandr Mikhailov—Dvornik (Caretaker)/Petr Ivanovich
Nikandr Moshchenko—Khokhol (Ukranian)
Nikolai Morozov—Vorobei (Sparrow)
Aleksei Oboleshev—Leshka
Maria Oshanina—Iakobin (Jacobin)
Georgii Plekhanov—Zhorzh/Orator (Orator)
Mikhail Popov—Rodionich
Georgii Preobrazhenskii—Iurist (Lawyer)
Aleksandr Semenovskii—Grazhdanin (Citizen)
Nikolai Sergeev—Sovetnik (Advisor)
Nikolai Shmeman—Nemets (German)
Iakov Stefanovich—Dmitro
Lev Tikhomirov—Tigrych (Little Tiger)/Starik (Old Man)
Iurii Tishchenko—Titych
Mikhail Trigony—Milord
Vasilii Troshchanskii—Martyshka
Nikolai Tiutchev—Tiut'ka
Innokentii Voloshenko—Petro, Volk (Wolf)
Vera Zasulich—Marfusha
Andrei Zheliabov—Boris/Taras/Zakhar
Aaron Zundelevich—Arkadii/Moisha

the activity of the particular member. The populists' spy in the Third Section, Kletochnikov, for example, was known to others as "Agent."

The populists did not by any means invent the falsification of documents. As Deich points out, "it had long been practiced here by different persecuted and hunted people, like sectarians, criminals, and vagrants."[53] Beginning in 1876, however, the populists brought document forgery to state-of-the-art excellence.[54] Their passports were of such quality that "illegals" could sometimes travel out of the country and return with them. While it is true that most "illegals" were eventually found and arrested, a few managed to survive for years with false papers. Mikhail Frolenko, for example, remained illegal from 1874 to 1881. Because forged papers became indispensable to the underground, their appropriation and fabrication became a cottage industry. Land and Freedom kept a stock of thousands of documents of various kinds that could be used in creating false identities. Their passport wing, which they jokingly referred to as "the Heavenly Chancery," was considered important enough that it was run, until his arrest, by the leading figure Oboleshov.[55] The St. Petersburg operation was the largest, but other "passport bureaus," like that run by Sergei Chubarov in Kiev, also produced high quality false documents, often in a matter of just two or three hours. If possible, the members of Land and Freedom possessed several different passports so that if one were compromised it would be possible to move to another city and register there to begin a new existence under a different identity.[56] The passport system helped to create the underground in part because it created an "alien" population within the center of society. As Debagorii-Mokrievich put it: "we considered the illegals to be the best element, since from such people we were certain to receive conspiratorial support and readiness for action."[57]

Disguise

Radical populism benefited from the fact that nihilism was so deeply associated with outward appearance. Since, as we have seen, nihilist protest involved the rejection of everyday social conformity, the nihilists often made political statements by means of dress, haircuts, mannerisms, speech, and other outward displays of difference. Years of such display had accustomed Russian society, even including many populists themselves, to conceive of radicalism as something externally visible, and it was not unusual for Russians to assume that those most capable of violence would also adopt the most anti-establishment forms of dress. When asked how he would recognize one of the socialist revolutionaries, a worker at the Winter Palace said, "You can recognize them right away. I dare say it's easy to recognize a person ready to attack with a knife."[58] This same worker was in fact speaking to Stepan Khalturin, who was disguised as a palace carpenter and busy preparing the dynamite that would soon demolish a section of the palace.

One reason the populists began to shed their distinctive "nihilist" garb when they returned to the city is the simple fact that such clothing made them more easily subject to arrest. While no law against dressing as a nihilist was ever promulgated, the policy of harassment against "nihilist types" was obvious. Nihilist garb even led to a kind of clothing-based police profiling. Lion, for example, was arrested as he "walked peacefully down some street, dressed in a simple summer shirt with high boots and without a haircut, in general looking rather nihilist."[59] Aleksandr Bogoliubov (Emelianov) was publicly whipped, lost his sanity, and eventually met his death in prison as a result of being arrested and incarcerated for taking part in the Kazan Square demonstration, although in fact he may never have participated but simply looked the part of a demonstrator because he was wearing plaid and a broad-brimmed hat.[60] An anonymous writer reported about the police at the Kazan Square demonstration that "they grabbed and beat everyone who outwardly looked like participants; the plaid of the male students and the modest outfits of female students served as sufficient evidence, so that a more bourgeois outfit, like a veil and a woman's hat could practically serve as a guarantee against arrest."[61] Since the populist underground was not located literally under the ground (at least most of the time), a foremost method of concealment was disguise, and for the members of Land and Freedom disguise meant blending in and looking ordinary. Where nihilist radicals had typically dressed as countercultural intellectuals in the 1860s, and as peasants and workers when they went out to the people in the early 1870s, by the late 1870s many of them had begun to dress with the express intent of fitting in with high-toned urban society.

As urban historians and sociologists have often pointed out, the modern metropolis is an ideal environment for the use of disguise. Lyn Lofland described the city as "a world of strangers, a world populated by persons who are personally unknown to one another."[62] This point may seem obvious, since it describes an extremely familiar aspect of the modern urban condition, but in historical terms being surrounded by absolute strangers is relatively new. The modern metropolis required a new skill set involving the ability to sum up people quickly through visual guesswork. In the city, people need to "know a great deal about one another by simply looking."[63] In this context, city dwellers seek to minimize social involvement in order to maximize social order, maintaining their "public privacy" by not butting into other peoples' business. They are "required to strike a balance between involvement, indifference and cooperation with one another."[64] Ignoring other people's affairs is one of the necessary preconditions of life in a large city. This built-in feature of urban life helps explain why although the Russian state sought to enlist the urban public in its attempts to counter radical populism, its efforts were largely a failure. Even the conservative novelist Dostoevsky and publisher Aleksandr Suvorin, in an oft-cited conversation, admitted to one another that neither would stand in the way of a terrorist attack.[65] Neither Dostoevsky nor Suvorin had any sympathy for left-wing populism; more likely they were expressing a version of Lofland's urban "social contract."[66] The fact that others knew how to mind only their own affairs allowed urban populists more easily to hide within the labyrinthine complexity of dense, busy, and impersonal metropolitan space.

In a related point, a modern urban environment is a space where it is not only possible to play multiple roles, "putting on different faces" to suit the situation at hand—it is even necessary at times to do so because of the anonymity of social interaction. This "role playing" may be extreme, as in the case of a man who returns home to his family after visiting a prostitute, or quite ordinary in the way that one displays a different attitude to different levels of acquaintances. Compared to the early modern city, in which European urbanites lived in socially mixed spaces where distinctions were maintained by clothing, bearing, and activity, in the later industrial metropolis, separation by region increased while sartorial separation diminished.[67] Where did reform-era St. Petersburg, both a pre-industrial court capital and a large urban center, fall within this schema? One could argue that St. Petersburg blended together aspects of both early modern and industrial social presentation. In order to form the underground, radical populists drew on elements of both.

The trend among radical populists, in particular the more politically active among them, was to blend in with the urban elite as seamlessly as possible. Mikhailov seems to have understood this imperative earlier than most. Once he began to direct Land and Freedom, he dropped "dressing like a genuine 'nihilist'" and began to dress "quite properly, accurately judging it better to spend several dozen [*neskol'ko desiatkov*] rubles on his clothing than to subject himself to unnecessary danger."[68] According to Tikhomirov, "when necessary, [Mikhailov] tried to produce and did produce an impression of a 'cultivated' man, committing suitable facts and phrases to memory."[69] In this way, industrial-era urban anonymity could serve as an effective mask. "These days," remarks a member of the Haymarket crowd in Dostoevsky's *Crime and Punishment*, "you can't figure out who's well-born and who isn't."[70] Problems with "reading the crowd" served the underground well because they made it difficult to differentiate an armed revolutionary from an ordinary citizen.

Mikhailov also began to persuade his comrades to dress conventionally and found them the money for new clothes, yet despite the fact that dressing unobtrusively was an obvious necessity for any underground organization, many were so committed to the nihilist image that they found the change difficult to accept. As mentioned earlier, Deich at first maintained cold relations with Plekhanov because he did not dress as a nihilist. The fact that Plekhanov dressed in a conventional way and seemed like a "well brought up young man" made him appear suspect to some of the other populists of his group, insufficiently prepared to fight for the cause.[71] It was difficult to give up the outward signs of the countercultural identity, even when it put underground radicals at a disadvantage. But eventually, the populist underground learned to drop the countercultural pretense almost entirely. As the revolutionaries became more aggressive, noted Aksel'rod, "even [their] external appearance was transformed: instead of the former dirty propagandist in a peasant blouse and high boots—before us stands a gentleman, quite properly dressed." At the same time, it should be noted, hidden beneath his proper attire, "from his belt hangs a dagger, and there's a revolver in his pocket."[72] By 1879, almost all the revolutionaries sought to blend in with ordinary urban society, even as they became outlaws within it. With weapons at the ready beneath their clothes, they rejected gruff nihilist manners: "judging by their dress, their gestures, their restrained speech . . . the stereotypical dissoluteness and edginess which people were accustomed to call 'nihilism' was no longer evident."[73]

At times, of course, especially when in danger of being recognized, disguises went even further. Beards were shaved, hair was dyed, uniforms were worn. As with the fixing of identity in the passport system, Russia's continued attachment to the outward trappings of personal identity through the use of clothing that clearly demarcated one's station and profession actually served members of the underground well by allowing them to appear as something completely different from what was expected. Even as late as the reform era, as Western European dress tended more and more toward a kind of undifferentiated bourgeois standard, in Russia it was still common to dress according to rank and *soslovie*, and the use of clothing as a necessary symbol of outward status was only just beginning to break down in this period.[74] The continued use of uniforms in Russia for rank and occupation sometimes enabled the radicals to cloak themselves in one or another familiar and unthreatening disguise. Once it became necessary to live "off the grid," dressing according to a certain stock "type" helped make it possible for radicals to go unnoticed. In the Russian urban sphere, at least relative to such cities as Paris and London, you were what you seemed to be. Georgii and Rosa Plekhanov, for example, using borrowed passports, passed themselves off as "provincial gentry, having come to the capital to consult with doctors."[75] Those like Plekhanova, who were not engaged in the more dangerous sorts of activity, still maintained the "look of a nihilist," but when she needed a disguise she purchased an "elegant outfit" and arranged her short hair in a red braid.[76] Kravchinskii, who had at times dressed like a peasant, now began to enjoy playing the role of a grand baron.[77] Anna Pribyleva-Korba recalled that Barannikov dressed like a strolling dandy, and Morozov, convinced of the usefulness of blending in, "with pleasure" agreed to a transformation of his wardrobe. To his amusement, he "started to look more like the attaché of a French ambassador than a Russian revolutionary."[78] He and others went into the streets "wearing top hats so they would take us as state officials."[79]

Conspiratorial Apartments

The use of disguises, false passports, false names, etc. was still not the most basic building block of the populist underground. The most indispensable component for maintaining independence in the face of an increasingly desperate manhunt was the creation of a secure space in which to live, meet, plan, and conduct operations. What the populists learned about concealing their views through the alteration of personal appearance, they also applied to the space in which they lived and operated. They constructed an unseen world within the world by establishing a network of disguised apartments throughout the city. This chain of "conspiratorial apartments" was the terra firma of the underground. Resting on the pose of everyday normalcy, the conspiratorial apartment provided a safe base of operations without which the populists could never have managed to portray themselves as a formidable opponent of autocratic power. Not all revolutionaries lived in conspiratorial apartments. Some lived in the homes of people sympathetic to the cause. Others boarded with unsuspecting landlords, lived in hotel rooms, or flopped somewhere in the back offices of certain businesses. But in order to meet, to publish documents, to fashion weapons, to store suspicious materials, and to live undetected with maximum freedom, the populists had to maintain a substantial square footage of concealed physical space. The network of conspiratorial apartments provided the subversive heterotopia of the underground with a sort of invisible encampment "behind enemy lines."

It allowed underground life to exist side by side with the rest of Russian society and yet to remain entirely distinct and undetected.

Sergei Kravchinskii's vivid description of the conspiratorial apartment in his *Underground Russia* can serve as an overview of its various functions. Aware of the location of one of these apartments, before entering Kravchinskii looks for a woman's umbrella placed in a certain window to signal that all is safe within. The umbrella noted, he is not satisfied, however, by its presence since the police have by now learned about the underground's use of such signals, and often after a raid return all items to their original places in order to lie in wait for visitors. Without appearing to stop, Kravchinskii continues to a backup signal located in a latrine at some distance from the apartment, a signal point his fellow populists refer to as "the information bureau." Here another pre-arranged signal indicates that the coast is clear. After a few more twists and turns to avoid random police spies on the street, he enters the apartment. Having followed the proper precautions, inside he is delighted to find "the kind of little feast the 'nihilists' allowed themselves from time to time as a respite from the nervous tension they constantly lived with." He goes on:

> The group was in excellent spirits and greeted me in the friendliest way, even though I had broken my "quarantine." I always loved these "feasts," happier and more animated than you can imagine. Everyone gathered here was an illegal. . . . They all had daggers and loaded revolvers at their waists and were ready, in case of a sudden attack, to defend themselves to their last drop of blood. . . . But, accustomed to constantly living under the sword of Damocles, after a while they stopped thinking about the danger. And maybe it was the danger itself that lent their merriment such a reckless and dashing character. Everywhere was heard laughter, loud conversations and jokes.[80]

Kravchinskii's description of this conspiratorial apartment captures its dual aspect: the need for extreme secrecy as well as the feeling of relative safety within.

A few conspiratorial residences were located on the city outskirts, which seemed as though they might have the advantage of distance from the watchful eyes of the police, but ultimately it was the urban apartment within the city center that became the go-to choice as a living and meeting place. Part of the preference for a central location, in spite of its proximity to the ever-expanding Third Section forces, involves the character of St. Petersburg itself. In the second half of the nineteenth century, St. Petersburg began its shift toward modern metropolis, not only in terms of population growth and densification but also through the introduction of new conveniences. Old dirt streets began to be paved, sidewalks were added, street lighting appeared in many neighborhoods, and the first horse-drawn public transportation system was created. Building at this time was dominated by the *dokhodnyi dom*, or rental apartment building, and the urban architecture of the middle of the nineteenth century was shifting away from "the majestic ensemble to the functional single-type complex."[81] As private capital-funded construction took over from earlier state-funded urban construction during the second half of the nineteenth century, the city began to acquire something of a new character: "Short wooden homes were gradually replaced by multi-story stone buildings. In place of single family homes appeared homes meant for a mass population. ... The Petersburg, Rozhdestvenskaia and Liteinaia regions of St. Petersburg took on the form and property of the living quarters of a large city."[82] By the middle of the 1870s, the vast majority of the city's inhabitants lived in apartments rather than free-standing homes.[83]

Wealth and number of inhabitants varied from neighborhood to neighborhood, but as in many European cities of the nineteenth century, the most typical pattern of variation in St. Petersburg was not horizontal division by neighborhood and region but vertical division by stories in buildings. The poor tended to be packed into the basement and upper floors, while the wealthy lived in apartments on the first floor and *bel étage*. James Bater's study of the St. Petersburg street directory revealed an unusual amount of intra-neighborhood diversity throughout the city. Even streets in the most elite neighborhoods "housed a contingent of some size from the lower orders." Ultimately Bater concluded that neighborhoods during the reform-era did not reflect the "substantial segregation based on socioeconomic factors" that would arise by the 1890s.[84] In Bater's words, at least in the early stages of industrialization, "the admixture of heterogeneity increased," and as a result, "the urban poor ... were literally everywhere."[85] Under these circumstances, "the topographical contrast between wealth and poverty was flattened out to a considerable degree, and it was easier for people of diverse backgrounds to occupy homes in close proximity to one another."[86]

In addition to diversity by neighborhood, St. Petersburg was characterized by what Daniel Brower dubbed the "fugitive populations" of nineteenth-century Russian cities, meaning large segments of the population capable of eluding official surveillance and control. In Brower's words, "the superficial appearance of compliance hid an extraordinary degree of disarray and disregard for both legal norms and state-imposed regulations."[87] Given both St. Petersburg's spatial diversity and underlying levels of disorder, it was possible for radicals to search out apartments in a wide variety of different neighborhoods and easily blend in. Some conspiratorial apartments were located in working class districts on the outskirts, some in the fashionable areas close to the center, and others were located where inexpensive housing was available. Together these apartments constituted a network of hidden spaces that formed a populist realm of underground autonomy. The map of conspiratorial apartments (below) suggests the populists favored both a congregation of apartments toward the center and a willingness to live in any centrally located district. To highlight the contrast, the locations of open, communal, as opposed to conspiratorial, apartments shows a very different geography that favored locations in inexpensive regions outside the city center, particularly around factory districts and within reach of educational institutions. The underground of Land and Freedom, then, was both everywhere and nowhere. It resembled a diffused, invisible village hidden within the available interstices of a large metropolis.

The evolution of the conspiratorial apartment took place gradually. It began with communes that maintained a low profile with respect to the police but were widely known and celebrated among young people. Such communes, as we have seen, were intended in part to project an image and serve as a model for others to follow, hence they were not particularly

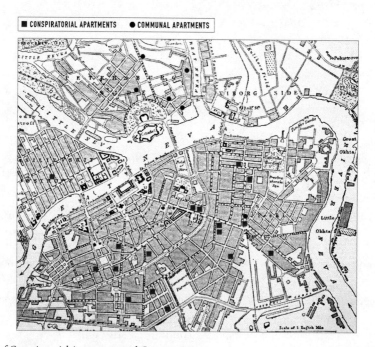

Map of Conspiratorial Apartments and Communes

carefully hidden. In the early 1870s the Chaikovtsy set up a few more carefully concealed apartments where members lived clandestinely in worker
regions. By the winter of 1873/1874 some of these apartments were used to
train students in useful trades in preparation for work in the village.[88] Many
of the same apartments would later become what Popov referred to as an
"information center" (*spravochnyi punkt*) for populists trying to find safe
lodgings in the city as they returned from the countryside.[89] Such locations
increasingly, as a result of arrests, needed to remain unknown to anyone
outside of populist circles. Like the blunt instrument of the passport system
that could be used as a weapon by the very people it was trying to regulate,
urban policing had been created as a tool to serve a purpose that did not
include detection of private residences. As populist attacks expanded, the
police added more and more patrols to public spaces like busy streets and
railroad stations.[90] It took the heavy machinery of state bureaucracy years
before it began to focus primary attention on the private residences that kept
the populists safe in the city.

Still, in the face of ever-expanding police pressure, how were the populists'
"safe houses" to remain hidden? First and foremost, they had to be unassuming. The appearance of quotidian normalcy was not limited to clothing
but also included shelter. As Tikhomirov explained, the concealed apartment that began to evolve for purposes of underground activism needed to
exhibit "an average environment, in no way distinct, living peacefully but
not shut off from the world so that sometimes there were guests, while from
time to time it was imperative to find a reason to let the caretakers in so they
could see that the apartment was in proper order and contained nothing
suspicious."[91] "The fundamental rule," according to Kravchinskii, "was as
much as possible not to hide, but on the contrary, to show the whole apartment as often as possible."[92] The best way to establish a sense of normalcy
was to give the appearance the apartment was rented by a husband and wife,
the family apartment being the most common and the least suspicious.[93]

The single most important of all the conspiratorial apartments, that on
Sapernyi Lane which housed the main printing press, makes an excellent
prototype. It was located on a small street in a quiet middle-class neighborhood. To Tikhomirov this was an ideal location: "rich people do not look
here for spacious halls; very poor families go elsewhere in the city in search
of small premises. But the spouse of some sort of middling official with a
salary of 1,000 rubles willingly would say: 'It's beautiful and quiet here, close
to the stores on Nevskii and Liteinyi; a street that in spite of its four-storey
homes is well lit and inexpensive.'"[94] When he ventured onto the street,
Bukh, the ostensible head of household, called himself "Mr. Lysenko" and

wore "a nice fur coat and gold pince-nez so comfortably situated on the nose that the caretaker would take off his hat at a distance to offer a respectful bow."[95] Maria Krylova played the role of his respectable wife, and yet another printer, Maria Griaznova, pretended to be their working-class cook.

Inside the apartment the rooms were set up to reflect a presumption of normalcy: "Entering through the front hall, the visitor would first notice a small room decorated with a large portrait of the tsar, beneath the portrait a sofa, a table surrounded by half a dozen chairs, and a large carpet—in a word the typical décor of a Russian family."[96] In addition, the apartment had thick walls that prevented the noise of the printing press from being heard on the street, large windows that enabled a good view of the surrounding streets, and a popular university professor for a neighbor who had students coming and going from his home, which offered a sort of social camouflage. Moreover, the apartment's dual exits, a feature of many more upscale Petersburg apartments (which possessed a main entrance and a service entrance) enabled a quick escape if necessary. Because the Sapernyi Lane apartment performed an important and difficult-to-conceal function, the populists went to great lengths to furnish it with everything from good china and comfortable furniture to wall clocks and a samovar.[97] The fictitious couple who ran the press also maintained friendly relations with their caretakers and tipped them well.[98]

State officials were not unaware of the importance of the conspiratorial apartment. The running meeting of ranking ministers originally convened to deal with the problem of radicalism after the Zasulich Affair stated that "stricter political control over the constantly increasing number of furnished apartments in Saint Petersburg" was necessary because "unreliable elements ... without passports live in them, and the police lack the legal sanction to enter the premises."[99] Behind events as usual, however, some state officials focused on open communes rather than disguised apartments. Even though all the revolutionaries now engaged in political violence had long since passed beyond communal living, one official proposed the eradication of "so-called communes where young men and women gather and live together in common," suggesting that such "dens of iniquity" be abolished and that all landlords tolerating them receive punishment.[100] At least some police officials were savvy enough to implement measures that fined any homeowners or landlords who rented out rooms to people without passports.[101] This approach did not, of course, have a great effect on an organization well equipped with false passports.

Ranking ministers also sought to enlist both landlords and caretakers in keeping a watch on their tenants as a patriotic service to the tsar.

One retired professor, alarmed by the rising tide of political violence, argued that landlords should act as police assistants, "as the closest and most natural observers, obligated to know everything undertaken within the bounds of their property."[102] For their part, caretakers were obvious choices for "eyes on the street" and had long been connected to the police as part of a chain of surveillance, but their allegiances varied widely, and they were as easily fooled as anyone by the populists' careful cultivation of a blandly ordinary façade. In 1879 the police added more caretakers to buildings and put some of them on the payroll with instructions to keep a close watch on those inside, an expensive measure that proved to have little benefit.[103]

The form and use of the conspiratorial apartment grew more intricate and effective over time. Conspiratorial apartments were most commonly used as domiciles for illegals, but they could also serve as meeting places for the core members of the organization, as storehouses for stockpiles of weapons and explosives, and even sometimes as depositories for ready-to-use disguises. Those apartments that were "strictly conspiratorial" would be carefully hidden and known to only a few members of the organization. In order to disguise these apartments, as Plekhanov put it, "the layout of the courtyard, the position of the entrance—all was taken into consideration."[104] Sometimes a sign would be hung in front to make it appear to be some sort of business.[105] In the famous case of the cheese shop involved in the assassination of Alexander II, the populists ran an actual business as a cover for tunneling under the street. Signals to show it was safe to enter conspiratorial apartments included open or closed windows and any previously agreed-upon object visible in the window, like a flowerpot or the umbrella described by Kravchinskii. A variety of such signs could be used in elaborate ways as methods of communication to inform members of the underground whether the apartment was unsafe, whether a meeting was taking place, or whether a raid had already happened.

As the underground developed, the uses of apartments multiplied. Sometimes Plekhanov would drop into one apartment, change into one of the worker's suits he kept there, and head off in proper attire to the factory or a meeting with workers.[106] By 1880 three different conspiratorial apartments were used to produce explosives.[107] Shiraev, a chemist assigned the task of producing sufficient amounts of dynamite, used his friendship with a student to get some free lab time at the university to carry out work for which the apartment was insufficient, but for the most part he was able to buy most of his materials at a store in St. Petersburg and to do his own work in the "innocuous" apartment itself.[108] In Shiraev's hidden homegrown laboratory, with the help of a few others he managed to produce, according to one source, ninety-six kilograms of high quality dynamite.[109]

Street Smarts

The architectural historian Boris Kirikov points out that as a result of intensive building in St. Petersburg, by the middle of the nineteenth century "the urban landscape lost its former openness and transparency. The many interconnections visible beyond the streets disappeared ... [and] an 'interiorization' took place that rendered urban space more cramped and closed off."[110] Similar processes were taking place throughout Europe in the nineteenth century as the pace of urbanization heated up. The increasing density and complexity of urban space made cities, in Richard Sennett's phrase, less "legible" than they had been before because they had grown so "quickly, enormously and messily."[111] Though urban historians have bemoaned this increased density for its role in rendering cities congested and unhealthy, for the purposes of the underground it proved as useful as the urban depersonalization described above. In an increasingly labyrinthine environment, knowing the city well and being able to navigate its contours with ease was an essential skill for those wishing to remain unseen.

Mikhailov insisted that every member of Land and Freedom learn techniques of urban orientation. His own ability to negotiate a city full of police agents was the stuff of legend. Tikhomirov celebrated Mikhailov's special genius for navigating urban space: "He saw everything on the street in a moment, from hundreds of faces he distinguished friends or 'the suspicious' and he could arrange it so that he himself was difficult to notice. For this he always had in his mind a store of previously noted shops, passable courtyards, and stairways with exits onto other streets. ... In cities he knew well like Moscow and Petersburg, he was literally uncatchable, like a beast in the forest. He could always disappear somewhere as though he'd slipped into the earth."[112] Members of the populist underground later offered a sample of Mikhailov's special talent:

> [Mikhailov] developed in himself the ability with one glance to distinguish a familiar face in a large crowd. He knew Petersburg like the fish knows its pond. He had created an enormous list of passageways through courtyards and homes (300 items) and knew it all by heart. ... One person, saved from arrest by A. D. [Mikhailov], told us how it happened: "I had to leave the apartment and soon noticed a stubborn tail following me. I sat down on a horse tram and then got into a carriage. Nothing helped. Finally I managed

to lose him by running through a market and jumping into a wagon on the other side. I lost my follower from view, but couldn't rest when all of a sudden a spy well-known to me got on the wagon . . . and followed me to the apartment from which I'd left. I was miserable, but at that very moment entirely unexpectedly I saw A. D. walking along the street. I hopped off the wagon and ran to catch up. I told him I was being followed and Mikhailov told me, without turning his head, to walk forward quickly. . . . He came up again and said 'No. 37, go in the yard, through the yard onto the Fontanka, No. 50, again go in the yard, go through and I'll catch up to you.'"[113]

After several twists and turns through both unfamiliar courtyards, he found Mikhailov already waiting for him on the other side. The tail was gone.

Mikhailov's legend as almost supernaturally evasive grew to greater proportions when he was temporarily arrested on October 31, 1878.[114] While being led to prison he freed himself from handcuffs, hit one of his captors over the head with them, escaped, lost himself in a crowd, jumped over a fence into a mud puddle, evaded the guards who tried to recapture him, and then with the help of a sympathetic student managed to escape. He remained free for the next two years.[115] Before he was finally apprehended, many members of Land and Freedom considered him too elusive to ever be caught, and his eventual capture seems to have been the result of excess confidence in his own ability to remain free.[116]

In reality, Mikhailov recognized that remaining underground was a game of numbers, that sooner or later every individual conspirator would be caught, so he did everything he could to increase the odds of evasion. The most important point was to develop an extensive mental map of the city. In his history of the New York underworld of the nineteenth century, Luc Sante points out that, as opposed to ordinary citizens, the outcasts of society (beggars, orphans, prostitutes, thieves) worked from a very different mental map of New York, a map that was "wrapped around hiding places and clandestine access to necessities."[117] One could say a similar thing about the illegals who had to develop their own ways of living in the city and their own distinct mental maps of St. Petersburg. When the police searched Mikhailov's apartment after he was captured, in addition to various weapons they found a store of maps of Russia and St. Petersburg with various routes of transit marked out on them.[118] Plekhanova recalled that Mikhailov "laid out for me the entire topography of Petersburg, indicating the homes with passable gates, and he taught me how to get away from spies when you see them behind your back."[119] Mikhailov sought to ensure that other members of the radical underground possessed something approximating his own skill at evading capture. To that end, since police agents were employed to follow suspected radicals home in order to discover the location of conspiratorial apartments, Mikhailov tested members of the underground by unexpectedly following them on the street in the same way the police would, and he scolded them if they failed to notice him.[120] He even gave impromptu eye exams, insisting that those without excellent eyesight had to buy a pair of glasses.[121]

A certain distinctive feature of Petersburg architecture came to the aid of populists seeking to evade police followers. Raskolnikov, the main character in Dostoevsky's *Crime and Punishment*, slips unnoticed into the apartment building in which he commits murder by shielding himself behind a cart in that transitional space common among St. Petersburg apartment buildings known as the *dvor* (courtyard). Members of the radical populist underground used the *dvor* for similar purposes of concealment. These Petersburg courtyards constitute a particularly significant social space in the city. A courtyard of at least thirty square *sazhen'* (around 1500 square feet) with access onto streets and/or other courtyards was mandated as a compulsory addition to building projects in the St. Petersburg planning regulations of 1857, and they became a characteristic feature of the city's pre-revolutionary apartment buildings.[122] In Soviet times these courtyards were often remembered nostalgically as a sort of hybrid public/private space in which one could feel both comfortably at home and yet able to see and be seen by neighbors and passers-by. As Kirikov suggested, the Petersburg *dvor* "had a distinctive and stubborn particularity . . . as a kind of interior beneath the open sky." It was "the behind the scenes 'inner space' of Petersburg."[123] Not only was the *dvor* a place for neighbors to meet one another, it was also a place where one found "peddlers, knife-sharpeners, organ grinders, street artists, idlers and beggars."[124] Architects of apartment buildings created courtyards in a plethora of different shapes and sizes. Sometimes they were fully enclosed, admitting only one entrance and exit, but in other cases they afforded passage through a second entry point or through the buildings themselves. As such, in their blending of public and private, the "wonderful labyrinths of the genuine Petersburg courtyards" served the underground well by allowing for movement in between public and semi-public space, as well as dual exits and connecting passageways for those who knew their form. All of these features helped ease escape.[125] When Plekhanov wanted to evade a police agent who was following him, he hired a driver to take him to a courtyard with an opening at both ends so that, walking through it, he could vanish from view. "Making use of such precautions," he wrote, "we could successfully undertake our affairs even in the most difficult times."[126]

Members of the underground had to learn these techniques, memorizing the locations of "passageways, courtyards open on both ends, familiar theaters and big crowds."[127]

Theaters and crowds were also useful since open public space was often the safest ground. In one sense, highly public space was safer even than a conspiratorial apartment. No matter how well organized and defended, if discovered the apartment could be put under secret surveillance and raided. With this defect of the conspiratorial apartment in mind, Mikhailov sometimes chose to meet people in particularly crowded places. He used the elegant shopping arcade Passazh, for example, as a place for what were potentially his most dangerous meetings with Kletochnikov, the populist spy inside the Third Section.[128] Other common public meeting places for potentially dangerous interactions included restaurants, taverns, or just a stroll along a busy boulevard. A Moscow group of populists in 1880 met in "cheap taverns, especially where crowds of coach drivers, salesmen, workers and other members of the public usually went."[129] When requested by the state to help eradicate the terrorist menace, some Petersburgers suggested they use public venues to ensnare them. One plan proposed by an unnamed merchant suggested that the police put on the payroll not just caretakers and landlords but also people with positions in a variety of public places, like waiters in restaurants and merchant shopkeepers, who would be in a position to listen in on conversations and report what they overheard.[130] This shopkeeper's suggestion may well have been self-serving, but it also might have been helpful. Little looks less suspicious than a public conversation over tea in a crowded café.

Fellow Travelers

The primary activities of the populists were managed and carried out by the Executive Committee, but concentric circles of assistance also lent great support to the operation as a whole. Outside the inner circle of the Executive Committee were those members of Land and Freedom not considered part of the core leadership but active and devoted participants. Another layer of more peripheral members, some of them students, served essentially as helpers auditioning for more central roles. A further outer layer consisted of those members of society willing to lend a hand but not considered candidates for inclusion. Because of their wealth and social prominence, some of these "fellow travelers" were very useful for Land and Freedom, which turned to them often. Kravchinskii called this group "that huge and diversified circle of friendly people which in Russia surrounds each and all of the conspirators."[131] Kravchinskii's term for them, referring to their willingness to shelter illegals, was "hiders" (*ukryvateli*), but the more common terms were "sympathizers" (*sochuvstvenniki*) and "fellow travelers" (*sputniki*).[132] The latter terms are more appropriate since fellow travelers did more than just harbor fugitives. They helped with funding, hosted meetings in their homes, received mail for those without an address, and even opened bank accounts for them in their own names.[133] All in all, as one populist memoir put it, they "eased the workload of the core and nourished the central organization with new strength."[134]

Part of the social support for the populists resulted from a sort of celebrity adulation they received in some quarters as a result of their reputation as self-sacrificing outlaws fighting for a noble cause. According to Figner, "surrounded by a whole layer of so-called sympathizers, behind whom usually followed people who enjoyed playing the liberal [*poliberalnichat'*] ... we did not feel like a sect isolated from the other parts of society."[135] Morozov believed that by late 1879 The People's Will had managed to attain a kind of heroic status in Russian society: "Everywhere ... especially among the youth, the only thing they talk about is the revolutionary movement getting off the ground and about the constant arrests among the students, and everywhere they are very sympathetic."[136] These statements no doubt exaggerate the adulation that greeted the populists at the height of the terror, but they certainly reflected the views of many. Whatever the level of public approval, as Lion pointed out, the radicals were relatively few in number and therefore considered it "extremely important to have 'sympathizers' and seek support among the influential circles of so-called 'society.'"[137]

Non-radical sympathizers appear over and over again in police reports and populist memoirs, but a few pertinent examples will serve to summarize their contribution to the underground. After the populist Andrei Presniakov escaped from prison in April of 1878, Plekhanova's friends, the elite and well-connected Semenskiis, "did not waver for a minute" to lodge him in disguise at their estate, "staying with him the whole time."[138] Later they thanked Plekhanova for the opportunity "to get acquainted with a person of such excellent, sensitive, delicate character."[139] This same couple would go on to shelter both the failed assassin Leon Mirskii and Mikhailov himself, as well as to contribute money to Land and Freedom. Such people were especially useful to illegals who did not reside in a conspiratorial apartment and "without a specific address, spent the night in turns now at one home, now at another of the many sympathizers."[140] Those like the Semenskiis were not willing to become part of a movement because the stakes of political protest were too high, but it cannot be denied that they supported the politics of underground political murder. Committed revolutionaries often disdained these contributors as "bourgeois." But their actions were not without risk. Semenskii, for example, wound up spending time in the Peter and Paul Fortress, which left him with a severe psychological illness.

Among the better known fellow travelers closely connected to Land and Freedom were the writers Vladimir Zlatovratskii, Gleb Uspenskii, and Nikolai Mikhailovskii, the last of whom wrote for the underground press and even served as the best man at Tikhomirov's wedding (held at the height of terrorist violence). Perhaps the most important of all the fellow travelers was Dr. Orest Weimar, involved in many aspects of the movement. Among other things, he stored weapons and illegal material, helped the populists procure the use of the race horse "Barbarian" for several of their exploits, served as the chief organizer of Kropotkin's escape from prison (literally driving the getaway carriage), and hid Vera Zasulich from the police before she went abroad. He did all of this while pursuing a highly respectable career as a medical doctor and professor. Such elite assistants were particularly useful to the movement because their standing in society created a sort of second shield to protect the populists from the police. Morozov pointed out about Weimar's concealment of Zasulich that it was nearly impossible to find her because she was in Doctor Weimar's apartment, "an enormous home on Nevsky" owned by someone "personally acquainted with the Empress."[141] Weimar was so tied in to the operation that he can almost be considered a part of it, and indeed the police ultimately connected him to an assassination attempt, arrested him, and sent him to prison, where he later died.[142] Other well-connected Petersburg fellow travelers included Aleksandr Ol'khin (a respected attorney), Nikolai Griboedov (an accountant at a governmental bank), the publisher Evgenyi Korsh, the noted feminist Anna Filosofova, the writer Vladimir Zotov, and Sofia Rubinshtein, sister to the great pianist Anton Rubinshtein. Such individuals braved the loss of stature and position by helping their underground friends, and some of them suffered more severe consequences.

Finally, it bears mentioning that students and politicized workers played a dual role as potential recruits and as active sympathizers. As Kravchinskii pointed out, populist organizations were able to replenish their numbers, which were always steadily diminishing as a result of arrests, precisely because the city had thousands of students and workers willing to step in. New recruits became especially easy to find in the late 1870s as Land and Freedom (and later The People's Will) attained greater and greater notoriety.[143] As arrests mounted with the expansion and intensification of police pressure, members remaining at liberty like Perovskaia and Zheliabov spent a great deal of time setting up circles among the students from which to recruit new members.[144] They even established a student circle directly connected to the Executive Committee. Figner was so sure of the importance of these student recruits that she believed "if the entire organization of The People's Will quit its destructive activity, then new volunteers or some sort of new organization would have appeared, which would have taken on itself the mission of killing the Tsar."[145]

Less tangibly, but perhaps no less importantly, the enthusiasm of young people helped sustain the movement. Plekhanova, for example, describes a young worker in the late 1870s, by the name "Marat," who seemed to enjoy the sheer adventure of underground activism: "His eyes burned with boldness and courage. He was always prepared for the most reckless exploits; he pasted proclamations to the wall under the nose of the police, and if they noticed and started to move in his direction, he got away from them with amazing dexterity. He liked to put up posters at night, and afterwards he would come home in rapture, as though after some beloved but dangerous sport."[146] The opportunity to locate and enlist the help of this diverse variety of sympathizers represented yet one more way a large and complex urban space helped sustain the populist underground.

Material Resources

Another absolutely essential pillar of underground operations was funding. To maintain unemployed people in respectable apartments, to purchase weapons, to publish a newspaper, and to carry out "disorganization" required a large amount of money. The amount required has been estimated as high as 10,000 rubles each month, but Mikhailov's records for the first half of 1879 show expenditures of approximately 1,200 rubles per months.[147] For obvious reasons of secrecy, reliable records of income and expenditure have been difficult to come by, though it is at least clear that the members of Land and Freedom considered the maintenance of sufficient funds to be a constant struggle. As Lion put it, "the need for money was chronic."[148] How did Land and Freedom and The People's Will manage to stay afloat? It must be acknowledged that information on their economic resources is sparse and sometimes contradictory, but we do have knowledge of general sources as well as certain specific contributions. To begin with, all the wealth and property of any member was understood (and stipulated in the regulations) to be the wealth and property of the entire organization. Outside funding sources varied widely, but here again the populists benefited from their urban location. Fellow Travelers were a consistent source of small donations, and the populists sometimes approached them for help with specific tasks.[149]

Beyond small donations, Land and Freedom actually managed to bring in some income by selling subscriptions to its publications, even though the publications were created primarily for propaganda purposes. They also profited from selling pictures of "revolutionary martyrs," meaning those who had died or been imprisoned for political activism.[150] The populists even secretly benefited from the proceeds of fund-raising parties like one event given by the Society for Inexpensive Apartments.[151] Another potential source of income was robbery, although the populists were not particularly successful with this method. In an initially successful robbery of the Kherson Treasury, led by Iurkovskii and Frolenko in June of 1879, they stole the enormous sum of 1,579,688 rubles. As the result of a mishap, however, most of the money was quickly recovered by the police. They seem to have managed to hold on to some 10,000 rubles.[152] Another failed robbery took place at the Kishinev Treasury in December of 1880.[153]

Because they failed to generate large sums elsewhere, it seems that the bulk of their funding was donated by the austere and self-sacrificing nobleman Dmitry Lizogub, who had holdings and properties that amounted to something in the neighborhood of 150,000 rubles. Though some accounts suggest Lizogub donated this much to Land and Freedom, it seems that nothing close to this amount made it into their coffers because of the difficulty in liquidating his property, and the fact that at least some of the proceeds were siphoned off by an unscrupulous intermediary. Estimates on how much of Lizogub's estate finally reached Land and Freedom vary widely.[154] Lizogub was arrested and executed in 1879, and most other infusions of capital seem to have come in the form of anonymous donations from wealthy supporters. Certain radicals from well-off families, like the Subbotina sisters, were also able to contribute large sums.[155] Another 23,000 rubles, according to Figner, were donated by the wealthy spouse of the Land and Freedom member Maria Iakimova.[156] And two members of Land and Freedom contracted a fictive marriage in order to bring in a 20,000 ruble dowry.[157] Perhaps because Mikhailov held the purse strings, nobody else ever knew precisely how much cash the organization had available.[158] One particularly interesting source on the subject of funding was Kletochnikov, who was well aware of the importance of capital for the continued viability of the underground struggle. In his post-arrest interrogation Kletochnikov stated that Mikhailov's work involved "primarily the financial operations of the party," and that the party needed approximately 50,000 rubles each year as a result of the fact that "the majority of illegals can scarcely have any side employment [and] live at the expense of the party." In addition, Kletochnikov held that the bulk of the funds came from the provinces (perhaps referring to the sale of Lizogub's estates), while the rest of it "is obtained in Petersburg by means of donations."[159]

Specialists

Another aspect of the discipline imposed on the underground was labor specialization. Various groups and individuals took specific tasks, and each of them remained relatively isolated from one another so that they could devote full attention to their own work while not compromising the work of other members. By accomplishing their separate goals in isolation from one another, they helped make Land and Freedom appear far more powerful than it otherwise would have. It also became more difficult to expose. Among the specialists in the organization were Aaron Zundelevich, a master at smuggling people and materials across the western border. Another specialty was that of Shiraev and Kibal'chich, chemists who produced much of the recently invented dynamite for use in attacks. Kibal'chich, who had a first-rate scientific mind, also invented and built the early hand grenades that were eventually used to assassinate the tsar. Sentenced to death for his part in the assassination, he spent the last weeks of his life working frantically in his prison cell to perfect his early design for a system of rocket propulsion.[160] Other distinct specialists included the staffs of the populist printing presses, which over time amounted to about a dozen individuals. These groups did the tedious work of typesetting and printing, working long hours and rarely leaving the apartments in which they labored to create the newspapers that conferred an aura of legitimacy on the revolutionaries. The printers in turn were isolated from the newspapers' writers and editors like Plekhanov, Tikhomirov, and Morozov. Another specialist role for a time was played by Valerian Osinskii, who, because the members of the underground were isolated from society, used his social connections to become the underground's information conduit. "Valerian served for us as an indefatigable newspaper reporter," wrote Aptekman, "penetrating into everything and taking from it anything useful to the circle. All day Valerian ran throughout Petersburg, travelling all over, inside and out. . . . He returned almost weighed down with news and hurried to share it with us."[161]

With little doubt, the most important of the specialists was Kletochnikov, who remained strictly isolated from the entire organization so as not to alert the staff of the Third Section to his collaboration with the revolutionaries. The insertion of Kletochnikov into the political police force proved a crucial reason for the success of the populists. In Kletochnikov, the police techniques of keeping watch on and control over the urban population were emulated by the radical populists. Kletochnikov infiltrated and then maintained surveillance on the Third Section just as they attempted to keep tabs on possible subversion within society. After his hiring had been engineered by Mikhailov, Kletochnikov entered service for the Third Section on January 25, 1879. He began working as a copyist two months later, at which point his rise in the ranks was rapid since he came across as both unobtrusive and reliable. He won a promotion in October, 1879, passing along part of his salary to The People's Will, and in April of 1880 he won the St. Stanislaus Medal for his services. In January of 1881, shortly before he was discovered and arrested, he received yet another raise.[162] Some of the information Kletochnikov provided, about people under suspicion or upcoming arrests, proved crucial for the maintenance of the underground.[163] Plekhanova referred to him as the populists' "guardian angel."[164] On Kletochnikov's information, for example, members of The People's Will found and murdered a police informant in their midst, and were able to avoid numerous planned searches and arrests.[165] According to Kletochnikov's testimony, he and Mikhailov would meet once a week in Kletochnikov's apartment. At other times they met in arranged public locations like the aforementioned Passazh, the Traktir "Sergeivskii" on Liteinyi Prospekt, the busy Isakova Café/Bakery on Malaia Sadovaia, and the fashionable restaurant "Palkin" on Sadovaia.[166]

Already by the fall of 1879 Kletochnikov had nearly full access to Third Section information. Some historians have held that the unheard of success of The People's Will was due almost exclusively to Kletochnikov, and it is true that he was, as Figner wrote, "entirely invaluable" to the organization.[167] But the notion that his efforts singlehandedly made the movement possible is a large exaggeration. The vast majority of the information he brought to Mikhailov was extraneous, since the Third Section itself remained mostly unaware of the underground's locations and membership and desperately pursued all avenues of information. Kletochnikov, moreover, reported his information orally, so that it could not be traced, and the fact he was able to pass along any useful information at all, amidst all the superfluous material, was mainly the result of his prodigious memory. In reading the notes that were kept from his reports to Mikhailov, it is clear that Kletochnikov brought in key pieces of information, but his information was accompanied by huge amounts of surplus data, which perhaps outnumbered the valuable information forty or fifty to one.[168] It is more accurate to see Kletochnikov as one valuable resource among many that helped the underground continue to operate for as long as it did.

* * *

All the functions, personnel, techniques, and tactics described above contributed to the maintenance of a secure underground. That underground in turn enabled the populists to wage a struggle to destabilize the government and win the sympathy of various sectors of Russian society. The underground was a remarkable tool. In the following chapter we will see how it was used to raise the profile of Land and Freedom (and its successor organization, The People's Will) through a series of violent and nonviolent operations that made the populists appear capable of acting against the state almost at will. In the final chapter, however, it will become apparent that, powerful as it was, the weapon of the underground never proved a successful tool for bringing about fundamental political change.

CHAPTER SEVEN

BATTLEGROUND PETERSBURG

The urban guerilla's aim is to attack the state apparatus of control at certain points and put them out of action, to destroy the myth of the system's omni-presence and invulnerability.

Baader-Meinhof Group

The majority of us had a single wish—a bloody fight against state power.

Aleksandr Mikhailov

AS A RESULT OF ALL these interconnected techniques that worked to maintain the autonomy of the underground, the populists managed to carry out a remarkable campaign to "disorganize" autocratic rule and make themselves appear a more powerful force than they were. The year 1878 witnessed four armed conflicts with the police, four assassination attempts against government officials (three of them successful), the founding of the Land and Freedom newspaper, assistance with at least two factory strikes, three attempted jailbreaks (two of them successful), the killing of a police informant, and the robbery of a treasury building. Much the same continued during the first half of the next year, but scattered attacks slowed down in the middle of 1879 when Land and Freedom split. The reformed party known as The People's Will went on to make assassination of the tsar its primary mission. From April 2, 1879, when Aleksandr Solov'ev first shot at and missed the tsar, radical populist attacks began to take on a more spec-tacular character. In November of that year, having tunneled beneath a rail line outside of Moscow, The People's Will blew up a royal train, though again the tsar was spared. In February 1880 the most shocking attack of all was carried out when The People's Will detonated a large store of dynamite in the basement of the Winter Palace itself, producing scores of victims. In all The People's Will carried out six attempts on the life of Alexander II between 1879 and the final, fatal attack of March 1, 1881.[1]

Amidst this litany of violent acts, so effective was the underground's concealment that its members began to develop a sense of impunity. So secure did they feel that they often took the liberty to behave like ordinary residents of the capital, believing that under assumed names and carrying false passports they could freely participate in public life. Mikhailov gave the members of his organization careful instructions to keep a low profile, but even he himself did not always follow these instructions, as would be demonstrated by his unnecessary arrest in November of 1880. Other members routinely ignored his warnings and went out together to restaurants, the theater, the opera, or visits to one another's disguised residences. Several populists, including Tikhomirov, Kibal'chich, and Ivanchin-Pisarev, wrote pseudonymous articles for the legal press. Under assumed names, Kibal'chich was a well-known participant on the staffs of the journals the *Word* (*Slovo*) and the *New Review* (*Novoe Obozrenie*) while Tikhomirov, one of the leaders of The People's Will, wrote for the well-known journals *Notes of the Fatherland,* the *Cause,* and *Russian Wealth* (*Russkoe Bogatstvo*).[2] Sofia Perovskaia surreptitiously sent theater tickets to her friends, which allowed her to meet and chat with them during intermission, even though (having escaped from armed custody a few months earlier) she was heavily sought after by the police.[3]

Far from the ideal revolutionary of Nechaev's "Catechism," enjoined to renounce "family, friends and loved ones," the revolutionaries of The People's Will formed close personal bonds, loved and despised one another, and shared a great deal of pleasant camaraderie. Their assumed names, manufactured passports, and fashionable attire offered them the possibility to live public lives under false identities. Under these circumstances, members of The People's Will did not forget in the heat of battle how to have a good time. At the height of the terror in 1880, a large group gathered together and ran up a bill at a first-rate Petersburg restaurant in order to hold a bountiful wedding celebration for Tikhomirov. The guest list included such high-profile fellow travelers as the publicist Nikolai Mikhailovskii. Similarly, Olga Liubatovich describes a boisterous New Year's Eve party at the home of the writer and sympathizer Gleb Uspenskii, with music, dancing, and singing into the night to the point that the neighbors complained.[4] The party came to a close with a rousing rendition of the Marseillaise.[5] Another New Year's party the year before had even included a tongue-in-cheek séance at which the members of The People's Will tried to raise from the dead the spirit of Nicholas I in order to discover how Alexander II would finally meet his demise.

None of this resembles the miserable, fugitive existence one might expect life in a terrorist underground would impose. Debagorii-Mokrievich recalled in his memoirs that "I started to enjoy this unsettled life. I loved to erase my tracks and feel the particular joy of cleverly succeeding at making a fool of the enemy following me."[6] The representative of the populist underground in Kravchinskii's *Career of a Nihilist* exulted in being part of the underground:

> that mysterious body which had undermined the Tzar's power beneath his very nose, and contrived to hide itself almost under the skirts of his gendarmes and policemen. There they stood, these myrmidons of the Tzar, sword and revolver in their belts, looking at them gravely as they passed by. But Andrey knew they were more likely to arrest half of the inhabitants of the capital, than to think that there was anything suspicious in two such bright and amiable young gentlemen. The sense of the fun of the thing blunted completely the sentiment of actual danger.[7]

This study is not, of course, intended as a narrative history of radical populism. The specific operations carried out by Land and Freedom and The People's Will have been described in detail elsewhere, but to understand how members of the populist underground made use of the city in carrying out their plans, the present chapter will analyze four actions taken by the populists over a five-year period: 1) the liberation of Petr Kropotkin from a prison hospital in 1876; 2) Kravchinskii's murder of Mezentsev in 1878; 3) the bombing of the Winter Palace, carried out by Stepan Khalturin; and 4) the long pursuit and eventual assassination of Alexander II in 1881. In each case a well-orchestrated manipulation of the urban environment enabled the operation successfully to attain its aim.

KROPOTKIN'S ESCAPE (1876)

In the summer of 1876, even before Land and Freedom had fully come into being and before an organized underground had taken shape, populist radicals exhibited their flair for street operations in organizing and successfully executing the liberation of Prince Petr Kropotkin from a prison hospital. The escape was carried out mainly by those "troglodytes" among the former Chaikovtsy who were still at large after the waves of arrests in 1874, and many of the people involved in the incident would go on to play important roles in Land and Freedom. Kropotkin, whose health was failing in prison and who had family connections among high officials, had been transferred to a military hospital in a quiet neighborhood near the Tavricheskii Garden, which made the task of freeing him far easier than it would have been to free him from the prisons and fortresses where political prisoners were usually held. Since Kropotkin was already a well-known figure in Russian society for his family connections, his scientific accomplishments, and his surprising arrest as a radical activist, to free him would serve as a confirmation of the populists' growing strength. The mission required elaborate planning and suffered from an initial failed attempt. As such, it served as a sort of training exercise in the development of underground operations.[8]

The original escape plan devised by Kropotkin himself was not particularly complicated. At a pre-arranged signal, Kropotkin was to run through the gate of the prison hospital, which opened for deliveries at specified times, climb onto a waiting carriage, and speed away. Kropotkin, however, was under constant surveillance with a sentry personally assigned to guard him at all times, and the planners had to take careful precautions and make extensive arrangements in order to bring the prison break to fruition. More than twenty people were involved in the operation, which as mentioned earlier was led by the populists' close associate Dr. Orest Weimar. On Kropotkin's afternoon walk in the prison yard, he was to receive some sort of signal from his team and dart for the open gate, where the carriage would be waiting. On June 29, the day planned for the escape, Kropotkin waited for a signal to run from his captors that never came. The signal he had expected was the release of a red helium balloon, but as it happens his comrades had failed to find a red toy balloon anywhere in the city. They tried to fashion their own helium balloon from gutta-percha and red dye, but it refused to rise a sufficient height above the prison-hospital wall. In the final analysis, theirs was a lucky failure for Kropotkin because they soon discovered that the street had been blocked by a delivery vehicle that would have made the escape impossible.

At this point they took time to regroup and devise a better method of signaling Kropotkin the moment to flee. The second attempt, made on the following day, was successful, and it turned out to be a great demonstration of the populists' resiliency and growing ability to manipulate the urban environment to their advantage. Particularly striking in the details of the second attempt was the way in which the organizers managed to dominate the entire local area in order to stymie prison safeguards and make a clean break. By prior arrangement, every other day for two weeks before the day set for the escape attempt, the carriage that would eventually speed Kropotkin away had driven up to the hospital, containing a male and a female disguised as a wealthy aristocratic couple. The driver was disguised as a coachman in full livery. The female passenger would step out and wait for a short while in order to accustom guards and any other observers to her regular presence. On the day of the escape attempt, the organizers decided to hire every cab they could locate for blocks in every direction so that it would be more difficult for anyone to follow the carriage as it escaped with Kropotkin. In addition, two populist operatives were given the job of distracting the local neighborhood policeman and the guard at the hospital gate. One of them diverted the policeman by playing the role of an ordinary clerk trying to rent a room, while the other pretended to be a drunk passerby waxing enthusiastic about the wonders of the microscope. At the same time another populist sat at the end of the street along which the carriage would escape, eating cherries held inside a hat. Were he to stop eating, it would signal that the road was blocked and the plan would have to be delayed. Yet another walked back and forth with a handkerchief, which he would stuff back into his pocket at the approach of any oncoming vehicle. High up above the prison yard in the upper story of a house, the populists had rented a room to use as a vantage point. With a clear view of the yard below a violinist stood at the window closely observing events as they unfolded. When he could see from watching the various signalers on the street that the coast was clear, he was to begin playing in order to signal the moment of escape.

As the plans developed, Kropotkin learned his own role in the escape attempt from an outside source. A female relative brought him a watch as a gift. As she left, she yelled out to him "Don't forget to check your watch." Once he did, inside the mechanism he discovered a tiny encoded message detailing his role in the escape. On the day of the escape, Weimar's brother, an accomplished violinist, stood in the window of the apartment observing events below him. When the carriage pulled up as usual, the violin began to play as the signal to run, but it suddenly stopped before Kropotkin could manage to approach the gate. A police patrol had passed by the hospital yard. After a pause for the police to move on, at the next favorable moment the violinist launched into a wild mazurka in an attempt to communicate in music to Kropotkin that the best possible time had now arrived. Having understood the signal, Kropotkin approached the gate. Throwing off his hospital robe, he dashed to the waiting carriage with his guards in hot pursuit. "Those watching," reported Kropotkin, "said that the guard was three steps behind me and that the bayonet he thrust forward came within a hair

Kropkin flees the yard. 1933 Akademia version of memoir by Prince Petr Kropotkin. (Kropotkin's drawing)

of touching me."[9] Kropotkin jumped in beside Weimar, who had hired the coach and sat waiting for him dressed in fashionable clothes. The horse harnessed for the escape was a recently retired race horse called "Barbarian," and it galloped off at such a pace that it nearly flipped the carriage at the first turn.

As the carriage sped through the streets, Kropotkin quickly put on a coat and top hat, and by the time the carriage had taken two turns from Suvorovskaia onto Tverskaia Street the prisoner Kropotkin had transformed into a "gentleman" riding placidly through the streets with his friend. As the carriage ambled along Tverskaia, two policemen actually saluted to them. Without any carriages available for hire, the prison guards could not follow them. From Tverskaia the carriage drove to a home on Nevskii Prospekt that had a back exit through a courtyard onto another street. Kropotkin and Weimar entered in the escape vehicle on one side and walked to another carriage waiting on the other side. At yet another location, Kropotkin's friends helped him change clothes once again and shave off his beard. Now confident in his disguise, and well aware that the best hiding place is often the least hidden of all, Kropotkin and the other participants went out to dine at the fashionable restaurant Donon. As the police searched in public places like the railroad station, or in the apartments of known associates of Kropotkin, the hunted fugitive dined in comfort at one of the best restaurants in St. Petersburg. Several days later, after hiding out in country houses in the dacha regions outside the city, Kropotkin left the country. Because the railroad stations in the Russian Empire were all on alert for him, he exited into Sweden across the Gulf of Bothnia from a remote sailing port in Finland. He arrived in England a month later. He was not to return to Russia until the age of seventy-four in 1917.

The success of Kropotkin's jailbreak was as disheartening for the government as it was an inspiration to the populist movement. It demonstrated for the first time that the populist radicals were capable of using intelligence and collective effort to embarrass the state and undermine its authority. The tsar himself took umbrage at the escape of such a noteworthy figure and gave orders that Kropotkin "must be found."[10] Figner recalled that the escape, as well as the fact that none of its participants were found or arrested, aroused "unprecedented animation" among the populists, especially since the task was accomplished without having to sacrifice any victims.[11] It also served as

Kropotkin and Weimar in disguise. 1933 Akademia version of memoir by Prince Petr Kropotkin. (Kropotkin's drawing)

a demonstration of the potential for a new kind of urban activism. The leadership of Weimar and the participation of his brother, although they never counted themselves members of the underground, exemplified the benefits of a dense environment in which possible sympathizers and helpers might collaborate. Because of its success, the freeing of Kropotkin emboldened further underground organization and activism. It also inspired a long succession of similar attempts to free prisoners; these escape attempts seem to have become the chief preoccupation of many populists between the time of Kropotkin's escape in 1876 and Zasulich's acquittal in 1878. A few other such attempts were successful, but most remained stuck in the planning stages or failed in execution. Kropotkin's successful escape also encouraged interest in a variety of new efforts to "disorganize" state power and demoralize the government. In this respect, it gave impetus to the construction of an elaborate and carefully concealed underground, which would help sustain such efforts and enable more of them to take place.

THE MEZENTSEV ASSASSINATION (1878)

In the summer of 1878, with the help of Mikhailov and other members of Land and Freedom, Sergei Kravchinskii set out to murder the head of the Third Section, Nikolai Mezentsev. The planned murder, ostensibly in retaliation for the execution of the populist Ivan Koval'skii, who had shot at and wounded a policeman in the course of a raid on a conspiratorial apartment in Odessa, was inspired by a desire for revenge. At least Kravchinskii presented it that way in the title of his pamphlet "A Death for a Death." But much more than avenging the death of an associate lay behind the attack. The plan was first concocted long before Koval'skii's execution, immediately in the wake of the Zasulich Trial, and its perpetrator had always had in mind its symbolic significance: the message murdering the head of the Third Section would send to the public. Thus, for example, rather than directly assassinate Mezentsev, Kravchinskii had considered challenging him to a duel. According to Kravchinskii's accomplice, Adrian Mikhailov, the original plan was to bring "pairs of revolvers, swords, and sabres [espadronov]" in order to force Mezentsev to participate "with his choice of any of these weapons."[12] Another option Kravchinskii considered was not the mere killing, but also the beheading, of Mezentsev, perhaps as a way to convey a graphic message about removing the "head" of the political police force, or at least as a way to signify that the assassination should be understood as the intentional execution of an enemy.[13]

As with the freeing of Kropotkin, a great deal of planning went into the murder of Mezentsev, even though its actual execution was fairly simple. Mikhailov had a "morning to night" watch placed on Mezentsev's activities, which discovered that he took a regular morning walk with an assistant through the central section of St. Petersburg.[14] The plan took shape that at Theater Square in the center of the city Kravchinskii was to approach Mezentsev, stab him in the abdomen, and jump into a waiting carriage. Were Mezentsev's assistant to attempt to stop Kravchinskii, another populist armed with a pistol would shoot at them. Kravchinskii's friend Morozov felt that to carry out such a plan in the middle of the day on crowded streets in the heart of the capital was a sure fire means of being captured or killed, but Kravchinskii and Mikhailov felt confident their precautions offered a good chance for escape.[15] Assassinating one of the leading figures in the imperial government in a highly public location in broad daylight would also send a strong message about the power and revolutionary potential of Land and Freedom. Kravchinskii attempted and failed to go through with the plan more than once, thwarted by the obvious moral difficulties of bringing oneself to kill in cold blood, but on August 4, 1878, he went through with the attack.

With help from accomplices on side streets signaling the movements of Mezentsev, Kravchinskii strolled toward his target from the opposite direction while pretending to read a newspaper. When he reached Mezentsev, he fatally stabbed him with an Italian stiletto specially designed for bear hunting. Mezentsev's assistant, Makarov, pursued Kravchinskii and hit him over the head with an umbrella, but Kravchinskii's accomplice Aleksandr Barannikov shot at Makarov, giving time for both assailants to flee the scene in a carriage, although Barannikov had to run after the carriage in order to jump on it as it sped away. The carriage, once again pulled by Barbarian, was driven by Adrian Mikhailov, dressed in the garb of an ordinary cab driver. Once in the carriage, as Tikhomirov later described it, "after two or three turns along the streets, they had completely hidden their trail and sank straightaway, like a rock in the water."[16] The dense and animated bustle in the heart of the city proved an excellent environment in which to murder with anonymity. A police analyst later followed Kravchinskii's getaway trail on a map of the city: "they went down Italianskaia and Sadovaia streets, crossed Nevsky, ran along the Imperial Library [Public Library], the Alexander Theatre, onto Theatre Street, and into the Apraksin Market; there they got out of the carriage and continued on foot, but at that point it had become impossible to follow their path precisely."[17] How, after murdering one of the top officials in the country, three assassins were able so quickly to disappear and return to underground invisibility was a puzzle the Third Section desperately hoped to solve. Two weeks before he was killed, when warned about the possibility of a retaliatory attack in response to the Koval'skii execution, Mezentsev had dismissed the danger, saying that "the power of the chief of police is still so great that the person of the chief is untouchable, the mystique of police power is still strong enough that such intentions belong to the realm of fantasy and ladies' gossip rather than reality."[18] If such a mystique had ever existed, it was now one of the casualties of Mezentsev's assassination. Kravchinskii's attack against a defenseless official would never be as easy again.

Not long after the murder, Kravchinskii published his explanatory pamphlet on Land and Freedom's press. "A Death for a Death" sought not only to justify the murder but also to explain why it had taken place. Reflective of the ideological incoherence that began to characterize Russian populism during its violent phase, Kravchinskii blames Russia's well-heeled public for his deed while at the same time trying to appeal to it for support. He defines "the bourgeoisie" as Russia's most significant problem and calls on the state to quit defending property owners, but at the same time he portrays the state itself as the mortal enemy of the radical populists. He presents the populists (whom he refers to here as "socialists") as a power in their own right, and grandly proclaims that they had "sentenced" Mezentsev to death. He threatens the autocracy in saying that, "as long as you continue to support the preservation of such unfettered lawlessness, our secret court, like the sword of Damocles, will eternally hang over your heads, and death will serve as the answer to every ferocious act against us."[19]

The populists had been judging state actions to be cruel and worthy of retribution at least since the early 1860s. What had changed all of a sudden to make violent attacks their new response? A valid answer to that question must emphasize both the social context of an attentive urban public and the sense of empowerment that arose from the underground's capacity to maintain security. Zasulich's acquittal seemed to have shown that society would not condemn violent acts against government officials, and by now the underground had created conditions whereby the populists could carry out such "death sentences" and remain free to carry out more of them when they chose. The turn to political violence, no matter what reasoning was used to justify it, arose not from doctrine but from anger, expediency, and a sense of impunity.

In the wake of the shocking murder, the city went into a military lockdown, and the police were reinforced with Cossack patrols and infantry soldiers. Kravchinskii was convinced he had maintained his anonymity to such a degree that, as he believed, "after the murder there [was] no greater danger than there had been before."[20] Less than a month after Mezentsev's death an anonymous letter was received by the Third Section that relentlessly mocked its ineptitude at locating the perpetrator. The letter is signed "Entirely yours, Sergei," and was either written by Kravchinskii himself, who was still in St. Petersburg at the time, or made to appear as though he had written it. Whoever wrote the letter, it reveals the state of exhilarating power some populists had come to feel as a result of their apparent ability to act without threat of punishment:

> You live in a city under siege! And it's all because of the nihilists and the midwives. Oh, I'd give it to them if only I had the strength and power! Especially that quiet Vera Zasulich who wouldn't hurt a fly! After all, all of this came from her. And just think how insulting. . . . I found out that not only have they found nothing, but they've even lost all hope of finding anything: the scoundrels were so agile and fast that not only could they not catch them, they couldn't even find a trace. They're probably somewhere now leisurely walking around the city or drinking tea with their short-haired lady friends, having a great laugh at the expense of the police, who grasp and grab and come up with nothing but thin air. . . . We think this must be a dirty business; we think someone on the police force is getting paid off. Somewhere out there they're well hidden, they keep horses, they even have a printing press. . . . They printed an announcement that says they have a newspaper, some sort of "Land and Freedom" it seems. They take subscriptions for a year and for half a year, and they do it in places and through people well known to the public. What impudence! The subscription rate is 6 rubles a year, 3 for half a year, and subscribers outside the city are kindly asked to include postage. It's all so direct and clearly expressed! Here the police are doing all they can to unravel the thread, but they just don't care about that. It's not their business! And what are the Cossacks looking for? No, it makes no sense to hold their lances out—just have them stand guard at every building and right away a nihilist or *nigilistka* [female nihilist] will crawl out from under the fence and stab them with their own lances![21]

Unlike "A Death for a Death," with its high-flown prose and ideological murkiness, this letter takes direct, sarcastic, even childish pleasure in the radicals' ability to attack state officials without repercussions. The contrast between the above mocking letter and "A Death for a Death" suggests that at least some populists were engaged in violent political acts not so much because of adherence to principle or a desire for revenge as because they had come to recognize that their ability to attack state officials now carried a much lower risk. One memoirist recalled that the Cossack patrols were finally removed once one of the Cossacks had his horse stolen out from under him while he was accepting a "few beers" from a seemingly friendly passerby.[22] The imposing authority of state power seemed to be ebbing rapidly.

It is tempting to give weight to the letter's taunts and attribute the underground's capacity to elude police capture to what seemed to be the sweeping ineptitude of the authorities. The tsar himself appears to have blamed the escape on the Third Section's incompetence, and he quickly replaced Mezentsev's successor when the latter failed to capture Kravchinskii. Two years later in the wake of the explosion at the Winter Palace, Alexander II approved the eradication of the Third Section as a government office. At times the radical populists managed to accomplish their goals with such apparent ease that it seems the police were incapable of doing their jobs, and a journey through the Third Section archives quickly reveals the large number of wild goose chases the political police went on by comparison to the number of their successful arrests. Police ineptitude existed, of course, as it has at many other times and places, and it will never be possible to decisively separate the strands of poor police work from skillful underground tactics, but we must not confuse inevitable blunders for general incompetence. For one thing, the police were often quite effective. Though they failed to capture Kravchinskii, in the wake of Mezentsev's assassination they arrested Olga Natanson and Oboleshov, two of the leaders of Land and Freedom. In fact they continued to make large numbers of arrests until they finally decimated The People's Will in 1881, a blow from which the radical populists never fully recovered.

Nor should we forget that the majority of populist operations were failures, often because of excellent policing that managed to thwart them. But of course the failures never receive a fraction of the attention shed on unexpected and/or notorious successes. As the populist Nikolai Tiutchev put it: "the long existence of an active revolutionary center is not explained by the disorganization of [the Third Section] . . . but mainly by the extremely strict fulfillment of the rules of conspiracy by every single member of Land and Freedom." It is difficult to disagree with Tiutchev that organization and discipline in the careful application of underground techniques outlined in the last chapter, allowed the populists in this era to keep one step ahead of the police, even if their period of ascendancy only lasted about three years. In fact, in contexts outside the radical populist movement of the late 1870s, the "dreaded" Third Section is often credited as the powerful police force that kept Russian revolutionary aspirations in check. Rather than fault the police and exalt radical populist tactics as essentially superior, it makes more sense to understand the relationship between the two rival organizations as a kind of tactical arms race in which radicals constantly sought new methods to undermine police restrictions while the police simultaneously worked to improve their controls. The rise of Land and Freedom and The People's Will marked a high point in underground superiority as a result of all the innovations described in the last chapter, but it was not a superiority that would last because the police were already catching up.

In certain ways, Mezentsev's "successful" murder marked an even more significant turning point in the populist movement than Zasulich's acquittal. The police were terrified. The new chief of police Seliverstov, writing four days after the killing, reported: "The underground press and a mass of intercepted letters threaten new murders in the near future. . . . Measures taken against anti-governmental agitation have met with no success and produced only unfortunate consequences. The evil grows by the day. The roots of that evil, uneradicated, penetrate deeper and deeper into the midst of the young generation."[23] Frolenko saw the Mezentsev assassination as the key moment when the movement began to shift from ideological persuasion to violent acts to achieve its aims.[24] Aware that violence worked as a means of publicizing their desire to fight, some populists were beginning to believe that a new way to bring down the government had fallen into their laps. They would grow increasingly enamored of these methods in spite of the fact that many important members were arrested as a result of the crackdown that took place in the wake of the Mezentsev assassination. From this point forward, more funds would be channeled to urban terror, hastening the schism between those members of Land and Freedom who wanted to maintain the original peasant-centered propaganda approach and those who favored violent urban insurrection against the state.

BOMBING THE WINTER PALACE (1880)

Before discussing the explosion at the Winter Palace, in this case it is important to point out the paucity of good sources about the event. The three men most involved in the plot—the bomber himself (Stepan Khalturin), Aleksandr Kviatkovskii, and Andrei Zheliabov—were all dead within three years of the bombing. None of them ever wrote about it in any detail. The other episodes described in this chapter are all known from several different sources, many of them from the participants themselves, but most of what we know about the bombing comes from the descriptions of a single writer, Lev Tikhomirov, who only knew what had happened by hearsay, although he claims to have gotten his story from Khalturin himself. Although

Tikhomirov's various descriptions of Khalturin and the bombing he carried out seem plausible, other former members of The People's Will objected to certain aspects of his description, calling the whole of it into question. But by the time they made their objections to Tikhomirov's account, Tikhomirov had already publicly renounced his populist beliefs and become a conservative monarchist. Because Tikhomirov's many published recollections of populist activities only rarely depart from other populist memoirs in terms of concrete detail, and because of his generally respectful (though certainly not approving) view of Khalturin, there is little reason to reject his account of events, even if it must be kept in mind that the story of the bombing has a less solid historical footing than others told here.[25]

The plan to assassinate the tsar by igniting dynamite inside his own palace did not originate with The People's Will. Khalturin, a carpenter and associate of the Chaikovskii Circle since the early 1870s, came up with the basic outline of the plan. Khalturin had been one of the most effective organizers in the workers movement that was just getting underway in the 1870s. He was a leading founder of the Northern Union of Russian Workers in 1879. The union was a large, if temporary, success that marked a turning point in the organization of Russian workers. It gathered hundreds of secret members, and with the help of the populist press it even managed to publish its own journal. Not long after it had begun, however, it was discovered and effectively dissolved by the Third Section (trade unions were forbidden under Russian law). Khalturin escaped arrest but found himself prevented from continuing to organize his fellow workers.

Understandably furious at having his successful organizing activities curtailed by the police, Khalturin wanted revenge. Under different circumstances he might simply have swallowed his anger, but at this moment in Russian history another option presented itself. In the late 1870s it was generally assumed on the left that the attacks of The People's Will were successfully destabilizing the autocracy, and Khalturin decided to throw his lot in with the organization that seemed to be enjoying such success against his enemies. In order to communicate the message that "workers are not fools and can appreciate the reality of the Tsar's false sympathy for the people," he began to pursue the same goal toward which by now many of the populists themselves had begun to strive: regicide.[26] Khalturin here took advantage of his ties within the increasingly interconnected urban environment. Where the populists had been able to make connections with workers and radicalize some of them, now he could easily turn back to them in order to get help avenging the government that had prevented him from organizing other workers. Were his venture to be successful, he would in turn contribute to the rising notoriety of populist terrorism. Moreover, his connections to the populists proved useful in that they enabled him to take advantage of an illegal status by assuming an alias and living under a false passport. Without such a false identity, he would not have been able to organize his fellow workers, nor would he have found a way to get close to the tsar.

Khalturin's possession of a false passport and his employable talent as a skilled craftsman offered him two tactical advantages over his friends among The People's Will. First of all, his clothing and speech made it seem as though he could never be identified as a student or "nihilist." He seemed to be a simple worker and did not appear, according to the nihilist stereotype, to be likely to adopt a false identity. Secondly, because his skill as a cabinetmaker was relatively high, he had sufficient connections among other workers to enable him to gain employment on the palace staff where no member of the intelligentsia would have been accepted. He managed to get into the palace first through a temporary assignment doing carpentry on the tsar's yacht. His varnishing work was of such quality that his first assignment paved the way for him to gain entry to the palace itself on the staff of the maintenance crew. Once Khalturin got access to the palace in September 1879 he began discussions with the Executive Committee of The People's Will to help him formulate the best plan of attack. At first he considered the possibility of murdering the Emperor with an axe, but the populists, at that time involved in various schemes to blow up the tsar's train, convinced him that the use of dynamite had a better chance of success.

From the time Khalturin began work in September until November of 1879, the royal family was living at its summer palace on the Crimean Peninsula, which allowed him easy access in and out of the palace and enabled him to move around remarkably freely within. His familiarity with the palace made it possible for him to devise a plan. His quarters were located in the basement precisely two floors beneath the tsar's dining room. Since the royal dinner schedule was well known and regular, he concluded it might be possible to assassinate the tsar by exploding a large amount of dynamite two floors below as the tsar dined above. The plan risked many lives, both because of those who would be dining with the tsar and because the floor in between held the quarters of the royal guards. Both levels would have to explode and collapse for the plan to be a success. The Executive Committee approved the plan, and one of its members, Kviatkovskii, began to act as Khalturin's go-between. A great deal of dynamite would be required to carry out the plan, so with Kviatkovskii's help Khalturin began to smuggle small amounts into the palace on a regular basis by various means, like placing it in the false bottom of a laundry basket. He would then store the dynamite under his pillow and in a chest near his bed, adding to it as often as possible. In the meanwhile, the technically gifted Kibal'chich worked on producing a glass tube to be used as a slow fuse.

At first the smuggling of small quantities was not particularly difficult, but security tightened when Kviatkovskii was arrested by the police as the result of an accidental discovery during a raid on the populists' underground press.[27] Although Kviatkovskii tried to burn as much material as possible before the police entered his conspiratorial apartment, they discovered among his papers a partially burned map of the interior of the Winter Palace with a red mark placed precisely on the section representing the tsar's dining room. Though unaware precisely what the map meant, the police correctly understood it as evidence of a conspiracy to attack the tsar in the palace itself. Kviatkovskii's arrest took place in November, and immediately police security tightened fiercely. New staff was hired to patrol the palace, and sudden searches were made of all staff and their quarters at surprise moments day and night. One would assume that at this point the police would discover Khalturin's store of dynamite and bring the plot to an end, but they did not discover the dynamite, and although smuggling in more became increasingly difficult, Khalturin managed to continue adding small amounts.

Part of the reason for the failure of the police involves the persona Khalturin adopted. A peasant by birth but by now a seasoned urbanite, Khalturin took on a role based on his false passport that identified him as a peasant from Olonetsk Province. At least to the satisfaction of the other members of the palace staff, he played the part of country bumpkin flawlessly. His fellow workers liked him but took him for a hopeless novice who needed everything about the sophisticated world of the capital and the court explained to him. A policeman was stationed with the workers in the very bunkroom where Khalturin was storing his dynamite, and he himself was so taken by his roommate that he tried to arrange a match between Khalturin and his own daughter. At Christmas of 1879, Khalturin even received a one hundred ruble bonus. It would seem likely that his naïve persona helped him survive the difficult period that ensued after the discovery of Kviatkovskii's map. Although Khalturin, like all other members of the palace staff, was subject to surprise inspections in the middle of the night and was searched every time he entered or left the palace (sometimes carrying dynamite), he still managed to evade detection. It seems to have been unthinkable to the palace guards that this simpleton could be involved in any sort of plot.

At one point when the tsar arrived earlier than expected, Khalturin found himself alone in a room with the man he planned to murder. He had his tools with him and later told Figner that he could easily have hit the Emperor over the head with his work hammer and ended his life at that moment.[28] Yet he could not bring himself to murder his nemesis in cold blood. Even a man who had designated himself the tsar's assassin found the charisma of his imperial station overwhelming. Khalturin even once took a small memento from the tsar as a souvenir.[29] Now the main concern in assassinating the tsar became the question of how much dynamite was necessary to blow up two floors of the palace. Khalturin believed he needed a huge amount, but Zheliabov, who had taken over Kviatkovskii's role as liaison, convinced him to use less in order to speed the process toward finally lighting the fuse as well as to minimize the number of innocent victims the explosion was sure to produce. Khalturin seems to have managed to bring in something on the order of one hundred pounds of dynamite. It was obviously a large amount, and Kibal'chich agreed that it would be sufficient to do the necessary damage, but Khalturin himself believed they needed more, reasoning that this was the only opportunity they would have to strike from within the palace itself. Eventually he accepted the will of Zheliabov and Kibal'chich and was prepared by late January 1880 to go ahead with the bombing. He stationed his dynamite-filled trunk as close as possible to two structural supports in his basement apartment in order to ensure the explosion would bring down the dining room.

At this point a new difficulty emerged that involved the timing of lighting the fuse when the tsar was at dinner but no other workers were with Khalturin in his dormitory. The timing presented obstacles for several days until on the 5th of February at around seven o'clock in the evening Khalturin left the palace and walked to the far end of the palace square. There he reported to Zheliabov that he had lit the fuse. No sooner had he spoken the words than a deafening explosion rang out. Windows shattered to pieces, and the palace immediately lost its gas lighting and went dark against the night sky, at which point small fires began to break out in various places throughout the building. In the dim light it was possible for Khalturin and Zheliabov to make out bodies being dragged outside. In all fifty-six people were wounded and eleven killed. Most of them were guards quartered in the room above Khalturin's, and a few were various palace servants. The actual target of the deadly explosion, however, went unharmed. Not only did the dining room sustain only minor damage, but the tsar had been delayed by another appointment, and neither he nor any of his family members had been present at the time of the explosion. When Khalturin learned of his failure, he was despondent and blamed Zheliabov for having convinced him to proceed with less dynamite than he thought necessary. As far as Khalturin had been concerned, it was worth the sacrifice of five-hundred lives as long as the main task was accomplished.[30]

The explosion at the Winter Palace produced a tremendous impression within Russia and around the world. It further damaged the reputation of the state as a dominating and unchallenged force, and it made The People's Will appear, as Tikhomirov put it, "all-powerful and ubiquitous."[31] The tsar had returned to his palace after many other reported plots, and two near misses, against his life. The Winter Palace seemed to be one of the few sanctuaries he had left against his attackers, and yet it became the scene of the bloodiest attack so far. It was at this point that alarm in government circles reached its zenith. The revolutionary movement seemed ever more capable of assassinating one of Europe's most powerful rulers. It hadn't killed him yet, but it did possess the astonishing capacity to infiltrate his own residence. Where could it not reach? Figner noted that at this point the glory of The People's Will grew to new heights among members of the public, and now it was generally assumed that "nothing was impossible" for its dreaded Executive Committee.[32]

Two days after the explosion, a widely distributed proclamation declared that the killing would not stop until the tsar granted the country a constituent assembly. Khalturin got away without repercussions, an outcome that also seemed to suggest that The People's Will was impervious to prosecution. In the wake of the bombing, the tsar and his ministers, acting in panic, began to make adjustments in the governing structure, and Loris-Melikov was appointed both to direct the changes and to put a more liberal face on the beleaguered government. As we will see, the Loris-Melikov reforms did not go as far as their contemporary reputation suggested, though the restructuring of state institutions was a clear indication that terrorism had the autocracy on its heels. Khalturin died two years later when in 1882 the government of Odessa had him quickly hanged for his part in the assassination of a public prosecutor. By that time the state under Alexander III was executing terrorists quickly by means of summary justice, and when Khalturin was killed under yet another assumed name six days after the murder he had committed, Russia did not even know he had been the perpetrator of the terrible explosion at the Winter Palace two years earlier.

THE ASSASSINATION OF ALEXANDER II (1879–1881)

After a string of assassinations and assassination attempts in 1878, both in the capital and in other provincial cities, by the spring of 1879 the members of Land and Freedom (soon to be re-formed as The People's Will) began to focus the entirety of their attention on the murder of the tsar. Assassination of the figure who both embodied and directed the state seemed to a growing number of them to be the best possible means of transforming Russia for the better, if only in some as yet uncertain way. From the time the populists began to pursue their royal target, most other violent attacks were put aside in order to concentrate all their energies on the difficult task of killing the increasingly well protected Emperor. Attempts would be made in the small city of Aleksandrovsk, as well as in Odessa and at a location along the railway outside of Moscow, but the most numerous and spectacular assassination attempts took place in St. Petersburg. Since possession of an underground space in the city made it possible for the populists to keep their enemies close at hand, St. Petersburg was the easiest place in which to organize and carry out their operations. It was also quite simply a location where the tsar spent a large amount of his time. Four of eight attempts on the life of the tsar took place in St. Petersburg, including the final successful assassination in the heart of the city not far from the palace.

The first assassination attempt was not carried out by members of Land and Freedom, but it was vetted and tacitly approved by them. Aleksandr Solov'ev, a populist who had spent years teaching and spreading propaganda in the village, had grown despondent over the apparent inability to bring about any change in the circumstances of the peasants. He came to the capital in February of 1879 in order to try a bolder measure. Profoundly inspired by Kravchinskii's assassination of Mezentsev the previous summer, which he had heard about while still working with peasants in Saratov Province, Solov'ev hatched a plan to assassinate the tsar. He believed that "the death of the emperor can bring about a change in public life," arguing that it would "clear the air, end the lack of trust in the intelligentsia and gain wide acceptance ... among the people."[33] This view rested on little more than wishful thinking, but it was coming to be accepted by a large number among the members of Land and Freedom as well. By 1879 a majority of party members were succumbing to the mystique of terror, almost as though the murder of a state official was an exercise of political power in and of itself. If so, the assassination of the tsar would be the most powerful "political act" available to them.

Solov'ev consulted with Mikhailov and other members of Land and Freedom, proposing his plan to kill the Emperor and stating that although he would like to receive their assistance, he would go forward with or without their help. Since several party members were already moving toward the idea of regicide while others remained adamantly opposed, Solov'ev's request for help sparked a debate in the party and began to expose a deep fissure in its ideological unity and personal amity. Those who opposed an attempt on the life of the tsar argued that even the consequences of success were highly unpredictable; many accurately predicted that a regicide would set back propaganda efforts in the village. Others had begun to believe that the statement such an attempt would make to the urban public and the peasants was their best chance of inciting rebellion, however unpredictable a form it might take. In the end it was decided that Solov'ev would not receive the public approval of Land and Freedom as a whole but that individual members had the right to support him if they chose to do so. Solov'ev received help tracking the tsar's movements in preparation for an attack, in purchasing the revolver he would use, and in procuring the poison he planned to take in case he was apprehended.[34]

Solov'ev said goodbye to the sympathetic members of Land and Freedom on April 1, the day before his assassination attempt, while Mikhailov moved the illegals out of the city in preparation for the possibility of severe reprisals. The next day Solov'ev met Alexander on his morning stroll on the Palace Square. He took five shots at the tsar from close range, but missed his target. Once he realized he was being fired on, the otherwise dignified Emperor ran in zigzags, fell, and crawled along the ground in order to avoid the bullets and managed to remain unharmed. Though Land and Freedom denied any connection to the assassination attempt, Mikhailov watched the entire event from a distance. Before he was seized by the police, Solov'ev swallowed the poison he had with him, but doctors forced it out of him with the help of an emetic. Under intense questioning and probably torture, he never confessed to the help he had received from the populists. He was executed in late May 1879.

The way Solov'ev formulated his plan to kill the tsar deserves attention because, as Mikhailov later admitted, it arose from the same mood of frustration that had begun to inspire other populists to consider regicide.[35] It was unclear to all the members of Land and Freedom what actual impact a successful assassination might have on the disposition of the peasants. Would they rise in revolt? Would they rally in support of the crown? Would they continue to remain indifferent to a political act in the far-off capital? Nobody knew. But Solov'ev did feel certain, as would later populists in pursuit of the tsar, that by wreaking havoc in government circles a regicide would "push forward the economic crisis," which would encourage peasant dissatisfaction. Inspired by his frustration with the apathy of the peasantry in removing itself from its difficult situation, Solov'ev had come to the conclusion that their further immiseration was the answer. Here was evident, as it would be at other times in the populist movement, a veiled contempt for the peasantry in whose name they waged their revolutionary struggle. The radical populists believed they knew what was in the best interest of the peasants and sometimes found their lack of revolutionary spirit galling.

Solov'ev's assassination attempt and the debate it aroused served to expose the divisions that would eventually split Land and Freedom into two distinct organizations (discussed in the next chapter). Once the split had taken place, the new organization of those populists who were devoted to a violent struggle against the state, now renamed The People's Will, began systematically to hunt down the tsar in order to bring about what they called his "execution." The first three attempts on the tsar's life involved a combination of two modern, industrial innovations: the railroad and dynamite. In the fall of 1879 The People's Will planned three separate attempts to tunnel beneath Russian railway lines in an attempt to blow up the tsar's carriage as he returned home from his summer residence on the Crimean Peninsula. The first attempt was planned for the outskirts of Odessa just after the tsar boarded the railway, and although the tunnel there had been partly completed this attempt had to be given up when it was learned the tsar's plans to travel through Odessa had changed. Another tunnel was built under the tracks at the city of Aleksandrovsk (today Zaporozhie). A group of revolutionaries led by Zheliabov bought a piece of property near the track, ostensibly in order to open a tannery. After a month of miserable digging in the mud below a railway embankment, they had created a tunnel in which their homemade bomb was ready to be discharged. As the royal train passed over on November 18, Zheliabov engaged the detonator, but for reasons that remain unknown, the charge did not explode.

The third attempt to assassinate the tsar on this same railway journey took place on the following day in a small town outside of Moscow. Here the populists had bought a house for 1,000 rubles. Playing the part of a merchant couple, Lev Gartman and Sofia Perovskaia had told their inquisitive neighbors that they would be digging a hole in order to put in an underground ice house. The house was approximately fifty yards from the railroad tracks, so here (with the help of about a dozen hands) they would be obliged to dig a long and elaborate tunnel in order to reach the necessary position directly beneath the tracks. It was an extremely difficult task that involved reinforcing the walls with wooden planks and putting in a ventilator so the tunnelers could breathe as they got further and further from the cellar room in which they began. Illuminated only by flickering candlelight in the low-oxygen mine and crawling along their stomachs in icy mud, they had to remove large amounts of earth while at times dealing with flooding from heavy snowfall and a cave-in that exposed the roof of the mine along an open road between the house and the tracks.[36] The chances of a collapse seemed so great that one of the diggers even brought poison with him in order to commit suicide in the event of a getting trapped.[37] After two months of work, about seventy-five pounds of explosives were laid under the tracks just in time for the arrival of the tsar's train. The populists knew approximately what time the railway entourage was supposed to pass by, but they could only guess in which car their intended victim would be traveling. This time the bomb ignited and a huge explosion rattled the area. It blew the train off the rails and overturned several wagons. As it turned out, however, the populists had chosen the wrong train. The car they blew up was a freight car carrying the goods of the tsar's household, while the tsar had passed by an hour earlier. In spite of their mistake, the railroad explosion in November 1879 enabled The People's Will to proclaim its strength as the state's formidable antagonist. Shortly after the explosion they sent out a proclamation to the amazed public that called for the tsar's death unless he chose to hand over the state to an elected parliament.

At the same time as these bombing attempts were underway, Khalturin was bringing dynamite into the Winter Palace, which was detonated three months later in February 1880. Another abortive attempt was made in Odessa in the spring of 1880, and that summer a huge amount of dynamite in four gutta-percha sacks was attached to the underside of the Kamennyi Bridge that ran over the Ekaterinskii (now Griboedov) Canal in St. Petersburg. The plan was set for August to explode the dynamite as the tsar passed over the bridge in his carriage, but the explosion never took place. One of the main participants claimed to have lost track of the time, though more likely he got cold feet at the last minute.

After these failed attempts, and a pause in operations during the fall and winter, the tsar finally succumbed on March 1, 1881, to a plot that involved months of preparations, new technology, careful background research, and elaborate orchestration.[38] In the plan that finally took the tsar's life, The People's Will used to the fullest extent their arsenal of techniques for capitalizing on the urban environment. First, in order to determine Alexander's movements a team of six operatives carried out a months-long time-motion study of the tsar's customary schedule and regular routes through the city. They constructed a detailed schematic of the hours and locations of his various comings and goings.[39] His most frequently traveled route passed along Malaia Sadovaia Street as he headed toward the Mikhailovskii manege to watch military drills. It was on this small street where the populists plotted the next attack.

In November 1880, two members of The People's Will, Iurii Bogdanovich and Anna Iakimova, carrying false passports and disguised as a young married couple by the name of Kobozev, moved to furnished apartments on Nevskii Prospekt. From there they began the process of renting a business at 56 Malaia Sadovaia and chose a storefront with an attached ground-level apartment in which to open a cheese shop, which they did in December at the rental price of 1,200 rubles per year. They moved in on January 7 and opened the store shortly thereafter. Certain visitors to the shop began to congregate at nightfall in the living quarters next door. These visitors, members of The People's Will, began the work of tunneling under the street. So that the light and noise of their labors could not be seen by people passing by, Bogdanovich and Iakimova boarded up the windows of the apartment on the pretext of making renovations. Building the tunnel first required that they quietly break through the cement wall of the apartment in order to dig down and underneath the street. Once the slow work of stealthily breaking through the wall was complete, they managed relatively quickly to build a tunnel into the middle of the street. At one point, however, they accidentally broke into a wooden sewer main, creating a stench so overpowering it was almost impossible to work in the mine. But braving the misery of the open sewer, they performed repairs to it and eventually managed to dig far enough under the street to plant their explosives.[40]

In this case, perhaps the most important thing the populists had going for them was the remarkable incompetence of the police force aligned against them. While Bogdanovich and Iakimova had been well chosen to look the part of young merchants, apparently they did not play their parts to perfection, and according to trial reports some neighbors felt they were doing their work "just for show."[41] For instance, it had not gone unnoticed by the local shop owners that they were, to borrow the understated words of Franco Venturi, "curiously ignorant about the various kinds of cheese."[42] On top of this, a local policeman noted with suspicion that an inordinate number of visitors were coming and going at various times of night, and a caretaker noted one of them covering his face with his collar. Their suspicions aroused, the district police decided to carry out an inspection on the pretext of a sanitary check. An engineer with a police escort searched the cheese shop and neighboring apartment, asking questions and opening containers. Somehow the inspectors failed to find the piles of barely covered dirt excavated from underneath the street that were gathered in boxes and barrels scattered around the store, underneath the sofa, and heaped up in large piles in the back. Iakimova came home after the surprise inspection to find Bogdanovich, who had been anxiously present throughout the inspection, dancing for joy.

As preparations for the attack went forward, The People's Will was falling apart. Though it appeared to the outside world that The People's Will remained an indomitable force, in reality by 1881 the police were closing in on them and making large numbers of arrests. In November 1880 Mikhailov, the party's vigilant defender and overseer, finally succumbed to a simple police trap that he should have known to avoid. The best explanation for how the "uncatchable" Mikhailov was finally caught lays the blame on his own hubris for believing himself impervious to capture. Perhaps even more damaging than Mikhailov's capture were the actions of two informants, who by the fall of 1880 had been giving information on The People's Will that was leading to arrest after arrest, including that of the valuable Kletochnikov, their eyes and ears in the Third Section, in early February 1881. The police had even discovered a map of the tsar's movements on the back of an envelope in a raided conspiratorial apartment.[43] Once Mikhailov was in prison, Zheliabov stepped in as the new de facto leader of The People's Will. He proved the equal of his predecessor in energy and competence but he was far less vigilant than Mikhailov had been. Only three days before the attack Zheliabov was arrested in the unsecured apartment of Mikhail Trigoni, a provincial member of The People's Will and one of the few members who did not use an alias and carry an illegal passport. Zheliabov's arrest left Sofia Perovskaia in charge, and it was she who made the final decision to go ahead with the assassination attempt on Sunday, March 1. The remaining populists knew they were in a race against time, and they acted accordingly.

Having failed more than once in their attempts to use underground explosives, this time the increasingly desperate members of The People's Will hedged their bets with a plan B as well as a plan C. This final assassination attempt was more elaborate and multi-faceted than any had been before. In case the underground explosives should fail to kill the tsar, they equipped four extra assailants with primitive, nitroglycerine hand grenades that had been invented by Kibal'chich. Two bomb throwers each were to be stationed at four corners of the block in order to converge on the carriage and finish the job. These bombs could only be thrown at close range, so that if the bomb throwers managed to escape being detonated by their own weapons, they were almost certain to be captured. It seems that as the ranks of the Executive Committee were thinned by arrests, the remaining members opted not to use themselves for the suicide mission of actually throwing the bombs. Zheliabov called for volunteers and claimed later to have received large numbers of people eager to play the role of assassin, but Zheliabov's claim seems heavily exaggerated since those chosen were far from seasoned veterans of the party. Young and unproven, those who were to carry the bombs posed a risk of upsetting the careful plans. The appointed list of four bombers was made up of Nikolai Rysakov, a nineteen-year-old student, Ignati Grinevitskii, a more tested twenty-four-year-old studying at the Technological Institute, Ivan Emelianov, another young student, and Timofei Mikhailov, the worker originally designated to throw the first bomb in order to indicate that the death of the tsar had been carried out "by the hand of the people." Should something go wrong with plan B, plan C was to be put into action. If the underground dynamite and the handheld bombs failed, Zheliabov would lie in wait to lunge out and attack the tsar face to face with a dagger and a pistol, the two weapons that served as the symbol of the Executive Committee. By the day of the assassination, however, this failsafe final precaution had been rendered moot by Zheliabov's arrest. No one else stepped forward to take his place.

To ensure they would not become complacent about their task, the Executive Committee never told the bomb throwers about the mine under Malaia Sadovaia. All four bomb throwers were relatively young and inexperienced, and each of them had very different reactions to the event itself. Rysakov, who as it turned out would throw the first bomb, behaved arrogantly at the scene of the crime, but after the bombing he would be slowly beaten into submission by the police until he began to turn in evidence on other members of The People's Will. Mikhailov, after he had received his bomb, thought better of his role in the assassination and chose to return his bomb to the conspiratorial apartment from which it came. Emelianov would never use his bomb, and he would be among the people who helped the tsar onto the sleigh that returned him to the palace to die. Grinevitskii was the oldest and most experienced of the bomb throwers. It was he who most clearly recognized the gravity of the event and wrote his revolutionary testimony a few days before the assassination. "Alexander II has to die," he wrote, "He will die, and we his enemies and murderers, will die with him. ... Fate has assigned to me an early death, and I will not see our victory. ... It is the work of the revolutionaries to burn away the flammable material that has accumulated, to throw a spark into the powder keg and then take all measures to insure that the uprising will end in success."[44] The combination of noble sacrifice and self-aggrandizement evident in Grinevitskii's testament captures something of the spirit of The People's Will in this era. The underground provided them with the invisibility necessary to carry out attacks on state officials, but they still had to find or generate the moral authority to be able to commit murder, not to mention the courage to sacrifice their own lives. It was Grinevitskii who threw the fatal explosive.

On the day after Zheliabov's arrest and the day before the assassination was to be carried out, those members of the Executive Committee who could be rounded up on short notice learned that not only had they lost the primary leader of the operation with the arrest of Zheliabov, but that Kibal'chich had not yet prepared the bombs to be used. They faced a choice between either going ahead with the assassination attempt under less than optimal conditions or waiting for a better opportunity as they continued to face the increasing threat of arrest. It had been conceded by all of them now that the rosy hopes some had harbored for a large revolutionary movement to greet the tsar's death would not soon materialize. All they had left was the desire to finish the mission they had begun nearly two years earlier and a vague hope that something as momentous as a regicide would produce some unknown revolutionary effect. In a state bordering on panic, the remaining members all agreed that the time to act was now or never.[45] Over the following fifteen hours Kibal'chich and other technicians began to construct the bombs at a feverish pace, and although Kibal'chich had tested some prototypes he was far from certain about their efficacy under real conditions.

On the next morning, Sunday, March 1, the tsar conferred with Loris-Melikov and his morganatic wife, Ekaterina Dolgorukaia, as to whether he should leave the palace and brave the possibility of an attack that afternoon. Both of them encouraged him to stay home because of recent rumors about a new assassination attempt, but because the police seemed to be closing in on The People's Will, the tsar felt optimistic enough to venture out. Part of his optimism involved the fact that he had that very morning finally signed Loris-Melikov's plans for increased (though still quite limited) popular participation in governance. Probably more importantly, the arrest of Zheliabov, already known to be one of the leaders of The People's Will, put the Emperor's mind at ease. Having heard about the suspicious cheese shop, Dolgorukaia did at least convince him to avoid Malaia Sadovaia Street. From that point forward plan A, like plan C, was already a dead letter. The assassination would have to rest alone on the hand grenades of plan B.

Snow covered the ground as the tsar headed out to the manege in the early afternoon to watch military drills. Perovskaia had given the bomb throwers their instructions in one of the conspiratorial apartments that morning, still expecting the tsar's carriage to pass along Malaia Sadovaia. The bombers were now told about the mine under the street and instructed to stand in wait on the four corners of the block where the cheese shop was located. Once the bomb under the street had exploded, they were to advance in unison toward the carriage and finish the job if the first explosion had not been successful. But when the tsar avoided Malaia Sadovaia, a new plan had to be put in operation with little time to spare. The tsar would have survived had he not chosen to make a short stop on Bolshaia Italianskaia Street in order to pay a visit to his aunt the Grand Duchess. Now there was no time for the bomb throwers to lose. Perovskaia had earlier instructed them, in case the tsar were to avoid Malaia Sadovaia, to meet on the short block of Mikhailovskaia Street just off Theater Square to receive new instructions. There by the prearranged signal of blowing her nose into her handkerchief, she notified them to regroup with their portable bombs at a location closer to the palace where the tsar was still very likely to pass by. The bombs were delicate and extremely dangerous. Kibal'chich's impressive design was engineered to explode easily on contact with the ground. As the bomb throwers rushed for six or seven blocks through the streets carrying their fragile bombs to their new stations, their movements through the central part of the city carrying strange packages past police guard posts serves as a reminder of the value of urban space as an environment in which suspicious acts often go unnoticed. Perovskaia now lined the throwers along the railing of the Ekaterinskii Canal embankment, while she herself stood on the opposite side of the canal in order to signal the moment for attack.

When the worker Mikhailov handed in his bomb, the young student Rysakov had become the first thrower. Around three o'clock in the afternoon, the tsar's carriage turned onto the street along the canal, and Perovskaia signaled again with her handkerchief that the moment had arrived. Rysakov hurled the first hand grenade under the wheels of the tsar's reinforced carriage, which traveled amidst a cortege of police officials and Cossack guards. The bomb exploded, throwing several escorts and unconnected passers-by to the ground and disabling the carriage. It killed both a Cossack guardsman and a passing delivery boy. Almost immediately the tsar's guards apprehended the bomb thrower, while the tsar himself, unharmed except for a small cut, got out of the carriage against advice and went to inspect the damage. Having looked over his vehicle and the site of the explosion, he expressed his condolences about the guard and the delivery boy, both of whom were lying mortally wounded on the ground. Next he went to examine Rysakov, who was being held against the embankment railing by several policemen, but he did not speak to his assailant. By this time a large crowd had formed around the explosion site near the Emperor.

As Alexander began to return to his carriage along the sidewalk next to the canal, Grinevitskii, who was standing against the canal railing and holding his strange package in his hands, awaited his victim's approach. Once the tsar had reached a distance of about four feet away, Grinevitskii hurled the bomb at his victim's feet. A large explosion rang out amidst the crowd.

As the smoke cleared, writhing bodies were strewn across the sidewalk and the street, and the snowy ground was brown with earth, speckled with bits of clothing, and red with blood. Many among the crowd were wounded and groaning in pain, though only one bystander died as the result of the second attack. Emelianov, still holding onto his bomb, stood to the side and watched. The tsar lay exposed, his outer clothing torn away, his legs blown to bits below the knee, bleeding profusely. Grinevitskii lay next to him, unconscious and dying. The head of the tsar's police guard, Colonel Dvorzhitskii, was injured as well. Close to the tsar, Dvorzhitskii could hear him quietly utter the words "help," and "it's cold, it's cold." Dvorzhitskii arose and managed to help others lift the tsar's body onto a sleigh. Alexander requested they return to the palace "to die there." As the sleigh sped off, it was later reported to have left a trail of blood in the snow all the way back to the tsar's splendid home. Alexander II died at home in the Winter Palace an hour and a half after the explosion.

* * *

It is hard to imagine just how terrifying The People's Will had become in the eyes of the state and the Russian public by this point. A rough analogy to the contemporary United States would suggest that in the space of three years a terrorist organization had managed to kill the director of the FBI, explode a deadly and destructive bomb inside the White House, assassinate the president and maim or kill many others besides. At the time of the assassination, moreover, they appeared to the public to have lost none of their strength and only threatened greater havoc and violence in the future. But for all their spectacular menace, in reality the assassination of Alexander II had now depleted their strength to the point that neither The People's Will in specific, nor radical populism in general, would ever regain the same stature and battle readiness they had maintained between 1878 and 1881. Within weeks Zheliabov, Perovskaia, and Kibal'chich had been executed, and nearly all the other Executive Committee leaders were incarcerated or abroad. Vera Figner, the one exception, had to regroup and attempt to salvage what was left of The People's Will in deep secrecy in Moscow.

CHAPTER EIGHT

THE ARMOR OF OUR INVISIBILITY

Underground Terror and the Illusion of Power

The educated part of the population, although small among us, is found in the center and thus has a strong position. In the same way that a small handful of good, bold archers on the high ground can stop a whole army, so we at the center of the state, shielded by the armor of our invisibility, can bring about a political revolution.

Nikolai Morozov

A S THE URBAN UNDERGROUND REACHED full force and Land and Freedom began to recognize its capacity to disrupt the status quo and create havoc in government circles, its increasing sense of power began to render Russian radical populism unrecognizable from what it had been only a few years earlier. From the middle of 1878, political violence would become the guiding force of radical populism, and as violence took on a momentum of its own, it began to dictate the direction of the movement as a whole. Those populists who remained devoted to the original doctrine that revolution had to arise exclusively from within the peasantry decided to separate from those devoted to violence against the state, and two separate organizations with entirely distinct aims emerged from the split. The faction that favored violent tactics, now newly named The People's Will, remained firmly anchored in the city and began to direct all its efforts toward undermining the autocracy in the belief they would be able to ride a wave of terror all the way to a full-blown revolution. Even though some among the populists were aware that their revolutionary aspirations rested on little more than vague hopes, several factors (the panicked reaction of the state, the uproar and sympathy within Russian society, the international notoriety of the movement) made it difficult to resist the belief that underground activism was, in one way or another, leading toward radical change. The conviction that they had discovered a new form of revolutionary power became the driving force behind the populist movement. This shift in mentality, which gave rise to the most notorious phase of radical populism under The People's Will, is the subject of the present chapter.

SCHISM

Beginning in the mid-1870s, Land and Freedom had continued to consolidate its center of operations more and more firmly in the city of St. Petersburg. At first the plan was to organize in the capital in order "to found a broad and powerful organization and then transfer [its] center of gravity to the village."[1] But such a transfer never materialized, and as urban "disorganization" activities expanded, Land and Freedom gradually began to split into two separate factions. Those who subscribed to the rural-based original principles of populism, many of whom remained in the countryside, came to be called "villagers" (derevenshchiki), while those who supported terror came to be called "urbanites" (gorodniki) or "politicals." Tikhomirov later described the developing schism between the two groups:

> The essence of the emerging difference consisted in the following. Those living among the people as teachers, village scribes, etc, were becoming less revolutionary. The more they lived together and united with the peasants, the less they thought about rebellion and began to consider a legal defense of the interests of the peasant. Those living in Petersburg, on the other hand, were more and more inflamed with revolution and thought more about struggle with the government. When after a long absence, former comrades met, one from the village and one from the city—they found themselves dissatisfied with one another. The "villagers" already had rather strange provincial manners, didn't take an interest in world affairs, and talked about the trivia of peasant life. From the point of view of the urbanites, they had "de-revolutionized." The Petersburger seemed to the "villager" practically a "liberal": he was used to proper attire and spoke about "politics" and was not indignant against "the kulak" or "the barin" but against "the government."

One expected him to start to "call for a constitution." And in the meantime, the urbanite had everything in his hands while the villager complained of inattention, not sending money, not supplying people, books.[2]

While these two separate cultures were emerging, as Shiraev noted, the very act of maintaining the underground and carrying out disorganization efforts created a kind of group unity among the urbanites: "terrorist acts, arranging demonstrations, operating the presses, etc., not only gave the members an opportunity to get to know each other better and draw close to one another, but also isolated them from the others [in the countryside]."[3] Even the term "troglodyte" came to mean something new around this time. Where it had once applied to those living illegally in the city, now it came to refer to those "stuck" in the isolation of the countryside.[4]

Those who tended to trust the power of ideas, and/or were averse to violence, held fast to the principles on which populism had originally been based. Those caught up in the social and political impact of terrorism, who yearned for rapid change, embraced the urban underground and its battle against the state.[5] The creation of the underground, the focus on violence, and the increasing concentration on the cities changed radical populism in such essential ways that Land and Freedom had become too ideologically divided to remain a sustainable organization. To the urbanites, peasant propaganda was painful and laborious, and it had not even amounted to much when the peasants were duped into rebellion in the Chigrin Affair, while the splendid success of underground activism in the cities had made Land and Freedom an entity that even the powerful autocratic state believed it was forced to reckon with. Because the enthusiasm generated by underground terror generated a seemingly unstoppable momentum, the original doctrinal basis of Russian populism still espoused by the villagers, for whom solidarity with the peasantry remained the *sine qua non* of the movement, was not so much refuted by the urban revolutionaries as it was ignored and put off until a later date.

As underground activism intensified, the process of centralization increased. At times the central leadership of Land and Freedom explicitly called upon rural populists to return to the center in order to help with urban efforts. Less directly, funding sources for rural propaganda began to dry up as the urbanites funneled more resources into their own activities. The desire to bolster the urban terror campaign at the expense of rural propaganda helps explain why, as Phillip Pomper noted, "at the moment when they achieved their greatest power as an organized oppositional force, the populists were furthest from their own ideological bases."[6] The two factions might have remained in a steady state of mutual displeasure, but the problem of funding brought the conflict to a head. As the urbanites grew more and more confident in the achievements of their terror campaign, they began to feel entitled to the bulk of the resources. After all, as Tikhomirov pointed out, "these means were acquired by us, the Petersburgers."[7] In the spring of 1879 a subset among the members of Land and Freedom formed a new secret organization within their secret organization called "Freedom or Death." This group espoused the necessity of political violence and would later become core leaders of "The People's Will."[8]

By this point Kviatkovskii, a central member of Freedom or Death, was arguing that the question of funding had become the most serious issue for Land and Freedom because society was getting involved and needed a push forward. As he saw it, the populists were standing at a historical crossroads, and the time had come when "a change of the state apparatus of some sort absolutely must take place, when society, even our society, gets agitated, begins to raise its head a bit."[9] With the stakes high, as Plekhanova noted, "Revolutionary terror, like an insatiable Moloch, requires more and more material, people and money."[10] In response to the shift of funds toward the city, those in the village began to feel isolated and ignored. Aksel'rod later described the growing rift from the "villager" point of view:

> The more and more the Petersburg members of Land and Freedom concentrated on themselves, the less and less concern they had for their comrades in the provinces: all resources and forces went to prison freeings and terrorist acts. ... Every member remaining among the peasants seemed to them to have been taken out of that frantic struggle to which they had given themselves with such enthusiasm. To the populists ... it seemed that the urbanites were getting wrapped up in fireworks, the brilliance of which attracted the youth away from the real business, from the midst of the people who so needed their strength.[11]

By early 1879, only a small fraction of Land and Freedom's funding was now directed toward those rural operations that, according to basic populist principles, justified their existence. One source notes that by the spring of 1879 only about one-seventh of Land and Freedom's available resources were going to pay for those carrying out work in the village.[12]

Tension mounted until in the spring of 1879 it had become clear that the organization as a whole would have to clarify its principles. A general meeting of core members was arranged for the provincial city of Voronezh in June, while shortly before that a core group among the urbanites assembled secretly in the city of Lipetsk to plan their strategy.[13] Once in Voronezh, at a picnic organized to make the populists appear to be urban pleasure seekers out for a country excursion, the two groups began to discover they had too little in common to be able to support the same vision.[14] As Frolenko put it, the members of Land and Freedom eventually realized that argumentation was pointless: "Russia is large and there's enough for everyone to do! Wouldn't it be better to separate in a brotherly fashion and let each follow his own path? Let the populists be active in the villages and the terrorists in the cities." The organizational split that eventually took place wound up a painful and protracted process, however, because according to Morozov, "in spite of the existence of a disparity in principles the feeling of comradery among us was strong."[15] By the fall of 1879 Land and Freedom had split into two distinct new organizations: "The People's Will," led by the urbanites, which continued to carry out a violent revolutionary struggle in the cities, and "The Black Repartition," composed of the villagers who opposed political violence and adhered to established populist doctrine.[16]

THE TURN TO VIOLENCE

In attempting to account for the rapid assumption of violent tactics beginning in 1878, many scholars have relied on one or another version of the notion that bloody actions were written into the "genetic code" of radical populism as a sort of dormant disease that would eventually erupt within the radical body politic. This view usually rests on examples of violent intent, like the "Young Russia" proclamation, with its call for blood, Bakunin's celebration of "creative destruction," or Nechaev's murder of Ivanov. But these incidents were anomalous and condoned by few among the populists. If the populist underground offered impunity for a variety of subversive acts—from publishing illegal proclamations and newspapers to revolutionary propaganda and successful jailbreaks—it was not in and of itself conducive to the adoption of violence. In fact, it is clear that the underground sphere would have remained much more secure had terrorist methods never been used. Large waves of arrests, the expansion of police forces, and harsh legal reprisals virtually always followed on the heels of a violent attack. Although the use of violent methods had long been entertained, especially in southern cities like Kiev and Odessa, the fondness for violence that became habitual in the year 1878 was decidedly new.[17] The vast majority of the radical populists had the kinds of gentle upbringing and elite education that were quite remote from the rougher parts of the world around them. Deich related how, inexperienced with weaponry and playing with a revolver, he accidentally came close to killing one of his comrades, and later a student connected to the populists in southern Russia was killed as the result of an accidental gunshot.[18] Thus it remains a crucial question why the use of violence emerged quickly, and quickly assumed a dominant role.

One common suggestion points to the widespread societal approval for Zasulich's attempt on the life of Trepov. Many have suggested that Zasulich's acquittal, along with the open approval expressed in court for her violent act, decisively transformed the murder of government officials into an accepted political tactic. While the Zasulich Trial played an important role in promoting the potential benefits of violent acts, we must also keep in mind the differences between Zasulich's deed and those later committed by self-avowed terrorists. Having fired on Trepov, Zasulich immediately gave herself up, and her legal defense and acquittal largely relied on the notion that she was acting as the avenger of an innocent victim. Thus Zasulich was celebrated by Russian society as a martyr who seemed to have acted alone in a fit of passion, motivated by a sense of moral outrage, and who welcomed her own punishment. The attacks carried out by Land and Freedom, in stark contrast, were the work of unknown assailants who, instead of throwing themselves on the mercy of the courts, escaped undetected back into the underground in order to carry out future operations. These were not isolated martyrs to justice so much as members of a disciplined organization collectively developing a systematic struggle intended to throw the government into turmoil and thereby precipitate revolution. In this regard, it is worth noting that Zasulich herself repudiated The People's Will's use of "terror" as a political weapon. She understood her own deed as unrelated to the pro-active (rather than reactive) political violence in which they engaged. The influence of Zasulich's assassination attempt was far from inconsequential, but the turn to systematic political violence requires a much more extensive explanation.

The common explanation for the turn to violence given by the populists themselves was that they were engaging in acts of revenge for fallen comrades. In "A Death for a Death" Kravchinskii justified his murder in Old Testament fashion as an act of vengeance for the hanging of Koval'skii two days earlier. Similarly, in his trial testimony of 1880, Kviatkovskii claimed that all populist violence was the result of "self-defense and the protection of party members."[19] While it is true that many hundreds of populists had been imprisoned and exiled, and a few dozen were executed for their part in terrorist activities, the notion that the populists were motivated primarily by vengeance for fallen comrades, though satisfying to their own heroic self-conception, is an inaccurate exaggeration. Kravchinskii's attack, as we have seen, had been planned and rehearsed long before Koval'skii's execution, and all the assassinations and attempted assassinations carried out by the urban populists were planned and exploited for maximum political impact. Most of the murders committed by The People's Will were less acts of revenge than acts of intimidation and political symbolism.

Other factors said to have inspired the turn to violence have included the impact of new technologies of violence. For example, far from unimportant for the rise of populist terrorism was the 1867 invention of dynamite by Alfred Nobel, which made possible many of the attacks that relied on explosives.[20] Interestingly, dynamite was on the whole a less successful method of assassination than handheld weapons in spite of its attraction as a producer of violent spectacle, but it certainly worked as a stimulus to the imaginations of terrorist revolutionaries. Others have proposed that war in the Balkans between 1875 and 1878 gave military experience and a taste for arms to those populists who had been involved, some of whom went on to introduce a fighting spirit to the rest of the group. Tikhomirov argued more generally, based on the 1877–1878 Russo-Turkish War, that the "military mood of the period … stirred up the instinct for battle among the revolutionaries."[21]

A more direct and important inspiration were the violent inclinations of the "rebel" group involved in the Chigrin Affair and other radical populists in southern cities such as Kiev and Odessa. Such populists as Debagorii-Mokrievich, Deich, Osinskii, and the Ivichevich brothers armed themselves as early as 1877 and began to favor the murder of police spies and government officials . They also invented the concept of an "executive committee" that existed to carry out the wishes of the larger organization Though it began as a fiction among the southern populists, "Executive Committee" would later be adopted as the name for the leadership circle of The People's Will, and it would develop a reputation as the main scourge of the Tsarist government. The southern populists certainly exhibited a greater inclination for arms and attacks, but their influence was not particularly persuasive in the north, and it certainly did not account for the adoption of violence as the all-encompassing focus of the revolutionary struggle in St. Petersburg. The southern populists lacked a disciplined organization and a well-protected underground. When Tikhomirov visited from the north, he found them living in "picturesque student disorder with visitors coming and going day and night." Political violence could not be successfully practiced this way, and they were quickly arrested and disbanded. Several of them were executed in 1879.

A more prosaic but probably more significant reason for the turn to violence involves the simple fact that for two decades the great majority of radicals had tried and failed to achieve tangible results using nonviolent forms of activism. The newspaper of The People's Will justified populist violence in these terms. It held that Russian radical populism turned to terror because of: "the complete impossibility of any kind of social activity to benefit the people, the complete impossibility to enjoy any kind of freedom of thought, freedom to live and breathe—all this forces Russian revolutionaries, Russian youth, in their convictions the most humanitarian and humane, to get involved in such a business that in its essence runs against human nature."[22] These frustrations were genuine, and the newfound ability to escape punishment and detection granted by the hidden heterotopia of the underground was such a powerful weapon that it grew difficult for many populists to resist using it. "Given our small forces," Mikhailov was reported to have said, "we have only one alternative: either entirely reject revolutionary activism or join in single combat with the state."[23] Frolenko put a similar point in different terms: "rather than perish from something trivial, better to accomplish some great deed that perhaps would clear the air and chase away the clouds hanging over everyone's head."[24]

I would argue that the turn to violence, the adoption of what would soon be called "terrorism," resulted more than anything else from a confusion between the populists' perceived and actual power. In other words, as they witnessed the remarkable effect they were having by frightening state officials and exercising what seemed to be potentially revolutionary strength, a core group among Land and Freedom members came to believe that by engaging in terrorist acts they were actually carrying out a serious revolutionary struggle. "A small group of people," as Deich would later point out, "managed to raise such a great commotion that it struck no less fear in the enormously powerful authorities than a hostile army of many thousands."[25] That "great commotion," the sensation of acting as an army of thousands, was seductive and easily mistaken for political power. The fever pitch of enthusiasm for terror was well expressed by Morozov in his article for The Land and Freedom Leaflet on the use of what in the spring of 1879 he still termed "political murder." Although one must keep in mind that not even every urban populist shared Morozov's unabashed enthusiasm for violent methods, this article offers a clear exposition both of the use of violence as a political tool and of the confidence many populists had begun to feel about its effectiveness as a battle tactic. Morozov's description of the new populist outlook is worth quoting at length:

Political murder is first of all an act of revenge. Only having avenged fallen comrades can a revolutionary organization look directly in the eyes of its enemies; only then does it become a whole and undivided force; only then does it rise to that moral height which is necessary to the freedom fighter [*deiatel' svobody*] in order to get the masses behind him. Political murder is the single means of self-defense under present conditions, as well as one of the best methods of agitation. Inflicting a blow at the very center of the government causes the whole system to tremble with dreadful force. Like an electric shock, in a moment it spreads its charge throughout the state and produces disorder in all its functions. When the supporters of freedom were few, they always closed themselves within a secret society. That secrecy lent them great strength. It gave a handful of bold people the possibility of struggling with millions of organized, overt enemies. . . . But when to this secrecy is introduced political murder as a systematic method of struggle, such people become truly terrifying to their enemies. The enemies must at each moment tremble for their lives, not knowing when and from where revenge will find them. Political murder is the fulfillment of revolution in the present moment. Underground forces "unknown to anyone" call to judgment highly placed criminals, decree upon them a death sentence, and the powerful of the world feel that the ground slips out from underneath them as, from the height of their powers, they fall into some dark and unknown abyss. . . . Who is there to fight with? Whom to defend oneself against? Upon whom to avenge one's rabid fury? Millions of bayonets, millions of servitors await an order, a single move of the hand. With one simple movement they are prepared to smother, to annihilate thousands of their own cohort. . . . But upon whom to direct this horrible discipline, created by centuries of growing state power? There's nobody there. It is unknown from where this punishing hand appeared which, having accomplished its execution, disappeared from whence it came—to some region nobody knows. Again it is peaceful and quiet. Only on occasion a corpse testifies to the recent catastrophe. The enemies feel their very existence has become impossible, they feel helpless amidst their great power. Political murder is the most terrifying weapon for our enemies, a weapon against which neither fearsome armies, nor legions of spies can help. This is why the enemies so fear it. This is why 3 or 4 successful political murders have forced our government to introduce martial law, to increase the divisions of police, to place Cossacks on the streets, to appoint district police to the villages—in a word to perform the sort of autocratic *salto mortale* to which they have not been compelled by years of propaganda, nor centuries of dissatisfaction in Russia, nor agitation among the youth, nor the thousands of cursed victims they have tormented in prison and exile. ... That is why we recognize political murder as one of the most important means of struggle against despotism.[26]

Morozov's glorification of murder in this article may well strike readers as coldly amoral, if not indeed sociopathic, but it is a fairly characteristic exposition of why terror came to absorb the interest of the urban populists.[27] It seemed they had discovered a source of righteous and unstoppable power. While a more diplomatic populist like Zheliabov went out of his way in court two years later to disavow Morozov's pro-terrorism position, the delight in a newfound power expressed so plainly and naïvely here captures well the spirit of radical populism at the height of its influence and notoriety.[28] For one thing, terror was clearly an effective tool for wreaking havoc among officials. The enthusiasm for terror was also expressed quite openly and directly in the underground newspaper of The People's Will. The lead articles for that publication between 1879 and 1881 exhibit an increasing tendency to gloat about both the destructive power and the imperviousness to capture of its fearful Executive Committee. The seemingly serene autonomy of the radicals, combined with their apparent potential to commit violent acts at any moment, served them as a justification to call upon all sectors of urban society (invoking the peasantry less and less) to join them in the revolutionary overthrow of the autocratic regime. It sometimes felt as though a revolution was already underway.

One might also note about Morozov's text that his enthusiasm for political murder is closely tied to the populists' spectral presence in the city. He seems to suggest that the greatest strength of the terrorists, and here the term "terrorist" is particularly apt, lies in their ability to strike without warning and without the state being able to avenge itself, thus magnifying the effect of violence by the horror of the unexpected. Without knowing who the enemies are, where they are, or when they will strike again, they rise to the level of something truly terrifying, almost supernatural, something that can induce the desire to capitulate for want of a sense of the true proportions of what one is fighting against. This capacity to rouse terror lay near the heart of the populists' confidence in terrorism as a method of struggle and, it must be said, infused their campaign with a morbid and joyful sense of superiority.

Although the point was never made explicitly, the delight they took in the undetectable nature of their enterprise may have found expression in some of the violent acts themselves. The People's Will grew particularly keen to carry out attacks by literally tunneling underground and demolishing their targets from underneath, as if out of nowhere. As a result, powerful people, to repeat Morozov's phrase, "feel that the ground slips out from underneath them as, from the height of their power, they fall into some dark and unknown abyss." Morozov wrote this before any underground bombing had taken place. Such tunneling operations were the most time-consuming and costly schemes The People's Will employed. Although underground dynamite never succeeded in causing major damage (unless we consider the workers' basement of the Winter Palace an underground space), it was used on several occasions and planned for others that never took place, almost as though the populists were physically recapitulating (below the earth/above the earth) the metaphorical underground that had given them their unexpected powers. And in another sense the underground and the bombs planted and detonated under the earth were themselves an expressive metaphor about the underground. It is at least worth considering that the populists grew enamored of the invisible attack almost as a statement in its own right: if our aims and principles are rendered invisible by a power that denies us the opportunity to express them, then our invisibility will turn against your blatant and unconcealed power and do it harm.

Many of the members of Land and Freedom had begun to understand themselves as existing in a state of war with the government, in which violence was to be expected from both sides. As P. H. Liotta and James F. Miskel point out, it is characteristic of those fighting against terrorism to express the frustration that, "if only the little bastards would just come out ... and fight like men, we'd cream them."[29] Such a comment expresses succinctly why an effective underground is a necessary component of terror-based insurrection. The People's Will understood and presented themselves as combatants in a state of war, and as in any combat situation, they recognized little need for a moral justification of their actions. Presenting themselves in a state of partisan warfare and imminent revolution, the glorification of heroic combat took on a momentum of its own. Underground publications continually presented the populist movement as a relative equal to the autocracy, even as a competitor for its power. They portrayed the overthrow of the government as a near-term inevitability. The populists sought to overcome their de facto weakness and incapacity to effect change by declaring themselves enemy combatants of the autocracy and defining violent attacks against state officials as a form of revolutionary struggle. Their decision was not dissimilar from what a modern Palestinian fighter has identified as the main advantage violent acts provide for a relatively weak force: "An armed action proclaims that I am here, I exist, I am strong, I am in control, I am in the field, I am on the map."[30] Rather than suffer in a state of powerlessness, The People's Will opted to embrace the illusory sense of power that isolated violent acts can confer.

Moreover, the empowering self-conception that they were engaged in a duel to the death with one of Europe's great powers encouraged the urban populists to operate on a sort of Manichaean moral basis in which otherwise immoral activities were justified by the fight against the absolute evil of the state. Many like Kravchinskii deeply romanticized their own actions, ascribing to themselves the characteristics of martyrs and heroes. Kravchinskii called the revolutionaries "noble, terrible, irresistibly fascinating."[31] For someone like Kravchinskii, as Shishko put it, "personal revolutionary heroism was a necessity."[32] Pribyleva-Korba later described the actions of The People's Will as "a holy deed [*sviatoi podvig*] which Mother Russia commanded."[33] The main character of Kravchinskii's *Career of a Nihilist* spoke in the cadences of a medieval saint: "If we have to suffer—so much the better! Our sufferings will be a new weapon for us. Let them hang us, let them shoot us, let them kill us in their underground cells! The more fiercely we are dealt with, the greater will be our following. I wish I could make them tear my body to pieces, or burn me alive on a slow fire in the market place."[34] It only added to the sense of personal heroism and noble sacrifice that the radical populists were lionized by certain segments of society. "Kravchinskii and Vera Zasulich became idols of the youth of that time and heroes in the eyes of the progressive part of society," wrote Morozov, "and not only I but hundreds of ardent hearts strove then to do something heroic or at least approximate the status of a helper to the unseen actors of that mysterious society."[35]

By contrast to the populists' growing prominence in this period, the state seemed to be growing increasingly inept. A published statement from The People's Will's Executive Committee in October 1879 argued that state power was growing fragile: "the Russian state is an iron colossus on feet of clay: it cannot rely on anyone's interests in the country; it lives entirely for itself and thus has no support from anyone. . . . The state can only be frightening to us until such time as we move against it with all our forces, for in that case behind us will be the entirety of thinking Russia."[36] Given the apparent power of the underground, alongside the apparent diminishment of public support for the state, it was not difficult to mistake terrorism for an effective revolutionary weapon. Since virtually all the urban populists acknowledged that "our forces were too small to stage a serious uprising in the street," terrorism seemed to provide an alternative means of revolutionary struggle that could be carried out by a small band.[37] Pribyleva-Korba said when she heard about the killing of Mezentsev that a feeling ran through her like "a bolt of lightning" that such methods would finally provide the means by which Russia could be freed.[38]

In these ways the populists began genuinely to believe that the government was weak enough, and so unsupported in society, as to be easily overthrown by their destabilization efforts. The newspaper of The People's Will conceived of underground terrorism as a force that endowed populism with an importance it could not otherwise possess:

> "The struggle with the state . . . turned out to be both possible and useful. Thanks to the battle with the state, the party acquired the right of citizenship; the government keeps it alone in mind, considers it alone worthy of attention. Neither national protests, nor the disparate objections of the village population, nor disorders among the urban population, nor spreading the idea of socialism among the people could ever force the state to expend its powers to the utmost, could not profoundly embarrass it."[39]

Underground assassinations, in other words, forced the state to pay attention. Murder gave voice to the voiceless. But in the end this sense of empowerment derived from the fallacy of confusing proximate results with end goals. Making the world take note was not in fact a step toward revolution, and the populists would be the first in a long line of terrorist true-believers to discover that their ability to wreak havoc was not the same as an ability to bring about fundamental change.

THE STATE AND THE UNDERGROUND

Once The People's Will had fully embarked on its path of revolutionary terrorism, it began to carry out the dual aims of undermining the state and inspiring revolutionary fervor in society. The tsar's brother, Grand Duke Konstantin Nikolaevich, wrote in his diary just after the Winter Palace explosion that "we are experiencing a time of terror like that of the French Revolution; the only difference is that Parisians in the Revolution looked their enemies in the eye whereas we do not see, do not know, do not have the slightest idea of their numbers."[40] Violent methods were unnerving state officials, and proof of this is not difficult to find. With each new attack the atmosphere of peril and uncertainty within the government grew thicker. By 1879 ranking ministers like Petr Valuev had come to feel that the state was threatened with collapse.[41] A Third Section officer described the unsettling mood that spread over the city as the attacks continued: "One felt as though by intuition that some great misfortune menaced the country. The spirits moved about amidst the noise and animation of the winter season in the capital. Nobody enjoyed a sense of confidence and security in the future. Financiers spent their money abroad, and foreign correspondents settled in St. Petersburg to bear witness to the battles between the revolution and the state."[42] Another official, Grigorii de Vollan, later recalled the situation in similar terms: "Terror was carried through St. Petersburg like the plague. Everyone found themselves as though in the grip of a horrible nightmare and unable to think about anything else. . . . Everyone was scared for their lives or their property. It seemed that one spark would set off a panic. Everything had become so electrified that at the sound of rumbling in the street, one's companion would go as white as a sheet. It was the same among the wealthy and the poor alike. Everyone was afraid of something; everyone awaited something."[43] On his return home from a Crimean vacation in June 1879, Miliutin found the government in a panic: "Even in the highest government circles they are talking about the necessity of radical reform, even uttering the word constitution; no one believes in the stability of the existing order of things."[44]

The state's panic was reflected in a series of top-level meetings that attempted, and continually failed, to find solutions to ward off the "revolutionary" menace. Ministerial conferences were typically convened in the direct aftermath of an attack, and officials, generally bereft of new ideas, almost always managed affairs in a reactive, rather than preventative, way. Old solutions that cropped up over and over again included increased censorship of newspaper articles critical of state policy, expansion of police forces, and limits on the number of students allowed into the capital.[45] Such ministerial inertia, however, was accompanied by a gradually increasing capacity to learn from past mistakes. In the wake of the Zasulich trial, typical solutions involved expanding the exile system, closing the more agitated institutes and universities, and sending infiltrators into underground populist organizations. After the murder of Mezentsev, however, more direct attention would be focused on preventing attacks on the street.[46] Valuev suggested a mounted police force could be effective in "averting and stopping crimes under circumstances that call for rapid movement," and police guard posts were increased along the most crowded streets in the center of St. Petersburg in an effort to ward off attacks.[47] The state also funneled a new allocation of 300,000 rubles to the Third Section for "counteracting propaganda" while detective forces were expanded and trained in the most current foreign methods of detection.[48] After the April 2, 1879, assassination attempt on the tsar, a new ukase expanded police powers to levels comparable to martial law. Where these powers were used with particular zeal in southern parts of the Empire, several populists were executed on political charges.[49] Some, like Dmitry Lizogub, were put to death for crimes that did not involve acts of violence.

Ministerial meetings in this era make it clear that the great obsession of state officials still remained public gatherings rather than terrorism. The fear of public assembly remained the autocratic government's bugbear even though the populists, recognizing the futility of public protest, had essentially abandoned public demonstrations once they had turned to political murder. Valuev was particularly interested in how the police could avert "anti-government agitation" at public gatherings like "funerals, popular festivals, and theatrical events."[50] Still frightened by the demonstrations that arose around the Zasulich trial, officials were fighting the last war rather than the one they were actually engaged in. After the Mezentsev assassination, a panel of leading officials began to include exile to the remote eastern province of Yakutsk as punishment for political crimes that included "street disorders or assemblies."[51] "Especially in Petersburg," read a report of the meeting, "it is as necessary to energetically eradicate any kind of ill-intentioned gathering as it is to deal harshly with participants. ... Only immediate investigation and punishment of the guilty parties will soothe public opinion, convincing [the city's] inhabitants that the presence of powerful leadership will preserve them from new outbreaks of disorder."[52] The state continued to maintain its dominance over expression in the public sphere, and its obsession with street demonstrations would persist all the way to the assassination of the tsar. After years of hidden attacks and virtually no populist attempts at public activism, two weeks before the assassination the top concern of the state's chief minister Loris-Melikov was the prevention of a possible street demonstration, although his fears had been prompted by nothing more than an anonymous rumor.[53] Even after the tsar's death, the obsession continued. Valuev remarked in his diary shortly after the assassination that "when it happened one expected demonstrations in the streets."[54]

Playing the very game they had learned from the underground, the state also began in 1878 to print a succession of appeals to the public, competing with the populists to gain the backing of those parts of the population that were, as one minister put it, "naturally" counterrevolutionary (those with an interest in maintaining law and order). Official Russia was growing increasingly alarmed that "in all social strata of the population there is appearing a kind of indistinct dissatisfaction that is seizing everyone. Everyone complains about something and seems to hope for and wait for some sort of change."[55] On August 20, 1878, two weeks after the assassination of Mezentsev, the state sent out a call to unite "the strength of all the estates of the Russian people in unanimous assistance in the effort to root out the evil."[56] Publishing such declarations, the state essentially acknowledged its growing vulnerability, affirming that the autocracy needed to "find support within society."[57] In June 1879, another ministerial conference proposed the creation of a state-run newspaper that would seek to "embolden and unify those elements of the population which naturally now and later would include intelligent and protective forces for countering revolutionary propaganda."[58] It was to be a daily paper, low in price and capable of counteracting "the harmful direction of the Russian periodical press."[59] Schemes of this sort are a classic counterinsurgency tactic. As a contemporary military strategist puts it, the aim is to set up "a competition with the insurgent for the right and the ability to win the hearts, minds and acquiescence of the population."[60] But in the case of a state that had long arrogated to itself the claim to exclusive rule, such appeals only strengthened the liberal argument that society needed to play a larger role in public affairs. Similar appeals ensued, typically as a response to one specific attack or another, in which case they were often followed by a populist counter-appeal to the public made through the underground press. To the public audience for these competing announcements, such appeals and counter-appeals must have suggested that the state and the populists were far closer in terms of real power and influence than they actually were. The liberal newspaper reporter G. K. Gradovskii, for example, characterized the situation as a war between two equal sides.[61]

The most shocking and effective terrorist act prior to the tsar's assassination was the explosion at the Winter Palace, which demonstrated with astonishing clarity the remarkable reach of the terrorist underground. As ever in reactive mode, Alexander shortly afterward appointed Loris-Melikov head of the "Supreme Executive Commission for the Preservation of State Order and Social Peace," with the primary mission of curtailing the terrorist threat. Loris-Melikov's appointment to oversee all branches of the government and reconstruct them as necessary was a not-so-subtle message from the Russian ruler that the Third Section and other government ministries had failed in their efforts to squelch populist terror.[62] Loris-Melikov took the blank check afforded him under the circumstances and used it boldly to remake the government in a way that would answer his mandate. The period of Loris-Melikov's ascendency was marked by sweeping powers combined with relatively liberal policies, for which it was dubbed "The Dictatorship of the Heart." Under Loris-Melikov the Third Section was abandoned and governmental structures were reshuffled so that Loris-Melikov became, as interior minister, Russia's de facto prime minister from August 1880 through May 1881.[63] Though his moderately liberal attempt to introduce a limited degree of popular representation into the governmental system did not amount to a "constitution," it was impossible not to notice that, as Zaionchkovskii put it, "it was the revolutionary struggle of the Populists that forced the government to soften the reign of police terror, and to transform Loris-Melikov himself into a unique kind of liberal bureaucrat."[64]

In describing his policies, Loris-Melikov emphasized the importance of winning the sympathy of society: "it is extremely important ... to find ways to involve society in the preparation of these reforms."[65] If some basic level of public participation were not satisfied, as he told the tsar, it would lead "if not to public disillusionment, then to apathy in civic affairs, and as the sad experience of recent years has shown, this apathy constitutes the best soil for anarchist propaganda."[66] Less than a week after Loris-Melikov's appointment, he published an appeal to society titled "To the Residents of the Capital," in which he stated that "I consider the support of society the main force strong enough to help the government to renew the proper flow of civic life."[67] Seeking to enlist Petersburgers in the struggle against terror, his appeal solicited suggestions from the entire urban population, and it received many written replies. Ideas flowed in for how to mitigate radical tendencies. They included predictable responses, such as strengthening the economy, improving the passport system, pardoning prisoners, improving primary education, and curtailing press criticism of the state. Other responses supported the reinforcement of traditional values by teaching a proper appreciation for Russia's history, conducting a campaign of religious indoctrination, giving awards for achievements in home economics, and coining a new medal with the tsar's likeness so the public would be able to purchase a constant reminder of his importance.[68]

Some letter writers even exhibited a certain awareness that urban space was enabling underground terrorism. One writer, for example, convinced that people tended to speak more openly and loosely about their private affairs while riding in train compartments, suggested that the police organize special observers in third-class carriages on railway lines connected to St. Petersburg where students and workers had a dangerous opportunity to meet and interact. Listening in on conversations between them would allow the police to weed out problems before they began. Another letter directly blamed an excess of public space for the terrorism problem, arguing that such venues as theaters, circuses, clubs, city gardens, taverns, bath houses, and popular festivals enabled unhealthy interaction among the members of separate estates.[69] In the end, Loris-Melikov's appeals did little to inhibit populist terror. For the populists, on the other hand, the Loris-Melikov administration created a breathing space when, as Figner put it, "the absence of police ... greatly facilitated our efforts among students and workers." It also enabled the expansion of ties between the populists and other sub-sections of society, even including connections within the military.[70]

URBAN SOCIETY AND THE UNDERGROUND

Convinced by their growing notoriety and impact on state policy that their actions were leading toward revolution, The People's Will came more and more to focus on preparing urban society to help with the transformation they hoped to unleash. Terror was not meant only to destabilize the state; it was a message to society intended, as expressed in the 1879 party program of The People's Will, "to undermine the fascination with government power, to offer unending proof of the possibility of struggle against the government, and by these means to raise the revolutionary spirit of the people and the faith in [our] success."[71] In the phrase "raising the revolutionary spirit of the people," the populists were no longer referring specifically to the peasantry. Those enamored with terror came to believe they could, in Kravchinskii's words, "move [The People's Will] from the conspiratorial underground out onto the street and the square."[72] The message they sent with their terrorist acts was becoming primarily a message to the educated, urban public, and this focus on the urban sector was encouraged by the increasing public sympathy for the apparent political successes of underground terror.[73] Whether or not it was an accurate assessment, the radicals perceived that "the liberal public conducted itself so that the revolutionaries could not but believe that they sympathized."[74] From the summer of 1878, radical populism began to make a constant stream of appeals to "the liberal public", calling upon it to "wake up from its long sleep and inaction and boldly stand on the side of the socialists."[75]

Figner captured well the mood of the urban public in this period: "Society, unable to see any escape from the existing situation, partly sympathized with the party, and partly saw it as an inescapable evil, but even in this case applauded the courage and creativity of the fighters."[76] Although it generally remained unarticulated, a mutually beneficial relationship developed in which moderate liberals allowed the radical populists to carry out a revolution they wanted but were unprepared to fight for, while radicals appealed to society for support, having learned to read public support as a sign of impending revolution. The ideological foundations and ultimate aims of liberals and populists differed profoundly, and the populists were fond of describing their relation to the liberals as a way of "exploiting" them for political purposes, but even so a liberal/radical rapprochement developed out of an awareness that each could benefit the other. It is at least clear that a significant subsection of urban society was disgruntled and prepared to take advantage of the discord being sown by the populists. Public dissatisfaction was prompted by several factors already alluded to: anger at the outcome of the Russo-Turkish War, a growing sense of the autocracy's incompetence, the mood of public spiritedness imparted by the various demonstrations in the mid-1870s, and the promise of political change suggested by the tsar's establishment of a constitutional regime in newly independent Bulgaria. Although he exaggerated, Frolenko even claimed that Russian society was so fed up with the status quo that "it entirely approved such things as the murder of Mezentsev."[77]

By the period of Loris-Melikov's ascendancy, liberal journalists were openly calling for the establishment of a *Zemskii Sobor* (a sort of Russian *Etats Généraux*), and they were finding ways to more or less openly call for a constitution.[78] A group of high-ranking nobles, professors, and even liberal officials responded to Loris-Melikov's call for help in dealing with the threat of terrorism by condemning the autocracy for having created its own miseries by limiting popular participation in public affairs. They called for some form of popular representation, freedom of the press, and argued that the only way to stop terror was to satisfy what one letter writer called "Russian society's thirst for public activity."[79] Even groups of left-leaning nobles were proclaiming that order would not be restored until Russia had similar forms of constitutional government "as already existed in Bulgaria and Finland."[80] Figner argued with some justification that Russian society "with astonishment and delight saw in [The People's Will] a warrior against the despotism of autocracy"[81] Aptekman, who returned to St. Petersburg from village work in the fall of 1879, found "almost universal sympathy of the liberal sphere for The People's Will."[82] As he saw it: "thinking society had accumulated much anger and indignation, from which it sought an escape—and this escape was found, it seemed to many, in that form of struggle which was being practiced by The People's Will."[83]

Nor were political liberals averse to turning the violent tactics of the populists to their own advantage by triangulating populist activities against the autocracy. They argued that "subversive underground protests" were a symptom of the state's denial of free speech. If the autocracy were to remove restrictions on speech, then "any kind of sedition will lose force and meaning because it will not be able to compete with activity, freedom, healthiness and legality."[84] Liberals disingenuously suggested that they would of course be helping the state in its fight against terrorists, except that their hands were tied because the absence of free speech deprived them of the power in which to combat the evil of terrorism. As the liberal *zemstvo* of Chernigov declared: "Chernigov Province with inexpressible distress proclaims its complete powerlessness to take any kind of practical measures in its struggle against the evil and considers it a civic duty to report this to the government."[85] Liberals contended that measures could be put in place to fight terrorism but that the state alone was too weak to implement them and needed the cooperation of society, noting pointedly that "Russia was no less ready for free institutions than Bulgaria."[86]

Although the populists often complained that liberals were profiting from their efforts and sacrifices while not risking the execution and exile they themselves faced, at the same time they benefited from liberal sympathy in other ways. Not only did they solicit funds, but the general admiration of the public bolstered their spirits through what Tikhomirov called "constant moral approval, strengthening them in the thought that they were only the front ranks [of a much larger movement]."[87] In general, radical populists kept their distance from political liberals, whom they considered representatives of the despised "bourgeoisie," in order to maintain the appearance of their traditional solidarity with the peasantry, but the distance diminished as the struggle centered more and more on the city. The newspaper of The People's Will, for instance, crowed about the respect populist radicalism received in society: "At the present time, under the present situation of our work, we are more than ever *absolutely and inarguably* a useful social force. Our work at present is not even party work but generally Russian. From here arises the general sympathy, or better to say, approval, that has never before been so wide as it is now."[88] Because of this apparent approval a populist like Sinegub, who on principle refused to engage in political violence, changed his mind. He was inspired by the capacity of The People's Will to arouse "a spirit of opposition" in Russian society: "only terrorist acts grabbed the attention of the politically frozen society."[89]

The more the populists attracted public attention, the more they came to reconceptualize their movement. Not only had the underground newspaper begun to openly request financial support from the public, but it also acknowledged a certain degree of dependence on urban society: "Either the state destroys the movement or the revolutionaries overthrow the state. But for that to happen it's necessary for the party to have widespread, active support."[90] With the formation of The People's Will, populism shifted further away from the peasant village and began to recognize "the necessity of penetrating the military, the bureaucracy, the *zemstva*, and the liberal professions in order to attract these elements to the struggle against the government."[91] In contrast to their original disdain for liberal politics, they now sought "insofar as possible to unite with local liberals and constitutionalists."[92] By 1880 the new organizational plan was to create a large number of subgroups from a variety of different backgrounds, which would form a web of influence throughout Russia. Kletochnikov, under police questioning in 1881, portrayed the aims of The People's Will in a similar way. Although he was insulated from the movement because of his delicate position within the Third Section, from conversations with Mikhailov and Tikhomirov he had gathered that "the main aim of their party at the present time was to strengthen and widen the party, to bring it, according to their expression, into battle readiness so that every city and even province would have a reliable circle, the members of which would try to get into the trust of all strata of society, so that it would be possible at the appointed hour to raise against the government an enormous mass of people all at once in various parts of Russia."[93] The People's Will now intended, it seemed to Kletochnikov, to foment an urban rebellion that might then spread to the countryside. The idea that society would follow them into revolution was based on little more than hope, but the novelty of the situation enabled radical populists to maintain faith in the coming revolution.

Certain populists pushed increasingly openly for one form or another of full reconciliation with liberalism. Those inclined in various ways toward liberal views included some of the most prominent members of the populist underground such as Osinskii (before his execution in 1879), Morozov, Zheliabov, Tikhomirov, Zundelevich, and Mikhailov. The argument among many ran that the populists could take advantage of liberal enthusiasm and then abandon the liberals when a revolutionary situation had been reached. As time went on, some of the populists began to accept the need for a political revolution in favor of liberal rights. When in 1878 Osinskii had raised the possibility of a revolution in favor of "political freedom," rather than insisting on the necessity of peasant rebellion, he met strenuous resistance from the members of Land and Freedom. Yet within a year of this time it had grown habitual among the urban populists to prioritize the struggle for political freedom in the capital before returning to propaganda among the peasantry. As Tikhomirov put it, "both personally and ideologically between the purely revolutionary and the constitutional movements it was impossible to draw a distinct line. Many of the terrorists were and announced themselves to be pure constitutionalists and many of the liberals were and called themselves socialists."[94]

In an influential article on debates over the term populism, Richard Pipes has portrayed the populist shift from support for a peasant-initiated revolutionary struggle in the countryside to revolutionary activism among various urban groups as an intellectual dispute over the meaning of populism.[95] Ideological debate continued, but pragmatic concerns far outweighed doctrinal disputes, at least among those populists left in The People's Will after the schism. Doctrine receded into the background as the immediate struggle for power came more and more to dominate their time and energy. During the division of Land and Freedom, Plekhanov loudly supported the logical populist strategy of maintaining the focus on peasants and workers, but no matter how he "argued, demonstrated, appealed to logic, and cited history" he was unable to change the minds of those who had come to advocate the benefits of political violence.[96] Plekhanov had populism's original ideals on his side, but he spoke in vain in opposition to the sensational effect that terrorism was producing on society and the government. "Sensing a truly new path to revolutionary activity," as Figner put it, the central membership of the party "more and more clearly came to accept the need to gain political freedom by means of active struggle against the state."[97] Zheliabov, of peasant origin, explicitly rejected the core populist concept of fomenting a peasant uprising. He told Aksel'rod, "I'm from the peasantry and I know the people. ... A peasant uprising would only create chaos in the country. It is hard to imagine what brutality, what savagery would arise here in the event of a rebellion. ... Our only problem at the moment is to gain a democratic constitution. For this the sympathy of society is necessary. We therefore must avoid those steps which could antagonize liberal social circles."[98] For his part, Morozov came to believe that "no widespread ideological activity for the good of the people is thinkable in Russia while she doesn't have freedom of speech and press, and while the entirety of the simple folk is illiterate or semi-literate and civic freedom among them isn't possible."[99]

Zheliabov and Morozov were in some respects outliers in The People's Will, but even Mikhailov came to favor a revolutionary overthrow of the autocracy and the institution of basic civil rights in order then to slowly introduce peasant-based socialism. This populist trend toward revolution based in liberal freedoms would be corroborated by the "Letter to Alexander III," which was written and distributed in large numbers a week after the assassination of Alexander II. This famous letter, which as Figner stated, "sufficiently characterized the general mood of the Petersburg members of the party during the period after March 1," attempted to strike a bargain with the new tsar.[100] It declared a cessation of terrorist activity in return for rights of speech and assembly and the institution of representative government. From prison, Mikhailov later wrote about the letter that "nothing more perfect has been produced by Russian revolutionary thought." He called it "the crowning accomplishment of the Executive Committee."[101] By this point, terrorist violence notwithstanding, The People's Will had come to resemble a liberal movement with its radical anarchist and socialist roots set aside for a later date.

Alongside its newfound comfort with liberal society, radical populism also began more adamantly to insist on the revolutionary importance of the industrial working class. According to the populist prejudice that had been relatively unquestioned only a few years earlier, workers had been "spoiled" by living in the city and had lost their "authenticity." Now the workers were becoming potential partners in revolution. Land and Freedom's 1878 party platform stated that "the urban worker population has an especially important significance for the Revolution; for its position as much as for its relatively considerable sophistication it must receive serious attention from the party."[102] In their premature optimism that workers were prepared to "close down factories, rouse the masses and get them out into the streets," the populists were overreaching, but their increasing emphasis on urban workers went hand in hand with the general tactical shift toward the urban center.[103] By 1879 Plekhanov was arguing almost the opposite of the original populist view, that workers were not debased peasants but instead represented "the flower of the village population."[104] Very much in keeping with his later adoption of Marxism, Plekhanov's interaction with the workers was leading him and others to see the working class as capable of engendering mass revolution. Mikhail Popov helped lead worker unrest at the Tornton Factory as early as March 1878, and Petr Tellalov in 1879 asserted that engaging in propaganda among the workers was "the essence of the program of The People's Will" because it was now more successful to introduce "the political ideal into the urban sphere."[105]

It was in the late 1870s that workers and full-time populist revolutionaries began to merge in various ways. At times workers and populists debated political questions together and read and spoke about the same books. Some workers (Khalturin was only one example) were fairly indistinguishable from the populists in their clothing, language, and political concerns.[106] Ultimately what we find in someone like Khalturin is the ability to move back and forth between worker and intelligentsia radicals, yet one must not exaggerate the convergence. In most cases an awareness of difference persisted, up to and including a sense of social and intellectual superiority on the part of the educated and well-connected populists. The trend, however, was toward a decreasing sense of distinction between different parts of the urban left.[107] Reginald Zelnik aptly referred to the emergent urban culture as a "climate of fluid, crossover identities."[108]

Simple urban proximity facilitated worker/populist interaction, as did the establishment of the aforementioned Northern Union of Russian Workers toward the end of 1878. This organization kept itself intentionally separate from the radical intelligentsia, but it was modeled on intelligentsia organizations with its own funds and its own library. The Northern Union possessed a large store of books and several separate libraries, including an informal interlibrary loan system in which a worker could get a book from another library by appealing to his own librarian in his own worker district.[109] Unlike those populists who remained ideologically tied to the concept of peasant socialism, the workers were more receptive to arguments in favor of liberal conceptions of political freedom. According to Tikhomirov, workers' attitudes about autocracy rapidly changed as a result of living in the city. About one group he wrote: "they had lived in Petersburg already a sufficiently long time to know a great deal about the tsar, and it wasn't very flattering for him. The peasant point of view, that the tsar always stands for the people, disappeared from them very quickly."[110] As they came to recognize such worker attitudes, members of The People's Will began to focus more of their propaganda efforts on the workers, who, they hoped, might be able to play a more decisive role in the movement. According to one contemporary source, "personal activity among the workers swallowed up a considerable amount of strength even at the very height of the terrorist struggle."[111] The pamphlet "Preparatory Work of the Party," published by the People's Will in the spring of 1880, boldly claimed that "if we can close the factories and workshops at the start of a revolt and move the masses out onto the streets, success is already half assured."[112]

How did The People's Will explain its rapid shift away from its doctrinal roots in support of peasant socialism and rural rebellion? The remaining writer and intellectual of the party (after Plekhanov had left to found Black Repartition), Tikhomirov struggled to fit the terrorist tactics of The People's Will into a framework of populist/socialist doctrine. Since then numerous historians have also wrestled to bring intellectual coherence to the rapidly evolving movement. The onerous task can be at least partially accomplished by excluding certain opinions, for example Morozov's advocacy for terrorist revolution or Zheliabov's constitutionalism, as uncharacteristic aberrations. Or one can highlight viewpoints found in the formal program or one of the underground newspapers as a clear reflection of "the" central tenets of the organization. Tikhomirov's main argument identified the state as "the greatest capitalist force in the country" and held that therefore attacking the state meant attacking the rising bourgeoisie itself. Intellectual historians have identified this view as a motivating force behind the actions of The People's Will, but under circumstances in which the radical populists were at least temporarily willing to ally with a liberal political program, the notion they were directly attacking "the bourgeoisie" rings hollow.

It makes little sense to ascribe the rapidly evolving tactics of The People's Will at this point to ideological repositioning. A variety of competing positions had arisen within the party, and actions rather than ideas had come to dominate the movement. That both the state and public opinion were sitting up and taking notice increasingly outweighed any need for an intellectual justification of violent activity. Thus once The People's Will had split off from the more ideologically orthodox populists, it came to maintain a "big tent" policy with respect to the political views of its members, even as it expected rigorous, almost military, adherence to secrecy, assigned duties, and the wellbeing of the party as a whole. Doctrinal orthodoxy was not a necessity for party membership, but steadfast devotion to the cause remained paramount. "On accepting new members," wrote Morozov about Land and Freedom, "we never asked them 'what do you think about social democracy, anarchism, communism and republicanism?' We asked them only 'Are you right now prepared to give your life, your personal freedom, and everything you own for the liberation of your motherland?'"[113] The formation of The People's Will further strengthened this tendency to downplay doctrine. Those engaged in terrorism were motivated less by ideology than by the desire, in one way or another, to act. "As a general rule," recalled Nikolai Bukh, "a unity of fundamental convictions was not required among the members; what was required was only unity in the practical implementation of the organization's aims."[114]

Having pointed out how ideologically divided were the members of The People's Will, Figner asserted that "what was common and grasped by everyone without exception was a spirit of action, a striving for active struggle and a feeling of indignation against passivity."[115] As Tikhomirov put it a bit more bluntly, "the terrorists themselves understood the meaning of their acts in a variety of different ways; they were not, after all, men of reason."[116] By contrast to "men of reason," the men and women of The People's Will saw themselves as insurgents already engaged in a life and death struggle against the government. They developed the practical method of terrorist violence as a means of carrying out what they considered almost a paramilitary struggle under conditions of limited manpower and limited weaponry. Pragmatic considerations therefore far outweighed adherence to doctrine. Kravchinskii made the necessity of this pragmatic focus explicit in *Underground Russia*: "Conspiracy in the Great Revolutionary Struggle is like guerrilla fighting in military warfare. Men are few, and all must be made use of. . . . The ground is confined, and therefore must be turned to the best account, and a good guerrilla soldier is the man who knows how to adapt himself to the exigencies of the ground and of the moment."[117]

TERRORISM: PROPAGANDA BY DEED AND SPECTACULAR VIOLENCE

Now that we have arrived at an understanding of the radical populists' complex and confused motivations, it should be easier to comprehend the specific practice of political violence in which the populist underground engaged. In some ways it is problematic to refer to their tactics by today's standards as a form of terrorism. The People's Will did not target political innocents and only willfully "terrorized" members of the state apparatus. Their methods were more similar to what today we would call the tactics of insurgency. While The People's Will did not engage in conflict with the military, they targeted the government as the enemy and sought a means to topple it through clandestine attacks. And yet despite their direct struggle against the state, the methods devised in Russia in the late 1870s are not far removed from some referred to as terrorism today. Most importantly, radical populism helped pioneer the connection between political violence and media-based publicity. The similarity to contemporary methods is made evident in Brigitte Nacos's analysis of the use of the media in recent terrorist attacks. According to Nacos, terrorist groups use the media to attain four aims: 1) to gain attention, 2) to gain recognition for their cause, 3) to gain a measure of respectability among a like-minded segment of the population, and 4) to gain a degree of legitimacy.[118] Although, as with most sub-national terror campaigns, their cause was ultimately unsuccessful, The People's Will did in fact achieve all these goals through the use of violence to send a message to the public.

Probably their most consequential innovation was the use of violence as political symbolism. The Russian radical populists did not invent the idea of "propaganda by deed," nor were they the first to conceptualize their violent attacks as spectacular events meant to arouse the attention of the public, but the term "propaganda by deed" came into widespread use in the late 1870s, paralleling the formation of Land and Freedom, and the language was in part the brainchild of their escaped associate Kropotkin. In practice, moreover, it was Russian radical populists who elevated these methods of political violence as a form of propaganda to previously unknown levels of effectiveness. It was in their innovative use of such violence that Russian populism contributed most directly to the history of terrorism as a method of revolutionary struggle.[119]

The word "terrorism" did not gain currency until after the attack on Mezentsev.[120] Even Morozov, whose articles were the first to justify and popularize the practice of "political murder," did not at first prefer the term "terrorism" since in 1879 it was still associated with violence from above. As he put it: "rule by means of terror, in my view, entirely belonged to the state and we fought an armed struggle against [the state]." To Morozov's dismay, however, the term "quickly spread among the public so that eventually I used it myself."[121] The roots of the word "terrorism" date to the Jacobin phase of the French Revolution, and indeed the association with French Revolutionary terror still predominated in the 1870s. Morozov's pamphlet "The Terrorist Struggle," written from abroad in 1880, includes three epigraphs, all culled from French Jacobin leaders attempting to formulate a justification for the revolutionary use of terror in 1793.[122] Each of these quotations concerns the individual's right to use violence against "tyrants," in spite of the fact that French Revolutionary terror was in fact used by the radical state in the service of its own aims and can itself be conceived as tyrannical. In his own text Morozov follows the lead of the Jacobins and describes terror as "a powerful love of freedom" and a comfort to the oppressed. Conflating the Committee of Public Safety and the populist pursuit of state officials, Morozov advocated for terrorism as a political leveling of the playing field: in the Russian case the use of terror came from below: "don't be afraid of the tsar, don't be afraid of despotic governments, [terrorism] says to humanity, because they are all powerless and helpless against secret, sudden murders."[123]

It is rather remarkable, given Morozov's reference to French Revolutionary terror, that he refuses to conceive of terror as a method available to any organization, large or small, state or non-state, with the inclination to use it. Like Karl Heinzen, who had appealed to the left in 1849 to invent deadly new weapons that would allow one "democrat" to kill a thousand "reactionaries," Morozov also seemed to believe that "the path to Humanity will pass through the zenith of Barbarity."[124] His naïve assumption that terror tactics could only be called forth by a "righteous" sense of justice was shortly afterward supported by another populist defense of terrorism in a pamphlet written by Gerasim Romanenko. Romanenko saw the populist use of terrorism as history "showing the exit" from oppression in the form of "terrorist revolution."[125] Citing terrorism's lower body count than what would likely be produced in an open revolutionary conflict, Romanenko even went so far as to call terror "smarter, more humane and consequently more ethical than a mass revolution."[126]

But if violence was to serve as a means of gaining political freedom, it had to be accepted as beneficial and humane by those members of society to whom it was meant to appeal as a political message. Premeditated murder, in other words, had to be transformed into an acceptable way to make a political statement. As early as February 1875, in organizational materials written before the formation of Land and Freedom, populists had set out a program that included plans to "arouse fear in the government and the privileged classes."[127] Even earlier, Ishutin had speculated in the mid-1860s about the need for "some kind of grand and terrifying fact to announce to the world the existence of a secret organization in Russia, to embolden and awaken the sleeping people."[128] The special irony of the use of terror to send a political message, an irony borne out time and again over the course of the last century and a half, is that while it never, or at least very rarely, leads to mass rebellion, it nearly always generates a great deal of attention that is all too easy to mistake for political success. This mistake was much easier to make when there did not yet exist a historical track record pointing to the limits of terrorist methods. Thus not only did underground terror go to the heads of the radical populists who engaged in it, but as it created greater and greater notoriety it even began to appeal to otherwise nonviolent intellectuals who had never before favored such tactics. Populist intellectuals like Lavrov, Mikhailovskii, and Vasilii Bervi-Flerovskii got swept up in its success and started to approve of it where they had not before. Even Plekhanov, who had strenuously rejected terrorist methods and helped to found The Black Repartition as a result, came to a degree to sympathize with the use of terror because of its apparently undeniable effectiveness.[129]

The rising popularity of The People's Will and its terrorist struggle gained added prestige from the fact that it succeeded in attracting tremendous international attention. The People's Will was especially admired by foreign radicals. The French anarchist Elisée Reclus called its members "the salt of the earth" and stated that "their devotion to duty, their contempt for death, their spirit of solidarity, their tranquility of soul amaze me, and I turn red in comparing myself to them."[130] In part because of such adulation, the terrorist campaign of The People's Will wound up serving as a spur for the spread of anarchist terrorism in Western Europe. It was only four months after the assassination of the tsar that anarchists at the London International Congress officially recognized "propaganda by deed" as a legitimate insurrectionary tool.[131] As early as 1879, foreign journalists began to pay close attention to "the revolution" that seemed to be taking place in Russia. Repeated attempts on the life of the tsar, as Figner wrote, "awoke at every level of Western European society an enormous interest and attention to the activities of the Russian revolutionary party."[132] Plekhanov would later concede about his ideological opponents in The People's Will that they had attained a degree of success simply in having attracted the attention of the globe.[133] The People's Will seemed, not only to its own members but also to many observers abroad, to have unlocked a new formula for effective revolutionary struggle.

Terror as "propaganda by deed" was not of course violence alone but violence combined with publicity. It was not an accident that the publication of fully fledged underground newspapers arose in lockstep with the emergence of underground terrorism, both coming into their own during the first half of 1878. Not only did the underground facilitate more extensive publication, but publication grew increasingly necessary as a means of justifying and explaining the use of violence. While small printing presses had been used by underground groups dating back to the early 1860s, these "pocket-sized" presses did not produce high-quality newsprint. That began to change in the late 1870s, when Land and Freedom first smuggled in a superior quality press which printed a newspaper that did not look a great deal different from the legal newspapers being printed at that time. Underground proclamations, pamphlets, leaflets, and newspapers all went out as regularly as possible on this press, even though such publication was a painstaking and expensive operation to carry out. The difficulty of underground publication notwithstanding, it was part of the plan to give all publications the greatest possible appearance of normalcy, as though the underground world had gained so much autonomy that its press was now as freely published and distributed as though it were printed legally.

The first journal the *Starting Point (Nachalo)* put a price of ten kopeks on its masthead (down from fifteen kopeks in the first issue), and it included some of the subsection headings that were common in the legal press of the day, like "Domestic Chronicle" and "Correspondence." The newspaper *Land and Freedom! (Zemlia i Volia!)* went even further, printing not just a monthly but a daily publication date on the masthead, even though it was actually published far less frequently. It offered subscription rates of 6 rubles per half year and a daily rate of 25 kopeks in St. Petersburg and 35 kopeks in the provinces. *Land and Freedom!* included a feuilleton (light journalism) section, and it frequently featured poetry. A separate publication, the *Land and Freedom Leaflet*, which began to be published as a result of dissenting views within the organization, was presented in terms which suggested that *Land and Freedom!* had so much of value to print that it now needed to be supplemented by yet one more newspaper. Such careful presentation seems to have been carried out partly tongue-in-cheek and partly as a method of appearing indomitable, both to the government and the public. The newspaper of The People's Will announced a long list of publications for sale, including proclamations, speeches, picture cards of revolutionary "heroes," and even classified government documents they managed to find and print.[134]

Mikhailov's assertion, cited in the introduction, that an underground press would convince the public of the power of the revolutionary movement, seemed correct. It is unclear exactly how many copies of each issue went out, and the quantity probably varied with each issue, but rough estimates put *Land and Freedom!* at 1,500–2,000 and the *People's Will* at 2,500–3,000.[135] Other publications had much higher print runs, up to 8,000 for the "Program of the Executive Committee" of The People's Will and a remarkable 13,000 copies of the letter sent to Alexander III after his father's assassination.[136] If these numbers can be trusted, at key moments populist underground publications were beginning to approach the print runs of the largest newspapers of the time, like the *Voice* and the *New Time*. According to Vera Zasulich, "The press operated for more than a year, regardless of the large sums allocated to discover it ... and *Land and Freedom!* was almost openly passed around Petersburg. Thanks to the organization, anyone in the 'public' with a sizable circle of acquaintances could certainly find people with connections to *Land and Freedom!*"[137] Mikhailov believed it essential to operate a press in order to reach out to members of the public and thereby in a sense include them in the effort to undermine the state. As he put it: "it was important to have a literature of agitation, so that using any notable fact of life, we could focus the attention of society and the party. ... It instilled in the party a greater unity of action and gave the populists initiative and leadership."[138]

In addition to their regular press, incidental proclamations were printed following specific events like terrorist attacks or government executions of populists. As we have seen, the radical proclamation dates back to the early 1860s as a method of propaganda, but the proclamations of the late 1870s were a rather new and distinct phenomenon in that they almost always commented on specific actions, and as soon after the fact as possible. In this way they served as the second step that transformed deed into propaganda. Going back as early as Osinskii's February 23, 1878, attack against state prosecutor Kotliarevskii, few violent acts were not followed by a proclamation to the public, either as part of the regular underground press, if the timing was right, or as a leaflet or pamphlet printed separately. Officials were furious about the success of these proclamations, complaining that the populists sent them out "everywhere and in great quantities" and "fearlessly attached them to private homes and even government buildings."[139] Without the accompanying proclamation, the use of terrorism would have made less sense.

Sometimes exhortations to the public were mild, pleading for sympathy and support. At other times they could reach the level of outraged demands, as in the case of a proclamation published after the May 25, 1878, murder of Baron Geiking: "Public! A moral obligation lies upon you to go over to the side of the people."[140] Populist proclamations typically addressed themselves to the general public, though some were addressed to specific groups such as students, workers, the military, and peasants. They tended to strike an orderly and respectful tone, justifying acts of violence as a sad but unfortunate necessity. Kravchinskii, for example, having assassinated Mezentsev, wrote in "A Death for a Death" that "killing is a deplorable thing." After the November 1879 explosion outside Moscow that narrowly missed the tsar's railway car, the ensuing proclamation read: "We appeal to all Russian citizens with the request to support our party in this struggle. . . . To defeat despotism and return to the people its rights and power, we need general support."[141] At the same time, proclamations sought to convey the insurmountable power of The People's Will as a revolutionary organization. One proclamation called The People's Will "an august, inaccessible, all-powerful body carrying on its activities behind an impregnable wall of secrecy."[142] It was in these ways that, as Norman Naimark has argued, "terrorism assumed the form of a fascinating and dangerous drama, played out for the benefit of educated Russians."[143]

Nancy Scheper-Hughes, Daniel Goldstein, and Jo Beall have referred to terrorism as "spectacular violence," meaning violence intended to create a spectacle that will broadcast a message.[144] One way to convey that message was through the proclamation, but it was also possible to convey a message through the violent act itself in combination with the assistance of a fascinated press. Even apart from political assassinations, the populists used violence quite consciously as a form of communication. When they discovered among them a police informant, Nikolai Reinshtein, Popov and an accomplice murdered him and, in order to insure that the message of his murder was clear, they carved the word "spy" (*shpion*) into his back with a knife. It has already been mentioned that murders sometimes represented by historians as revenge killings, like Zasulich's attempt on Trepov and Kravchinskii's murder of Mezentsev, were planned originally as message killings. Trepov's assassination was to be part of a double murder and Mezentsev was not only to be killed but also beheaded. As the importance of following acts of violence with explanatory proclamations suggests, the populists were well aware of the theatrical effect produced by their violent actions. Klements, in attempting to convince Kravchinskii to leave St. Petersburg after killing Mezentsev, cared about more than just Kravchinskii's safety. He was also intent on preserving what might be called the "public image" of the assassination: "You yourself see what kind of an enormous impression was produced by your attack on Mezentsev on the square, precisely thanks to the fact that they still cannot find you. If you're arrested, three fourths of the significance of your act is lost."[145]

In spite of the admiration for peasant simplicity that lay at the foundation of populist doctrine, during the late 1870s radical populism came to be known for its technological sophistication. To tunnel under railroad tracks and city streets, to blow up trains, and to demolish parts of the Winter Palace forcefully illustrated the technical expertise of the populists, and thus seemed to confirm their power and importance. It was the railroad and telegraph, moreover, that enabled them to spread their urban movement throughout Russia when the need arose. It is relevant in this respect that dynamite so quickly came to play a key role. The People's Will could have continued using the revolver of a Zasulich or the dagger of a Kravchinskii, but the spectacular appeal of dynamite proved irresistible. According to Frolenko, had the tsar not been assassinated in an extraordinary fashion, "it would not have created such an impression ... [and] would not have announced a step forward in the revolutionary movement."[146] The use of dynamite created a new kind of violence, not only horrifying in its powers of destruction, but also impossible to limit to single targets and thus liable to generate "collateral damage" to buildings, vehicles, and innocent bystanders. In this respect, explosives, which killed innocents in more than one populist attack, contributed to the symbolic violence of populist terrorism. While they regretted the loss of innocent lives, The People's Will also profited from "collateral" murders in the sense that the death of uninvolved human beings contributed to the shock of the spectacle and the attention it generated.

With respect to spectacular violence today, it would be difficult to state for certain which method has the most potent and shocking effect. Options chosen by terrorists have included the assassination of high-ranking officials, the destruction of famous buildings, the use of simultaneous, concerted attacks, and graphic acts of violence like televised beheadings.[147] Arguably the most shocking method, developed after the period under consideration here, has been intentional attacks against innocent victims. Such attacks are horrifying both in their apparent senselessness and because any member of a targeted population can imagine becoming the next victim.[148] For the populists, targeting innocent civilians does not seem to have been suggested and probably would have been counterproductive in the extreme, but in reform-era Russia it was difficult to conceive of a target more spectacular than the tsar himself. A regicide had the advantage of being justified and minimized as an attack against an impersonal state rather than against another human being. Even more importantly, in autocratic Russia a regicide was quite nearly the overthrow of the regime itself in that policy was to an extent dictated by the personal will of the ruler. "His reason, his power," wrote Figner of the tsar, "is placed higher than the height of the reason and power of millions of people."[149] The subjects of the Russian Empire had, in their various ways, internalized the idea of the tsar as the embodiment of state power. Although the state had many detractors and Alexander II was embattled for reasons both personal and political, his personal importance to ordinary Russian subjects remained enormous. Even the populists who helped to assassinate him sometimes wrote about their encounters with him in reverent tones.

It is not often enough pointed out just how nonsensical it was to hope to ignite a peasant rebellion by assassinating the tsar, but the absurdity itself speaks eloquently about the position the radical populists now found themselves in. The only way any peasant revolt had yet been effectively encouraged was "in the name of the Tsar." Could killing the tsar now be seen as a way to promote revolution in the countryside? Though some populists continued to harbor the hope that a regicide could ignite a peasant revolution, it seems that most had already rejected this justification. Alexander II was arguably the single most potent symbol in Russia, and regicide seemed the most spectacular form of political violence possible. In pursuing regicide they believed they had discovered a fight that could make a difference. If nothing else it would serve as a demonstration of the might of populist revolution. On this basis more than any other, for nearly two years, from the summer of 1879 to March 1, 1881, The People's Will put the majority of its resources and energies into accomplishing Alexander's assassination. Targeting the person of the tsar was attacking the essential nature of the Russian Empire, and once The People's Will had fastened on regicide, the effort was not abandoned until the act was completed.

In the aftermath of the assassination, The People's Will explained the reason for their act in the aforementioned letter from the Executive Committee to Alexander III. This letter was not only sent out in thousands of exemplars, but it was also printed in a single pristine copy on vellum and sent in a formal envelope directly to the new tsar himself. At the same moment, several other proclamations were printed in smaller numbers and addressed to the workers, the Russian population as a whole, and even to "European society."[150] The letter to Alexander III was written in collaboration between

Tikhomirov, one of the few remaining leaders of The People's Will at large, and Nikolai Mikhailovskii, the most widely read left-wing publicist of this era.[151] It combined both an appeal to public sympathy and a declaration of the inevitability of revolution. Aspiring to assuage the public's anger at the assassination, the letter acknowledged the new tsar's grief and referred to him as "a citizen and an honest man." At the same time, however, it declared its intent to fan the flames of revolutionary conflict if elections to convene a national assembly were not swiftly declared. The letter revealed the full extent of changes that had taken place since underground terror had become the *modus operandi* of radical populism. It appealed directly to the tsar, but by its language and by the fact of printing and distributing nearly twice as many copies as had been printed before, it demonstrated the populists' deep concern for the approval of the educated public.

Should we conclude from this absence of ideological consistency that the tail of underground terrorism had begun by the late 1870s to wag the dog of the populists' initial aim of stimulating peasant-centered rebellion? To an extent the cliché captures the situation The People's Will found itself in. Commitments had been sworn, and the lumbering machinery of regicidal assassination, once set in motion, would not stop turning. To return to an epoch of questioning and irresolution would have seemed a clear defeat at this point. Their enthusiasm was no longer generated by ideology. It arose from tactical successes and the illusion of power. Ideologically, perhaps, most populists continued to hope for an eventual turn to peasant socialism, but in practical terms, and by this time pragmatism was paramount, they had come to accept the need for electoral politics and representative government. Underground terror had remade the populists who invented it.

CONCLUSION

I T HAS BEEN THE BURDEN of this study to explain how the radical populist underground came into being. Because of this I have intentionally limited discussion of underlying ideological motivations. In the previous chapter, I tried to suggest that the how—the strategies and tactics of populism—even began to shape the ideological principles of the actors involved. Throughout the book I have argued that the ideology of radical populism, notwithstanding its core set of values condemning social injustice and championing the innate revolutionary potential of the peasantry, was undogmatic, open-ended and malleable. Indeed, this undoctrinaire quality of populist activism would continue to be one of its tactical strengths. It facilitated the populists' remarkable capacity to shift with changing circumstances, enabling quick adaptation to whatever methods proved most effective for revolutionary activism. Ideological flexibility did not help them fulfill the original revolutionary goals of populism, but it did allow the populist movement to become something it wished to be: "a new generation of intelligentsia youth unconnected from the traditions of the old society ... that took on its young shoulders the heavy burden of struggle against a washed up regime."[1]

On the other hand, it may well be that such an ideologically rudderless movement never had the capacity to lead a revolution. While populism was, at least at times, a more widely accepted alternate political principle than liberalism in autocratic Russia, it was liberalism that led the Revolution of 1905 and Bolshevik Marxism that took over the Revolution of 1917. Nor was radical populism, as some have suggested, part of a long, interconnected tradition of conspiratorial activism that linked subversive movements in European history from Babeuf to Buonarroti to Blanqui, and from there to The People's Will and Bolshevism.[2] From a broad perspective, the landscape of European revolutionary activity may appear interconnected, and at times the populists learned certain techniques through study of earlier models, but upon closer examination Russian radical populism was only tenuously connected to radical movements in other parts of Europe. The populists reacted to local and immediate problems and created their movement with the materials at hand in reaction to conditions as they found them.

It was for this reason that radical populism developed in a dialectical process of trial, error, regrouping, and reconfiguration until it reached a stage of explosive intensity that flared up like a Roman candle in the late 1870s and just as quickly burned itself out. In 1926, a half century after the events described here, Frolenko catalogued the activities of his fellow populists (in southern cities) in the following outline:

> Having begun with the distribution of books in 1872, we then fight for the rights of workers and spread propaganda among them in 1873. Quitting this for a time in 1874 we go to the people. In 1875 we're settled there and establish a firmer footing for propaganda. Later in 1876 we begin to incite rebellion, but now without propaganda. In 1877–1878 we turn to terror, not however abandoning those in the villages, and clad as workers we penetrate the factories and workshops. The year 1879 sees Solov'ev's assassination attempt and there begins an organized attack on the Tsar. A political program appears and the party of The People's Will is born.[3]

Others would have recalled events in somewhat different fashion, depending on their personal experience, but in this simple list of events Frolenko captures the essence of reform-era radical populism. It was a movement that continually transformed itself in order to popularize its cause, seeking in one way or another to move toward revolution. Stuck in their urban bastion between the rock of peasant resistance to their revolutionary goals and the hard place of autocratic power, populist radicals were forced constantly to remake themselves, now as demonstrators in the public sphere, now as agitators in the countryside, now as "teachers" of urban workers, now as book distributors, now as underground terrorists.

This lurching from one concerted effort to another, as I have tried to show, had its roots in shifting ways of taking advantage of the urban environment in which populism took shape. The available possibilities—from use of the city's "public stage" in the early 1860s to the discovery of its hidden interstices in the late 1870s—were not simple and singular processes; they were overlapping, interconnected, and constantly in tension with one another. Most obviously, the spread and intensification of underground organizations occurred side by side with the struggle to make use of the tantalizing but restricted and dangerous (given the autocracy's intransigence) arena of the public sphere. At the same time, the ideologically informed drive to transcend the urban sphere in communion with the world of the Russian peasantry was a constant shaping factor. The apparent failure of any one large-scale revolutionary strategy tended to promote rapid shifts toward new solutions until the final stage combined underground self-protection with spectacular, publicized violence, a violence that presented to the world a model of revolutionary terrorism that in many ways has been followed ever since. Why The People's Will culminated in an organized underground wielding surprise attacks as its main weapon was summed up by Tikhomirov in the 1880s: "The state took energetic measures . . . but it could not do any harm to conspirators hidden in dark recesses; it only gave them publicity."[4]

At least some members of The People's Will genuinely believed that the assassination of the tsar would provoke a popular uprising. On the night of the assassination some of them were surprised to discover no signs of insurrection on the city streets.[5] The fact that no uprising occurred, whether in the city or the countryside, yet again brought profound disappointment in populist circles. Maria Oshanina reacted with a statement that summarizes the position many populists had reached by this point: "I love and at the same time hate the Russian peasants for their obedience and patience."[6] On the other hand, many other populists were not at all surprised that no uprising occurred. During the days leading up to the assassination, one plan had been to stage street demonstrations directly after the attack, but in fact what played out just after the assassination was better captured by the crowd that accosted a man in a student uniform and tried to hang him from a lamp post.[7] Figner later admitted that The People's Will was well aware it lacked sufficient numbers to organize any sort of street demonstration.

According to Figner, only a minority among The People's Will, those who were "accustomed to reap where they did not sow," expected any kind of peasant rebellion to arise as a result of the tsar's murder.[8] She claimed instead that most had reduced their revolutionary aspirations to gaining certain concessions from the government that would amount to "the curtailment of reaction," a minimization of their original grand objectives that is well attested to in the letter sent to Alexander III.[9] Like many terrorists who came after them, they believed the fear they inspired could operate as an instrument with which to extract at least some political demands, but they found instead that terror tends to bring about a retrenchment of the opponent's original positions. As Golovina-Iurgenson later admitted, "Terrorist acts ... systematically led to the reinforcement of reaction."[10] For their part, orthodox populists remaining in the countryside well understood that regicide would not inspire revolt and could potentially lead to a backlash. These "villagers" had long argued that a struggle against the tsar could ignite an angry reaction against them, making their work more difficult.[11] Their predictions proved true.

In reaction to the assassination, the autocratic regime (though for a time it perceived The People's Will as an ongoing threat) used the fear of terrorist violence to accomplish a quick shift toward reactionary conservatism and political intransigence. In the wake of his father's assassination, Alexander III cracked down on radical populism in a way that Alexander II had never dared to. Laws known as the provisional regulations of August 14, 1881, were designed specifically to contain the terrorist threat, introducing a version of martial law more extreme than what had existed under Alexander II. The new laws made it possible, for example, without a trial to exile a suspected revolutionary for up to five years.[12] Such laws were renewed over and over again, and the autocracy continued its stubborn fight to suppress "treason" until the Revolution of 1905 (partially and temporarily) undermined its control. In the end, the terror campaign of 1878–1881 had intensified political reaction and arguably helped to lengthen the tenure of autocratic power.[13]

It must be noted that a "popular" reaction to the assassination did take place in the form of one of Russia's most virulent pogroms, and The People's Will was not without responsibility for these attacks. The above-mentioned Gerasim Romanenko, who had published an article in support of terrorism in 1880, without the consent of remaining members of The People's Will published a proclamation in August of 1881 in Ukrainian under the banner of The Executive Committee that intentionally fanned the already out-of-control flames of popular violence against Jews. Full of vicious slurs and calls for violence, Romanenko's proclamation directly incited further attacks. Although the proclamation was denounced by the few remaining leaders of The People's Will, who even tried to order existing copies burned, Romanenko's proclamation does reflect a genuine ambiguity about the pogroms among the radical populists. That ambiguity rested on three points: 1) an abiding antisemitism among some of them that is evident in certain publications, 2) a neo-Slavophile conviction that the Russian peasant had almost mystical access to a consciousness higher than that of the intelligentsia and thus could not be gainsaid, and 3) the vain hope that perhaps the inchoate lashing out of the peasantry against Jews was an initial phase in the coming revolution, a sort of antisemitic Russian version of the French Revolutionary Great Fear. It is a revealing point that the Jewish populist Grigorii Goldenberg in 1879 had requested the support of the organization in order to make an attempt on the life of the tsar, but the other aspirant to that role, Solov'ev, argued successfully that Russian Jews would suffer if Goldenberg were to commit the act. The populists, in other words, had long been aware that their actions could ignite anti-Jewish sentiment in the countryside.[14] Whatever the views of particular individuals among them, The People's Will did not strive mightily to end the pogroms their assassination had inadvertently unleashed. In essence, they treated Jewish victims as "collateral damage."[15]

Underground tactics enabled the populists to project an image of power far out of proportion to their actual strength. The effect of that image is clearly visible in the panic within government circles that was unleashed by the assassination. Although in fact the potential of The People's Will was already in rapid decline, for months after the assassination, state officials had come to perceive the invisible menace of the terrorists as a persistent threat, and they acted accordingly. During the weeks that immediately followed the assassination, soldiers lined the streets of St. Petersburg in even greater numbers than had been seen before.[16] They established roadblocks and checkpoints at many street corners, and even dug trenches around the Winter Palace to set a protective perimeter. The new tsar himself was not to be found in the Winter Palace during several weeks after his father's assassination because he had retreated to the Gatchina Palace, about twenty-five miles outside the city. Terrified by persistent rumors that a new bombing would take place at Alexander II's funeral procession, the police placed a multitude of soldiers on the streets and had all windows closed that faced the procession so that it became nearly impossible for mourners to see the funeral cortege pass by.[17] Officials even took to heart the legend that the revolutionaries planned to kill the new tsar at his coronation and, contradicting established custom, refused to announce the momentous occasion. When it finally did take place more than two years after the assassination in May 1883, it was conducted at a distant remove from bystanders.[18]

The climate of fear was misplaced, but it served as a reminder that terror had managed to achieve its intermediary goal of making The People's Will appear to be a powerful revolutionary force. The populists had become heroic figures to many, and terror seemed to have put them on a stage side by side with the only institution that really mattered in Russia: the autocratic state. The desperate desire for influence where it is not otherwise available is one of the unfortunate temptations of terrorism, a classic "weapon of the weak." The seductive notion that political violence can replace impotence with importance is one reason why, since the late 1870s, terrorist methods of political struggle have never really gone away. Terrorism has arisen at different times and places across the globe, most often where political influence is either restricted or entirely unavailable. In the end, The People's Will, like most subsequent political organizations that have adopted political violence, found a notoriety-generating way to fight the battle, but never found a way to win the war. The creation of underground space coupled with violence against political figures not only gave the revolutionaries a general sense of power; it also gave them specific, tangible powers: the power to "shock and awe" the public, the power to terrify the state to the extent that it was pushed into a period of "crisis," the power to generate international attention and convince foreign observers that Russia was in a state of revolution. These powers were in and of themselves a seductive reason to continue the violent campaign, even as the original aims of that campaign were dissolving into incoherency.

By highlighting the conditions created by large-scale urbanization, I have tried to show here why the subversive heterotopia of the organized underground proved to be such an effective weapon. As Henri Lefebvre points out, the state's monopoly over the space of its territory is also a monopoly on violence. In his words, within the principle of sovereignty, "the state lays claim to a monopoly on violence. . . . Sovereignty implies 'space', and what is more it implies a space against which violence, whether latent or overt, is directed—a space established and constituted by violence." Lefebvre has in mind here all sovereign states, but there is an important distinction to be made between states that have electoral and other mechanisms for change and those that refuse to acknowledge the possibility of change without consent from above. Such states are not only "constituted by violence" but boldly display their wealth, bureaucratic control, and military power as the symbol of their unassailable authority. Under circumstances in which peaceful propaganda is prohibited by force, it seems little wonder that the power gained by underground space resulted in confronting physical force with physical force. In this respect, one might argue that violence was a nearly inevitable result of a movement intent on disrupting an autocratic empire. By creating a covert heterotopia and using it as a lever to apply violent force against state power, the populist underground was able to demonstrate that the "all-powerful" autocracy was not entirely all-powerful. Mikhailov accepted this achievement as a satisfactory outcome of the movement he led and would soon die for: "Our endeavors and successes have done their work," he wrote from prison, "they have exposed the weaknesses of the monarchy."[19]

That the underground itself was the populists' most powerful tool of sub-version is eloquently attested to by the fact that, during the frenzied year after the assassination, both the police and a large movement of socially elite defenders of autocracy began to adopt the very underground methods that had been employed by their populist nemeses. The Degaev-Sudeikin affair that brought down much of the remaining part of The People's Will by 1883, and ended in the death of Police Chief Georgii Sudeikin, played out almost entirely in an underground setting. Appointed head of the police prior to Alexander's 1881 assassination, Sudeikin devised a strategy that accepted the existence of the underground as a necessary evil and attempted to work inside of it in order to destroy the populist movement from within. Sudeikin believed the only way to overcome The People's Will was to penetrate it with the use of techniques the populists had themselves pioneered. He found a way to infiltrate and eventually dominate The People's Will by uniting in secretive collaboration with Sergei Degaev (one of the organization's post-assassination leaders) in effect becoming a part of the organization himself. Like the populists, Sudeikin made use of forged passports and disguises, maintained several different clandestine residences, never living in them for longer than a few weeks, and intentionally met with radical populists only in public places or inside his carriage as it moved through the streets.

Sudeikin's infiltration efforts were remarkably successful. With the coop-eration of Degaev, the police under his leadership soon came to direct and control the populist underground, even publishing issues of The People's Will newspaper. In the end, Sudeikin himself was seduced by the power of the underground into thinking he could make himself more powerful than the tsar and able to rule Russia in secret by maintaining control of both the underground revolutionary and underground police forces at the same time.[20] Apparently Sudeikin even went so far as to plan the assassinations of ranking government officials, particularly those he did not like or whom he believed might interfere with his grandiose plans for attaining power.[21] Degaev once remarked about Sudeikin: "How much he could have done if only he'd been a revolutionary!"[22] Sudeikin's death in 1883 resulted from the mistake of getting too closely intertwined with the organization he was originally attempting to subvert. Eventually, he was discovered and assas-sinated by members of the People's Will acting under Tikhomirov's orders from abroad. Degaev helped to murder Sudeikin, and for his role in the murder he was spared the charge of having double-crossed the remaining members of The People's Will. He was allowed to go free so long as he abided by the stipulation that he must leave Europe on a permanent basis. Degaev died many years later under the name Alexander Pell as a widely admired instructor of mathematics at the University of South Dakota. Undergraduates there still receive the Dr. Alexander Pell Scholarship.

Equally revelatory of the underground's significance in this period is the fact that less than two weeks after the assassination was carried out, a new organization was formed that used underground techniques in the service of the tsar as a means of combating the populist underground. Led by high-ranking government officials, military officers, and members of the nobility and the royal family, this organization, called the Holy League (*Sviashchennaia Druzhina*), sought to protect Alexander III by weeding out and destroying radical populist subversion. The organization appears to have been the early-career brainchild of the celebrated government minister Sergei Witte, who wrote a letter shortly after the assassination that suggested the necessity of creating a counterterrorist underground as the only means available to combat the revolutionaries.[23] Witte's idea was quickly adopted at the highest levels, and his counterterrorist underground came into being in the weeks following the assassination.

To a remarkable extent the Holy League was modeled on the structure of The People's Will, with an executive committee, its own underground newspapers, strict secrecy, plans for violent attacks against the populist leadership, and cells of five individuals each, known by anonymous numbers rather than by their own names. In contrast to the populist underground, the Holy League did not, of course, struggle to find funding. It also quickly reached larger numbers than had ever existed in The People's Will, with over 700 members and thousands of supporters and assistants. Its headquarters in the capital was located at the Yacht Club. The remaining members of the People's Will recognized the irony of the Holy League and declared in print that "the government is openly taking the form of a secret conspiracy against the people's freedom."[24] The conservative minister Pobedonostsev eventually came to believe that the Holy League was more dangerous to the state than the populists themselves had been.[25] But in spite of its serious intent, ample funding, and sizable constituency, The Holy League savored of leisured gentlemen playing at espionage, almost as though they harbored a certain envy of the cloak and dagger tactics (and international notoriety) of The People's Will.

The assassination and its aftermath marked a turning point in the fortunes of The People's Will. The party ambled along for several years, severely crippled and unable to regenerate the levels of organization and influence it enjoyed during its initial year and a half of existence. But the demise of The People's Will was far from the demise of populist terrorism. The mold stamped in this epoch of terrorist battle appealed to future generations of radicals, rendering political violence a recurrent feature of late-imperial Russia. As the political police, since the time of Loris-Melikov known as the *Okhrana*, continued to learn from and imitate the tactics designed by Land and Freedom and The People's Will, an underground battle raged for decades between the two forces. From the 1880s through to the First World War, a confused jumble of anti-autocratic populists, terrorists, propaganda and counterpropaganda, police agents, provocateurs, expropriators, spies, double agents, moles, and informers succeeded in taking thousands of lives on both sides. Officials were assassinated in large numbers, radicals were executed in large numbers, but both the populists and the autocracy wound up history's losers in the early twentieth century.[26]

Vera Figner was a founder and leader of the populist underground. She lived almost to the age of ninety, and later in life she came to grasp the deep destructiveness of the violent methods she had favored in her youth:

> Violence . . . is never accompanied by a softening of manners. It creates bitterness, hones fierce instincts, awakens evil impulses and leads to treachery. Humanitarianism and magnanimousness are incompatible with it. And in this way the government and the party, having entered into a virtual hand-to-hand combat, competed to corrupt the surrounding world. On the one side, the party proclaimed all tactics acceptable in the struggle against the state, that in this instance the ends justify the means. They also created a cult of the bomb, the gun, and the sanctified terrorist. Murder and the scaffold captured the minds of the youth, and the weaker their nerves and more difficult their lives, all the more did revolutionary terror throw them into a state of ecstasy.[27]

Figner was right. By the late 1870s frustration, impatience, and delusions of grandeur were in the vanguard of the movement. But as senseless as it may have been for political violence to become an end in itself, as I have tried to suggest throughout this book, there was a logic to the development of radical populism. The awareness of social inequality and injustice, magnified within urban, countercultural enclaves, and compounded by a political system that offered very little outlet for protest or the expression of opinion, created conditions that made a war of assassinations seem a viable way forward. The state (via reforms, education) and society (via press, industrialization, urbanization) were opening up space for public interaction and encouraging the participation of society, while at the same time state officials, continuing in the autocratic tradition, limited speech and refused to allow public space to be used for unsanctioned purposes. Demonstrations were squashed, and even mild forms of independent opinion were discouraged. Under these circumstances, one does not need to search out obscure impulses to comprehend the reasons for the turn to underground violence, however contemptible a phenomenon.

Even Fyodor Dostoevsky, one of the most formidable opponents of populist ideology and activism, believed he could imagine the route that would lead a person of good conscience to the adoption of political violence. Shortly before his own death, which predated the assassination of the tsar by less than a month, he told Aleksei Suvorin that the main character of *The Brothers Karamazov* would return in a sequel to become an anarchist and assassinate the tsar.[28] To envision such a cruel destiny for Alyosha Karamazov, one of his most conscientious and morally driven characters, amounted to a declaration that, at least in some cases, the adoption of violent tactics could be chosen for ethical, if misguided, reasons. But among the real radical populists of Russian history, the turn to terrorism did not rest on a foundation of ethics alone. The choices the populists made in the 1860s and 1870s reflected a much more familiar phenomenon: young people in changing times casting about recklessly in search of a way to usher in a better world.

Notes

INTRODUCTION

1. Vera Figner, *Zapechatlennyi trud: Vospominaniia*, vol. 1 (Moscow: Mysl', 1964), 281.

2. Here the term "populist" is being used in a relatively broad sense. Most broadly it can refer to all intellectuals and activists who saw Russian peasants as the fount of Russian identity. Most narrowly, as pointed out by Richard Pipes and others, the term was not really used until the late 1870s and only latterly applied to a broader movement going back to the 1860s. Pipes, "Narodnichestvo: A Semantic Inquiry," *Slavic Review* 3 (September, 1964): 441–458. The problem here is finding an adequate name for the movement as a whole. For good reason neither anarchist nor revolutionary nor radical nor nihilist fits the bill. Therefore for purposes of this book, the conventional term populist, often "radical populist," will be maintained. See below (p. 10) for a more detailed explanation.

3. Nicholas Riasanovsky and Mark Steinberg, *A History of Russia*, 8th ed. (New York, Oxford University Press, 2011), 378.

4. Nikolai Morozov, *Povesti moei zhizni*, vol. 2 (Moscow, 1962), 412–413.

5. Isaiah Berlin, *Russian Thinkers* (London: Penguin Books, 1994), 126.

6. Ibid., 221.

7. Much of the analysis of the Russian populist intelligentsia is rooted in the essays collected in the volume *Vekhi*, published in 1909. See Marshall Shatz and Judith Zimmerman, trans. and ed., *Signposts: A Collection of Articles on the Russian Intelligentsia* (Irvine, CA.: Charles Schlacks Jr., 1986).

8. A convincing interpretation of this view is found in Laurie Manchester, *Holy Fathers, Secular Sons: Clergy, Intelligentsia, and the Modern Self in Revolutionary Russia* (DeKalb: Northern Illinois University Press, 2008).

9. See, for example, Semen Frank, "The Ethic of Nihilism" in *Signposts*, 131–155.

10. This view pervades Soviet historiography in spite of its problematic relationship to the historical figures of populism.

11. This explanation has particular resonance with respect to the "going to the people" movement and the views of one of its inspirers, Petr Lavrov.

12. Peter Zaionchkovsky, *The Russian Autocracy in Crisis, 1878–1882*, trans. Gary Hamburg (Gulf Breeze, FL.: Academic International Press, 1979).

13. Two scholars in particular who have emphasized the importance of the city were Richard Wortman in *The Crisis of Russian Populism* (Cambridge: Cambridge University Press, 1967) and Deborah Hardy in *Land and Freedom: The Origins of Russian Terrorism* (London: Greenwood Press, 1987).

14. Scholars in different disciplines have sought in a variety of ways to refine use of the term "underground" and to explain its relationship to the city. While all such possible distinctions are far from being clarified into any kind of unified concept, undergrounds have been connected to associations ranging from criminal underworlds and bohemian countercultures to revolutionary insurrections and even various underground physical spaces. Fascinating and important connections link these disparate (mostly urban) phenomena. Useful studies include Dick Hebdige, *Subculture: The Meaning of Style* (London: Routledge, 1979), David Pike, *Metropolis on the Styx: The Underworlds of Modern Urban Culture* (Ithaca, NY: Cornell University Press, 2007); Luc Sante, *Low Life: Lures and Snares of Old New York* (New York: Farrar, Srauss, Giroux, 1991); Rosalind Williams, *Notes on the*

Underground (Cambridge: MIT Press, 1990); Elizabeth Wilson, *Bohemians: The Glamorous Outcasts* (New Brunswick: Rutgers University Press), 2000; Sarah Wise, *The Italian Boy: A Tale of Murder and Body Snatching in 1830s London* (London: MacMillan, 2005).

15. Those belonging to the peasant estate made up some 80 plus percent of the population of the Russian Empire in the 1860s.

16. On Herzen, see Martin Malia, *Alexander Herzen and the Birth of Russian Socialism* (Cambridge: Harvard University Press, 1961).

17. On the problem of overcoming Russian backwardness while staving off capitalism, see Andrzej Walicki, *The Controversy over Capitalism* (Oxford: Clarendon Press, 1969).

18. Debates did take place, such as those in the 1870s between Lavrovists and Bakuninists about the revolutionary potential of the peasantry, but even this debate was couched in the shared view that a peasant-based revolution was both a necessity and an inevitability.

19. Lev Tikhomirov, *Vospominaniia* (Moscow, 1927), 133–134.

20. Ibid., 134. It should be noted here that Tikhomirov wrote his memoirs after having repudiated populism and become a staunch conservative, which might make his disavowal of ideology seem politically motivated. His recollections of concrete facts, however, usually dovetail with those of populists who kept the faith, and his jaundiced view of the activities of his youth rings at least as true as some of the starry-eyed celebrations of the heroic struggle offered in the memoirs of several of his contemporaries.

21. This concern for reputation and influence helps explain why memoirs written by revolutionary populists, in sharp contrast to the work of later historians, tend to downplay ideology and focus instead on practical matters. These memoirs, written between 1882 and the 1920s, are absorbed in the questions that most concerned the radical populists at the height of their influence: how to gain and hold on to power, how to inflame the public's anger against the state, how to instigate a mass peasant uprising (or at least appear capable of instigating one), and how to stay out of the hands of an increasingly powerful police force.

22. Martin Malia, "What is the Intelligentsia?" *Daedalus*, vol. 89, no. 3 (1960): 444.

23. Claudia Verhoeven, *The Odd Man Karakozov* (Ithaca: Cornell University Press, 2009), 23.

24. The basic argument in the *Signposts* essays was later articulated at greater length, and taken further into the 20th century, by one of the book's essayists, Nikolai Berdiaev, in *The Origin of Russian Communism* (London: Geoffrey Bles, 1937).

25. Unfortunately, the umbrella category *raznochintsy* had little relationship to Marx's reading of class-based social change, no direct connection to the advance of capitalism, and even the various social groups that could be shoehorned into the category were only partially responsible for revolutionary thought and activity.

26. S. S. Volk, *Narodnaia Volia* (Moscow: Nauka, 1966), 7. It is only fair to note here that toward the end of his life Marx himself, excited by the revolutionary potential that seemed abundant in Russia as a result of the successes of The People's Will, also tried to envision ways in which an agrarian revolution might take place in Russia in contrast to the way he saw revolution playing out in the west. See Teodor Shanin, ed., *Late Marx and the Russian Road* (New York: Monthly Review Press, 1983), 79–126.

27. Avraham Yarmolinsky, *Road to Revolution* (Princeton, NJ: Princeton University Press, 1957) and Franco Venturi, *The Roots of Revolution*, trans. Francis Haskell (Chicago: University of Chicago Press, 1960).

28. James Billington devised a nice label for this historiographical tradition in the title of his book *Fire in the Minds of Men* (Transaction, 1980), which treats a faith in ideas as one of the essential (and unfortunate) features of modern European history, and in which Russian radicals are featured as an important case in point.

29. John Doyle Klier, *Russians, Jews, and the Pogroms of 1881–1882* (Cambridge: Cambridge University Press, 2011), 155.

30. Daniel Brower, *Training the Nihilists: Education and Radicalism in Tsarist Russia* (Ithaca: Cornell University Press, 1975).

31. Barbara Alpern Engel, *Mothers and Daughters: Women of the Intelligentsia in Nineteenth-Century Russia* (Cambridge: Cambridge University Press, 1983).

32. Abbott Gleason, *Young Russia: The Genesis of Russian Radicalism in the 1860s* (Chicago: University of Chicago Press, 1980).

33. See, for example, Joseph Bradley, *Voluntary Associations in Tsarist Russia: Science, Patriotism and Civil Society* (Cambridge: Harvard University Press, 2009); Edith Clowes et al., eds., *Between Tsar and People: Educated Society and the Quest for Public Identity in Late-Imperial Russia* (Princeton, NJ: Princeton University Press, 1991); and Boris Mironov, *Sotsial'naia istoriia Rossii perioda imperii: XVIII–nachalo XX v.: Genezis lichnosti, demokraticheskoi sem'i, grazhdanskogo obshchestva i pravovogo gosudarstva* (Moscow: Bulanin, 1999).

34. Verhoeven, *Odd Man.*

35. Ana Siljak, *Angel of Vengeance: The "Girl Assassin," the Governor of St. Petersburg and Russia's Revolutionary World* (New York: St. Martin's Press, 2008).

36. E. I. Shcherbakova, *Otshchepentsy: Put' k terrorizmu* (Moscow: Novyi Khronograf, 2008). Similarly, Oleg Budnitskii compiled a collection of documents in the 1990s, written by familiar figures in the populist movement, that stresses their contribution to "the history of terrorism in Russia." Budnitskii, *Istoriia terrorizma v Rossii v dokumentakh, biografiiakh, issledovaniiakh* (Rostov na Donu: Feniks, 1996). At the same time the focus on the social and intellectual history regarding the intelligentsia has also shifted—for example, toward religion and social origins in Manchester, *Holy Fathers*; toward place and sociability in John Randolph, *The House in the Garden: The Bakunin Family and the Romance of Russian Idealism* (Ithaca: Cornell University Press, 2007); and toward the question of faith in Victoria Frede, *Doubt, Atheism and the Nineteenth-Century Russian Intelligentsia* (Madison: University of Wisconsin Press, 2011).

37. Such issues run throughout Foucault's work, but for a useful theoretical discussion of them, see Michel Foucault, *"Society Must Be Defended": Lectures at the Collège de France, 1975–1976*, trans. David Macey (New York: Picador, 1997), 1–19.

38. I will mention in passing that from an ethical standpoint I find populist actions both politically understandable and morally troubling, but I intend to leave political and moral judgments to the reader.

39. Jeremy Crampton and Stuart Elden, eds., *Space, Knowledge and Power: Foucault and Geography* (Burlington: Ashgate, 2007).

40. Chris Philo, "Michel Foucault" in *Key Thinkers on Space and Place* (Los Angeles: Sage Publications, 2004), 165.

41. Paul Rabinow, ed., *Foucault, Power/Knowledge* (New York: Vintage Press, 1980), 149.

42. Edward Soja, *Postmodern Geographies: The Reassertion of Space in Critical Social Theory* (London: Verso Press, 1989), 79.

43. On the history of suburbanization, see Robert Fishman, *Bourgeois Utopias: The Rise and Fall of the Suburb* (New York: Basic Books, 1989).

44. Fedor Dostoevsky, *Prestuplenie i nakazanie* (Moscow: Izdatel'stvo 'Act,' 2009), 76. Also see Adele Lindenmeyr, "Raskolnikov's City and the Napoleonic Plan," *Slavic Review* (1976): 37–47.

45. On the cultural functions of large cities, see, for example, Lewis Mumford, *The City in History* (New York: Harcourt Inc., 1961), 561–563.

46. For an overview, see Eklof, Bushnell, and Zakharova, *Russia's Great Reforms, 1855–1881* (Bloomington: Indiana University Press, 1994).

47. The point is discussed in James Bater, *St. Petersburg: Industrialization and Change* (London: Edward Arnold, 1976) and Daniel Brower, *The Russian City between Tradition and Modernity* (Berkeley: University of California Press, 1990).

48. This sense of rapid dissolution was captured in the diary of N. V. Nikitenko, in which he complains of the "drunken crowds" and the "vile antics in the taverns, on the streets and in the market-place." Aleksandr Nikitenko, *Diary of a Russian Censor*, trans. Helen Saltz Jaboson (Amherst: University of Massachusetts Press, 1975), 275, 287. It is also reflected in fictional works, like those of Vladimir Krestovskii and Dostoevsky.

49. Alexandra Staub, "St. Petersburg's Double Life: The Planners' versus the People's City," *Journal of Urban History* 31, no. 3 (2005): 336.

50. Matt Houlbrook, *Queer London: Perils and Pleasures in the Sexual Metropolis, 1918–1957* (Chicago: University of Chicago Press, 1957).

51. Claude Fischer and Robert K. Merton, *The Urban Experience* (New York: Harcourt, Brace Jovanovich, 1976), 35–37.

52. Among many other studies, see, for example, Bradley, *Voluntary Associations*; Katia Dianina, "The Firebird of the National Imaginary: The Myth of Russian Culture and Its Discontents," *Journal of European Studies* 42, no. 3 (2012): 223–244; Adele Lindenmeyr, *Poverty Is Not a Vice: Charity, Society and the State in Imperial Russia* (Princeton, NJ: Princeton University Press, 1996); Louise McReynolds, *The News under Russia's Old Regime: The Development of a Mass-Circulations Press* (Princeton, NJ: Princeton University Press, 1991); McReynolds, *Russia at Play: Leisure Activities at the End of the Tsarist Era* (Ithaca: Cornell University Press, 2003); Murray Frame, *School for Citizens: Theatre and Civil Society in Imperial Russia* (New Haven: Yale University Press, 2006); Sally West, *I Shop in Moscow: Advertising and the Creation of Consumer Culture in Late Tsarist Russia* (DeKalb: Northern Illinois University Press, 2011).

53. Hans Rogger, *Russia in the Age of Modernization and Revolution* (London: Longman, 1983), 132.

54. Hardy, *Land and Freedom*, xii.

55. On the romantic roots of populism, see Dmitry Likhachev, *Reflections on Russia*, trans. Christina Sever (Boulder: Westview Press, 1991), 16.

56. Nikolai Chernyshevsky, *What Is To Be Done?*, trans. Michael R. Katz (Ithaca: Cornell University Press, 1989), 279.

57. Cited in Wortman, *Crisis*, 4.

58. Zasulich, "Nechaevskoe delo," *Gruppa "Osvobozhdenie truda"* 2 (1924): 26.

59. A. P. Pribyleva-Korba and Vera Figner, eds., *Narodnovolets Aleksandr Dmitrievich Mikhailov* (Leningrad, 1925), 86.

60. The term comes from Foucault's lecture translated into English as "Of Other Spaces," trans. J. Miskowiec, *Diacritics* (Spring 1986): 22–27.

61. See, for instance, Freerk Boedeltje, "The Other Spaces of Europe: Seeing European Geopolitics through the Disturbing Eye of Foucault's Heterotopias," *Geopolitics* 17, no. 1 (2012): 1–24; Michiel Dehaene and Lieven De Cauter, eds., *Heterotopia and the City: Public Space in a Postcivil Society* (New York: Routledge, 2008); Kevin Heatherington, *The Badlands of Modernity: Heterotopia and Social Ordering* (New York: Routledge, 1997); Miglena Nikolchina, *Lost Unicorns of the Velvet Revolutions: Heterotopias of the Seminar* (New York: Fordham University Press, 2012); Edward Soja, *Thirdspace* (Malden, MA: Blackwell Publishing, 1996).

62. For a discussion of Foucault's relationship to space and geography, see Stuart Eldon and Jeremy W. Crampton, *Space, Knowledge and Power: Foucault and Geography* (Burlington: Ashgate, 2007) and Edward Soja, *Thirdspace*, 145-63.

63. As Edward Casey has noted, "to make a difference in the social fabric, a heterotopia must possess a focus for the applications of force. This focus is found in the marginal location of the heterotopia itself: from this location, force can be exerted more effectively than if it stemmed from the center of the circumstance." Casey, *The Fate of Place: A Philosophical History* (Berkeley: University of California Press, 1997).

64. I differ with Soja here on the point that all heterotopia are meant to "detonate" and "deconstruct." In my reading of Foucault many spaces referred to as heterotopia have the precise function of maintaining the status quo. See Soja, *Thirdspace*, 163.

65. It is worth noting here that some scholars might read the term "subversive heterotopia" as a redundancy. For example, as M. Christine Boyer, points out, all heterotopia are meant to contest, compensate for, or "purify" neutral or conventional space, so heterotopia may be seen as ipso facto subversive. While this may be true of a space like a bohemian district, in my view two aspects of the revolutionary underground call for a modifier like "subversive." First, such an underground is not meant as a heterotopia in Foucault's sense of a separate space to exist side by side with other spaces.

It is used as an instrument to change the entire space. Second, the underground is temporary. Once it has achieved its goals, there is no longer any reason for it to exist. It functions as a heterotopic space in every way, but its aim is to nullify the need for its own existence, ultimately to subvert itself. See Boyer, "The Many Mirrors of Foucault" in Dehaene and De Cauter, *Heterotopia*, 53–54.

66. David Harvey, *Social Justice and the City* (London: Arnold, 1973), 13.

67. Sergei-Stepniak Kravchinskii, "Podpoil'naia Rossiia," reprinted in *Grozovaia tucha Rossii*, (Saint Petersburg: Novyi Kliuch, 2001). The title of this book is intended, in part, as a refinement or reorientation of Kravchinskii's memoir. On Kravchinskii's memoir also see Lynn Ellen Patyk, "Remembering 'The Terrorism': Sergei Stepniak-Kravchinskii's 'Underground Russia,'" *Slavic Review* (2009).

68. Three studies that examine Russian terrorism after this period are Anna Geifman, *Thou Shalt Kill: Revolutionary Terrorism in Russia, 1894–1917* (Princeton, NJ: Princeton University Press, 1995); Norman M. Naimark, *Terrorists and Social Democrats: The Russian Revolutionary Movement under Alexander III* (Cambridge: Harvard University Press, 1983); and Oleg Budnitskii, *Terrorizm v rossiiskom osvoboditel'nom dvizhenii: Ideologiia, etika, psikhologiia (vtoraia pol. XIX–nachalo XX v.)* (Moscow: Rosspen, 2000).

CHAPTER 1

1. Jurgen Habermas, *The Structural Transformation of the Public Sphere: An Inquiry into a Category of Bourgeois Society*, trans. Thomas Burger (Cambridge: The MIT Press, 1999), 7.

2. A fuller picture of the diverse public culture that emerged in late-imperial Russia has been coming together for more than two decades in studies far too numerous to mention. Clowes et al. (*Between Tsar and People*) examine the topic from numerous angles. Bradley, *Voluntary Associations* offers the most sophisticated historiographical analysis of the topic.

3. See Marc Raeff, *Origins of the Russian Intelligentsia: The 18th Century Nobility* (New York: Harcourt, Brace and World, 1966).

4. The gradual but unmistakable growth of an autonomous nobility under Catherine II is covered in Isabel de Madariaga, *Russia in the Age of Catherine the Great* (New Haven: Yale University Press, 1981).

5. Lewis Mumford, *The City in History* (New York: Harcourt, 1961), 377–379 and 386–391.

6. On the baroque city and political power, see Marcel Henaff and Tracy B. Strong, *Public Space and Democracy* (Minneapolis: University of Minnesota Press, 2001), 1–28.

7. It should be pointed out that St. Petersburg's monumental architecture is mostly classical in style and built in a later age. However, the city's underlying structure, put in place to exalt royal grandeur, has its genesis in the blueprint of the baroque era of Peter the Great.

8. Iu. A. Egorov, *The Architectural Planning of St. Petersburg*, (Athens, OH: Ohio University Press, 1969), 90–94.

9. On the principle of *reguliarnost'*, see James Cracraft, *The Petrine Revolution in Russian Architecture* (Chicago: University of Chicago Press, 1988), 257–258.

10. All the same, it must be kept in mind that the city's grandeur and monumentality were ideals rather than a finished reality. A short walk off the beaten path could reveal the squalor behind the façade, and the process of building the monumental space was a far more haphazard affair than its projected grandeur and opulence would seem to suggest.

11. Pavel Svin'in, "Kratkaia zapiska o novostiakh, naidennykh izdatelem O. Z. v stolitse po vozvrashchenii svoem nyneshnim letom iz puteshestviia," *Otechestvennye zapiski* no. 31 (1828): 498–514 and Astolphe Marquis de Custine, *Empire of the Czar: A Journey through Eternal Russia* (New York: Doubleday, 1989), 151–152.

12. Mumford, *The City*, 390.

13. Ibid., 370.

14. Solomon Volkov, *St. Petersburg: A Cultural History* (New York: Simon and Schuster, 2010), 26.

15. Nikolai Gogol, "Nevsky Prospect," *The Complete Tales of Nikolai Gogol,* vol. 1, trans. Constance Garnett (Chicago: University of Chicago Press, 1985), 297–238.

16. See Arthur L. George, *St. Petersburg: Russia's Window to the Future* (New York: Taylor Trade Publishing, 2003), 287.

17. Richard Wortman, *Scenarios of Power: Myth and Ceremony in Russian Monarchy from Peter the Great to the Abdication of Nicholas II* (Princeton, NJ: Princeton University Press, 2006), 143.

18. A. P. Shevyrev, "Kul'turnaia sreda stolichnogo goroda. Peterburg i Moskva" in *Ocherki Russkoi kul'tury XIX veka* (Moscow: Izd. Moskovskogo universiteta, 1998), 78.

19. M. V. Nechkina, *Dekabristy* (Leningrad, 1984), 59.

20. Here it is important to note that the Decembrists did have plans to attack the Winter Palace and even considered assassinating Nicholas I, but they did not have the willpower or personnel to follow through.

21. In Marc Raeff, *The Decembrist Movement* (Englewood Cliffs, NJ: Prentice-Hall, 1966), 61.

22. Ibid.

23. Ibid., 66.

24. Wortman, *Scenarios,* 54, 135, and 191.

25. George Munro, *The Most Intentional City: St. Petersburg in the Reign of Catherine the Great* (Cranbury, NJ: Associated University Presses, 2008), 17.

26. Works that have examined the non-normative aspects of the city from a wide and fascinating variety of perspectives include V. N. Toporov, *Peterburgskii tekst russkoi literatury: Izbrannye trudy* (Sankt-Peterburg: Iskusstvo, 2003), 7–118; Iu. M. Lotman, "Simvolika Peterburga i problemy semiotiki goroda" in *Semiotika goroda i gorodskoi kul'tury* (Tartu: Tartu University Press, 1984); Nikolai Antsiferov, *Byl i mif Peterburga* (Petrograd: Brokgauz i Efron, 1924); Mark Steinberg, *Petersburg Fin de Siècle* (New Haven: Yale University Press, 2011); Volkov, *St. Petersburg*; Arthur and Elena George, *St Petersburg: Russia's Window to the Future* (London: Taylor, 2003); W. Bruce Lincoln, *Sunlight at Midnight: St. Petersburg and the Rise of Modern Russia* (New York: Basic Books, 2002); and Grigorii Kaganov, *Sankt-Peterburg: Obrazy prostranstva* (St. Petersburg: Indrik, 1995).

27. This is not to say that scholars have entirely avoided the more normative historical development of the city. Those who have approached St. Petersburg as part of a more conventional process of urbanization include Bater, *St. Petersburg*; Brower, *Russian City*; Julie Buckler, *Mapping St. Petersburg* (Princeton, NJ: Princeton University Press, 2005); Munro, *The Most Intentional City*; Gerald Surh, *1905 in St. Petersburg: Labor, Society and Revolution* (Stanford, CA: Stanford University Press, 1989); and Reginald Zelnik, *Labor and Society in Tsarist Russia: The Factory Workers of St. Petersburg, 1855–1870* (Stanford, CA: Stanford University Press, 1971).

28. See Joseph Bradley, *Muzhik and Muscovite: Urbanization in Late-Imperial Russia* (Berkeley: University of California Press, 1985), 9. The other country with two such cities was the United States.

29. See Bater, *St. Petersburg,* 68, 161, 310.

30. Ibid., 158–166. Venturi maintains that between 1869 and 1881 the population of St. Petersburg went from 668,000 to 928,000. Another measure suggests that between 1869 and 1881 the city's population grew from 667,900 to 861,300. See O. S. Grintsevich, "Proekty planirovki Peterburga vtoroi poloviny XIX–nachala XX vekov," *Arkhitekturnoe nasledstvo* 9 (Leningrad, 1959).

31. Ibid., 90.

32. James Bater, "Between Old and New: St. Petersburg in the Late-Imperial Era," Michael Hamm, ed., *The City in Late Imperial Russia* (Bloomington: Indiana University Press, 1986), 51.

33. See V. A. Fedorov, *Istoriia Rossii, 1861–1917* (Moscow: Vysshaia shkola, 2001), 84–86.

34. Zelnik, *Labor and Society,* 214.

35. Boris Kirikov, *Arkhitektura Peterburgskogo moderna: Osobniaki i dokhodnye doma* (Saint Petersburg: Zhurnal Neva, 2003), 145.

36. E. I. Kirichenko, *Russkaia arkhitektura, 1830–1910* (Leningrad, 1982), 153.

37. Zelnik, *Labor and Society,* 49–54.

38. Ibid., 241.

39. Vladimir Mikhnevich, *Iazvy Peterburga* (Sankt-Peterburg: Limbus Press, 2003), 95 and 112–15.

40. Bater, *St. Petersburg*, 208. "It should also be noted that in a later period of even more intensive growth in the early 20th century, the perception of turmoil and disorientation in the city of St. Petersburg had grown even more acute. For a recent discussion see Steinberg, *Petersburg Fin de Siecle*."

41. Nikitenko, *Diary*, 275.

42. Egorov, *Architectural Planning*, 197.

43. See N. V. Kireev, "Transport, torgovliia, kredit" in *Ocherki Istorii Leningrada. tT 2 period kapitalizma, vtoraia polovina XIX veka*, Moscow, 1957), 152.

44. Mikhnevich, *Iazvy*, 384.

45. Zelnik, *Labor and Society*, 255.

46. Mikhnevich, *Iazvy*, 113.

47. See Georg Simmel, "The Metropolis and Mental Life" in Miles, Hall and Borden, eds., *The City Cultures Reader* (New York: Routledge, 2000), 12–19.

48. See Fischer, *Urban Experience*, 30–31.

49. Cited in Kornei Chukovskii, *Liudi i knigi shestidesiatykh godov* (Leningrad, 1934), 99.

50. Nikolai Shelgunov, *Vospominaniia* (Leningrad, 1967), 110.

51. Mikhnevich, *Iazvy*, 63.

52. W. Bruce Lincoln, *The Great Reforms: Autocracy, Bureaucracy and the Politics of Change in Imperial Russia* (DeKalb, IL: Northern Illinois University Press, 1990), xi.

53. Alfred Rieber, "Interest Group Politics in the Era of the Great Reforms" in Eklof et al., *Russia's Great Reforms, 1855–1881* (Bloomington: Indiana University Press, 1994), 79.

54. See Lincoln, *Great Reforms*, 46–60.

55. Ibid., 116

56. Ibid., 124–131.

57. David Saunders, *Russia in the Age of Reaction and Reform* (New York: Longman, 1992), 269.

58. Cited in Daniel Orlovsky, *The Limits of Reform: The Ministry of Internal Affairs in Imperial Russia, 1802–1881* (Cambridge: Harvard University Press, 1981), 75.

59. Cited in N. I. Iordanskii, *Konstitutsionnoe dvizhenie 60-kh godov* (St. Petersburg, 1906), 31.

60. Ibid., 117.

61. Shelgunov, *Vospominaniia*, 131–133.

62. E. N. Vodovozova, *Na zare zhizni: Memuarnye ocherki i portrety*, vol. 2 (Leningrad, 1964), 38.

63. On *The Contemporary*, see William F. Woehrlin, *Chernyshevskii: The Man and the Journalist* (Cambridge: Harvard University Press, 1971), 95.

64. Eliseev, "O literaturnoi bogeme shestidesiatykh godov" in M. A. Antonovich and G. Z. Eliseev, *Shestidesiatye gody* (Moscow: Akademiia, 1933), 475.

65. Eliseev, "O literaturnoi bogeme," 479.

66. Vodovozova, *Na zare zhizni*, 38.

67. M. M. Klevenskii, "Vertepniki," *Katorga i ssylka* 10 (1928): 20.

68. Ibid., 27.

69. GARF, f. 109, op. 3-a, dd. 2990–3014.

70. Ibid., 2997.

71. Ibid., 2996.

72. Ibid., 2990 and 2996.

73. Cited in Shcherbakova, *Otshchepentsy*, 31.

74. See N. Nikoladze, "Vospominaniia o shestidesiatykh godakh," *Katorga i ssylka* 34 (1927): 32

75. M. K. Lemke, *Ocherki osvoboditel'nogo dvizheniia "shestidesiatykh godov"* (St. Petersburg, 1908), 201.

76. For instance, the Third Section forbid the opening of a bookstore by E. P. Pechatkin who, in petitioning to open the store, was investigated by the police because of his connections to radical circles (GARF, 109, op. 1-a, f. 278). On surveillance of bookstores, see Jonathan Daly, *Autocracy under Seige: Security Police and Opposition in Russia, 1866–1905* (DeKalb, IL: Northern Illinois University Press, 1998), 23.

77. See I. E. Berenbaum, "Knizhnyi magazin A. A. Cherkesov i ego rol' v osvoboditel'nom dvizhenii 1860-kh g. v Rossii" in S. G. Luppov and N. V. Paramonova, eds., *Knigotorgovoe i bibliotechnoe delo v Rossii* (Leningrad, 1981), 55–60.

78. See R. A. Somina, *Nevskii Prospekt: Istoricheskii ocherk* (Leningrad, 1959), 113.

79. Shelgunov, *Vospominaniia*, 134.

80. Ivan Pryzhov, "Peterburg i Moskva" in *Ocherki, stat'i pis'ma* (Moscw, 1934), 277.

81. GARF, 109, op. 1-a, f. 353.

82. See *Sankt-Peterburg, Petrograd, Leningrad: entsiklopedicheskii spravochnik* (Saint Petersburg, 1992), 662.

83. Ibid., 662. Also see L. F. Panteleev, *Iz vospominanii proshlogo* (Moscow, 1934), 211.

84. Cited in Charles Ruud and Sergei Stepanov, *Fontanka 16: The Tsars' Secret Police* (Montreal: McGill-Queen's University Press, 1999), 27.

85. B. Bazilevskii (V. Bogucharskii), ed., *Gosudarstvennye prestupleniia v Rossii v XIX veke* (Stuttgart, 1903), 203.

86. Nikoladze, "Vospominaniia," 32.

87. V. Sorokin, "Vospominaniia starogo studenta," *Russkaia Starina* (November, 1906): 449–450.

88. A. M. Skabichevskii, *Literaturnye vospominaniia* (Moscow: Agraf, 2001), 137.

89. Ibid., 466.

90. Ibid., 175.

91. Ia. V. Abramov, *Nashi voskresnye shkoly* (Saint Petersburg, 1900), 27.

92. Zelnik, *Labor and Society*, 174–175.

93. Z. P. Bazileva, "K istorii pervykh arteli raznochintsev," *Voprosy istorii sel'skogo khoziaistva* (Moscow, 1961), 206.

94. Cited in Zelnik, *Labor and Society*, 183.

95. Z. P. Bazileva, "Arkhiv semei Stasovykh" in *Revoliutsionnaia situatsiia* (Moscow, 1965), 440.

96. Patrick Alston, *Education and the State in Tsarist Russia* (Stanford, CA: Stanford University Press, 1969), 44–45.

97. Quoted in Shcherbakova, *Otshchepentsy*, 40.

98. Quoted in Venturi, *Roots*, 332.

99. O. V. Aptekman, *Obshchestvo "Zemlia i Volia" 70-kh gg. Po lichnym vospominaniiam* (Petrograd, 1924), 420–421.

100. Sorokin, "Vospominaniia," 443.

101. Susan Morrissey, *Heralds of Revolution: Russian Students and the Mythologies of Radicalism* (Oxford, UK: Oxford University Press, 1998), 25. Morrissey describes the *skhodka* as a venue for debate but also as a method of determining the students' "general will."

102. Cited in M. Lemke, *Ocherki osvoboditel'nogo dvizheniia "shestidesiatykh godov"* (Saint Petersburg, 1908), 469–470.

103. Pryzhov, "Peterburg i Moskva," 275.

104. Sergei Tatishchev, *Imperator Aleksandr II. Ego zhizn' i tsarstvovanie* (Moscow: Tranzitkniga, 2006), 885.

105. Shelgunov, *Vospominaniia*, 241–242.

106. See P. A. Zaionchkovskii, ed., *Dnevnik P. A. Valueva Ministra Vnutrennykh Del* (Moscow, 1961), 117.

107. The precise number of participants is unclear, but several witnesses commented on the large crowds observing and partly participating in the demonstration.

108. See Zaionchkovskii, ed., *Dnevnik Valueva*, 117.

109. Cited in Iu. I. Gerasimova, "Krizis pravitel'stvennoi politiki v gody revoliutsionnoi situatsii i Aleksandr II" in *Revoliutsionnaia situatsiia* (1962), 103.

110. Vydrin, R., *Osnovnye momenty studencheskogo dvizheniia v Rossii* (Sankt-Peterburg, 1908), 16.

111. Cited in Gleason, *Young Russia*, 141.

112. Sorokin, "Vospominaniia," 456–464.

113. B. S. Itenberg, *Dvizhenie revoliutsionnogo narodnichestva* (Moscow, 1965), 286.

114. Gleason, *Young Russia*, 158.

115. Bazilevskii, ed., *Gosudarstvennye prestupleniia*, 201.

116. Zelnik, *Labor and Society*, 178.

117. Zaionchkovskii, ed., *Dnevnik Valueva*, 388.

118. It is worth pointing out here that the reform era did witness a rise in social initiative within tolerated voluntary associations. These did not satisfy the ambitions of radicals, but they did gradually grow into a significant realm of public activity in their own way. See Bradley, *Voluntary Associations*, and Adele Lindenmeyr, "The Rise of Voluntary Associations during the Great Reforms: The Case of Charity" in Eklof et al., eds., *Great Reforms*, 264–279.

119. Zelnik, *Labor and Society*, 194.

120. See Wortman, *Scenarios of Power*, vol. 2, 72–91.

121. On celebrations staged by the autocracy, in addition to Wortman, see Zaionchkovskii, ed., *Dnevnik Valueva*, 82; Olga Maiorova, *From the Shadow of the Empire: Defining the Russian Nation through Cultural Mythology* (Madison: University of Wisconsin Press, 2010), 114; and Ia. N. Dlugolenskii, *Vek Dostoevskogo* (Sankt-Peterburg, 2007), 109–110.

122. On Chernyshevskii's civil execution, also see M. P. Sazhin, *Vospominaniia* (Moscow, 1925), 16–18; Laura Engelstein, "Revolution and the Theater of Public Life in Nineteenth-Century Russia" in I. Wolloch, ed., *Revolution and the Meaning of Freedom in the Nineteenth Century* (Stanford, CA: Stanford University Press, 1996), 331–332; and Gleason, *Young Russia*, 226–228.

123. See F. V. Volkhovskii, "Na Mytninskoi ploshchadi" in A. N. Tsamutali and S. S. Volk, eds., *Shturmany budushchei buri* (Leningrad, 1983), 248–253.

124. Such sympathetic crowds returned at the public sentencing related to the Karakozov and Nechaev affaris. There was a sufficiently large and varied public at the sentencing of Ishutin on October 3 or 4, 1866, that Third Section officials expressed anxiety about the potential for a public demonstration erupting. See GARF, 109, op. 1-a, d. 299.

125. M. S. Al'tman, *Ivan Gavrilovich Pryzhov. Ocherki, stat'i, pis'ma* (Moscow, 1934), 100–101.

126. GARF, 109, op. 1-a, d. 652.

127. GARF, 109, op. 3-a, d. 277.

128. For a listing of the various proclamations, see "Proklamatsii 60-kh godov," *Byloe* 4 (May, 1903): 6–8.

129. Vladimir Burtsev, *Za sto let: Sbornik po istorii politicheskikh i obshchestvennykh dvizhenii v Rossii* (London, 1897), 45–46.

130. Panteleev, *Iz vospominanii*, 242.

131. Cited in Shelgunov, *Vospominaniia*, 333.

132. Burtsev, *Za sto let*, 34.

133. Shelgunov, *Vospominaniia*, 350.

134. Ibid.

135. Gerasimova, "Krizis," 102.

136. V. Bogucharskii, *Aktivnoe narodnichetsvo semidesiatykh godov* (Moscow, 1912), 44.

137. Panteleev, *Iz vospominanii*, 246.

138. Bogucharskii, ed., *Gosudarstvennye prestupleniia*, 229.

139. Lev Deich, *Za polveka*, 60.

140. Sergei Bulgakov, "Heroism and Asceticism (Reflections on the Religious Nature of the Russian Intelligentsia)" in *Signposts: A Collection of Articles on the Russian Intelligentsia*, trans. and ed. Marshall Shatz and Judith Zimmerman (Irvine, CA.: Charles Schlacks Jr., 1986), 19.

CHAPTER 2

1. Brower, *Training the Nihilists*, 118.

2. The best source on the importance of the sons of clergymen is Manchester, *Holy Fathers*. An old argument that Manchester has convincingly revived suggests that in the nihilist struggle to counteract the dominance of the nobility, the training and values of a seminary education had a strong influence.

3. Brower, *Training the Nihilists*, 121

4. Richard Stites, *The Women's Liberation Movement in Russia: Feminism, Nihilism, and Bolshevism, 1860–1930* (Princeton, NJ: Princeton University Press, 1978), 100.

5. Sergei Kalinchuk, "Psikhologicheskii faktor v deiatel'nosti 'Zemli i Voli' 1870-kh godov," *Voprosy istorii* 3 (1999): 47.

6. Stephen Greenblatt, *Renaissance Self-Fashioning from More to Shakespeare* (Chicago: University of Chicago Press, 1980).

7. Aleksandr Skabichevskii, quoted in Gleason, *Young Russia*, 143.

8. On Nikol'skii, see Venturi, *Roots*, 333. On Lutsernov, see V. A. Anzimirov, *Kramol'niki* (Moscow, 1907), 11–12.

9. Greenblatt, *Renaissance Self-Fashioning*, 113.

10. Ibid., 2nd ed., 2009, xi–xviii.

11. Michel Foucault, "What is Enlightenment?," in Paul Rabinow, ed., *The Foucault Reader* (New York: Pantheon Books, 1984), 42.

12. Greenblatt, *Renaissance Self-Fashioning*, 7–8.

13. For two self-fashioning projects prior to the reform era, although described in somewhat different terms, see Iurii Lotman, "The Decembrist in Daily Life" in Nakhimovsky, ed., *The Semiotics of Russian Cultural History* (Ithaca: Cornell University Press, 1985) and Randolph, *The House in the Garden*.

14. Chernyshevsky, *What Is To Be Done?*, 255.

15. D. I. Pisarev, *Literaturnaia kritika v trekh tomakh*, vol. 2 (Leningrad, 1981), 369.

16. Bulgakov, "Heroism and Asceticism" in *Signposts*, 34.

17. For an in-depth and insightful reading of the novel, see Andrew M. Drozd, *Chernyshevksii's "What Is To Be Done?": A Reevaluation* (Chicago: Northwestern University Press, 2001). This study takes *What Is To Be Done?* seriously as a work of art, emphasizing its irony and ambiguity over its polemical message and, with some justification, reading the narrative's undertone as its dominant aspect. Drozd even goes so far as to suggest that the "how-to" message that appealed to contemporaries and has been the dominant interpretation of the novel for generations was never Chernyshevskii's primary aim. This reinterpretation seems to me at once fascinating and excessive, but even if it is accurate with respect to Chernyshevskii's intent, it still has little to do with the reception of the novel and its impact on the nihilism of the 1860s.

18. Skabichevskii, *Vospominaniia*, 291.

19. Irina Paperno, *Chernyshevskii and the Age of Realism: A Study in the Semiotics of Behavior* (Stanford, CA: Stanford University Press, 1988), 37.

20. Nikolai Berdyaev, *The Russian Idea*, trans. R. M. French (London: Geoffrey Bles, 1947), 123.

21. Pisarev, *Literaturnaia kritika*, vol. 1, 230.

22. Ibid., 238.

23. Ibid., 258.

24. Petr Kropotkin, *Memoirs of a Revolutionist* (Boston: Houghton Mifflin, 1962), 195.

25. Wilson, *Bohemians*, 174.

26. Gleason, *Young Russia*, 131.

27. Paperno, *Chernyshevskii*, 18.

28. Kavelin's letter to Herzen, cited in N. N. Hovikova, "N. G. Chernyshevskii i Komitet 'Velikorussa'" in *Revoliutsionnaia situatsiia v Rossii v 1859–1861 gg.* (Moscow, 1960), 299–300.

29. Nikolai Charushin, *O dalekom proshlom: Iz vospominanii o revoliutsionnom dvizhenii 70-ikh godov 19 veka* (Moscow, 1973), 44.

30. Berlin, *Russian Thinkers*, 230.

31. Skabichevskii, *Vospominaniia*, 290.

32. Cited in Brower, *Training the Nihilists*, 167.

33. Skabichevskii, *Vospominaniia*, 290.

34. Chernyshevskii, *What Is To Be Done?*, 49.

35. Pisarev, *Literaturnaia kritika*, 391.

36. Ibid., 384.

37. Cited in Paperno, *Chernyshevskii*, 27.

38. Skabichevskii, *Vospominaniia*, 291.

39. Chernyshevskii, *What Is To Be Done?*, 211.

40. Ibid., 212.

41. For a discussion of Mikhailov, see Stites, *Women's Liberation*, 38–48.

42. See the description in A. Kornilova-Morozova, "Perovskaia i osnovanie kruzhka chaikovtsev," *Katorga i ssylka* 22 (1926): 10–16.

43. On the Alarchin Courses, see Engel, *Mothers and Daughters*, 112.

44. Cited in Saunders, *Russia in the Age of Reaction*, 314.

45. Ibid., 49.

46. Ibid., 87.

47. Vodovozova, *Na zare zhizni*, 196.

48. Ibid., 222.

49. Shcherbakova, *Otshchepentsy*, 53.

50. V. K. Debagorii-Mokrievich, *Ot buntarstva k terrorizmu* (Moscow, 1930), 9.

51. E. Dubenskaia, "Dmitrii Aleksandrovich Klements," *Katorga i ssylka* 5 (1930): 173.

52. Tikhomirov, *Vospominaniia*, 94.

53. Richard Sennett, *The Fall of Public Man* (New York: W. W. Norton, 1974).

54. Christine Ruane, *The Empire's New Clothes: A History of the Russian Fashion Industry, 1700–1917* (New Haven: Yale University Press, 2009), 151.

55. Morozov, *Povesti*, vol. 2, 138.

56. Gleason, *Young Russia*, 271.

57. B. P. Koz'min, *Revoliutsionnoe podpol'e v epokhu "belogo terrora"* (Moscow, 1929), 141.

58. Vladimir Mikhnevich, *Nashi znakomye* (Saint Petersburg, 1884), 91.

59. Skabichevskii, *Vospominaniia*, 292.

60. See Kalinchuk, "Psikhologicheskii faktor," 48.

61. Cited in William C. Brumfield, "Sleptsov Redivivus" *California Slavic Studies* 9 (1976): 40.

62. Kalinchuk, "Psikhologicheskii faktor," 50.

63. Peter Pozefsky, *The Nihilist Imagination: Dmitry Pisarev and the Cultural Origins of Russian Radicalism (1860–1868)* (New York: Peter Lang Publishing, 2003), 13.

64. Henri Murger, *Bohemian Life*, trans. George. B. Ives (Philadelphia: George Barrie and Son, 1899), xi.

65. Wilson, *Bohemians*, 28.

66. Emile Durkheim, *Suicide: A Study in Sociology*, trans. John Spaulding (London, 1952).

67. See, for the obvious example, David Riesman, Nathan Glazer, and Reuel Denny, *The Lonely Crowd* (New Haven: Yale University Press, 2001).

68. Georg Simmel, *Conflict and the Web of Group Affiliations*, trans. Reinhard Bendix (Glencoe, IL: The Free Press, 1955), 163.

69. Karp et al., *Being Urban: A Sociology of City Life*, 2nd ed. (New York: Praeger, 1991), 134.

70. Fischer, *Urban Experience*, 199.

71. Umberto Eco, "Towards a Semiotic Inquity into the Television Message" (1965). Cited in Dick Hebdige, *Subculture: The Meaning of Style* (New York: Routledge, 1979), 105.

72. Shcherbakova, *Otshchepentsy*, 4.

73. Hebdige, *Subculture*, 102.

74. Ibid., 102. Hebdige is interested here in the role of commodities, but norms of any sort can be substituted.

75. Kornilova-Morozova, "Perovskaia," 19.

76. Vera Zasulich, *Vospominaniia* (Moscow, 1931), 18.

77. Bazileva, "Arteli," 204–212.

78. Quoted in Deborah Hardy, *Petr Tkachev, The Critic as Jacobin* (Seattle: University of Washington Press, 1977), 35.

79. Pribyleva-Korba and Figner, eds., *Mikhailov*, 87.

80. Zasulich, "Nechaevskoe delo," 25.

81. A good description of communal life is found in Kornilova-Morozova, "Perovskaia," 16–17.

82. Ibid., 17.

83. A lengthy, if tendentious, description of the commune can be found in the memoirs of one of its inhabitants: E. I. Zhukovskaia, *Zapiski* (Moscow: Agraf, 2001).

84. Discussed in A.Ia. Panaeva, *Vospominaniia* (Moscow: Khudozhestvennaia literatura, 1972), 330–336.

85. Cited in Brower, *Training the Nihilists*, 222.

86. On the commune's problems, see Chukovskii, *Liudi i knigi* (Moscow, 1958), 221–249.

87. Brower, *Training the Nihilists*, 222.

88. GARF, f. 109, op, 1-a, d. 563.

CHAPTER 3

1. E. S. Vilenskaia, *Revoliutsionnoe podpol'e v Rossii 60-e gody XIX v.* (Leningrad, 1965), 84.

2. See I. E. Barenbaum, *N. A. Serno-Solov'evich (1834–1866): Ocherk knigotorgovoi i knigoizdatel'skoi deiatel'nosti* (Moscow, 1961).

3. Deich, *Za polveka*, 272.

4. B. P. Koz'min, *Nechaev i Nechaevtsy*, (Moscow, 1931), 22.

5. See, for example, Zemfir Ralli-Arbore, "Sergei Gennad'evich Nechaev," *Byloe* 7 (1906).

6. For example, a multi-volume series, M. V. Nechkina, ed., *Revoliutsionnaia situatsiia v Rossii v 1859–1861 gg.* vols. 1–6 (Moscow, 1960–1974), was published to celebrate the one hundredth anniversary of the so-called "first revolutionary situation."

7. Venturi, *Roots*, 253–284.

8. Various names have been added to and subtracted from this list of core members. For a detailed discussion of the initial organization, see M. V. Nechkina, "Vozniknovenie pervoi 'Zemli i Voli'" in *Revoliutsionnaia situatsiia*, 283–298.

9. See E. S. Vilenskaia, "Novye arkhivnye materialy o deiatel'nosti 'Zemli i Voli'" in Nechkina, ed., *Revoliutsionnaia situatsiia*, vol. 3, 38–50.

10. Ibid., 45.

11. See V. I. Neupokoev, "Vazhneishii programmnyi dokument 'Zemli i voli' 60-kh XIX veka," *Revoliutsionnaia situatsiia v Rossii v 1859–1861 gg.* (Moscow, 1960), 538.

12. Cited in Vilenskaia, *Podpol'e*, 111.

13. Burtsev, *Za sto let*, 68.

14. L. F. Panteleev, *Vospominaniia* (Leningrad, 1958), 339.

15. See Iu. V. Kulikov, "Voprosy revoliutsionnoi programmy i taktiki v proklamatsii 'Molodaia Rossiia'" in Nechkina, ed. *Revoliutsionnaia situatsiia v Rossii* (1962), 245–249.

16. Ibid., Neupokoev, "Vazhneishii programmnyi dokument," 538.

17. Sleptsov, cited in Tsamutali, *Shturmany*, 311–312.

18. Panteleev, cited in Tsamutali, *Shturmany,* 271.

19. Herzen, cited in Venturi, *Roots*, 275.

20. Ibid., 268.

21. R. V. Filippov, *Revoliutsionnaia narodnicheskaia organizatsiia N. A. Ishutina i I. A. Khudiakova* (Moscow, 1964), 25–26.

22. Ibid., 32.

23. Ibid., 36.

24. Ibid., 65.

25. Ibid., 51.
26. Ibid., 138.
27. Cited in Verhoeven, *Odd Man*, 36.
28. For a detailed discussion of some of these enterprises, see E. S. Vilenskaia, "Proizvoditel'nye assotsiatsii v Rossii v seredine 60-kh godov XIX-v." *Istoricheskie zapiski* 68 (1961).
29. Filippov, *Organizatsiia*, 148.
30. Ibid., 51.
31. Ibid., 54 and 159–160.
32. Ibid., 160–162.
33. M. M. Klevenskii and K. G. Kotel'nikov, eds., *Pokushenie Karakozova: Stenograficheskii otchet po delu D. Karakozova, I. Khudiakova, N. Ishutina*, vol. 1 (Moscow-Leningrad, 1928–1930), 208.
34. Ibid., 208.
35. Ibid., 106.
36. Filippov, *Organizatsiia*, 173.
37. Vilenskaia, *Podpol'e*, 393–394.
38. Bazilevskii, ed., *Gosudarstvennye prestupleniia*, 251 and 265.
39. Cited in Filippov, *Organizatsiia*, 68.
40. Bazilevskii, ed., *Gosudarstvennye prestupleniia*, 252.
41. Venturi, *Roots*, 334.
42. Filippov, *Organizatsiia*, 89.
43. Shcherbakova, *Otshchepentsy*, 56.
44. Klevenskii and Kotel'nikov, eds., *Pokushenie*, 28.
45. Verhoeven, *Odd Man*, 32.
46. Klevenskii and Kotel'nikov, eds., *Pokushenie*, 87. Alfred Nobel did not take out a patent for dynamite until 1867.
47. Testimony of D. A. Iurasov, May 31, 1866. Cited in Budnitskii, *Istoriia terrorizma*, 41–42.
48. Vilenskaia, *Podpol'e*, 397–398.
49. Ibid., 398.
50. See conflicting testimony in Klevenskii and Kotel'nikov, eds., *Pokushenie*, 69–72.
51. Ibid., 209.
52. Filippov, *Organizatsiia*, 146. Verhoeven argues that Karakozov's attempt at "propaganda by deed" played a seminal role in the advent of terrorist methods.
53. Verhoeven, *Odd Man*, 147–149 and note, 213.
54. Filippov, *Organizatsiia*, 75.
55. Cited in Daly, *Autocracy*, 19.
56. A striking example of that exaggeration appears in John Merriman, *The Dynamite Club: How a Bombing in Fin-de-Siècle Paris Ignited the Age of Modern Terror* (Boston: Houghton Mifflin Harcourt, 2009), in which a distinguished historian claims that Nechaev "founded" The People's Will, an organization with which he had nothing to do and that came into being several years after his incarceration. See 47.
57. Budnitskii, *Istoriia terrorizma*, 47–49.
58. Bazilevskii, ed., *Gosudarstvennye prestupleniia*, 337.
59. Ibid., 334.
60. Ibid., 337.
61. N. F. Bel'chikov, "S. G. Nechaev v sele Ivanove v 60-e gody," *Katorga i ssylka* 1 (1925), 134–152.
62. Zasulich, "Nechaevskoe delo," 31.
63. Ralli-Arbore, "Nechaev," 137–138.
64. Zasulich, *Vospominaniia*, 30.
65. Tikhomirov, *Vospominaniia*, 50.
66. Zasulich, "Nechaevskoe delo," 42–46.
67. Bazilevskii, ed., *Gosudarstvennye prestupleniia*, 335.
68. Zasulich, *Vospominaniia*, 28–33.

69. Koz'min, *Nechaevtsy*, 108.

70. Zasulich, "Nechaevskoe delo," 50. Nechaev even sent a false inspector from the supposed revolutionary leadership to "report" on the activities of the Petrovskii students.

71. Zasulich, *Vospominaniia*, 37.

72. Koz'min, *Nechaevtsy*, 104.

73. Zasulich, *Vospominaniia*, 27.

74. Koz'min, *Nechaevtsy*, 116–117.

75. Ibid., 24.

76. Ibid., 108.

77. Cited in Venturi, *Roots*, 361.

78. See I. E. Barenbaum, "Knizhnyi magazin A. A. Cherkesova i ego rol' v osvoboditel'nom dvizhenii 1860-kh gg. v Rossii" in S. G. Luppov and N. V. Paramonova, *Knigotorgovoe i bibliotechnoe delo v Rossii v XVII-pervoi polovine XIX v.*(Leningrad, 1981), 52–68.

79. Koz'min, *Nechaevtsy*, 22.

80. Bazilevskii, ed., *Gosudarstvennye prestupleniia*, 333.

81. Ibid., 335.

82. Zasulich, *Vospominaniia*, 47.

83. Zasulich, "Nechaevskoe delo," 58.

84. Ibid.

85. Zasulich, *Vospominaniia*, 56.

86. Zasulich "Nechaevskoe delo," 69.

87. See N. V. Chaikovskii, *Religioznye i obshchestvennye iskaniia* (Paris, 1929), 39.

88. Aksel'rod, *Perezhitoe i peredumannoe*, I (Berlin, 1923), reprint edition, 74.

89. Kornilova-Morozova, "Perovskaia," 27.

90. Chaikovskii, *Religioznye*, 49.

91. Ibid., 41.

92. Charushin, *O dalekom proshlom*, 108.

93. Kropotkin, *Memoirs*, 201.

94. Aksel'rod, *Perezhitoe*, 75.

95. Bogucharskii, *Aktivnoe*, 152.

96. Aksel'rod, *Perezhitoe*, 135.

97. Kravchinskii, "Podpol'naia Rossiia," 105.

98. Ibid., 106.

99. Aksel'rod, *Perezhitoe*, 153.

100. On Aleksandrov, see Kornilova-Morozova, "Perovskaia," 18.

101. Kropotkin, *Memoirs*, 210.

102. Morozov, *Povesti*, 298.

103. Leonid Shishko, *Sergei Mikhailovich Kravchinskii i Kruzhok Chaikovtsev: Iz vospominanii i zametok starogo narodnika* (St. Petersburg, 1906), 37.

104. Charushin, *O dalekom proshlom*, 221.

105. E. Dubenskaia, "Dmitrii Aleksandrovich Klements," *Katorga i ssylka* 5 (1930): 170.

106. Kropotkin, *Memoirs*, 202.

107. Morozov, *Povesti*, 83.

108. Kornilova-Morozova, "Perovskaia," 25. See also Chaikovskii, *Religioznye*, 48.

109. S. Sinegub, *Zapiski chaikovtsa* (Moscow-Leningrad, 1929), 37–84.

110. S. N. Valk et al., eds., *Revoliutsionnoe narodnichestvo 70-kh godov XIX veka Tom I 1870–1875* (Moscow, 1964), 220. Also see Kornilova-Morozova, "Perovskaia," 14.

111. Kropotkin, *Memoirs*, 203.

112. Paul Miliukov, "The Beginnings of the Revolutionary Movement" in Miliukov, et al., *History of Russia: Reforms, Reaction, Revolutions*, trans. Charles Lam Markmann (New York: Funk and Wagnalls, 1969), 64.

113. Charushin, *O dalekom proshlom*, 221.

114. Valk et al., eds., *Revoliutsionnoe narodnichestvo* vol. 1, 221.

115. Tikhomirov, *Vospominaniia*, 54.

116. Shishko, *Kravchinskii*, 13.

117. Charushin, *O dalekom proshlom*, 221.

118. Kropotkin, *Memoirs*, 202.

119. On this religious offshoot of the movement to the people, see K. A. Solov'ev, *Ia skazal: Vy bogy* (Moscow, 1998).

120. Chaikovskii, *Religioznye*, 62.

121. Ibid., 64.

122. See Kornilova-Morozova, "Perovskaia," 18.

123. Kropotkin, *Memoirs*, 211.

124. Tikhomirov, *Vospominaniia*, 79.

125. Kropotkin, *Memoirs*, 214.

126. Ibid., 218.

127. Ibid., 325.

128. Chaikovskii, *Religioznye*, 82.

129. Ibid., 66–68.

CHAPTER 4

1. S. N. Krivenko, cited in Wortman, *Crisis*, 27.

2. Idealization of the peasantry, in a variety of different forms, was a defining aspect of Russian populism even in its most radical forms, but it is important to keep in mind that idealization was far from simple and uniform, and over time it often shaded into disappointment and disillusion. Cathy Frierson's *Peasant Icons: Representations of Rural People in Late 19th Century Russia* (New York: Oxford University Press, 1993) gives the most complex and nuanced reading of intelligentsia's perceptions of the peasantry in this era.

3. Itenberg, *Dvizhenie*, 267.

4. Chernyshevskii, *Polnoe sobranie sochinenii T. VII* (Moscow, 1939), 889.

5. On Zaichnevskii, see Kulikov, "Molodaia Rossiia," 245; on Peterson, see Vilenskaia, *Podpol'e*, 212.

6. Kropotkin, *Memoirs*, 199.

7. While Bakunin and Lavrov gave impetus and direction to the ventures into the countryside, they were equally inspired by the work of Vasilii Bervi-Flerovskii, in particular his *The Position of the Working Class in Russia*.

8. In the late 1860s, Bakunin argued in a series of articles that Russian revolutionaries needed to work among the people in order to incite a mass rebellion. See Robert Cutler, ed., *The Basic Bakunin* (New York: Prometheus Books, 1992).

9. Lavrov espoused these ideas most forcefully in his "Historical Letters" of 1870. See *Historical Letters*, trans. James P. Scanlan (Berkeley: University of California Press, 1967).

10. Cited in Itenberg, *Dvizhenie*, 179.

11. Stepan Shiraev, "Avtobiograficheskaia zapiska i pis'ma," *Krasnyi arkhiv* 7 (1924): 78.

12. Charushin, *O dalekom proshlom*, 201.

13. GARF, F. 109, op. 3-a, d. 3010.

14. Plekhanov, "Russkii rabochii v revoliutsionnom dvizhenii" in *Sochinenia*, vol. 3 (Moscow, 1923), 123.

15. For the period of the 1860s, see Zelnik, *Labor and Society*, 200–239.

16. A. A. Kviatkovskii, "Avtobiograficheskoe zaiavlenie A. A. Kviatkovskogo" *Krasnyi arkhiv* 1 (1926): 161.

17. Shishko, *Kravchinskii*, 32.

18. Charushin, *O dalekom proshlom*, 141.

19. Plekhanov, "Russkii rabochii" in *Sochineniia*, vol. 3 (Moscow, 1923), 123.

20. Ibid., 132.

21. Deich, *Za polveka* II, 278.

22. Plekhanov, "Russkii rabochii," 137.

23. Deich, *Za polveka* II, 278.

24. Plekhanov, "Russkii rabochii," 136–137.

25. Bazilevskii, ed., *Gosudarstvennye prestupleniia*, 463.

26. Ibid., 463.

27. Ibid., GP, 461–462.

28. S. F. Kovalik, cited in Itenberg, *Dvizhenie*, 168.

29. Burtsev, *Za sto let*, 98.

30. M. Frolenko, "Chaikovskii i ego bogochelovechestvo," *Katorga i ssylka* 26 (1926): 220. Also see Charushin, *O dalekom proshlom*, 173. The early journey of Kravchinskii and Rogachev was widely reported on in numerous memoirs.

31. Ibid., 200.

32. Katerina Breshkovskaia, *Hidden Springs of the Russian Revolution* (Stanford, CA: Stanford University Press, 1931), 17.

33. Mikhail Frolenko, "Khozhdenie v narod, 1874" *Katorga i ssylka* 11 (1924): 12.

34. Charushin, *O dalekom proshlom*, 200.

35. Ibid., 172.

36. Shishko, *Kravchinskii*, 28–29.

37. Cited in Itenberg, *Dvizhenie*, 186.

38. Charushin, *O dalekom proshlom*, 202.

39. Deich, *Za polveka*, 60.

40. Zasulich, *Vospominaniia*, 35.

41. Dmitrii Klements, *Iz proshlogo. Vospominaniia* (Moscow, 1925), 123.

42. Ivanchin-Pisarev, *Iz vospominanii o "Khozhdenii v narod"* (St. Petersburg, 1907), 6. Italics in original.

43. Burtsev, *Za sto let*, 130.

44. Ibid., 131.

45. Vladimir Korolenko, *The History of My Contemporary*, trans. Neil Parsons (Oxford, UK: Oxford University Press, 1972), 178.

46. Cited in Itenberg, *Dvizhenie*, 130.

47. Debagorii-Mokrievich, *Ot buntarstva*, 38.

48. Wortman, *Crisis*, 18.

49. Lev Tikhomirov, *Zagovorshchiki i politsiia* (Moscow, 1930), 40–41.

50. Figner, *Zapechatlennyi trud*, 153.

51. Charushin, *O dalekom proshlom*, 202.

52. Kravchinskii, "Podpol'naia Rossiia," 38.

53. O. V. Aptekman, *Obshchestvo "Zemlia i Volia" 70-kh gg. Po lichnym vospominaniiam* (Petrograd, 1924), 91.

54. Kravchinskii, "Podpol'naia Rossiia," 38.

55. Frolenko, "Chaikovskii." 217–223.

56. Charushin, *O dalekom proshlom*, 214.

57. Cited in Shcherbakova, *Otshchepentsy*, 101.

58. Morozov, *Povesti*, 89.

59. Aksel'rod, *Perezhitoe*, 112–113.

60. Plekhanov, "Russkii rabochii," 134.

61. Brower, *Training the Nihilists*, 143. Note that Brower is referring to the number of people who were arrested.

62. Aptekman, *Obshchestvo "Zemlia i Volia,"* 49.

63. Debagorii-Mokrievich, *Ot buntarstva*, 38.

64. Aksel'rod, *Perezhitoe*, 114.

65. Debagorii-Mokrievich, *Ot buntarstva*, 64–65.

66. S. A. Viktorova-Val'ter, "Iz zhizni revoliutsionnoi molodezhi" *Katorga i ssylka* 11 (1924), 67.

67. Charushin, *O dalekom proshlom*, 145.

68. Viktorova-Val'ter, "Iz zhizni," 65.

69. On this trend across the 19th century in Western Europe, see, for example, Malcolm Andrews, *The Search for the Picturesque: Landscape Aesthetics and Tourism in Great Britain, 1760–1800* (Stanford, CA: Stanford University Press, 1989); Jonas Frykman and Orvar Lofgren, *Culture Builders: A Historical Anthropology of Middle Class Life* (New Brunswick, NJ: Rutgers University Press, 1987); and Nicholas Green, *The Spectacle of Nature: Landscape and Bourgeois Culture in Nineteenth-Century France* (Manchester, UK: Manchester University Press, 1990); and Thomas Lekan, *Imagining the Nation in Nature: Landscape Preservation and German Identity, 1885–1945* (Cambridge: Harvard University Press, 2004).

70. See Christopher Ely, *This Meager Nature: Landscape and National Identity in Imperial Russia* (DeKalb, IL: Northern Illinois University Press, 2002); Louise McReynolds, "The Prerevolutionary Russian Tourist" in Gorsuch and Koenker, eds., *Turizm: The Russian and East European Tourist Under Capitalism and Socialism* (Ithaca, NY: Cornell University Press, 2006); and Willard Sunderland, *Taming the Wild Field: Colonization and Empire on the Russian Steppe* (Ithaca, NY: Cornell University Press, 2004), 160–174.

71. Aptekman, *Obshchestvo "Zemlia i Volia,"* 133.

72. Aksel'rod, *Perezhitoe*, 113.

73. Morozov, *Povesti*, 99.

74. Ibid., 152–153.

75. G. F. Cherniavskaia-Bokhanovskaia, "Avtobiografiia," *Katorga i ssylka* 42 (1928): 54.

76. Deich, *Za sto let*, 166.

77. Lopatin, cited in Shcherbakova, *Otshchepentsy*, 100.

78. Plekhanov, "Russkii rabochii," 128.

79. Morozov, *Povesti*, 176.

80. N. A. Golovina-Iurgenson, "Moi vospominaniia," *Katorga i ssylka* 6 (1923): 32.

81. Daniel Field, "Peasants and Propagandists in the Russian Movement to the People of 1874," *Journal of Modern History* (1987): 437.

82. Figner, *Zapechatlennyi trud*, 153.

83. Ibid., 153 and 164.

84. Valk et al., eds., *Revoliutsionnoe narodnichestvo*, vol. 1, 145–151.

85. Tikhomirov, *Zagovorshchiki*, 34.

86. Klements, *Iz proshlogo*, 123–126.

87. Frolenko, *Zapiski semidesiatnika* (Moscow, 1927), 323.

88. Figner, *Zapechatlennyi trud*, 99.

89. Ibid., 101.

90. Cherniavskaia-Bokhanovskaia, "Avtobiografiia," 54.

91. Deich, *Za polveka* I, 174.

92. Plekhanov, "Russkii rabochii," 137.

93. Aptekman, *Obshchestvo "Zemlia i Volia,"* 266.

94. Ibid., 266.

95. P. Semeniuta, "Iz vospominanii ob A. I. Zheliabove," *Byloe* 4 (1906): 219.

96. Figner *Zapechatlennyi trud*, 154.

97. Morozov, *Povesti*, vol. 2, 264–265.

98. Figner, *Zapechatlennyi trud*, 205.

99. Deich, *Za polveka* II, 62

100. Aptekman, *Obshchestvo "Zemlia i Volia,"* 383.

101. Quoted in Hardy, *Land and Freedom*, 91.

102. Morozov, *Povesti*, vol 2, 262.

103. Pribyleva-Korba and Figner, eds., *Mikhailov*, 101.

104. Cited in Field, "Peasants and Propagandists," 419.

105. Debagorii-Mokrievich, *Ot buntarstva*, 114.

106. Frolenko, *Zapiski*, 60.

107. Figner, *Zapechatlennyi trud*, 177.

108. Cited in Hardy, *Land and Freedom*, 91.

109. See discussion in Ivanchin-Pisarev, who worked closely with Solov'ev, *Iz vospominanii*, 243–244.

110. M. M. Chernavskii, "Demonstratsiia 6 dekabria 1876 goda," *Katorga i ssylka* 4 (1926): 10.

111. See Bogucharskii, ed., *Gosudarstvennye prestupleniia*, 243–244.

112. Figner, *Zapechatlennyi trud*, 275.

113. Debagorii-Mokrievich, *Ot buntarstva*, 126–127.

114. Ibid., 74.

115. Quoted in Daniel Field, *Rebels in the Name of the Tsar* (Boston: Houghton-Mifflin, 1976), 164.

116. It should be noted that Bakunin himself did not share their view.

117. Ibid., 137.

118. Debagorii-Mokrievich, *Ot buntarstva*, 138.

119. Ibid., 156.

120. Deich, *Za polveka* II, 68–69.

121. Ibid., 66.

122. Debagorii-Mokrievich, *Ot buntarstva*, 155.

123. Ibid., 155.

124. Deich, *Za polveka* II, 247.

125. "Ot ispolnitel'nago komiteta," in *Narodnaia Volia 1* (October 1879) in B. Bazilevskii, ed., *Literatura partii Narodnoi Voli* (Paris, 1905), 4.

126. Tatishchev, *Imperator Aleksandr II*, 895.

127. Mikhail Frolenko, cited in Kalinchuk, "Psikhologicheskii faktor," 52.

128. Debagorii-Mokrievich, *Ot buntarstva*, 118.

129. Philip Pomper, *The Russian Revolutionary Intelligentsia*, 2nd Edition (Wheeling, IL: Harlan Davidson, 1993), 124.

130. Charushin, *O dalekom proshlom*, 190.

CHAPTER 5

1. S. A. Nikitin, *Slavianskie komitety v Rossii v 1858–1876 godakh* (Moscow, 1960).

2. On the public response to the war, see ibid. Also V. M. Khevrolina, "Revoliutsionnoe narodnichestvo i natsional'no-osvoboditel'noe divizhenie na Balkanakh v 1875–1876" in *Slavianskoe vozrozhdenie* (Moscow, 1966) and I. V. Koz'menko "Russkoe obshchestvo i aprel'skoe Bolgarskoe vosstanie 1876 g.," *Voprosy istorii* 5 (1947).

3. See McReynolds, *The News*, 73–87. She writes, "Atrocities committed by Ottoman Turks ... furnished the crucible that caused the Russian mass-circulation press to come of age" (73). Also see Effie Ambler, *Russian Journalism and Politics, 1861–1881; the Career of Aleksei S. Suvorin* (Detroit: Wayne State University Press, 1972), 34–35.

4. "Na Strazhdushchikh Slavian!" *Delo* 8 (August, 1876), 99–100; "Zapiski profana," *Otechestvennye zapiski* 10 (October, 1876), 249–250

5. *Vestnik Evropy*, (October, 1876).

6. Cited in S. A. Nikitin, ed. *Osvoboditel'naia bor'ba iuzhnykh slavian i Rossiia* I (Moscow, 1960), 470.

7. Astrid Tuminez, *Russian Nationalism since 1856: Ideology and the Making of Foreign Policy* (Lanham MD: Rowan and Littlefield Publishers, 2000), 89.

8. A. L. Narochnitskii, ed., *Rossiia i natsional'no-osvoboditel'naia bor'ba na Balkanakh, 1875–1878* (Moscow, 1978), 12 and 60–61.

9. See, for example, D. A. Miliutin, *Dnevnik* (Moscow: Rosspen, 2009), 27–178.

10. Ibid., 100.

11. "Na Strazhdushchikh slavian!," *Delo* 8 (1876): 96–99.

12. *Golos* 204 (July 25, 1876) and *Novoe vremia* 144 (July 24, 1876). *Novoe vremia* reported that a run of 20,000 portraits of Cherniaev were published in July and sold out on the first day. See *Novoe vremia* 130 (July 10, 1876).

13. *Golos* 231 (August 22, 1876).

14. Nikitin, *Slavianskie komitety*, 321.

15. Klements, *Iz proshlogo*, 135.

16. *Otechestvennye zapiski* 10 (October, 1876).

17. On the importance of the mass-circulation press in facilitating a sense of national identity, see Benedict Anderson, *Imagined Communities* (New York: Verso, 2006), 22–36.

18. Boguchevskii, "Russkoe osvoboditel'noe dvizhenie i voina za osvobozhdenie Bolgarii," *Sovremennik*, 1911, quoted in Narochnitskaia, ed., *Rossiia*, 157.

19. A reasonable estimate from a Third Section memo places the number of demonstrators at a Petersburg send-off at more than 2,000. In Moscow they may have been much larger. Moscow's governor-general, V. A. Dolgorukov, put the number of one at 10,000. See Nikitin, ed., *Osvoboditel'naia bor'ba*, 364, 373.

20. *Golos* 242 (Sept. 2, 1876).

21. Nikitin, ed., *Osvoboditel'naia bor'ba*, 317.

22. Ibid., 373.

23. Narochnitskii, ed., *Rossiia*, 157.

24. Nikitin, ed., *Osvoboditel'naia bor'ba*, 322. The Kazan Chief of Police, A. N. Zhitkov, worried that public prayer could allow agitators to stir up discontent with the government. See Narochnitskii, ed., *Rossiia*, 165.

25. Konstantin Pobedonostsev, *Pis'ma Pobedonostseva k Aleksandru III*, vol. 1 (Moscow, 1925), 49.

26. Narochnitskii, ed., *Rossiia*, 128.

27. Nikitin, ed., *Osvoboditel'naia bor'ba*, 373.

28. Ibid., 333.

29. *Golos* 211 (August 1, 1876).

30. Miliutin, *Dnevnik*, 123.

31. Nikitin, ed., *Osvoboditel'naia bor'ba*, 333–334.

32. Ibid., 361.

33. Narochnitskii, ed., *Rossiia*, 16.

34. Nikitin, ed., *Osvoboditel'naia bor'ba*, 379.

35. N. A. Naidenov, *Vospominaniia o vedennom, slyshannom i ispytannom*, vol. 2 (Newtonville, MA: Oriental Rsearch Partners, 1976), 157.

36. *Golos* 238 (August 29, 1876).

37. Nikitin, ed., *Osvoboditel'naia bor'ba*, 470.

38. *Novoe vremia* 201 (Sept. 19, 1876).

39. *Golos* 237 (August 28, 1876).

40. Cited in M. Popruzhenko, "Obshchestvennoe nastroenie v Rossii nakanune Osvoboditel'noi voiny" in *Proslava na osvoboditelnata voina* (Sofia, 1929), 295–296.

41. Nikitin, ed., *Osvoboditel'naia bor'ba*, 336.

42. "Zapiski profana," *Otechestvennye zapiski* (October, 1876), 238.

43. Narochnitskii, ed., *Rossiia*, 177.

44. *Otechestvennye zapiski* 10 (October, 1876), 235.

45. Nikitin, ed., *Osvoboditel'naia bor'ba*, 39.

46. Quoted in Venturi, *Roots*, 567.

47. M.A,. Timofeev, "Perezhitoe," *Katorga i ssylka*. 57 (1929): 96–99.

48. Plekhanov, "Russkii rabochii," 150.

49. Chernavskii, "Demonstratsiia," 12.

50. Cited in Volk, *Narodnaia Volia*, 66.

51. Nikolai Morozov, *Terroristicheskaia bor'ba* (London, 1980), 5.

52. Aptekman, *Obshchestvo "Zemlia i Volia,"* 182.

53. GARF f. 109, op. 1-a, d. 714, 3–4.

54. Pribyleva-Korba and Figner, eds., *Mikhailov*, 100–101.

55. Frolenko, *Zapiski*, 170.

56. S. P. Shvetsov (Marusin), "Iz proshlogo: Pervye ulichnye demonstratsii v Peterburge" in *Narodnyi vestnik* 2 (1906): 45.

57. Aptekman, *Obshchestvo "Zemlia i Volia,"* 324.

58. The earliest charter is reprinted in Valk et al., eds., *Revoliutsionnoe narodnichestvo*, 27–33. See also Aptekman, *Obshchestvo "Zemlia i Volia,"* 194–200.

59. Figner, *Zapechatlennyi trud*, 143.

60. Figner, *Zapechatlennyi trud*, 177.

61. A. L. Narochnitskii, "Berlinskii kongress, Rossiia i iuzhnye slaviane," *Novaia i noveishaia istoriia* 2 (1979): 72–84.

62. Volk, *Narodnaia Volia*, 58. See also P. E. Shchegolev, "Iz istorii 'konstitutsionnykh veianii' v 1879–1881 gg.," *Byloe* 12 (1906): 262–284.

63. Morozov, *Povesti*, vol. 2, 273.

64. Tikhomirov, *Vospominaniia*, 97.

65. Georgii Plekhanov, "Vospominaniia ob A. D. Mikhailove" in Pribyleva-Korba and Figner, eds., *Mikhailov*, 64.

66. Bazilevskii, *Literatura*, 73.

67. Valk et al., eds., *Revoliutsionnoe narodnichestvo*, 13.

68. Ol'ga Liubatovich, "Dalekoe i nedavnoe: Vospominaniia iz zhizni revoliutsionerov, 1879–1881," *Byloe* 5 (1906): 227.

69. Lev Tikhomirov, "Neskol'ko myslei o razvitii i razvetvlenii revoliutsionnykh napravlenii," *Katorga i ssylka* 3 (1926): 119.

70. GARF, 109, 1878, d. 502 t.1 (4), 151.

71. GARF 109, op. 3-a, d. 277. Also see I. Bekker, "Demonstratsiia dolgushintsev na Konnoi ploshchadi," *Katorga i ssylka* 2 (1926): 67–77.

72. Engelstein, "Theater of Public Life," 337.

73. Shelgunov, *Vospominaniia*, 241.

74. Koz'min, *Nechaevtsy*, 168.

75. Ibid., 184.

76. See Kravchinskii, "Podpol'naia Rossiia," 40–41.

77. Figner, *Zapechatlennyi trud*, 146.

78. Ibid., 146–147.

79. Described in David Footman, *Red Prelude: The Life of the Terrorist Zhelyabov* (New Haven: Yale University Press, 1945), 66.

80. Sofya Kovalevskaya, *Nihilist Girl*, trans. Natasha Kolchevska (New York: Modern Language Association of America, 2001), 104.

81. Deich, "Valerian Osinskii," 25. Also see Deich, "G. V. Plekhanov v 'Zemle i Vole'" *Gruppa "Osvobozhdenie truda,"* 3 (1925), 48.

82. Valk et al., eds., *Revoliutsionnoe narodnichestvo*, vol. 1, 370.

83. Ibid., 152.

84. Burtsev, *Za sto let*, 133.

85. Golovina-Iorgenson, "Moi vospominaniia," *Katorga i ssylka* (1923): 103.

86. GARF 109, op 1-a, f. 714, 8.

87. Ibid., 13.

88. Miliukov, *Alexander II*, 66.

89. A description of the Kievan funeral march is found in GARF, f. 109, 1878, d. 94, 15–16. The police themselves were baffled by the significance of the event but concluded that it "bears some kind of political nature."

90. Shevtsov, *Iz proshlogo*, 48.

91. Ibid., 49.

92. Aptekman, *Obshchestvo "Zemlia i Volia,"* 185.

93. Shevtsov, *Iz proshlogo*, 51.

94. Deich, *Za polveka* II, 303.

95. Chernavskii, "Demonstratisiia," 10–12.

96. Tom Trice, "Rites of Protest: Populist Funerals in Imperial St. Petersburg, 1876–1878," *Slavic Review* 60 (Spring 2001): 53.

97. Deich, *Za polveka* II, 308.

98. Pribyleva-Korba and Figner, eds., *Mikhailov*, 111.

99. Aptekman, *Obshchestvo "Zemlia i Volia,"* 188.

100. For an in-depth analysis, see M. M. Chernavskii, "Demonstratsiia 6 dekabria 1876 goda: Po vospominaniiam uchastnika," *Katorga i ssylka* 28–29 (1926) and Pamela Sears McKinsey, "The Kazan Square Demonstration and the Conflict between Russian Workers and Intelligenty," *Slavic Review* (1985): 83–103.

101. Siljak, *Angel*, 167.

102. Chernavskii, "Demonstratsiia," 13.

103. GARF, f. 112, op. 1, d. 170, 354–355.

104. Cited in McKinsey, "Demonstratsiia," 96.

105. GARF, f. 112, op. 1, d. 170, 354.

106. Chernavskii, "Demonstratsiia," 18.

107. GARF, f. 112, op. 1, d. 170, 354–355.

108. A. N. Bibergal', "Vospominaniia o demonstratsii na Kazanskoi ploshchadi," *Katorga i ssylka* 12 (1928): 27.

109. As, for example, described in Daly, *Autocracy*, 21–22.

110. RGIA, f. 1282, op. 1, d. 416, 7.

111. GARF, 109, op. 1-a, d. 718, 6.

112. Ibid.

113. See Sinegub, *Zapiski*, 33.

114. On the increasing number of workers in St. Petersburg in the 1870s, see D. G. Kutsentov, "Naselenie Peterburga. Polozhenie peterburgskikh rabochikh" in *Ocherki istorii Leningrada* (Moscow, 1957), 182–190.

115. Golovina-Iurgenson, "Moi vospominaniia," 30.

116. Plekhanov, "Russkii rabochii," 131.

117. Ibid., 132–133.

118. Plekhanov, "Russkii rabochii," 134. Italics in original.

119. Ibid.

120. Ibid., 182.

121. See Saunders, *Russia in the Age of Reaction*, 315.

122. Rosa Plekhanova, "Periferinnyi kruzhok 'Zemli i Voli'" *Gruppa "Osvobozhdenie truda"* 4 (1926),103. See also Aptekman, *Obshchestvo "Zemlia i Volia,"* 321 and M. R. Popov, *Zapiski zemlevol'tsa* (Moscow, 1933), 177.

123. Popov, *Zapiski*, 104.

124. GARF, 109, op. 1-a, f. 803, 30. For a description of these events, see Plekhanov, "Russkii rabochii," 157–161.

125. GARF, 109, op. 1-a, f. 718, 30.

126. Plekhanov, "Russkii rabochii," 167.

127. Miliutin, *Dnevnik*, 406.

128. N. N. Shebeko, *Chronique du mouvement socialiste en Russie, 1878–1887* (St. Petersburg: Imprimerie officielle du Ministère de l'intérieur, 1890), 15.

129. On the European and American reception of the acquittal, see Siljak, *Angel*, 279–299.

130. Bogucharskii, *Revoliutsionnaia zhurnalistika semidesiatykh godov*, 34.

131. Tikhomirov, "Neskol'ko myslei," 119.

132. Plekhanov, "Vospominaniia ob A. D. Mikhaikove" *Sochineniia*, vol. 1 (Moscow, 1923), 161.

133. GARF, f. 109, 1878, d. 502 t. 1 (4), 154.

134. V. A. Anzimirov, *Kramol'niki* (Moscow, 1907), 28–29. A verst was slightly longer than a kilometer.

135. The underground publication *Nachalo* immediately made this claim, supported by the fact that the conservative journalist Mikhail Katkov referred to the beatings as the "answer" of the masses to the "scandal" of the Zasulich Trial, a notion that seems far-fetched at best. See Bogucharskii, *Revoliutsionnaia zhurnalistika*, 29–30.

136. Tikhomirov, *Konstitutsionalisty v epokhu 1881 goda* (Moscow, 1895), 30.

137. Morozov, *Povesti*, vol. 2, 228.

138. Ibid., 261–262.

139. Aptekman, *Obshchestvo "Zemlia i Volia,"* 326.

140. Cited in Frolenko, *Zapiski*, 170.

141. Valk et al., eds., *Revoliutsionnoe narodnichestvo*, 56–57. Italics are in original.

142. GARF, 109, op. 1-a, f. 803, 56.

143. Ibid., 47.

144. Morozov, *Povesti*, vol. 2, 76.

145. Kravchinskii, "Podpol'naia Rossiia," 47.

146. Ibid., 55.

147. Plekhanov, "Russkii rabochii," 166.

CHAPTER 6

1. Figner, *Zapechatlennyi trud*, 298–299.

2. Kibal'chich, cited in Volk, *Narodnaia Volia*, 220.

3. Deich, *Za polveka* II, 303. For a different interpretation of the term that involves the concealment of conspiratorial apartments as though they were caves, see Kornilova-Morozova, "Perovskaia," 30. Tikhomirov believed the name had to do with their lack of sophistication, but this is unsupported elsewhere and clearly inaccurate.

4. Precise details about the original organization of this group are murky. Figner and Aptekman both cover the period in detail, and Deborah Hardy in *Land and Freedom* seeks to pull together the various strands on its formation.

5. Figner, *Zapechatlennyi trud*, 141–142.

6. Deich, *Za polveka* II, 302.

7. GARF 109, opo 1-a, d. 714, 3.

8. Berlin, *Russian Thinkers*, 232.

9. See Aksel'rod, *Perezhitoe*, 153–154. Deich referred to Natanson as the "last salvation" of the populists because his emphasis on organization at this time opened a new organization and allowed them to form a new approach to political activism, *Za polveka*, II, 100.

10. Aksel'rod, *Perezhitoe*, 154.

11. Figner, *Zapechatlennyi trud*, 138.

12. Cited in Lev Deich, "Valerian Osinskii," *Katorga i ssylka* 54 (1929): 10.

13. V. Figner, "Mark Andreevich Natanson," *Katorga i ssylka* 56 (1929): 142.

14. Zasulich, *Vospominaniia*, 87. Here Zasulich is citing the impressions of Kravchinskii, who had returned from abroad in the spring of 1878.

15. Figner, "Natanson," 141.

16. It should be noted that the name "Executive Committee" was only adopted in 1879 in imitation of a name devised by a group of southern radicals who had intended, in rather Nechaevian fashion, to make the populists appear more imposing than they actually were. A smaller group of de facto leaders had already directed "Land and Freedom" since its inception. They did not call themselves an "ispolnitel'nyi komitet" but rather used the terms "rasporiaditel'naia komissiia" or "administratsiia." After the term had gained notoriety through its connection to a violent attack, the northern populists adopted it for its mysterious and threatening reputation.

17. Tikhomirov, *Vospominaniia*, 126.

18. Pribyleva-Korba and Figner, eds., *Mikhailov*, 43.

19. Aptekman, *Obshchestvo "Zemlia i Volia,"* 327.

20. Pribyleva-Korba and Figner, eds., *Mikhailov*, 45.

21. E. Serebriakov, *Obshchestvo 'Zemlia i Volia'* (Geneva, 1894), 8.

22. See A. P. Pribyleva-Korba, *Narodnaia Volia: Vospominaniia o 1870–1880-kh gg.* (Moscow, 1926), 42.

23. GARF, f. 112, op. 1, d. 504, 345.

24. Bukh, "Pervaia tipografiia 'Narodnoi Voli'" *Katorga i ssylka* 57 (1929): 57.

25. Figner, *Zapechatlennyi trud*, 229.

26. Ibid., 181–184.

27. On the concentric circles of membership in Land and Freedom and The People's Will, see Pribyleva-Korba, *Narodnaia Volia: Vospominaniia*, 44–45.

28. For a copy and the history of their ustav, see S. N. Valk, ed., *Arkhiv "Zemli i Voli" i "Narodnoi Voli"* (Moscow, 1930), 53–89.

29. Pribyleva-Korba and Figner, eds., *Mikhailov*, 131.

30. Tikhomirov, *Vospominaniia*, 123.

31. Aptekman, *Obshchestvo "Zemlia i Volia,"* 197

32. Rosa Plekhanova, "Periferinnyi," 114.

33. Pribyleva-Korba and Figner, eds., *Mikhailov*, 134–135.

34. Soja, *Postmodern Geographies*, 63.

35. Ibid.

36. Pribyleva-Korba and Figner, eds., *Mikhailov*, 146.

37. Shcherbakova, *Otshchepentsy*, 118.

38. Foucault, "Of Other Spaces," 24.

39. Casey, *Fate*, 300.

40. Foucault, *Reader*, 142.

41. On imperial passport laws, see Mervyn Matthews, *The Passport Society: Controlling Movement in Russia and the USSR* (Boulder, CO: Westview Press, 1993), 1–13.

42. See Mikhnevich, *Iazvy*, 662.

43. V. G. Chernukha, *Pasport v Rossii 1719–1917* (Sankt-Peterburg, 2007), 120.

44. Charles Steinwedel, "Making Social Groups, One Person at a Time: The Identification of Individuals by Estate, Religious Confession, and Ethnicity in Late Imperial Russia" in Jane Capland and John Torpey, eds., *Documenting Individual Identity* (Princeton, NJ: Princeton University Press, 2001), 75.

45. Stepniak, *The Career of a Nihilist*, (New York: Harper's, 1889), 58.

46. Debagorii-Mokrievich, *Ot buntarstva*, 131.

47. See Valk, ed. *Arkhiv*, 32.

48. Deich, *Za polveka* II, 46.

49. Ibid., 43–44.

50. Ibid., 48.

51. RGIA, f. 112, op. 1, d. 504, 338.

52. S. Lion, "Ot propagandy k terroru" *Katorga i ssylka* 13 (1924): 10.

53. Deich, *Za polveka* II, 45.

54. Mikhailov began to organize the production of false documents around the time of the Kazan Cathedral demonstration. See P. E. Shchegolev, ed., *Pis'ma narodovol'tsa A. D. Mikhailova* (Moscow, 1933), 222.

55. For a record of passports and other papers available, their type and relative "quality," etc., see Valk, ed., *Arkhiv*, 339–349.

56. Deich, *Za polveka* II, 47.

57. Debagorii-Mokrievich, *Ot buntarstva*, 135.

58. Tikhomirov, *Zagovorshchiki*, 179.

59. Lion, "Ot propagandy," 10.

60. Chernavskii, "Demonstratsiia," 19.

61. Mikhailov also participated in the demonstration and later claimed he was not arrested because he was wearing "proper clothing." See Shchegolev, ed., *Pis'ma*, 202.

62. See Lyn Lofland, *A World of Strangers: Order and Action in Urban Public Space* (New York: Basic Books, 1973), 3.

63. Ibid., 22.

64. See Karp et al., *Being Urban*, 108–110.

65. Cited in Dlugolenskii, *Vek Dostoevskogo*, 264.

66. Lofland, *A World of Strangers*, 140–157.

67. Ibid., 29–91. Also see Richard Senett, *The Fall of Public Man* (New York: Norton, 1974).

68. Plekhanov, *Sochineniia*, vol. 1, 153–157 and Pribyleva-Korba and Figner, eds., *Mikhailov*, 62.

69. Tikhomirov, *Vospominaniia*, 95.

70. Dostoevskii, *Prestuplenie i nakazanie*, 519.

71. Cited in Kalinchuk, "Psikhologicheskii faktor," 50.

72. Aksel'rod, *Perezhitoe*, 323.

73. Liubatovich, "Dalekoe," 215.

74. Bater, *St. Petersburg*, 193. According to Bater, as far as clothing was concerned, "the existing social order was still intact. Not even the emancipation upset the status quo."

75. Plekhanova, "Nasha Zhizn' do emigratsii" *Gruppa "Osvobozhdenie truda"* 6 (1928): 97.

76. Plekhanova, "Periferinnyi," 117–118.

77. Golovina-Iurgenson, "Iz dalekogo proshlogo," *Katorga i ssylka* 8 (1925): 103.

78. Pribyleva-Korba, *Narodnaia Volia: Vospominaniia*, 50. Morozov, *Povesti*, vol. 2, 111.

79. Morozov, *Povesti*, vol. 2, 371.

80. Kravchinskii, "Podpol'naia Rossiia," 73–75.

81. Kirichenko, *Russkaia arkhitektura*, 146.

82. Grintsevich, "Proekty," 58.

83. Vladimir Mikhnevich, *Peterburg ves' na ladoni*, (Saint Petersburg, 1874), 135.

84. Bater, *St. Petersburg*, 198–200. Also see Bater, "Between Old and New: St. Petersburg in the Late-Imperial Era" in Michael Hamm, ed., *The City in Late Imperial Russia* (Bloomington: Indiana University Press, 1986), 67.

85. Bater, "Between Old and New," 70–71.

86. Shevyrev, "Kul'turnaia sreda," 91.

87. Brower, *Russian City*, 23.

88. Morozov, *Povesti*, vol. 2, 77.

89. Popov, *Zapiski*, 56.

90. GARF 110, op. 3, d. 1594.

91. Tikhomirov, *Vospominaniia*, 136.

92. Kravchinskii, "Podpol'naia Rossiia," 169.

93. Morozov, *Povesti*, vol. 2, 228.
94. Tikhomirov, *Zagovorshchiki*, 151.
95. Sof'ia Ivanova-Boreisha, "Pervaia Tipografiia 'Narodnoi Voli,'" *Byloe* 9 (1906): 5.
96. Tikhomirov, *Zagovorshchiki*, 153.
97. Bukh, "Tipografiia," 68–69.
98. Ivanova-Boreisha, "Pervaia tipografiia," 2.
99. GARF 109, op. 1-a, d. 742, 7.
100. RGIA, 1282, op. 1, d. 416, 117–118.
101. Zaionchkovskii, *Russian Autocracy*, 49.
102. O. V. Budnitskii, *Politicheskaia politsiia i politicheskii terrorizm: Sbornik dokumentov* (Moscow, 2001), 108–109.
103. Tatishchev, *Imperator Aleksandr II*, 926. Tatishchev claimed this measure cost the city more than a million rubles.
104. Pribyleva-Korba and Figner, eds., *Mikhailov*, 62.
105. Popov, *Zapiski*, 244.
106. Plekhanova, "Periferinnyi," 108.
107. Volk, *Narodnaia Volia*, 259.
108. Shiriaev, "Avtobiograficheskaia zapiska," 94–95. The store was called "Schtoll and Schmidt."
109. R. M. Kantor, "Dinamit Narodnoi Voli," *Katorga i ssylka* 57 (1929): 118–128.
110. Kirikov, *Arkhitektura*, 127.
111. Richard Sennett, *The Conscience of the Eye: The Design and Social Life of Cities* (New York: Norton, 1990), 190–191.
112. Tikhomirov, *Vospominaniia*, 95. Deborah Hardy's study of Land and Freedom stresses the theme of Mikhailov's elusiveness in ways that were extremely helpful for the present work.
113. Pribyleva-Korba and Figner, eds., *Mikhailov*, 46–47.
114. See Shebeko, *Chronique*, 46.
115. Aptekman, *Obshchestvo "Zemlia i Volia,"* 330–331. Also see Shebeko, *Chronique*, 46.
116. Pribyleva-Korba and Figner, eds., *Mikhailov*, 51. On Mikhailov's arrest, also see GARF, f. 112/op. 1/504. Mikhailov was apprehended in a photo studio when he went to claim photographic copies of other revolutionaries he had made for distribution.
117. Sante, *Low Life*, 303.
118. GARF, f. 112, op. 1, d.504.
119. Plekhanova, "Periferinnyi," 92.
120. Bukh, "Tipografiia," 73.
121. Cited in Hardy, *Land and Freedom*, 46
122. E. I. Kirichenko, "O nekotorykh osobennostiakh evoliutsii gorodskikh mnogokvartirnykh domov vtoroi poloviny XIX-nachala XX vv.," *Arkhitekturnoe nasledstvo* 15 (1963): 154.
123. Kirikov, *Arkhitektura*, 48–49.
124. Ibid., 53.
125. E. D. Iukhneva, *Peterburgskie dokhodnye doma: Ocherki iz istorii byta* (Moscow: Tsentrpoligraf, 2008), 85.
126. Plekhanov, "Russkii rabochii," 149–150.
127. Anzimirov, *Kramol'niki*, 95.
128. GARF, f. 112, op. 1, d. 504.
129. Anzimirov, *Kramol'niki*, 143.
130. RGIA, f. 1282, op. 1, d. 642, 189–191.
131. Stepniak, *Career*, 292.
132. Kravchinskii, "Podpol'naia Rossiia," 149.
133. Morozov, *Povesti*, vol. 2, 375.
134. M. A. Timofeev, "Perezhitoe: Otryvok iz vospominanii o semidesiatykh godakh," *Katorga i ssylka* 57 (1929): 100.

135. Figner, *Zapechatlennyi trud*, 221.

136. Morozov, *Povesti*, vol. 2, 140–141.

137. Lion, "Ot propagandy," 14.

138. Plekhanova, "Periferinnyi," 104.

139. Ibid., 105.

140. Morozov, *Povesti*, vol. 2, 311.

141. Ibid., 278.

142. See GARF, f. 94, op. 1, ed. kh. 16.

143. Kravchinskii, "Podpol'naia Rossiia," 206.

144. Volk, *Narodnaia Volia*, 339.

145. Figner, *Zapechatlennyi trud*, 222.

146. Plekhanova, "Periferinnyi," 98.

147. Valk, ed., *Arkhiv*, 126–145.

148. Lion, "Ot propagandy," 15.

149. See Aptekman, *Obshchestvo "Zemlia i Volia,"* 315.

150. GARF, 109, op. 1-a, 868.

151. GARF, 109, op. 1-a, d. 868, 871.

152. Described in Footman, *Red Prelude*, 97.

153. Volk, *Narodnaia Volia*, 261.

154. Deich, for example, suggests that the populists received only 10,000 rubles. See Deich, "Valerian Osinskii," *Katorga i ssykla*, 54 (1929): 12–13. Tikhomirov, who was much more closely connected to Mikhailov, suggests that tens of thousands of rubles came from Lizogub. *Vospominaniia*, 124.

155. Yarmolinsky, *Road*, 244–245.

156. Figner, *Zapechatel'nyi trud*, 193.

157. A. V. Iakimova, "Gruppa 'Svoboda ili Smert,'" *Katorga i ssylka* 24 (1926): 15.

158. On Lizogub's contributions, see Volk, *Narodnaia Volia*, 260.

159. GARF, f. 112, op. 1, d. 504, 345–346.

160. Cherniak, *Nikolai Kibal'chich: Revoliutsioner i uchenyi* (Moscow, 1960), 80–91.

161. Aptekman, *Obshchestvo "Zemlia i Volia,"* 234–235.

162. Valk, ed., *Arkhiv*, 24–29.

163. For the extensive notes taken from Kletochnikov's information, see ibid., 160–224.

164. Plekhanova, "Okhota za G. V. Plekhanovym," *Gruppa "Osvobozhdenie truda"* 3 (1925): 310.

165. GARF, f. 112, op. 1, d. 504, 354.

166. GARF, f. 112, op.1, d. 504, 340.

167. Figner, *Zapechatlennyi trud*, 237.

168. See Valk, ed., *Arkhiv*, 160–224.

CHAPTER 7

1. English language histories that cover some or all of these events include Hardy, *Land and Freedom*; Ulam, *In the Name of the People*; Venturi, *Roots*; and Yarmolinsky, *Road*.

2. A.Ia. Cherniak, *Nikolai Kibal'chich: Revoliutsioner i uchenyi* (Moscow, 1960), 52–56; Tikhomirov, *Vospominaniia*, 81.

3. See Sof'ia Ivanova, "Vospominaniia o S. L. Perovskoi," *Byloe* 3 (1906): 87.

4. Liubatovich, "Dalekoe," 124.

5. Yarmolinsky, *Road*, 273.

6. Debagorii-Mokrievich, *Ot buntarstva*, 339.

7. Stepniak, *Career*, 49.

8. Kropotkin's liberation has been described in many sources, including his own memoirs, 251–258. One of the most complete and compelling discussions of Kropotkin's escape is found in Martin A. Miller, *Kropotkin* (Chicago: University of Chicago Press, 1976), 120–29. Also see A. Ivanchin-Pisarev, "Pobeg kn. P. A. Kropotkina," *Byloe* 1/13 (January 1907): 37–42.

9. Kravchinskii, "Podpol'naia Rossiia," 143.

10. Kropotkin, *Memoirs*, 257.

11. Figner, "Natanson," 144.

12. Cited in Volk, *Narodnaia Volia*, 79.

13. Deich, *Za polveka*, 106–107; Tikhomirov, *Vospominaniia*, 119.

14. Deich, "Aaron Zundelevich," *Gruppa "Osvobozhdenie truda"* 2 (1924), 191.

15. Morozov, *Povesti*, vol. 2, 16.

16. Tikhomirov, *Vospominaniia*, 119.

17. Described in Shebeko, *Chronique*, 31. This text seems to have been modeled on the original report found in GARF F 94, op 1, d. 48, 1.

18. General V. D. Novitskii, *Iz vospominanii zhandarma* (Priboi, 1929), 83. Mezentsev's sense of urgency was also dampened by the fact that he believed "at the present time the main center of socialist-democratic propaganda must be considered Kiev, Odessa and Kharkov," as he wrote a week before he was stabbed: GARF, 109, op. 3-a, f. 694.

19. Kravchinskii, "'Smert' za smert'" in Shcherbakova, *Otshchepentsy*, 178.

20. From Morozov, *Povesti*, vol. 2, 334.

21. GARF, 109, op. 1-a, d. 734.

22. L. Ursynovich, *Klochki vospominanii. Al'manakh "Krasnaia Nov'"* (1925): 336.

23. GARF, 109, op. 1-a, 791.

24. Frolenko, addendum to Morozov, "Vozniknovenie 'Narodnoi Voli,'" *Byloe* 12 (1906): 25.

25. Tikhomirov's three main accounts of the bombing are found in his memoir, *Zagovorshchiki*, and an earlier article titled "Teni proshlogo: Stepan Khalturin," *Katorga i ssylka* 25 (1926).

26. Tikhomirov, "Teni proshlogo," 86.

27. GARF, 94, op. 1, ed. khr. 16.

28. Figner, *Zapechatlennyi trud*, 209.

29. Liubatovich, "Dalekoe," 127.

30. Tikhomirov, *Zagovorshchiki*, 180.

31. Tikhomirov, "Teni proshlogo," 96.

32. Figner, *Zapechatlennyi trud*, 221.

33. Ibid., 171.

34. While Mikhailov did not admit to this assistance in his testimony from prison, other members in later years admitted helping Solov'ev with the revolver and poison. See, for example, Morozov, *Povesti*, vol. 2, 416.

35. Pribyleva-Korba and Figner, eds., *Mikhailov*, 127.

36. Ibid., 138–141.

37. Cited in Yarmolinsky, *Road*, 255.

38. The most useful text on the assassination itself is taken from transcripts of the trial that took place later in the same month of the assassination and is based on both testimony given and evidence collected as a result of arrests and interrogations: *Protsess 1-ogo marta 1881-go goda* (Saint Petersburg, 1906).

39. Discussed in A. Tyrkov, "K sobytiiu 1 marta 1881 goda," *Byloe* 5 (1906): 147–149.

40. For a descrption of the preparations, see A. Iakimova, "Iz dalekogo proshlogo," *Katorga i ssylka* 8 (1925), 9–17.

41. *Protsess*, 23.

42. Venturi, *Roots*, 709.

43. V. Ia. Bogucharskii, "1-e marta—3-a aprelia 1881 goda," *Byloe* 3 (1906): 15.

44. Quoted in Volk, *Narodnaia Volia*, 113.

45. For a description of this final meeting, see Figner, *Zapechatlennyi trud*, 260–261.

CHAPTER 8

1. Plekhanov, *Sochineniia*, vol. 1, 164.
2. Tikhomirov, *Vospominaniia*, 125–126.
3. Shiraev, "Avtobiograficheskaia zapiska," 86.
4. Liubatovich, "Dalekoe," 217.
5. For a detailed exposition of the dispute, see Hardy, *Land and Freedom*, 107–123.
6. Pomper, *Revolutionary Intelligentsia*, 130.
7. Tikhomirov, *Vospominaniia*, 129.
8. Iakimova, "Gruppa 'Svoboda ili Smert,'" 14–16.
9. Valk, ed., *Arkhiv*, 104.
10. Plekhanova, "Nasha zhizn," 66.
11. Aksel'rod, *Perezhitoe*, 322–323.
12. Valk, ed., *Arkhiv*, 15.
13. This meeting was an obvious case of subterfuge committed by a subgroup of the members of an organization that was supposed to be open and devoted to all other members of the organization. In and of itself the pre-meeting in Lipetsk is a powerful example of the tactical and ideological split that had arisen during the previous year. Those not invited to the meeting, like Sofia Perovskaia, were understandably outraged.
14. The best account of the meeting, as well as the problems that led to it and its aftermath, is found in Hardy, *Land and Freedom*.
15. Morozov, *Povesti*, vol. 2, 417.
16. It should be noted that "The People's Will," or *Narodnaia Volia*, might just as well be translated as "The People's Freedom." Since the word "will" better captures the double meaning of the Russian word *volia*, it is retained here.
17. In the north as well certain revolutionaries closely connected to Land and Freedom had espoused the use of violent methods from as early as the mid 1870s. The most ardent early exemplar of this tendency was Iosif Kablits, leader of a group Klements dubbed "bomb throwers" [*vspyshkopuskateli*]. Kablits eventually went to England in order to learn the manufacture of dynamite, but he was never successful. His influence over the members of Land and Freedom in this period was minimal.
18. Deich, *Za polveka* II, 63–65.
19. Burtsev, *Za sto let*, 182.
20. The use of dynamite for industrial purposes made Nobel a wealthy man, but its use as a weapon took him by surprise. When his brother died in 1888, a newspaper mistakenly published an obituary about Nobel himself that castigated him for the wave of terrorist violence that began with the Russian populists and resulted in part from his invention. Hoping to rectify the situation, he endowed the Nobel Peace Prize.
21. Tikhomirov, *Vospominaniia*, 86.
22. Bazilevskii, ed., *Literatura*, 188.
23. Plekhanova, "Periferinny," 115.
24. Frolenko, *Zapiski*, 102.
25. Deich, "G. V. Plekhanov," 53.
26. Bogucharskii, *Revoliutsionnaia zhurnalistika*, 282–283.
27. Other members of The People's Will publicly disavowed Morozov's enthusiasm for political violence, most notably Zheliabov in his trial testimony for his part in the assassination of Alexander II. By that point, however, it was in the interest of The People's Will to present themselves as reasonable revolutionaries using violence only as a last resort. Morozov was notable as one of the most naïve of the radical populists, but his naïveté is best seen as a somewhat embarrassing tendency to speak the unvarnished truth that other, subtler figures were able to couch in more elegant, if less comprehensible, language. In fact, without turning to some of the more direct statements made by Morozov, the urban populists' adamant adoption of political violence becomes difficult to make sense of.

28. On Zheliabov's refutation of Morozov's influence during his murder trial, see *Protsess*, 218–219. It is interesting to note that in spite of his disavowal of Morozov's full embrace of terrorism, he went on to say, drawing on the language of August Comte, that as the populist movement evolved over the course of the 1870s it shifted from its metaphysical phase to a level of mature "positivism" in its embrace of underground terrorism.

29. Liotta and Miskel, "Digging Deep: Environment and Geography as Root Influences for Terrorism" in James J. F. Forest, ed, *The Making of a Terrorist: Recruitment, Training and Root Causes*, vol. 3 (Santa Barbara: Praeger Security International, 2006), 256.

30. Jerrold M. Post, "'When Hatred is Bred in the Bone': The Sociocultural Underpinnings of Terrorist Psychology" in Forest, ed., *Making of a Terrorist*, Vol. 2, 22.

31. This passage comes from the English version of Underground Russia for which Kravchinskii used his pseudonym "Stepniak." See Stepniak, *Underground Russia: Revolutionary Profiles and Sketches from Life* (New York: Charles Scribner's Sons, 1883), 39. In his essay "Heroism and Asceticism," Sergei Bulgakov reads this romanticism as a symptom of the entire Russian intelligentsia, unable, according to him, to settle for the role of modest worker. See Schatz, *Signposts*, 26–31.

32. Shishko, *Kravchinskii*, 11.

33. A. P. Pribyleva-Korba, "Ispolnitel'nyi komitet 1879–1881 gg.," *Katorga i ssylka* 24 (1926), 28.

34. Stepniak, *Career*, 250.

35. Morozov, *Povesti*, vol. 2, 378–379.

36. Bazilevskii, ed., *Literatura*, 6.

37. Figner, *Zapechatlennyi trud*, 261.

38. Pribyleva-Korba, A. P. *Narodnaia Volia: Vospominaniia*, 30.

39. Bazilevskii, ed., *Literatura*, 186.

40. Zaionchkovskii, *Russian Autocracy*, 92.

41. Volk, *Narodnaia Volia*, 59.

42. Shebeko, *Chronique*, 203.

43. G. A. de Vollan, "Ocherki proshlago" *Golos Minuvshago* 4, (April 1914): 139–140.

44. Volk, *Narodnaia Volia*, 59.

45. RGIA, f. 1282, op. 1, d. 416, 45.

46. Miliutin, *Dnevnik*, 462.

47. GARF, f. 110, op. 3, d. 1617, 2–14.

48. Zinaida Peregubova, "Departament politsii i mestnye uchrezhdeniia politicheskogo rozyska (1800–1917)" in *Politicheskii sysk Rossii 1800–1917* (Moscow: Rosspen, 2000), 279.

49. Daly, *Autocracy*, 26.

50. GARF f. 110, op. 3, d. 1617, 9, 46; and RGIA f. 1282, op 1d. 416, 54.

51. Tatishchev, *Imperator Aleksandr II*, 900; Volk, *Narodnaia Volia*, 55.

52. GARF, f. 109, 1878, d. 502, t. 1, 161.

53. RGIA f. 1282, op. 1, d. 105, 1.

54. Zaionchkovskii, *Krizis samoderzhaviia na rubezhe 1870–1880-kh godov* (Moscow, 1964), 301.

55. GARF, f. 109, op 1-a, d. 909, 2.

56. *Pravitel'stvennyi vestnik*, (August 20, 1878).

57. Zaionchkovskii, *Russian Autocracy*, 47.

58. GARF, f. 109, op. 1-a, 909, 3–4.

59. RGIA, f. 1282, op. 1, d. 416, 45.

60. David Kilcullen, "Twenty-Eight Articles: Fundamentals of Company-Level Counterinsurgency," *Marine Corps Gazette* 90, no. 7 (2006), 29.

61. G. K. Gradovskii, *Itogi (1862–1907)* (Kiev, 1908), 54.

62. Daniel T. Orlovsky, *The Limits of Reform: The Ministry of Internal Affairs in Imperial Russia, 1802–1881* (Cambridge: Harvard University Press, 1981), 173–178.

63. Ibid., 178–189.

64. Zaionchkovskii, *Russian Autocracy*, 143.

65. Ibid., 181.
66. Ibid., 184.
67. Cited in Tatishchev, *Imperator Aleksandr II*, 920.
68. RGIA, f. 1282, op. 1, d. 642.
69. Ibid., 426.
70. Figner, *Zapechatlennyi trud*, 232–233.
71. Valk et al., eds., *Revoliutsionnoe narodnichestvo*, 173.
72. Kravchinskii, "Podpol'naia Rossiia," 216.
73. A potentially important contribution to the relationship between radical populist terrorism and Russian society came to the attention of the present author too late for inclusion in this study, but it is worthy of reference here: Iuliia Safronova, *Russkoe Obshchestvo v zerkale revoliutsionnogo terror, 1879-1881 gody* (Moskva: Novoe Literaturnoe Obozrenie, 2014).
74. Tikhomirov, "Neskol'ko myslei," 119.
75. Cited in Volk, *Narodnaia Volia*, 77.
76. Figner, *Zapechatlennyi trud*, 285.
77. Frolenko, *Zapiski*, 171.
78. Gradovskii, *Itogi*, 68–73.
79. RGIA, f. 642, op. 1, f. 643, 152–53 and 224.
80. Cited in the diary of Count Aleksei Bobrinskii. See M. Murzanova, "Vospominaniia A. A. Bobrinskogo (1880–1881 gody), *Katorga i ssylka* 76 (1931): 91. Bobrinskii himself only shortly before the tsar's assassination was publicly equating love of country with "full legal and civic freedoms and lawful self-government."
81. Ibid., 220–221.
82. Aptekman, *Obshchestvo "Zemlia i Volia,"* 379.
83. Ibid., 380.
84. Itenberg, *Dvizhenie*, 37.
85. Cited in Tikhomirov, *Konstitutsionalisty*, 34.
86. Zaionchkovskii, *Russian Autocracy*, 129.
87. Tikhomirov, *Konstitutsionalisty*, 16.
88. Bazilevskii, ed., *Literatura*, 103. Italics in original.
89. Sinegub, *Zapiski*, 223–224.
90. Bazilevskii, ed., *Literatura*, 103.
91. Figner, *Zapechatlennyi trud*, 144–145.
92. Tikhomirov, *Konstitutsionalisty*, 65.
93. GARF, f. 112, op. 1, f. 504, 344.
94. Tikhomirov, *Konstitutsionalisty*, 16.
95. Pipes, "Narodnichestvo," 441–449.
96. This description of Plekhanov's efforts is found in Deich, "G. V. Plekhanov," 60.
97. Figner, *Zapechatlennyi trud*, 178–179.
98. Aksel'rod, *Perezhitoe*, 361.
99. Morozov, *Povesti*, vol. 2, 325.
100. Figner, *Zapechatlennyi trud*, 268.
101. Shchegolev, ed., *Pis'ma*, 216.
102. Burtsev, *Za sto let*, 159–160.
103. Ibid., 160.
104. Cited in Aptekman, *Obshchestvo "Zemlia i Volia,"* 353–354.
105. Cited in Volk, *Narodnaia Volia*, 304.
106. Reginald E. Zelnik, "Workers and Intelligentsia in the 1870s: The Politics of Sociability" in Zelnik, ed. *Workers and Intelligentsia in Late-Imperial Russia* (Berkeley: UC Berkeley Press, 1999), 32–33.
107. Ibid., 41–42.

108. Ibid., 45.

109. Plekhanov, *Sochineniia*, vol. 1, 185.

110. Tikhomirov, *Zagovorshchiki*, 24.

111. Cited in Volk, *Narodnaia Volia*, 287.

112. Bazilevskii, ed., *Literatura*, 286.

113. Morozov, "Vozniknovenie," 28.

114. Bukh, "Tipografiia," 66–67.

115. Figner, *Zapechatlennyi trud*, 203.

116. Tikhomirov, *Vospominaniia*, 104.

117. Stepniak, *Underground*, 90.

118. Brigitte L Nacos, "Mediated Terror: Teaching Terror through Propaganda and Publicity" in Forest, ed., *Making of a Terrorist*, Vol. 2, 101–102.

119. On the origins of the concept of "propaganda by deed," see Marie Fleming, "Propaganda by the Deed: Terrorism and Anarchist Theory in Late Nineteenth-Century Europe," *Terrorism: An International Journal* 4 (1980): 1–23.

120. Deich, *Za polveka*, I, 304.

121. Morozov, *Povesti*, vol. 2, 418.

122. See Morozov, *Terroristicheskaia bor'ba* (London, 1880).

123. Ibid., 8.

124. A translation of Heinzen's article "Murder" can be found in Walter Laqueur, ed., *Voices of Terror: Manifestoes, Writings and Manuals of Al-Qaeda, Hamas and Other Terrorists from Around the World and Throughout the Ages* (New York: Reed Press, 2004). For a discussion of Heinzen's role as a seminal figure in the development of terrorist tactics, see Martin Miller, *The Foundations of Modern Terrorism: State, Society and the Dynamics of Political Violence* (Cambridge: Cambridge University Press, 2013), 54–57.

125. V. Tarnovskii (Romanenko), *Terrorizm i rutina* (London, 1882), 10.

126. Tarnovskii, *Terrorizm*, 19. Also see S. Valk, "G. G. Romanenko," *Katorga i ssylka* 11 (1928): 36–50.

127. Valk et al., ed., *Revoliutsionnoe narodnichestvo*, vol. 1, 122.

128. Filippov, *Organizatsiia*, 75.

129. Volk, *Narodnaia Volia*, 236.

130. Cited in Fleming, "Propaganda by the Deed," 9.

131. Ibid., 10.

132. Figner, *Zapechatlennyi trud*, 245–246.

133. Volk, *Narodnaia Volia*, 104.

134. See the announcement reprinted in Bazilevskii, ed., *Literatura*, 99.

135. Shebeko, *Chronique*, 62–63. Also see Ulam, *In the Name of the People*, 334 and Venturi, *Roots*, 665.

136. Volk, *Narodnaia Volia*, 260.

137. Zasulich *Vospominaniia*, 88.

138. Pribyleva-Korba and Figner, eds., *Mikhailov*, 123.

139. GARF, f. 109, 1878, d. 504.

140. GARF, f. 109, op. 1-a, d. 785.

141. Burtsev, *Za sto let*, 173.

142. Cited in Yarmolinsky, *Road*, 233.

143. Norman M. Naimark, "Terrorism and the Fall of Imperial Russia," *Terrorism and Political Violence* Vol. 2, No. 2 (Summer, 1990): 172.

144. See Beall, "Cities, Terrorism and Development," *Journal of International Development* 18 (2006), 109.

145. Cited in Morozov, *Povesti*, vol. 2, 362–363.

146. Frolenko, "Nachalo narodnichestva," *Katorga i ssylka* 24 (1926): 22.

147. On Al Quaeda's targeting of such landmarks as the Eiffel Tower, Big Ben, and the Statue of Liberty, see Nacos, "Mediated Terror," 102.

148. Martin A. Miller has described this trajectory toward more spectacular forms of terrorism in *Foundations*. Miller emphasizes that such fear-inducing tactics are wielded by states as well as subnational groups like The People's Will. Also see Bruce Hoffman, *Inside Terrorism* (New York: Columbia University Press, 2006) and John Merriman, *The Dynamite Club: How a Bombing in Fin-de-Siècle Paris Ignited the Age of Modern Terror* (New York: Houghton Mifflin, 2009).

149. Figner, *Zapechatlennyi trud*, 281.

150. S. Livshits, "Podpol'nye tipografii 60-kh, 70-kh i 80-kh godov," *Katorga i ssylka* 50 (1928): 70.

151. A. Pribyleva-Korba, "Nekotoryia dannyia o 'Pis'me Ispolnitel'nago komiteta k Aleksandru III,'" *Byloe* 6 (June, 1906): 234–236.

CONCLUSION

1. Ursynovich, *Klochki*, 331.

2. The underlying connections between ideologically inspired subversive movements constitute a theme of Billington's *Fire in the Minds of Men*. See above.

3. Frolenko, "Nachalo," 26.

4. Tikhomirov, "Neskol'ko myslei," 119.

5. Volk, *Narodnaia Volia*, 114.

6. Ibid., 223.

7. Murzanova, "Vospominaniia Bobrinskogo," 98.

8. Figner, *Zapechatlennyi trud*, 284.

9. Ibid.

10. Golovina-Iurgenson, "Iz dalekogo proshlogo," 106.

11. Yarmolinsky, *Road*, 227.

12. See Naimark, "Terrorism," 183.

13. On the lasting impact of these laws, see Richard Pipes, *Russia under the Old Regime* (New York: Scribner, 1974), 305–318.

14. M. Frolenko, "O Gol'denberge," *Katorga i ssylka* 57 (1929): 281. Also see Morozov, *Povesti*, vol. 2, 416.

15. For a wide-ranging discussion of the populist reaction to the pogroms, see Klier, *Russians, Jews, and the Pogroms*, 155–173.

16. See Murzanova, "Vospominaniia Bobrinskogo," 104–106.

17. See Wortman, *Scenarios*, vol. 2, 198.

18. Ibid., 212–224. As Wortman points out, the two years between the start of Alexander III's rulership and his coronation were "the longest interval between accession and coronation in the dynasty's history."

19. Shchegolev, ed., *Pis'ma*, 202.

20. On relations between Degaev and Sudeikin, see Richard Pipes, *The Degaev Affair: Terror and Treason in Tsarist Russia* (New Haven: Yale University Press, 2005).

21. Ibid., 87–90.

22. Cited in Zasulich, *Vospominaniia*, 79.

23. Stephen Lukashevich, "The Holy Brotherhoood: 1881–1883," *American Slavic and East European Review* 18/4 (Dec. 1959): 491.

24. Yarmolinsky, *Road*, 303.

25. Ibid., 305.

26. After the initial phase of populist terrorism described in this book, in spite of the effective autocratic crackdown, terrorism became a sort of ingrained habit among Russian radicals for decades to

come. Its continued history has been described at length in more than one study. See Anna Geifman, *Thou Shalt Kill: Revolutionary Terrorism in Russia, 1894–1917* (Princeton, NJ: Princeton University Press, 1995) and Norman Naimark, *Terrorists and Social Democrats: The Russian Revolutionary Movement under Alexander III* (Cambridge: Harvard University Press, 1983).

27. Figner, *Zapechatlennyi trud*, 285.

28. See Joseph Frank, *Dostoevsky: The Mantle of the Prophet, 1871–1881* (Princeton, NJ: Princeton University Press, 2002), 727.

Bibliography

ARCHIVES

GARF

Fond 94 Verkhovnaia rasporiaditel'naia komissiia po okhraneniiu gosudarstvennogo poriadka i obsh-
chestvennogo spokoistva. 1880.
Fond 95 Sledstvennaia komissiia 1862 g. po delam o rasprostranenii revoliutsionnykh vozvannii i
propagande. 1862–1871.
Fond 102 Departament politsii ministerstva vnutrennykh del. 1880–1917.
Fond 109 Tret'e otdelenie sobstvennogo ego imperatorskogo velichestva kantseliarii. 1826–1880.
Fond 110 Shtab otdel'nogo korpusa zhandarmov. 1827–1917.
Fond 112 Osoboe prisutstvie pravitel'stvuiushchego senata dlia suzhdeniia del o gosudarstvennykh
prestupleniiakh i protivozakonnykh soobshchestvakh

RGIA

Fond 1282 Kantseliariia Ministertsva Vnutrennykh Del
Fond 1286 Departament Politsii Ispolnitel'noi MVD
Fond 1287 Khoziaistvennyi Departament MVD
Fond 1405 Ministerstvo Iiustitsii
Fond 1410 Veshchestvennye Dokazatel'stva po Delam Ministerstva Iiustitsii
Fond 1488 Plany i Chertezhi Grazhdanskoi Arkhitektury

CONTEMPORARY PERIODICALS

Delo
Golos
Narodnoe delo
Nedelia
Novoe vremia
Obshchee delo
Obshchina
Otechestvennye zapiski
Pravitel'stvennyi vestnik
Vpered

MEMOIRS, DIARIES, NOVELS, AND PRIMARY SOURCE DOCUMENTS

Aksel'rod, P. B. *Perezhitoe i peredumannoe*. Berlin, 1923.
Al'tman, M. S. *Ivan Gavrilovich Pryzhov. Ocherki, stat'i, pis'ma*. Moscow, 1934.

Antonovich, M. A., and G. Z. Eliseev. *Shestidesiatye gody*. Moscow, 1933.

Anzimirov, V. A. *Kramol'niki. Khronika radikal'nykh kruzhkov 70-kh gg*. Moscow: I. D. Sytin, 1907.

Aptekman, O. V. *Obshchestvo "Zemlia i Volia" 70-kh gg. Po lichnym vospominaniiam*. Petrograd, 1924.

Ashenbrener, M.Iu. "Voenno-revoliutsionnaia organizatsiia partii Narodnoi-Voli." *Katorga i ssylka* 7 (1923).

Bibergal', A. N. "Vospominaniia o demonstratsii na Kazanskoi ploshchadi." *Katorga i ssylka* 12 (1928).

Breshkovskaia, Katerina. *Hidden Springs of the Russian Revolution*. Translated by Lincoln Hutchinson. Stanford, CA: Stanford University Press, 1931.

Budnitskii, O. V. *Istoriia terrorizma v Rossii v dokumentakh, biografiiakh, issledovaniiakh*. Rostov na Donu: Feniks, 1996.

———. *Politicheskaia politsiia i politicheskii terrorizm: Sbornik dokumentov*. Moscow, 2001.

Bukh, N. K. "Pervaia tipografiia 'Narodnoi Voli.'" *Katorga i ssylka* 57 (1929).

Burtsev, Vladimir. *Za sto let: Sbornik po istorii politicheskikh i obshchestvennykh dvizhenii v Rossii*. London, 1897.

Chaikovskii, N. V. *Religioznye i obshchestvennye iskaniia*. Paris, 1929.

Charushin, Nikolai. *O dalekom proshlom: Iz vospominanii o revoliutsionnom dvizhenii 70 godov 19 veka*. Moscow, 1973.

Chernavskii, M. M. "Demonstratsiia 6 dekabria 1876 goda: Po vospominaniiam uchastnika." *Katorga i syylka* 28–29 (1926).

Cherniavskaia-Bokhanovskaia, G. F. "Avtobiografiia." *Katorga i ssylka* 42 (1928).

Chernyshevsky, Nikolai. *What Is To Be Done?* Translated by Michael R. Katz. Ithaca: Cornell University Press, 1989.

Debagorii-Mokrievich, V. K. *Ot buntarstva k terrorizmu*. Moscow, 1930.

De Custine, Marquis Astolphe. *Empire of the Czar: A Journey through Eternal Russia*. New York: Doubleday, 1989.

Deich, Lev. "Aaron Zundelevich." *Gruppa "Osvobozhdenie truda"* 2 (1924).

———. "G. V. Plekhanov v 'Zemle i Vole.'" *Gruppa "Osvobozhdenie truda"* 3 (1925).

———. "Valerian Osinskii." *Katorga i ssylka* 54 (1929).

———. *Za polveka*. Berlin, 1923.

De Vollan, G. A. "*Ocherki proshlago.*" *Golos minuvshago na chuzhoi storone* 4 (1914).

Dostoevskii, Fedor. *Prestuplenie i nakazanie*. Moscow: Izdatel'stvo 'Act,' 2009.

Dubenskaia, E. "Dmitrii Aleksandrovich Klements." *Katorga i ssylka* 5 (1930).

Eliseev, G. Z. *Sochineniia v dvukh tomakh*. Moscow, 1894.

Figner, V. "Mark Andreevich Natanson." *Katorga i ssylka* 56 (1929).

———. *Zapechatlennyi trud: Vospominaniia I*. Moscow: Mysl', 1964.

Filippov, R. V. *Revoliutsionnaia narodnicheskaia organizatsiia N. A. Ishutina-I. A. Khudiakova 1863–1866*. Petrozavodsk: Karel'skoe knizhnoe iz-vo, 1964.

Frolenko, M. "Chaikovskii i ego bogochelovechestvo." *Katorga i ssylka* 26 (1926).

———. "Khozhdenie v narod, 1874." *Katorga i ssylka* 11 (1924).

———. "Nachalo narodnichestva." *Katorga i ssylka* 24 (1926).

———. "O Gol'denberge." *Katorga i ssylka* no. 57 (1929).

———. *Zapiski semidesiatnika*. Moscow, 1927.

Gogol, Nikolai. "Nevsky Prospect." *The Complete Tales of Nikolai Gogol. Volume 1*. Translated by Constance Garnett. Chicago: University of Chicago Press, 1985.

Golovina-Iurgenson, N. A. "Iz dalekogo proshlogo." *Katorga i ssylka* 8 (1925).

———. "Moi vospominaniia." *Katorga i ssylka* 6 (1923).

Gradovskii, G. K. *Itogi (1862–1907)*. Kiev, 1908.

Iakimova, A. V. "Gruppa 'Svoboda ili smert.'" *Katorga i ssylka* 24 (1926).

———. "Iz dalekogo proshlogo." *Katorga i ssylka* 8 (1925).

Ivanchin-Pisarev, A. *Iz vospominanii o "Kozhdenii v narod."* St. Petersburg, 1907.

———. "Pobeg kn. P. A. Kropotkina." *Byloe* 1 (1907).

Ivanova, Sof'ia. "Vospominaniia o S. L. Perovskoi." *Byloe* 3 (1906).

Ivanova-Boreisha, Sof'ia. "Pervaia tipografiia 'Narodnoi Voli'." *Byloe* 9 (1906).

Khudiakov, Ivan. *Zapiski Karakozovtsa*. Moscow, 1930.

Klements, Dmitrii. *Iz proshlogo. Vospominaniia*. Moscow, 1925.

Klevenskii, M. M., and K. G. Kotel'nikov, eds. *Pokushenie Karakozova: Stenograficheskii otchet po delu D. Karakozova, I. Khudiakova, N. Ishutina i dr*. Seriia Politicheskie protsessy 60–80 gg. Moscow-Leningrad: Izdatel'stvo Tsentrarchiva RSFSR, 1928–1930.

Koni, A. F. *Vospominaniia o dele Very Zasulich*. Moscow, 1933.

Kornilova-Morozova, A. "Perovskaia i osnovanie kruzhka chaikovtsev." *Katorga i ssylka* 22 (1926).

Korolenko, Vladimir. *The History of My Contemporary*. Translated by Neil Parsons. Oxford, UK: Oxford University Press, 1972.

Kovalevskaya, Sofya [Sofiia Kovalevskaia]. *Nihilist Girl*. Translated by Natasha Kolchevska. New York: Modern Language Association of America, 2001.

Kravchinskii (Stepniak), Sergei. *The Career of a Nihilist*. New York: Harper's 1889.

———. *Grozovaia tucha Rossii*. Saint Petersburg: Novyi Kliuch, 2001.

Kropotkin, Petr. *Memoirs of a Revolutionist*. Boston: Hoghton Mifflin, 1962.

Kviatkovskii, A. A. "Avtobiograficheskoe zaiavlenie A. A. Kviatkovskogo." *Krasnyi arkhiv*, 1 (1926).

Lavrov, Petr. *Historical Letters*. Translated by James P. Scanlan. Berkeley: University of California Press, 1967.

Lion, S. "Ot propagandy k terroru." *Katorga i ssylka* 13 (1924).

Liubatovich, Olga. "Dalekoe i nedavnoe: Vospominaniia iz zhizni revoliutsionerov, 1879–1881." *Byloe* 5 (1906).

Livshits, S. "Podpol'nye tipografii 60-kh, 70-kh i 80-kh godov." *Katorga i ssylka* 50 (1928).

Mikhnevich, Vladimir. *Iazvy Peterburga*. Sankt-Peterburg: Limbus Press, 2003.

———. *Nashi znakomye*. Saint Petersburg, 1884.

———. *Peterburg ves' na ladoni*. Saint Petersburg, 1874.

Miliutin, D. A. *Dnevnik*. Moscow: Rosspen, 2009.

Morozov, Nikolai. *Povesti moei zhizni*. Moscow, 1962.

———. *Terroristicheskaia bor'ba*. London, 1980.

———. "Vozniknovenie 'Narodnoi Voli.'" *Byloe* 12 (1906).

Murzanova, M. "Vospominaniia A. A. Bobrinskogo (1880–1881 gody)." *Katorga i ssylka* 76 (1931).

Naidenov, N. A. *Vospominaniia o vedennom, slyshannom i ispytannom*. Newtonville, MA: Oriental Research Partners, 1976.

Narochnitskii, A. L., ed. *Rossiia i natsional'no-osvoboditel'naia bor'ba na Balkanakh, 1875–1878*. Moscow: Nauka, 1978.

Nikitenko, Aleksandr. *The Diary of a Russian Censor*. Translated by Helen Saltz Jacobson. Amherst: University of Massachusetts Press, 1975.

Nikitin, S. A., ed. *Osvoboditel'naia bor'ba iuzhnykh slavian i Rossiia*. Moscow, 1960.

Nikoladze, N. "Vospominaniia o shestidesiatykh godakh." *Katorga i ssylka* 34 (1927).

Novitskii, General V. D. *Iz vospominanii zhandarma*. Moscow, 1991.

Panaeva, A.Ia, *Vospominaniia*. Moscow: Khudozhestvennaia Literatura, 1972.

Pankratova, V. "1 marta 1881 goda." *Byloe* 3 (1926).

Panteleev, L. F. *Iz vospominanii proshlogo*. Moscow, 1934.

Pisarev, D. I. *Literaturnaia kritika v trekh tomakh*. vol. 2. Leningrad, 1981.

Plekhanov, Georgii. *Sochineniia*. Vols. 1 and 3. Moscow, 1923.

Plekhanova, Rosa, "Nasha zhizn' do emigratsii." *Gruppa "Osvobozhdenie truda"* 6 (1928).

———. "Okhota za G. V. Plekhanovym." *Gruppa "Osvobozhdenie truda"* 3 (1925).

———. "Periferinnyi kruzhok 'Zemli i Voli.'" *Gruppa "Osvobozhdenie truda"* 4 (1926).

Pobedonostsev, Konstantin. *Pis'ma Pobedonostseva k Aleksandru III*. Vol. 3. Moscow, 1925.

Popov, M. R. *Zapiski zemlevol'tsa*. Moscow, 1933.

Pribyleva-Korba, A. P. "Ispolnitel'nyi komitet 1879–1881 gg." *Katorga i ssylka* 24 (1926).

———. *Narodnaia Volia: Vospominaniia o 1870–1880-kh gg*. Moscow, 1926.

———. "Nekotoryia dannyia o 'Pis'me Ispolnitel'nago Komiteta k Aleksandru III.'" *Byloe* 6 (1906).

Pribyleva-Korba, A. P., and Vera Figner, eds. *Narodnovolets Aleksandr Dmitrievich Mikhailov*. Leningrad, 1925.

Protsess 1-ogo marta 1881-go goda. Saint Petersburg, 1906.

Ralli-Arbore, Z. "Sergei Gennad'evich Nechaev." *Byloe.* 7 (1906).

Sazhin, M. P. *Vospominaniia.* Moscow, 1925.

Semeniuta, P. "Iz vospominanii ob A. I. Zheliabove." *Byloe* 4 (1906).

Shatz, Marshall, and Judith Zimmerman, trans. and ed. *Signposts: A Collection of Articles on the Russian Intelligentsia.* Irvine, CA: Charles Schlacks Jr., 1986.

Shchegolev, P. E., ed. *Pis'ma narodovol'tsa A. D. Mikhailova.* Moscow, 1933.

Shebeko, N. N. *Chronique du mouvement socialiste en Russie, 1878–1887.* St. Petersburg: Imprimerie officielle du Ministère de l'intérieur, 1890.

Shelgunov, Nikolai. *Vospominaniia.* Leningrad, 1967.

Shevtsov (Marusin), S. P. "Iz proshlogo: Pervye ulichnye demonstratsii v Peterburge." *Narodnyi vestnik* 2 (1906).

Shiraev, Stepan. "Avtobiograficheskaia zapiska i pis'ma." *Krasnyi arkhiv* 7 (1924).

Shishko, Leonid. *Sergei Mikhailovich Kravchinskii i Kruzhok Chaikovtsev: Iz vospominanii i zametok starogo narodnika.* St. Petersburg, 1906.

Sinegub, Sergei. *Zapiski chaikovtsa.* Moscow-Leningrad, 1929.

Skabichevskii, A. M. *Literaturnye vospominaniia.* Moscow: Agraf, 2001.

Sorokin, V. "Vospominaniia starogo studenta." *Russkaia starina* 2 (1906).

Stepniak (Kravchinskii), Sergei. *The Career of a Nihilist.* New York: Harper's, 1889.

Svin'in, Pavel. "Kratkaia zapiska o novostiakh, naidennykh izdatelem O. Z. v stolitse po vozvrashchenii svoem nyneshnim letom iz puteshestviia." *Otechestvennye zapiski* 31 (1828).

Tagantsev, N. S. "Iz perezhitogo." *Byloe* 9 (1918).

Tarnovskii (Romanenko) V. *Terrorizm i rutina.* London, 1882.

Tikhomirov, Lev. *Konstitutsionalisty v epokhu 1881 goda.* Moscow, 1895.

———. "Neskol'ko myslei o razvitii i razvetvlenii revoliutsionnykh napravlenii." *Katorga i ssylka* 3 (1926).

———. "Teni proshlogo: Stepan Khalturin." *Katorga i ssylka* 25 (1926).

———. *Vospominaniia.* Moscow, 1927.

———. *Zagovorshchiki i politsiia.* Moscow, 1930.

Timofeev, M. A. "Perezhitoe: Otryvok iz vospominanii o semidesiatykh godakh." *Katorga i ssylka* 57 (1929).

Titova, A. A., ed. *Nikolai Vasil'evich Chaikovskii: Religioznye i obshchestvennye iskaniia.* Paris: 1929.

Tiutchev, N. S. "Razgrom Zemli i Voli v 1878. Delo Mezentsova." *Byloe* 8 (1918).

Tsamutali, A. N., and S. S. Volk, eds. *Shturmany budushchei buri.* Leningrad, 1983.

Tyrkov, A. "K sobytiiu 1 marta 1881 goda." *Byloe* 5 (1906).

Ursynovich, L. *Klochki vospominanii. Al'manakh "Krasnaia nov'."* 2 (1925).

Valk, S. N., ed. *Arkhiv "Zemli i Voli" i "Narodnoi Voli."* Moscow, 1930.

Valk, S. N. et al., eds. *Revoliutsionnoe narodnichestvo 70-kh godov XIX veka Tom I 1870–1875.* Moscow, 1964.

Viktorova-Val'ter, S. A. "Iz zhizni revoliutsionnoi molodezhi." *Katorga i ssylka* 11 (1924).

Vodovozova, E. N. *Na zare zhizni: Memuarnye ocherki i portrety.* Leningrad, 1964.

Zaionchkovskii, P. A., ed. *Dnevnik P. A. Valueva Ministra Vnutrennykh Del.* Moscow, 1961.

Zasulich, Vera. "Nechaevskoe delo." *Gruppa "Osvobozhdenie truda"* 2 (1924).

———. *Vospominaniia.* Moscow, 1931.

Zhukovskaia, Ekaterina Ivanovna. *Zapiski: Vospominaniia.* Moscow: Agraf, 2001.

SECONDARY SOURCES

Abbott, Robert. "Crime, Police, and Society in St. Petersburg." *Historian* 40 (1977).

Ambler, Effie. *Russian Journalism and Politics, 1861–1881; the Career of Aleksei S. Suvorin.* Detroit: Wayne State University Press, 1972.

Baedarida, Francois, and Anthony Sutcliffe. "The Street in the Structure and Life of the City." *Journal of Urban History* 6 (1980).

Barenbaum, I. E. "*Knizhnyi magazin A. A. Cherkesova i ego rol' v osvoboditel'nom dvizhenii 1860-kh g. v Rossii.*" In S. G. Luppov and N. V. Paramonova (eds.), *Knigotorgovoe i bibliotechnoe delo v Rossii v XVII–pervoi polovine XIX v.* Leningrad, 1981.

———. "*N. A. Serno-Solov'evich (1834–1866): Ocherk knigotorgovoi i knigoizdatel'skoi deiatel'nosti.*" Moscow, 1961.

Baron, Samuel. *Plekhanov: Father of Russian Marxism.* Stanford, CA: Stanford University Press, 1963.

Bater, James. *St. Petersburg: Industrialization and Change.* London: Edward Arnold, 1976.

Beall, Jo. "Cities, Terrorism, and Development." *Journal of International Development* 18 (2006).

Bekker, I. "Demonstratsiia dolgushintsev na Konnoi ploshchadi." *Katorga i ssylka* 2 (1926).

Bel'chikov, N. F. "S. G. Nechaev v sele Ivanove v 60-e gody." *Katorga i ssylka.* 1 (1925).

Berlin, Isaiah. *Russian Thinkers.* London: Penguin Books, 1994.

Bogucharskii, V. [B. Bazilevskii]. *Aktivnoe narodnichetsvo semidesiatikh godov.* Moscow, 1912.

———, ed. *Gosudarstvennye prestupleniia v Rossii v XIX veke.* Stuttgart, 1903.

Bradley, Joseph. *Muzhik and Muscovite: Urbanization in Late-Imperial Russia.* Berkeley: University of California Press, 1985.

———. *Voluntary Associations in Tsarist Russia: Science, Patriotism and Civil Society.* Cambridge: Harvard University Press, 2009.

Brower, Daniel R. *The Russian City between Tradition and Modernity.* Berkeley: University of California Press, 1990.

———. *Training the Nihilists: Education and Radicalism in Tsarist Russia.* Ithaca: Cornell University Press, 1975.

Brumfield, William. "Sleptsov Redivivus." *California Slavic Studies* 9 (1976).

Budnitskii, O. V. *Terrorizm v rossiiskom osvoboditel'nom dvizhenii: Ideologiia, etika, psikhologiia (vtoraia pol. XIX–nachalo XX v.).* Moscow: Rosspen, 2000.

Casey, Edward. *The Fate of Place: A Philosophical History.* Berkeley: University of California Press, 1997.

Chernavskii, M. M. "Demonstratsiia 6 dekabria 1876 goda." *Katorga i ssylka* 4 (1926).

Cherniak, A.Ia. *Nikolai Kibal'chich: Revoliutsioner i uchenyi.* Moscow, 1960.

Chernukha, V. G. *Pasport v Rossii 1719–1917.* Sankt-Peterburg: Liki Rossii, 2007.

Chukovskii, Kornei. *Liudi i knigi shestidesiatykh godov.* Leningrad, 1958.

Clowes, Edith et al., eds. *Between Tsar and People: Educated Society and the Quest for Public Identity in Late-Imperial Russia.* Princeton, NJ: Princeton University Press, 1991.

Cracraft, James. *The Petrine Revolution in Russian Architecture.* Chicago: University of Chicago Press, 1988.

Crampton, Jeremy, and Stuart Elden, eds. *Space, Knowledge and Power: Foucault and Geography.* Burlington: Ashgate, 2007.

Crisp and Edmondson, eds. *Civil Rights in Imperial Russia.* Oxford: Clarendon Press, 1989.

Daly, Jonathan. *Autocracy under Seige: Security Police and Opposition in Russia, 1866–1905.* DeKalb, IL: Northern Illinois University Press, 1998.

De Madariaga, Isabel. *Russia in the Age of Catherine the Great.* New Haven: Yale University Press, 1981.

Dianina, Katia. "The Firebird of the National Imaginary: The Myth of Russian Culture and Its Discontents." *Journal of European Studies* 42 (2012).

Dlugolenskii, Ia. N., *Vek Dostoevskogo.* Sankt-Peterburg: Izdatel'stvo Pushkinskogo Fonda, 2007.

Egorov, Iu. A. *The Architectural Planning of St. Petersburg.* Translated by Eric Dluhosch. Athens, OH: Ohio University Press, 1969.

Eklof, Ben, John Bushnell, and Larissa Zakharova. *Russia's Great Reforms, 1855–1881.* Bloomington: Indiana University Press, 1994.

Engel, Barbara Alpern. *Mothers and Daughters: Women of the Intelligentsia in Nineteenth-Century Russia.* Cambridge: Cambridge University Press, 1983.

Engelstein, Laura. "The Dream of Civil Society in Tsarist Russia: Law, State, and Religion." In *Civil Society before Democracy: Lessons from Nineteenth-Century Europe*, edited by N. Bermeo and P. Nord. Lanham, MD: Rowan and Littlefield, 2000.

———. "Revolution and the Theater of Public Life in Nineteenth-Century Russia." In I. Wolloch (ed.), *Revolution and the Meaning of Freedom in the Nineteenth Century*. Stanford, CA: Stanford University Press, 1996.

Field, Daniel. "Peasants and Propagandists in the Russian Movement to the People of 1874." *Journal of Modern History* 59 (1987).

———. *Rebels in the Name of the Tsar* (Boston: Houghton-Mifflin, 1976).

Filippov, R. V. *Revoliutsionnaia narodnicheskaia organizatsiia N. A. Ishutina-I. A. Khudiakova 1863–1866*. Petrozavodsk: Karel'skoe knizhnoe iz-vo, 1964.

Fischer, Claude, and Robert K. Merton. *The Urban Experience*. New York: Harcourt, Brace Jovanovich, 1976.

Fishman, Robert. *Bourgeois Utopias: The Rise and Fall of the Suburb*. New York: Basic Books, 1989.

Fleming, Marie. "Propaganda by the Deed: Terrorism and Anarchist Theory in Late Nineteenth-Century Europe" *Terrorism: An International Journal* 4 (1980).

Footman, David. *Red Prelude: The Life of the Terrorist Zhelyabov*. New Haven: Yale University Press, 1945.

Forest, James J. F., ed. *The Making of a Terrorist: Recruitment, Training, and Root Causes*. Santa Barbara: Praeger Security International, 2006.

Foucault, Michel. "Of Other Spaces" Translated by J. Miskowiec. *Diacritics* (Spring 1986).

———. *"Society Must Be Defended": Lectures at the Collège de France, 1975–1976*. Translated by David Macey. New York: Picador, 1997.

Frame, Murray. *School for Citizens: Theatre and Civil Society in Imperial Russia*. New Haven: Yale University Press, 2006.

Frank, Joseph. *Dostoevsky: The Mantle of the Prophet, 1871–1881*. Princeton, NJ: Princeton University Press, 2002.

Frede, Victoria. *Doubt, Atheism and the Nineteenth-Century Russian Intelligentsia*. Madison: University of Wisconsin Press, 2011.

Frierson, Cathy. *Peasant Icons: Representations of Rural People in Late 19th Century Russia*. New York: Oxford University Press, 1993.

Geifman, Anna. *Thou Shalt Kill: Revolutionary Terrorism in Russia, 1894–1917*. Princeton, NJ: Princeton University Press, 1995.

George, Arthur L. *St. Petersburg: Russia's Window to the Future*. New York: Taylor Trade Publishing, 2003.

Gleason, Abbott. *Young Russia: The Genesis of Russian Radicalism in the 1860s*. Chicago: University of Chicago Press, 1980.

Greenblatt, Stephen. *Renaissance Self-Fashioning from More to Shakespeare*. Chicago: University of Chicago Press, 1980.

Grintsevich, O. S. "Proekty planirovki Peterburga vtoroi poloviny XIX–nachala XX vekov." *Arkhitekturnoe nasledstvo* 9 (1959).

Habermas, Jurgen. *The Structural Transformation of the Public Sphere: An Inquiry into a Category of Bourgeois Society*. Translated by Thomas Burger. Cambridge: The MIT Press, 1999.

Hamm, Michael, ed. *The City in Late Imperial Russia*. Bloomington: Indiana University Press, 1986.

Hardy, Deborah. *Land and Freedom: The Origins of Russian Terrorism*. London: Greenwood Press, 1987.

———. *Petr Tkachev, the Critic as Jacobin*. Seattle: University of Washington Press, 1977.

Harvey, David. *Social Justice and the City*. London: Arnold, 1973.

Hebdige, Dick. *Subculture: The Meaning of Style*. London: Routledge, 1979.

Henaff, Marcel, and Tracy B. Strong. *Public Space and Democracy*. Minneapolis: University of Minnesota Press, 2001.

Houlbrook, Matt. *Queer London: Perils and Pleasures in the Sexual Metropolis, 1918–1957*. Chicago: University of Chicago Press, 1957.

Itenberg, B. S. *Dvizhenie revoliutsionnogo narodnichestva*. Moscow, 1965.

———. *Revoliutsionery i liberaly Rossii*. Moscow, 1990.

Iukhneva, E. D. *Peterburgskie dokhodnye doma: Ocherki iz istorii byta*. Moscow: Tsentrpoligraf, 2008.

Izmozik, V. C. *Zhandarmy Rossii*. Sankt-Peterburg: Neva, 2002.

Kalinchuk, Sergei. "Psikhologicheskii faktor v deiatel'nosti 'Zemli i Voli' 1870-kh godov." *Voprosy istorii* 3 (1999).

Kantor, R. M. "Dinamit Narodnoi Voli." *Katorga i ssylka* 57 (1929).

———. "K istorii revoliutsionnogo dvizheniia 1870–1880-kh godov." *Katorga i ssylka* 24 (1926).

Karp, D. A. et al. *Being Urban: A Sociology of City Life*. 2nd ed. New York: Praeger, 1991.

Kilcullen, David. "Twenty-Eight Articles: Fundamentals of Company-Level Counterinsurgency." *Marine Corps Gazette* 90/7 (2006).

Kirichenko, E. I. "O nekotorykh osobennostiakh evoliutsii gorodskikh mnogokvartirnykh domov vtoroi poloviny XI –nachala XX vv." *Arkhitekturnoe nasledstvo* 15 (1963).

———. *Russkaia arkhitektura, 1830–1910*. Leningrad, 1982.

Kirikov, Boris. *Arkhitektura Peterburgskogo moderna: osobniaki i dokhodnye doma*. Saint Petersburg: Zhurnal Neva, 2003.

Klevenskii, M. M. "Vertepniki." *Katorga i ssylka* 10 (1928).

Klier, John Doyle. *Russians, Jews, and the Pogroms of 1881–1882*. Cambridge: Cambridge University Press, 2011.

Kornilov, A. A. *Obshchestvennoe dvizhenie pri Aleksandre II (1855–1881)*. Moscow, 1909.

Koz'min, B. P. *Nechaev i Nechaevtsy*. Moscow, 1931.

———. *Revoliutsionnoe podpol'e v epokhu "belogo terrora."* Moscow, 1929.

Koz'menko, I. V. "Russkoe obshchestvo i aprel'skoe Bolgarskoe vosstanie 1876 g." *Voprosy istorii* 5 (1947).

Kuz'min, D. "Kazanskaia demonstratsiia 1876 g." *Katorga i ssylka* 5 (1928).

Laqueur, Walter, ed. *Voices of Terror: Manifestoes, Writings, and Manuals of Al-Qaeda, Hamas and Other Terrorists from Around the World and Throughout the Ages*. New York: Reed Press, 2004.

LeFebvre, Henri. *The Production of Space*. Translated by Donald Nicholson-Smith. Oxford: Blackwell Publishing, 1991.

Lemke, M. K. *Ocherki osvoboditel'nogo dvizheniia "shestidesiatykh godov."* St. Petersburg, 1908.

Likhachev, Dmitry. *Reflections on Russia*. Translated by Christina Sever. Boulder: Westview Press, 1991.

Lincoln, W. Bruce. *The Great Reforms: Autocracy, Bureaucracy, and the Politics of Change in Imperial Russia*. DeKalb, IL: Northern Illinois University Press, 1990.

Lindenmeyr, Adele. *Poverty Is Not a Vice: Charity, Society, and the State in Imperial Russia*. Princeton, NJ: Princeton University Press, 1996.

———. "Raskolnikov's City and the Napoleonic Plan." *Slavic Review* 1 (1976).

Lofland, Lyn. *A World of Strangers: Order and Action in Urban Public Space*. New York: Basic Books, 1973.

Lukashevich, Stephen. "The Holy Brotherhoood: 1881–1883." *American Slavic and East European Review* 18 (1959).

Maiorova, Olga. *From the Shadow of the Empire: Defining the Russian Nation through Cultural Mythology*. Madison: University of Wisconsin Press, 2010.

Malia, Martin. *Alexander Herzen and the Birth of Russian Socialism*. Cambridge: Harvard University Press, 1961.

———. "What is the Intelligentsia?" *Daedalus* 89 (1960).

Manchester, Laurie. *Holy Fathers, Secular Sons: Clergy, Intelligentsia, and the Modern Self in Revolutionary Russia*. DeKalb: Northern Illinois University Press, 2008.

Matthews, Mervyn. *The Passport Society: Controlling Movement in Russia and the USSR*. Boulder, CO.: Westview Press, 1993.

Mazour, Anatole G. *The First Russian Revolution, 1825: The Decembrist Movement, Its Origins, Development, and Significance*. Stanford, CA: Stanford University Press, 1964.

McKinsey, Pamela Sears. "The Kazan Square Demonstration and the Conflict between Russian Workers and *Intelligenty*." *Slavic Review* 1 (1985).

McReynolds, Louise. *The News under Russia's Old Regime: The Development of a Mass-Circulations Press.* Princeton, NJ: Princeton University Press, 1991.

———. *Russia at Play: Leisure Activities at the End of the Tsarist Era.* Ithaca: Cornell University Press, 2003.

Merriman, John. *The Dynamite Club: How a Bombing in Fin-de-Siècle Paris Ignited the Age of Modern Terror.* Boston: Houghton Mifflin Harcourt, 2009.

Miliukov, et al. *History of Russia: Reforms, Reaction, Revolutions.* Translated by Charles Lam Markmann. New York: Funk and Wagnalls, 1969.

Miller, Martin. *The Foundations of Modern Terrorism: State, Society, and the Dynamics of Political Violence.* Cambridge: Cambridge University Press, 2013.

Mironov, Boris. *Sotsial'naia istoriia Rossii perioda imperii: XVIII–nachalo XX v.: Genezis lichnosti, demokraticheskoi sem'i, grazhdanskogo obshchestva i pravovogo gosudarstva.* Moscow: Bulanin, 1999.

Morrissey, Susan. *Heralds of Revolution: Russian Students and the Mythologies of Radicalism.* Oxford, UK: Oxford University Press, 1998.

Mumford, Lewis. *The City in History.* New York: Harcourt Inc., 1961.

Munro, George. *The Most Intentional City: St. Petersburg in the Reign of Catherine the Great.* Cranbury, NJ: Associated University Presses, 2008.

Naimark, Norman N. "Terrorism and the Fall of Imperial Russia." *Terrorism and Political Violence* 2 (1990).

———. *Terrorists and Social Democrats: The Russian Revolutionary Movement under Alexander III.* Cambridge: Harvard University Press, 1983.

Nechkina, M. V. *Dekabristy.* Leningrad, 1984.

———, ed. *Revoliutsionnaia situatsiia v Rossii v 1859–1861 gg.* Vols. 1–6. Moscow, 1960–1974.

Nikitin, S. A. *Slavianskie komitety v Rossii v 1858–1876 godakh.* Moscow, 1960.

Orlovsky, Daniel. *The Limits of Reform: The Ministry of Internal Affairs in Imperial Russia, 1802–1881.* Cambridge: Harvard University Press, 1981.

Paperno, Irina. *Chernyshevskii and the Age of Realism: A Study in the Semiotics of Behavior.* Stanford, CA: Stanford University Press, 1988.

Peregubova, Zinaida. "Departament politsii i mestnye uchrezhdeniia politicheskogo rozyska (1800–1917)." *Politicheskii sysk Rossii 1800–1917.* Moscow: Rosspen, 2000.

Philo, Chris. "Michel Foucault." In *Key Thinkers on Space and Place,* edited by Phil Hubbard and Rob Kitchin. Los Angeles: Sage Publications, 2004.

Pike, David. *Metropolis on the Styx: The Underworlds of Modern Urban Culture.* Ithaca, NY: Cornell University Press, 2007.

Pipes, Richard. *The Degaev Affair: Terror and Treason in Tsarist Russia.* New Haven: Yale University Press, 2005.

———. "Narodnichestvo: A Semantic Inquiry." *Slavic Review* 3 (1964).

———. *Russia under the Old Regime.* New York: Scribner, 1974.

Pomper, Philip. *The Russian Revolutionary Intelligentsia.* 2nd ed. Wheeling, IL: Harlan Davidson, 1993.

Popruzhenko, M. "Obshchestvennoe nastroenie v Rossii nakanune Osvoboditel'noi voiny." *Proslava na osvoboditelnata voina.* Sofia: 1929.

Pozefsky, Peter. *The Nihilist Imagination: Dmitry Pisarev and the Cultural Origins of Russian Radicalism (1860–1868).* New York: Peter Lang Publishing, 2003.

Rabinow, Paul, ed. *The Foucault Reader.* New York: Pantheon Press, 1980.

Raeff, Marc. *Origins of the Russian Intelligentsia: The 18th Century Nobility.* New York: Harcourt, Brace and World, 1966.

———. *The Decembrist Movement.* Englewood Cliffs, NJ: Prentice-Hall, Inc. 1966.

Randolph, John. *The House in the Garden: The Bakunin Family and the Romance of Russian Idealism.* Ithaca: Cornell University Press, 2007.

Riasanovsky, Nicholas, and Mark Steinberg. *A History of Russia.* 8th ed. New York: Oxford University Press, 2011.

Riesman, David, Nathan Glazer, and Reuel Denny. *The Lonely Crowd*. New Haven: Yale University Press, 2001.

Rogger, Hans. *Russia in the Age of Modernization and Revolution*. London: Longman, 1983.

Rowland, Daniel. "Urban in-migration in late 19th century Russia." In *The City in Russian History*, edited by Michael F. Hamm. Lexington: University Press of Kentucky, 1976.

Ruane, Christine. *The Empire's New Clothes: A History of the Russian Fashion Industry, 1700–1917*. New Haven: Yale University Press, 2009.

Russo, Paul. "Golos 1878–1883: Profile of a Russian Newspaper." PhD diss., Columbia, 1974.

Ruud, Charles, and Sergei Stepanov. *Fontanka 16: The Tsars' Secret Police*. Montreal: McGill-Queen's University Press, 1999.

Sante, Luc. *Low Life: Lures and Snares of Old New York*. New York: Farrar, Srauss, Giroux, 1991.

Saunders, David. *Russia in the Age of Reaction and Reform*. New York: Longman, 1992.

Savitch, H. V. "An Anatomy of Urban Terror: Lessons from Jerusalem and Elsewhere." *Urban Studies* 3 (2005).

Seddon, J. H. *The Petrashevtsy: A Study of the Russian Revolutionaries of 1848*. Manchester, UK: Manchester University Press, 1985.

Sennett, Richard. *The Conscience of the Eye: The Design and Social Life of Cities*. New York: Norton, 1990.

———. *The Fall of Public Man*. New York: W. W. Norton, 1974.

———. *The Uses of Disorder: Personal Identity and City Life*. New Haven: Yale University Press, 1970.

Serebriakov, E. *Obshchestvo 'Zemlia i Volia.'* Geneva, 1894.

Shchegolev, P. "Iz istorii 'konstitutsionnykh veianii' v 1879–81." *Byloe* 12 (1906).

Shcherbakova, E. I. *Otshchepentsy: Put' k terrorizmu*. Moscow: Novyi Khronograf, 2008.

Shevyrev, A. P. "Kul'turnaia sreda stolichnogo goroda. Peterburg i Moskva." In *Ocherki Russkoi kul'tury XIX veka*. Moscow: Izd. Moskovskogo universiteta, 1998.

Siljak, Ana. *Angel of Vengeance: The "Girl Assassin," the Governor of St. Petersburg and Russia's Revolutionary World*. New York: St. Martin's Press, 2008.

Simmel, Georg. *Conflict and the Web of Group Affiliations*. Translated by Reinhard Bendix. Glencoe, IL: The Free Press, 1955.

———. *The Sociology of Georg Simmel*. New York: Simon and Schuster, 1950.

Soja, Edward. *Postmodern Geographies: The Reassertion of Space in Critical Social Theory*. London: Verso Press, 1989.

———. *Thirdspace*. Malden, MA: Blackwell Publishing, 1996.

Somina, R. A. *Nevskii Prospekt: Istoricheskii ocherk*. Leningrad, 1959.

Staub, Alexandra. "St. Petersburg's Double Life: The Planners' versus the People's City." *Journal of Urban History* 31 (2005).

Stites, Richard. *The Women's Liberation Movement in Russia: Feminism, Nihilism, and Bolshevism, 1860–1930*. Princeton, NJ: Princeton University Press, 1978.

Tatishchev, Sergei. *Imperator Aleksandr II. Ego zhizn' i tsarstvovanie*. Moscow: Tranzitkniga, 2006.

Trice, Tom. "Rites of Protest: Populist Funerals in Imperial St. Petersburg, 1876–1878." *Slavic Review* 60 (2001).

Ulam, Adam. *In the Name of the People*. New York: Viking Press, 1977.

Venturi, Franco. *The Roots of Revolution*. Translated by Francis Haskell. Chicago: University of Chicago Press, 1960.

Verhoeven, Claudia. *The Odd Man Karakozov*. Ithaca: Cornell University Press, 2009.

Vilenskaia, E. S. "Proizvoditel'nye assotsiatsii v Rossii v seredine 60-kh godov XIX-v." *Istoricheskie zapiski* 68 (1961).

———. *Revoliutsionnoe podpol'e v Rossii 60-e gody XIX v*. Leningrad: 1965.

Volk, S. S. *Narodnaia Volia, 1879–1882*. Moscow, 1966.

Volkov, Solomon. *St. Petersburg: A Cultural History*. New York: Simon and Schuster, 2010.

Von Borcke, Astrid. "Violence and Terror in Russian Revolutionary Populism: The Narodnaya Volya." Mommsen and Hirschfeld, *Social Protest, Violence and Terror in Nineteenth-and Twentieth-century Europe*. London: Macmillan 1982.

Walicki, Andrzej. *The Controversy over Capitalism*. Oxford: Clarendon Press, 1969.

West, Sally. *I Shop in Moscow: Advertising and the Creation of Consumer Culture in Late Tsarist Russia*. DeKalb: Northern Illinois University Press, 2011.

Williams, Rosalind, *Notes on the Underground*. Cambridge: MIT Press, 1990.

Wilson, Elizabeth. *Bohemians: The Glamorous Outcasts*. New Brunswick: Rutgers University Press, 2000.

Woehrlin, William F. *Chernyshevskii: The Man and the Journalist*. Cambridge: Harvard University Press, 1971.

Wortman, Richard. *The Crisis of Russian Populism*. Cambridge: Cambridge University Press, 1967.

———. *Scenarios of Power: Myth and Ceremony in Russian Monarchy from Peter the Great to the Abdication of Nicholas II*. Princeton, NJ: Princeton University Press, 2006.

Yarmolinsky, Avraham. *Road to Revolution*. Princeton, NJ: Princeton University Press, 1957.

Zaionchkovsky, Petr. *The Russian Autocracy in Crisis, 1878–1882*. Translated by Gary Hamburg. Gulf Breeze, FL.: Academic International Press, 1979.

Zelnik, Reginald. *Labor and Society in Tsarist Russia: The Factory Workers of St. Petersburg, 1855–1870*. Stanford, CA: Stanford University Press, 1971.

———, ed. *Workers and Intelligentsia in Late-Imperial Russia*. Berkeley: UC Berkeley Press, 1999.

Index

Z